BARR

IELTS®

INTERNATIONAL ENGLISH LANGUAGE TESTING SYSTEM

FOURTH EDITION

Dr. Lin Lougheed
Teachers College
Columbia University

Publishing Globally

NEW AGE INTERNATIONAL (P) LIMITED, PUBLISHERS

New Delhi • Bangalore • Chennai • Cochin • Guwahati
Hyderabad • Kolkata • Lucknow • Mumbai
Visit us at www.newagepublishers.com

Acknowledgments

Directions in the model tests used with permission of the IELTS partners. The chart on page 6 is reprinted from the IELTS Handbook with permission of the IELTS partners.

The author gratefully acknowledges the comments and suggestions of ELT teachers and IELTS administrators around the world. The suggestions of Mary Hernandez of ELS Language Center, Santa Monica, California, have been especially helpful. The author would also like to thank Elisabeth Gillstrom of ELS Language Centers, Grand Rapids, Michigan, for her assistance.

The author wishes to thank the following organizations, institutions, bloggers, and clearinghouse for their kind permission to use their source material. If we neglected to list your name, please contact us so we can correct that omission.

(page 304) Less Television, Less Violence and Aggression, TV-Free America, *www.tvturnoff.org/lessviolence.htm*.

(page 308) Issues Affecting the Southern Resident Orcas from Declining Fish Populations, The Whale Museum (*www.whalemuseum.org*).

(page 422) Adult Intelligence, by Phillip Ackerman, ED410228, ERIC Clearinghouse on Assessment and Evaluation, Washington, DC, 1996.

BARRON'S IELTS with MP3 CD, 4th Edition by Dr. Lin Lougheed

Fourth Indian Sub-Continent Edition: 2018 by **New Age International (P) Ltd., Publishers**

This special low-priced edition is for sale in **India, Bangladesh, Bhutan, Maldives, Nepal** and **Sri Lanka** only.

Originally Published in the *United States of America.*

BRANCHES

- **Bangalore** 37/10, 8th Cross (Near Hanuman Temple), Azad Nagar, Chamarajpet, Bangalore-560 018
  Tel.: (080) 26756823, Telefax: 26756820, **E-mail: bangalore@newagepublishers.com**
- **Chennai** 26, Damodaran Street, T. Nagar, Chennai-600 017
  Tel.: (044) 24353401, Telefax: 24351463, **E-mail: chennai@newagepublishers.com**
- **Cochin** CC-39/1016, Carrier Station Road, Ernakulam South, Cochin-682 016
  Tel.: (0484) 2377303, Telefax: 4051304, **E-mail: cochin@newagepublishers.com**
- **Guwahati** Hemsen Complex, Mohd. Shah Road, Paltan Bazar, Near Starline Hotel, Guwahati-781 008
  Tel.: (0361) 2513881, Telefax: 2543669, **E-mail: guwahati@newagepublishers.com**
- **Hyderabad** 105, 1st Floor, Madhiray Kaveri Tower, 3-2-19, Azam Jahi Road, Near Kumar Theater, Nimboliadda Kachiguda, Hyderabad-500 027, Tel.: (040) 24652456, Telefax: 24652457
  E-mail: hyderabad@newagepublishers.com
- **Kolkata** RDB Chambers (Formerly Lotus Cinema) 106A, 1st Floor, S.N. Banerjee Road, Kolkata-700 014
  Tel.: (033) 22273773, Telefax: 22275247, **E-mail: kolkata@newagepublishers.com**
- **Lucknow** 16-A, Jopling Road, Lucknow-226 001
  Tel.: (0522) 2209578, 4045297, Telefax: 2204098, **E-mail: lucknow@newagepublishers.com**
- **Mumbai** 142C, Victor House, Ground Floor, N.M. Joshi Marg, Lower Parel, Mumbai-400 013
  Tel.: (022) 24927869, Telefax: 24915415, **E-mail: mumbai@newagepublishers.com**
- **New Delhi** 22, Golden House, Daryaganj, New Delhi-110 002
  Tel.: (011) 23262368, 23262370, Telefax: 43551305, **E-mail: sales@newagepublishers.com**

ISBN: 978-93-87477-00-1

C-18-01-11080

Printed in India at SAP PRINT SOLUTIONS PVT. LTD., Mumbai.

PUBLISHING GLOBALLY
NEW AGE INTERNATIONAL (P) LIMITED, PUBLISHERS
7/30 A, Daryaganj, New Delhi-110002
Visit us at **www.newagepublishers.com**
(CIN: U74899DL1966PTC004618)

CONTENTS

1 Introduction

Over 2.2 million people take IELTS each year. There are more than 1,000 test centers that administer IELTS in over 140 countries around the world. Today it is one of the most accepted international exams for academic qualification, professional licensing, and immigration. You can learn more about IELTS by visiting the official website at *www.ielts.org.*

Purpose

IELTS is available for people who need to demonstrate their English language proficiency for specific purposes. There are two formats of IELTS to choose from depending on your needs. You should take the Academic Training modules if you are planning to apply to an international university where English is the spoken language. The Academic Training modules are also used as a measure of professional language proficiency for educators, nurses, veterinarians, and other professionals. The General Training modules are more suitable if you want to work, live, or study at a secondary institution in an English-speaking country.

There is a new test called IELTS Life Skills for those applying for a UK visa. This test measures a test taker's speaking and listening skills. More information on this immigration-specific test can be found at *www.ielts.org.*

Test Takers

International students represent the highest percentage of candidates who take IELTS. An IELTS score is a recognized measurement of English proficiency at over 7,000 institutions around the world. Government departments and businesses around the globe also require an IELTS or equivalent score for employment or immigration. Medical professionals who want to work overseas in the UK may take the IELTS test.

Skills Tested

IELTS consists of four sections that test the full range of English language skills—Reading, Writing, Listening, and Speaking. The Listening and Speaking sections are the same for both the Academic and General Training modules. The Reading and Writing sections are different in the Academic and General Training modules. These four modules are examined in detail in this book.

Language Tested

IELTS is an international test. The English used in the test and heard on the audio can be British, American, Australian, or New Zealand English. The language tested will be comprehensible to any learner of English.

In this book, we point out the common differences between American English and the English used in other parts of the world. Footnotes are provided to show differences in spelling and usage. Whatever spelling you use when writing your test answers, the examiners will accept, as long as you are consistent throughout.

International users of English are aware of differences in usage and spelling. Most international users understand that *colour* is written *color* in American English and that *organize* is written *organise* in British English. Because of films, international magazines, travel, and the Internet, we know that *apartment* and *flat* and *gas* and *petrol, downtown* and *city centre* are synonyms. We know that an American form is *filled out* and in Britain it is *filled in.* In Britain, a family could take a *holiday* at the *sea.* In America, *vacationers* go to the *beach* for a *vacation*; in New Jersey, they go to the *shore.* We may use one synonym, but we understand the other without problem.

We know that the cultural institutions of English-speaking countries are organized (*organised*) differently. American and Australian students study for a *semester* or a *term*; British students study for a *term.* In Canada and Britain, students get *marks*; in America, they get *grades.* A British *public* school is a *private* school in America. In America, a building begins on the *first* floor. In Britain, one starts at the *ground* floor. In America, a friend is a *pal* or a *buddy.* In Australia, people call each other *mate* in conversation, whether they are friends or not. We can understand these differences from the context. Their meanings will not be misunderstood.

Some of the common usage differences in this book are:

American English	British English
math	maths
college major	subject
city hall	town hall
pharmacy	chemist
parking garage/lot	car park
movies/film	film
movie theater	cinema
sidewalk	pavement
cell phone	mobile phone
graduated from college	left college
school/college/university	college/university
checkroom	cloakroom
check	cheque
downtown	city centre

Some of the common spelling differences in this book are:

	American English	British English		American English	British English
Suffixes	-yze -ize -or -am -ck -er	-yse -ise -our -amme -que -re	Prefixes	co re	co- re-
			Doubling of Consonants	traveling labeled	travelling labelled
			Use of Dipthong *ae*	anesthesia	anaesthesia

USING THIS BOOK

You can study the material in this book in many ways. You can study it in a class; you can study it by yourself starting with the first page and going all the way to the end; or you can study only those parts where you know you need extra help.

Here are some suggestions for getting the most out of *Barron's IELTS.*

- Look over the Table of Contents so you have an idea of what is in the book.
- Take a Model Test so you understand where you need more help.
- Become familiar with the directions for IELTS. Get to know what the task is. This will help you move quickly through the test.
- Study efficiently. If you don't have much time, only study where you need extra help.
- Use the strategies. These strategies will help you score well on IELTS.
- Use the explanatory answers. These answers will explain why an answer choice is wrong. For many of the items, the answers will only be approximate. Your answer need not match the one provided as a sample.
- Study a little every day. Don't fall behind. Keep at it.

QUESTIONS AND ANSWERS ABOUT IELTS

Should I take the Academic or General Training exam?

It is important that you choose the correct test on your application form. The institution or agency that will be receiving your scores will tell you which exam to take. If you are planning on taking an undergraduate or postgraduate course at an English college or university, you should take the Academic Training exam. Your entrance to an institution will be based on this exam. You might also need to take the Academic Training exam if you are taking the IELTS for professional purposes. Check with your organization to find out what its requirements are. The General Training exam tests the English language communication skills or general communication skills that are needed for those who want to live and work in English-speaking countries. Although the Reading and Writing modules of the Academic exam measure the candidate's ability to function in a higher educational institution, a range of educational and social contexts are used in the Listening and Speaking sections of both tests. The Listening and Speaking sections are the same in both the Academic and General tests.

Where can I take IELTS?

More than 1,000 test centers around the world administer IELTS. All test centers are run by the British Council, IELTS Australia, or Cambridge University. Some testing centers also offer off-site testing for large groups if prior arrangements are made with IELTS. Contact your local examination center or visit *www.ielts.org* to find out where the nearest IELTS test center is located.

Where can I find information about registering for the test?

You can contact your nearest examination center or visit the official IELTS website (*www.ielts.org*) for more information about application procedures and the location of a test center near you.

How much does it cost to take IELTS?

Test fees are set centrally by the British Council and its partners. The fees are generally set for a year at a time. You can find out the cost to take IELTS in your currency by contacting your test center. If for some reason you cannot take the test, contact your test center as soon as possible.

Is this a paper-and-pencil test or is there a computer-based version?

As of May 2005, a computer-based IELTS (CB IELTS) became available at select test centers around the world. These tests are usually administered on alternative dates to the paper test. If you are taking the CB IELTS, you will take the Listening and Reading modules on the computer. If you are worried about your typing abilities, you have the option of doing the Writing section on paper. The Speaking section will still be administered face-to-face. CD-ROM versions of the CB IELTS are available for practice. See *www.ielts.org* for a list of test centers that offer the computer-based version.

How long is the test?

The complete IELTS takes 2 hours and 45 minutes. The Listening, Reading, and Writing modules are taken in one sitting. There are no breaks. The Speaking module may be taken within seven days before or after the other modules. It is usually taken the same afternoon or within two or three days. You will have to arrange for the Speaking module at your test center.

What can I take into the testing room?

On your desk you will be allowed only pencils and erasers (*rubbers*). (On the paper-based test, the answer sheet for the Listening and Reading modules must be written in pencil as parts of the answer sheet will be scanned by a computer.) You cannot use correction fluid. You also may not borrow or lend pens or pencils during the test. There will be a designated area for you to put your other personal belongings. You will not be allowed to have any electronic devices such as cell (*mobile*) phones in the testing room.

What identification is required?

You will need to have two forms of identification (such as a valid photo ID card, passport, driver's license, student ID, or national ID) with you when you register, as well as on test day. When you take the Speaking module, you will have to present your photo ID again. In the United States, only your passport is required.

How can I find out my results?

Your test results will be sent to your home address or your educational institute within two weeks of taking the test. Your overall band score will be given on the Test Report Form, as will a breakdown of your scores in the four separate sections. On the IELTS registration form, you can designate up to five institutions, agencies, or individuals to receive your Test Report Form. There will be a charge for additional reports.

What is a band?

You cannot pass or fail IELTS. The test is scored on a band scale. A band is a level of ability. In each section, you can score anywhere from a band of 0 (nonuser) to a band of 9 (expert user). In the Listening and Reading modules, a mark is given for each correct answer. This number is then converted into a band using a conversion table. Overall scores are an average of all four sections and can be given in whole or half bands.

How can I interpret my band scores?

A general description of the competency level for each of the nine bands is reprinted from the IELTS website with permission. Scores are reported in whole or half bands. The overall band requirement for each institution or government body may be different. A band of 6.5 or 7 is a common requirement for university admission.

9	Expert user	Has fully operational command of the language: appropriate, accurate, and fluent with complete understanding.
8	Very good user	Has fully operational command of the language with only occasional unsystematic inaccuracies and inappropriacies. Misunderstandings may occur in unfamiliar situations. Handles complex detailed argumentation well.
7	Good user	Has operational command of the language, though with occasional inaccuracies, inappropriacies, and misunderstandings in some situations. Generally handles complex language well and understands desired reasoning.
6	Competent user	Has generally effective command of the language despite some inaccuracies, inappropriacies, and misunderstandings. Can use and understand fairly complex language, particularly in familiar situations.
5	Modest user	Has partial command of the language, coping with overall meaning in most situations, though likely to make many mistakes. Should be able to handle basic communication in own field.
4	Limited user	Basic competence is limited to familiar situations. Has frequent problems in understanding and expression. Is not able to use complex language.
3	Extremely limited user	Conveys and understands only general meaning in very familiar situations. Frequent breakdowns in communication occur.
2	Intermittent user	No real communication is possible except for the most basic information using isolated words or short formulae in familiar situations and to meet immediate needs. Has great difficulty understanding spoken and written English.
1	Nonuser	Essentially has no ability to use the language beyond possibly a few isolated words.
0	Did not attempt the test	No assessable information provided.

*Reprinted from the IELTS Handbook with permission of the IELTS partners.

How long is my score valid?

An IELTS score is generally recognized for two years. Some institutions may accept your score after two years if you can provide proof that you have maintained your English language proficiency. If you are applying for admission to a post-secondary institution, your last test score will be used.

When can I retake the test?

You may repeat the test whenever and as often as you wish. However, some studies suggest that three months may be the minimum amount of time that average learners need to improve their band score. During these three months, candidates must continue their efforts to improve their English through class study or self-study.

How can I improve my score on each of the test sections?

Most importantly you must read, write, speak, and listen to English on a regular basis. *Barron's IELTS* will help you achieve your goal.

Where can I find extra help?

For test tips and new vocabulary words, follow Dr. Lin Lougheed on Twitter @LinLougheed.

Want your essays posted to Facebook for feedback from others? Post them directly at *www.facebook.com/EssaysTOEFL.IELTS* or search on Facebook for "**IELTS and TOEFL Essay Writing.**"

Preparing for IELTS 2

→ A STUDY CONTRACT
→ EXAM DAY TIPS

A STUDY CONTRACT

You must make a commitment to study English. Make a contract with yourself. A contract is a document that establishes procedures. You should not break a contract—especially a contract with yourself.

- Print your name below on the first line.
- Write the total amount of time you will spend each week studying English and the time for each skill area. Think about how much time you have to study every day and every week and make your schedule realistic.
- Sign your name and date the contract on the last lines.
- At the end of each week, add up your hours. Did you meet the requirements of your contract?

IELTS STUDY CONTRACT

I, ______________________________________, promise to study for IELTS. I will begin my study with *Barron's IELTS*, and I will also study English on my own.

I understand that to improve my English I need to spend time using English.

I promise to study English ________________ a week.

I will spend _______ hours a week listening to English.

I will spend _______ hours a week writing English.

I will spend _______ hours a week speaking English.

I will spend _______ hours a week reading English.

This is a contract with myself. I promise to fulfill the terms of this contract.

____   ______________________

Signed   Date

Self-Study

Here are some ways you can study English on your own. Put a check mark next to the ones you plan to try. Space is included for you to add some of your own ideas.

Listening

- ☐ Watch podcasts on the Internet
- ☐ Watch news websites: CNN, BBC, NBC, ABC, CBS
- ☐ Watch YouTube
- ☐ Listen to CNN and BBC on the radio
- ☐ Watch movies and TV in English
- ☐ Listen to music in English
- ☐ ________________________________
- ☐ ________________________________

Speaking

- ☐ Describe what you see and do out loud
- ☐ Practice speaking with a conversation buddy
- ☐ Use Skype to talk to English speakers
- ☐ ________________________________
- ☐ ________________________________

Writing

- ☐ Write a daily journal
- ☐ Write a letter to an English speaker
- ☐ Make lists of the things you see every day
- ☐ Write descriptions of your family and friends
- ☐ Write e-mails to website contacts
- ☐ Write a blog
- ☐ Leave comments on blogs
- ☐ Post messages in a chat room
- ☐ Use Facebook and Twitter
- ☐ ________________________________
- ☐ ________________________________

Reading

- ☐ Read newspapers and magazines in English
- ☐ Read books in English
- ☐ Read academic articles in English
- ☐ Read informational brochures and pamphlets in English
- ☐ Do web research on topics that interest you
- ☐ Follow blogs that interest you
- ☐ ________________________________
- ☐ ________________________________

Examples of Self-Study Activities

Whether you read an article in a newspaper or on a website, you can use that article in a variety of ways to practice reading, writing, speaking, and listening in English.

- Read the article.
- Paraphrase and write about it.
- Give a talk or presentation about it.
- Record or make a video of your presentation.
- Listen to or watch what you recorded. Write down your presentation.
- Correct your mistakes.
- Do it all again.

PLAN A TRIP

Go to *www.concierge.com*
Choose a city, choose a hotel, go to that hotel's website and choose a room, then choose some sites to visit. (*reading*) Write a report about the city. (*writing*) Tell why you want to go there. Describe the hotel and the type of room you will reserve. Tell what sites you plan to visit and when. Where will you eat? How will you get around?

Now write a letter to someone recommending this place. (*writing*) Pretend you have to give a lecture on your planned trip. (*speaking*) Make a video of yourself talking about this place. Then watch the video and write down what you said. (*listening*) Correct any mistakes you made and record the presentation again. Then choose another city and do this again.

SHOP FOR AN ELECTRONIC PRODUCT

Go to *www.cnet.com*
Think of an electronic product you need to buy. Write a list of features you want the product to have. (*writing*) Find the electronic product online and read about it. (*reading*) Compare the features you want with the features of the product.

Now, write an e-mail to a friend explaining why you chose this product. (*writing*) Pretend to call a friend and explain your reasons. (*speaking*) Make a video of yourself talking about the product. (speaking). Then watch the video and write down what you said. (*listening*) Correct any mistakes you made and record the presentation again. Then choose another product and do this again.

DISCUSS A BOOK, A CD, A PRODUCT

Go to *www.amazon.com*
Choose a book or CD or any product. Read the item's description and reviews. (*reading*) Write a report about the item. Tell why you want to buy one or why it is interesting to you. Describe its features.

Now write a letter to someone recommending this product. (*writing*) Pretend you have to give a talk about this product. (*speaking*) Make a video of yourself talking about this product. Then watch the video and write down what you said. (*listening*) Correct any mistakes you made and record the presentation again. Then choose another item and do this again.

DISCUSS ANY SUBJECT

Go to *simple.wikipedia.org*
This website is written in simple English. Pick any subject and read the entry. (*reading*)

Write a short essay about the topic. (*writing*) Give a presentation about it. (*speaking*) Make a video of yourself giving the presentation. Then watch the video and write down what you said. (*listening*) Correct any mistakes you made and record the presentation again. Choose another topic and do this again.

DISCUSS ANY EVENT

Go to *news.google.com*
Google News has a variety of links. Pick one event and read the articles about it. (*reading*)

Write a short essay about the event. (*writing*) Give a presentation about it. (*speaking*) Make a video of yourself giving the presentation. Then watch the video and write down what you said. (*listening*) Correct any mistakes you made and record the presentation again. Then choose another event and do this again.

REPORT THE NEWS

Listen to an English language news report on the radio or watch a news program on TV. (*listening*) Take notes as you listen. Write a summary of what you heard. (*writing*)

Pretend you are a news reporter. Use the information from your notes to report the news. (*speaking*) Make a video of yourself giving the presentation. Then watch the video and write down what you said. (*listening*) Correct any mistakes you made and record the presentation again. Then listen to another news program and do this again.

EXPRESS AN OPINION

Read a letter to the editor in the newspaper. (*reading*) Write a letter in response in which you say whether or not you agree with the opinion expressed in the first letter. Explain why. (*writing*)

Pretend you have to give a talk explaining your opinion. (*speaking*) Make a video of yourself giving the talk. Then watch the video and write down what you said. (*listening*) Correct any mistakes you made and record the presentation again. Then read another letter to the editor and do this again.

REVIEW A BOOK OR MOVIE

Read a book (*reading*) or watch a movie. (*listening*) Think about your opinion of the book or movie. What did you like about it? What didn't you like about it? Who would you recommend it to and why? Pretend you are a book or movie reviewer for a newspaper or a website. Write a review of the book or movie with your opinion and recommendations. (*writing*)

Give an oral presentation about the book or movie. Explain what it is about and what your opinion of it is. (*speaking*) Make a video of yourself giving the presentation. Then watch the video and write down what you said. (*listening*) Correct any mistakes you made and record the presentation again. Then read another book or watch another movie and do this again.

SUMMARIZE A TV SHOW

Watch a TV show in English. (*listening*) Take notes as you listen. After watching, write a summary of the show. (*writing*)

Use your notes to give an oral summary of the show. Explain the characters, setting, and plot. (*speaking*) Make a video of yourself speaking. Then watch the video and write down what you said. (*listening*) Correct any mistakes you made and record the presentation again. Then watch another TV show and do this again.

EXAM DAY TIPS

- Read all communication from the test center carefully. You may receive directions or advice on nearby hotels.
- Be early. Give yourself more than enough time to get to the test center. If you live far away, you may want to arrive the night before. Then you can relax without worrying about being late.
- Be comfortable. Don't wear clothes that don't fit or don't feel good.
- Don't bring unnecessary items with you to the testing center. The only things you will be allowed to take into the testing room are pencils and erasers (*rubbers*), your identification, and possibly a bottle of water. Everything else, including handbags, coats, jackets (even blazers or other jackets normally worn indoors), and cell (*mobile*) phones, will have to be left outside the testing room.
- You will have to bring identification with you to the testing site. The test administrators normally ask for a passport. You will be asked to arrive at the testing center at least 30 minutes ahead of time for check-in and identification check. Anyone who arrives late will not be admitted to the test.
- The Listening, Reading, and Writing parts of the test last about 3 hours altogether. You will have to remain in your seat in the testing room during this entire period of time, even if you finish the test early.
- You will be permitted to leave the room to go to the restroom if necessary. Raise your hand and quietly ask the person in charge for permission to leave the testing room. Do not disturb the other test takers.
- The last part of the test is the Speaking part. It takes up to 20 minutes. This is a face-to-face interview, so each test taker will be assigned a time for his or her interview. You probably won't know the time for your interview until the day of the test, so you need to be prepared to spend most of the day at the testing center.

Listening Module 3

→ **QUICK STUDY**
- **Overview**
- **Question Types**
- **Listening Tips**
- **Completing the Blanks**

→ **LISTENING SKILLS**
- **Skill 1—Making Assumptions**
- **Skill 2—Understanding Numbers**
- **Skill 3—Understanding the Alphabet**
- **Skill 4—Distinguishing Similar Sounds**
- **Skill 5—Listening for Descriptions**
- **Skill 6—Listening for Time**
- **Skill 7—Listening for Frequency**
- **Skill 8—Listening for Similar Meanings**
- **Skill 9—Listening for Emotions**
- **Skill 10—Listening for an Explanation**
- **Skill 11—Listening for Classifications**
- **Skill 12—Listening for Comparisons and Contrasts**
- **Skill 13—Listening for Negative Meaning**
- **Skill 14—Listening for Chronology**

→ **ANSWER EXPLANATIONS**

QUICK STUDY

OVERVIEW

There are four sections to the Listening module. There are 40 questions altogether. The audio will last approximately 30 minutes.

During the test, you will be given time to read the questions *before* you hear the audio. As you listen, you should write your answers on your question paper. Do not wait until the end. The answers in the audio follow the order of the questions. If you hesitate and think about one question, you may miss the next question. The audio keeps going.

At the end of each section, you will be given 30 seconds to check your answers. At the end of the Listening Module, you will have an additional 10 minutes to transfer your answers from your question paper to the official answer sheet. You must transfer your answers. If you don't transfer your answers, your answers will not be counted and you will not receive a listening score.

The Listening modules are the same for both the Academic and the General Training versions of IELTS.

Listening Module		
Sections	**Topics**	**Speakers**
1	General, everyday topics	Conversation between two people
2	General, everyday topics	One person
3	School or training-related topics	Conversation between two or more people
4	School or training-related topics	One person

QUESTION TYPES

There are a variety of question types on the IELTS Listening module. You will find examples of these types in this chapter.

- Multiple choice
- Short answer
- Sentence completion
- Chart completion
- Flowchart completion
- Graphs
- Tables
- Making notes
- Summarizing[1]
- Labeling[2] diagrams, plans, and maps
- Classification
- Matching
- Selecting from a list

[1]British: Summarising
[2]British: Labelling

LISTENING TIPS

1. Learn and understand the directions by using this book and the Model Tests it contains. Use your time during the test to study the questions, not the directions.
2. Study the different types of questions. Be prepared for what the question might ask you to do. Be prepared to complete a sentence, check[1] a box, or choose a letter.
3. Take notes in your question booklet as you listen. You can circle possible answers and change your mind later when you transfer your answers to the answer sheet.
4. If you don't know an answer, guess.
5. After answering, preview the next set of questions. Make assumptions about what you think you will hear.
6. When you make assumptions, ask yourself: *Who? What? When? Where?* and *How?*
7. The correct answer is often repeated, but the words will not be written exactly as they are heard. The test will use paraphrases and synonyms.
8. A lot of information given in the conversations and lectures is not tested. Try to listen only for answers to the questions.
9. Don't get stuck on a question. If you didn't hear the answer, go on.
10. The answers are given in order. For example, if you hear the answer to question 10, but didn't hear the answer for question 9, you missed question 9. You will not hear the answer later. Guess the answer to question 9 and move on.
11. When you write a word in a blank, you must spell the word correctly. It doesn't matter if you use British or American spelling. It must be spelled correctly or you will get a lower score.
12. Mark your answers carefully. If you are asked to give a letter (e.g., *A*), don't answer with a phrase.
13. Pay attention when speakers correct themselves. The second statement is usually the one that contains the correct answer.
14. Incomplete or shortened answers (e.g., times and dates) will be marked as incorrect.
15. Remember that answers that exceed word limits (even use of *a* and *the*) will be marked as incorrect.
16. A variety of accents are used, including British, American, and Australian. Practice listening to different types of native speakers.
17. Practice[2] listening for a full half hour. Concentrate. Do not let your mind wander. Can you repeat main ideas and details from what you heard? Can you summarize what you heard?

[1]British: tick a box
[2]British: practise

COMPLETING THE BLANKS

Number of Words and Spelling

Many IELTS test takers do not correctly complete the blanks. Some test takers use more than the suggested number of words, or they do not spell the answer correctly.

If you make these mistakes, you will lose points. Be careful when you complete blanks. You may know the correct answer, but if you don't spell it correctly or if you add additional words, you will get a lower score.

NUMBER OF WORDS

Complete the sentence below. Write NO MORE THAN THREE WORDS *for each answer.*

Incorrect: While on the subway, the boy lost his favorite leather wallet.
Correct: While on the subway, the boy lost his wallet.

The incorrect answer above counts as four words. Four words will count against you. You can use fewer than three words, but you cannot use more than three words.

WORD CHOICE

Complete the sentence below. Write NO MORE THAN THREE WORDS *for each answer.*

Incorrect: The ceremony will be held in in a beautiful/lovely resort hotel.
Correct: The ceremony will be held in a beautiful hotel.

The incorrect answer above counts as six words. The word *in* is repeated. Using *beautiful/lovely* counts as two words. If there are two possible words with similar meaning, choose the best word for your answer. Do not use a slash. The adjective *resort* is not necessary to the statement.

TIP

You can practice your spelling by taking dictation. Listen to the audio in this book. Write down everything you hear. Check your spelling in the audio script in the back of this book.

SPELLING

Complete the sentence below. Write NO MORE THAN THREE WORDS *for each answer.*

Incorrect: The scientists discovered a cancer treetment.
Correct: The scientists discovered a cancer treatment.

You must spell the words correctly. A misspelled word will count against you. You can use British or American spelling, but you must spell the word correctly.

Questions 1–10

The following statements are not completed correctly. Write the correct answer. Write NO MORE THAN THREE WORDS *for each answer.*

1 The shelves were filled with with fruts and fresh vegetables.

The shelves were filled with fruits and vegetables.

In the incorrect sentence, *with* is repeated, *fruits* is misspelled, the adjective *fresh* is not necessary to the statement, and there are five words instead of three.

2 Cynthia lives near to the train stattion.

Cynthia lives near ....

3 If you return a library book late, you must ....pay a fine of 25 cents[1] a day..... .

If you return a library book late, you must ....

4 Their trip was spoiled[2] because of ......it was bad/terrible weather...... .

Their trip was spoiled because of ....

5 The fountain is in the center of the ....beautiful, sunny roses garden..... .

The fountain is in the center of the ....

6 Students ....they usually can choose/decide.... the topic for their essay.

Students .... the topic for their essay.

7 ....More or less ten thousend of.... visitors come to the museum each year.

.... visitors come to the museum each year.

8 If you don't understand the assignment, you should ....have to ask the professor.... for help.

If you don't understand the assignment, you should .... for help.

9 Roberto was excited about ....about taking a trip to Alaska.... .

Roberto was excited about ....

10 Many northern song birds ....spend the long witer.......... in Mexico.

Many northern song birds .... in Mexico.

Verb, Noun, and Pronoun Agreement

The words you write in a blank must match the rest of the sentence in tense, number, and gender. Don't use a singular verb when a plural verb is required. Don't use a singular noun when a plural noun is required. Don't use a masculine pronoun to refer to a feminine or neutral antecedent. You may know the correct answer, but if you don't use correct grammar, you will get a lower score.

VERB AGREEMENT

Incorrect: The scientists at the research hospital ..is looking.. for a cure.
Correct: The scientists at the research hospital ..are looking.. for a cure.

The incorrect answer above uses a singular verb *is.* A plural verb *are* refers to the plural subject *scientists.* The singular noun *hospital* is the object of the preposition *at,* not the subject of the sentence.

SINGULAR/PLURAL NOUN

Incorrect: They ordered five ..shirt.. .
Correct: They ordered five ..shirts.. .

The incorrect answer above uses a singular noun *shirt.* A plural noun *shirts* is needed because of the plural number *five.* (See Writing Skills, Skill 27—Plural Nouns on page 189 for more study.)

[1]U.S. CURRENCY: 100 CENTS IN ONE DOLLAR
[2]AMERICAN: ruined

PRONOUN AGREEMENT

Incorrect: The patients have confidence in his doctors.
Correct: The patients have confidence in their doctors.

The incorrect answer above uses a singular pronoun *his*. A plural pronoun *their* refers to the plural subject *patients*. (See Writing Skills, Skill 23—Pronouns on page 183 for more study.)

Questions 1–10

The following statements are not completed correctly. Write the correct answer. Write **NO MORE THAN THREE WORDS** *for each answer.*

1 Unlike most other ducks, wood ducks build thier nest in trees.
Unlike most other ducks, wood ducks .... in trees.

2 The new compact laptop computer is very popular among busines traveler.
The new compact laptop computer is very popular among ....

3 Bananas grow in in a tropicale climates.
Bananas grow in ....

4 Fruit cost moor in the winter than in the summer.
Fruit .... in the winter than in the summer.

5 Mrs. Smith donated his old close to charity.
Mrs. Smith donated .... to charity.

6 Students in this class have to must take two exam this semester.[1]
Students in this class have to .... this semester.

7 The college professor bought new house.
The college professor bought ....

8 Mr. and Mrs. Rodgers took his vacations[2] in August this year.
Mr. and Mrs. Rodgers .... in August this year.

9 Every house have a garden in the back.
Every house .... in the back.

10 The female dragonfly likes to lay their eggs under water.
The female dragonfly .... under water.

[1]BRITISH: term
[2]BRITISH: holiday

Articles

When completing a blank, you must use an article—*a, an, the*—if grammar requires it. An article counts as one word, just like any other word you may put in a blank.

When referring to something in general, you can use a plural noun without an article, or you can use a singular noun with *a* or *an*. If you use a non-count noun, do not use an article when speaking in general.

Incorrect: Child needs good nutrition to grow up healthy.
Correct: Children need good nutrition to grow up healthy.
Correct: A child needs good nutrition to grow up healthy.

When referring to specific people, places, or things, use *the* with a singular, plural, or non-count noun.

Incorrect: Homework that Mrs. Smith gives in her math class is very challenging.
Correct: The homework that Mrs. Smith gives in her math class is very challenging.

Questions 1–10

The following statements are not completed correctly. Write the correct answer. Write NO MORE THAN THREE WORDS *for each answer.*

1 We have to complete all assignment in this class before the end of the semester.

We have to complete .... in this class before the end of the semester.

2 A moth usually fly at night.

.... usually fly at night.

3 The professor showed us a butterfly. Butterfly had beautiful colors.

The professor showed us a butterfly. .... had beautiful colors.

4 The old library building is too small, and it needs many repairs. Therefore, the City Council is talking about building the new library.

The old library building is too small, and it needs many repairs. Therefore, the City Council is talking about building ....

5 The air pollution is a serious problem in many large cities around the world.

.... is a serious problem in many large cities around the world.

6 Animals living near the Arctic has special adaptations for the cold climate.

.... living near the Arctic has special adaptations for the cold climate.

7 Keep your ticket with you at all times. To get a discount at the museum gift shop, show a ticket to the gift shop clerk.

Keep your ticket with you at all times. To get a discount at the museum gift shop, show .... to the gift shop clerk.

8 An information in this book will help you pass the course.

.... in this book will help you pass the course.

9 The gold is a precious metal that is valued by people everywhere.

.... is a precious metal that is valued by people everywhere.

10 Pet parrot requires a lot of care and attention.

.... requires a lot of care and attention.

Gerunds, Infinitives, and Base Form Verbs

When you write a verb, you must use the correct form. The main verb of a sentence has a verb tense. Other verbs in a sentence might be in the gerund, infinitive, or base form.

GERUNDS (VERB + *ING*) CAN BE USED AS THE SUBJECT OF A SENTENCE. GERUNDS CAN FOLLOW CERTAIN VERBS. THEY CAN ALSO FOLLOW PREPOSITIONS.

Incorrect: Eat sweets can cause weight gain and other health problems.
Correct: Eating sweets can cause weight gain and other health problems.

Incorrect: Many tourists enjoy to visit the museum.
Correct: Many tourists enjoy visiting the museum.

Incorrect: They are interested in learn about history.
Correct: They are interested in learning about history.

INFINITIVES (*TO* + VERB) OFTEN FOLLOW ADJECTIVES. INFINITIVES ALSO FOLLOW CERTAIN VERBS.

Incorrect: During a blizzard, it is important keeping warm.
Correct: During a blizzard, it is important to keep warm.

Incorrect: He expected returning to school in the autumn.
Correct: He expected to return to school in the autumn.

BASE FORM VERBS FOLLOW MODALS.

Incorrect: You can to find information in the university library.
Correct: You can find information in the university library.

Questions 1–10

The following statements are not completed correctly. Write the correct answer. Write NO MORE THAN THREE WORDS *for each answer.*

1 We will finish read this novel before the end of the semester.

We will finish .... before the end of the semester.

2 He plans arrive in Chicago at 10:00.

He .... in Chicago at 10:00.

3 She should wait until after dinner going to the gym.

She should wait until after dinner .... to the gym.

4 All visitors must having a ticket to enter the museum.

All visitors must .... a ticket to enter the museum.

5 Pay a deposit will secure the apartment for you.

.... will secure the apartment for you.

6 It's easier get reservations at the hotel during the winter season.

It's easier .... at the hotel during the winter season.

7 Marvin felt nervous about gave his report in front of the class.

Marvin felt nervous about .... in front of the class.

8 You cannot missing more than three classes during the semester.

You cannot .... three classes during the semester.

9 Sarah failed the class because she was confused about fulfills the lab requirement.

Sarah failed the class because she was confused about .... requirement.

10 They hoped saw alligators during their tour of the Everglades.

They hoped .... during their tour of the Everglades.

TIP

Study Skills 17 and 18 on Stress in the Speaking Module, pages 265–266. These skills will help you understand how stress changes the meaning of words or sentences. This will help you when you listen as well.

LISTENING SKILLS

Skill 1—Making Assumptions

In order to understand a conversation, you should focus on two things: the speakers and the topic. To score well on the IELTS, you should determine what you know and what you need to know.

As you listen to a conversation, you must make some assumptions about the speakers and the topic. You want to know *who*, *what*, *when*, *where*, and *why*.

Assumptions About the Speaker	Assumptions About the Topic
Who are they?	*What* are they talking about?
What is their relationship?	*What* happened?
Where are they?	*What* might happen?
What do they plan to do?	
What did they do?	
What are their feelings?	
Why are they talking?	

To help you make these assumptions, you should scan the questions in your Listening Test booklet quickly and ask yourself: *Who? What? When? Where?* and *Why?* By looking for the answers to these general questions, you will discover what you know and what you need to know.

During the test, you will have about 20 seconds to look over these questions. Use that time to make assumptions about the listening passage. Read the question first. Then read the exercise on "Assumptions" on page 26. Do the exercises. Finally, listen to the conversation and test your assumptions.

Track 1

PRACTICE 1

Questions 1–5

Quickly read each question. Then complete the Assumptions exercises on page 26.
Finally, listen to the conversation and test your assumptions.
Complete the form below.
Write NO MORE THAN THREE WORDS AND/OR A NUMBER *for each answer.*

Woodside Apartments[1]

Tenant Application Form

Example
Type of apartment requested: ....One bedroom........

Last name[2] **1** .... First name ....James..............

Address 1705 **2** .... Street, Apt. **3** ....

Phone: Home: .....721-0584..... Work: **4** ....

Date of birth **5** .... 12, 1978[3]

Questions 6–8

Choose three letters, ***A–G****.*

What features will James get with his apartment?

A study
B balcony
C garage parking space[4]
D storage space
E exercise club
F fireplace
G washing machine

Questions 9–10

Complete the sentences.
Write NO MORE THAN THREE WORDS *for each answer.*

The apartment will be ready next **9** ....

James will have to pay **10** .... of the first month's rent as a deposit.

[1]BRITISH: Flats
[2]BRITISH: surname
[3]BRITISH: day month, year; AMERICAN: month day, year
[4]BRITISH: parking place

Assumptions

Answer the questions below by making assumptions about the speaker and topic. Write NO MORE THAN THREE WORDS *for each answer.*

Who? ....
What? ....
When? ....
Where? ....
Why? ....

Circle the clues in Practice 1 on page 25 that help you make these assumptions. No answers are provided in the answer key.

Assumption 1—James wants to rent a one-bedroom apartment at the Woodside Apartments.

How do we know his first name is James?
How do we know he wants to rent?
How do we know he wants a one-bedroom apartment?
How do we know the name of the building?

Assumption 2—He is a prospective tenant.
How do we know he is a prospective tenant?

Assumption 3—The apartment is not ready yet.
How do we know the apartment is not ready?

Assumption 4—He will have to pay a deposit.
How do we know there is a deposit?

Now listen to the audio and answer the questions for Practice 1 on page 25.

We don't know this:
Write the number of the question from Practice 1, questions 1–10 on page 25 next to the question you have to answer.

A. What is James's last name? Question ......1......
B. What street does he live on? Question ....
C. What is his work telephone number? Question ....
D. What month was he born? Question ....
E. What features will he get with his apartment? Question ....
F. When will the apartment be ready? Question ....
G. How much is the deposit? Question ....

Now listen to the conversation. Listen for the answers you don't know.

Track 2

PRACTICE 2

Questions 11–13

Before you listen to the audio, look over the questions and make assumptions. Try to find the answers to *Who? What? When? Where?* and *Why?*

Assumptions

Find the answers to Who? What? When? Where? and Why?

Who are the speakers?
What are they talking about?
When is something happening?
Where is something happening?
Why are they having a conversation?

Complete the information about the museum.
Write NO MORE THAN THREE WORDS AND/OR A NUMBER *for each answer.*

Jamestown Museum of Art
Information for Visitors

Entrance Fees: Adults $ **11** ....
Children $ **12** ....
Entrance is free for senior citizens on **13** ....

Hours
Tues–Thur 11:00 A.M.–5:00 P.M.
Fri 11:00 A.M.–7:00 P.M.
Sat–Sun 10:00 A.M.–6:00 P.M.
Mondays and holidays closed

Questions 14–18

Fill in the missing information on the map of the museum.
Write NO MORE THAN THREE WORDS *for each answer.*

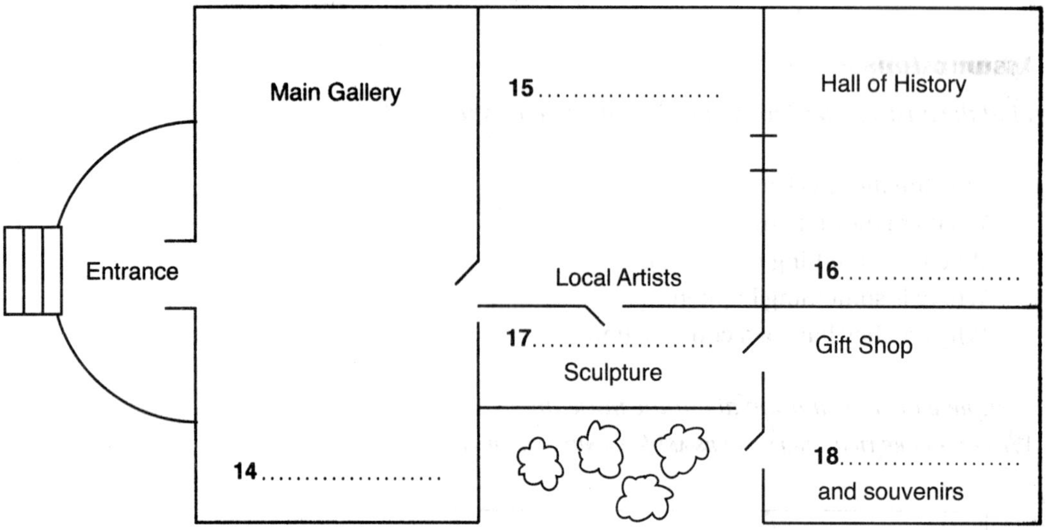

Questions 19–20

Complete the notice below.
Write NO MORE THAN THREE WORDS *for each answer.*

Notice to museum visitors.
The following areas are restricted.
Hall of History: Closed for **19** .... Will reopen in April.
20 .... : Museum staff offices. Employees only.
All others must have an appointment.

We know this from reading Practice 2, questions 11–20 on pages 27–28.

The Jamestown Museum of Art has varied hours of operation, but it is closed on Monday and holidays. There are four galleries. One gallery has local art. The other has sculpture. There is a gift shop. The Hall of History will reopen in April. The Museum staff offices are open only by appointment to non-staff members.

Answer these questions.

Write NO MORE THAN THREE WORDS *for each answer.*

Who? ....

What? ....

When? ....

Where? ....

Why? ....

Circle the clues in Practice 2 on pages 27–28 that help you make these assumptions. No answers are provided in the answer key.

We don't know this:

Write the number of the question in Practice 2, questions 11–20 on pages 27–28 next to the question you have to answer.

A.	What is the admission price for adults?	Question .....11.....
B.	What is the admission price for children?	Question ....
C.	When is there no admission fee for senior citizens?	Question ....
D.	What kind of art is in the Hall of History?	Question ....
E.	In which gallery is local art located?	Question ....
F.	What kind of art is in the Main Gallery?	Question ....
G.	In which gallery is sculpture located?	Question ....
H.	What besides souvenirs is sold in the gift shop?	Question ....
I.	Why is the Hall of History closed?	Question ....
J.	Where are the staff offices located?	Question ....

Skill 2—Understanding Numbers

Many of the questions on the IELTS Listening Module ask you to remember, identify, and/or write numbers that you hear. This is an easy skill to practice, but a difficult one to perfect.

You will hear: Flight 33 leaves from Gate 13 Concourse C3.

You will see: *Write the number you hear.*

What is the flight number? ....33....

Many numbers sound alike. Here are a few easily confused numbers. Say them out loud.

3	13	30	33	4	14	40	44	6	16	60	66

Try to use the context to make a guess about what you are hearing. When you look over the questions to make assumptions about the topic, pay attention to those questions that ask for specific numbers. Listen carefully for those numbers.

Track 3

Questions 1–5

Listen for the numbers and answer the questions.
Write a number in the blank or *choose the correct letter,* **A**, **B**, *or* **C**.

1

Credit Card Charge Form

Card Holder:	Roger Wilcox
Address:	13 High Street
Card Number:	....

2 How many seats are there in the new theater?

A 200
B 250
C 500

3

Name	Phone
Roberts, Sherry	....

4 How much will the woman pay for the hotel room?

A $255
B $265
C $315

5

Lost Luggage Report

Passenger name: Richard Lyons

Flight number: ....

Track 4

Questions 6–15

Listen to these telephone numbers. Pay attention to the way three different speakers say the same number.

6	703-6588	**11**	637-0550
7	744-1492	**12**	265-1811
8	202-9983	**13**	287-6216
9	671-4532	**14**	455-3021
10	824-1561	**15**	305-8480

Now write the numbers you hear.

6 .... **11** ....

7 .... **12** ....

8 .... **13** ....

9 .... **14** ....

10 .... **15** ....

Skill 3—Understanding the Alphabet

Many of the questions on the IELTS Listening module ask you to remember, identify, and/or write letters of the alphabet that you hear. This is a good skill to practice for the test and for real life.

You will hear:

Speaker 1: Is your name spelled[1] L-I-N or L-Y-N-N?
Speaker 2: Actually, it's Lynne with an e.

You will see: *Write the name you hear.*

What is the person's name? ....Lynne........

Track 5

Questions 1–6

Circle the correct spelling of the name you hear.

1	Tomas	Thomas
2	Maine	Main
3	Patty	Patti
4	Roberts	Robertson
5	Springfield	Springvale
6	Nixon	Dixson

Track 6

Questions 7–12

Complete the statements.
Write NO MORE THAN THREE WORDS AND/OR A NUMBER *for the answer.*

7

Order Form

Name **A** ....Green........
Credit Card Number **B** ....

8

Telephone Directory

Barney's Discount Store 673-0982
A .... Theater **B** ....

[1]British: spelt

9

Hotel Serenity

Albert Street (Private Bag 91031)
Auckland 1, New Zealand
Tel: (9) 309-6445

Reservations

Name: Roberta **A** ....

Room number 304 ....

Price **B** £ ....

10

Royale Theater
Ticket Order Form

Name: Peter Park ....

Address: 75 **A** .... Street

City: Riverdale ....

Seat number: **B** ....

11

Professor: Dr.[1] **A** ....

Office hours: T, Th 3:00–5:00

Office number: **B** ....

12

Addresses

W

Name: Wild Flower Society ....

Address: **A** .... State Street

City: **B** ....

[1]BRITISH: No period after Dr

Skill 4—Distinguishing Similar Sounds

Some words sound similar to each other, but they are different. For speakers of certain languages, some sounds are more difficult to distinguish than others.

Native Language	Difficult Sounds	Examples
Arabic	p and b	pan / ban
Russian	d and t	door / tore
Spanish	sh and ch	wish / which
Japanese	l and r	lot / rot
Thai	v and w	vet / wet
Korean	th and s	thin / sin

English vowels can be difficult to distinguish for speakers of almost any language. Here are some commonly confused English vowel sounds:

i and ee	ship / sheep
a and e	pat / pet
e and ay	debt / date
o and aw	boat / bought
a and u	bat / but

It is always a good idea to practice distinguishing similar sounds in English. This will help you choose the correct spelling of a word. Determine which sounds give you the most difficulty and look for minimal pairs drills online and in books that will help you practice them. These are exercises that focus on two similar but different sounds.

Track 7

PRACTICE 1

Read and listen to these commonly confused words. In each pair, the only difference is one sound.

bath / path
cub / cup
lice / rice
chip / ship
match / mash
tear / dare
wet / wed
thumb / some
math / mass
din / ding
jam / yam
west / vest
flow / flaw
cat / cut
chit / cheat
set / sat

PRACTICE 2

Listen to the sentence and circle the word you hear.

p/b

1 beach / peach
2 back / pack
3 stable / staple
4 cab / cap

l/r

5 lane / rain
6 alive / arrive
7 clown / crown
8 light / right

ch/sh

9 choose / shoes
10 cheat / sheet
11 ditch / dish
12 much / mush

t/d

13 tore / door
14 tied / dyed
15 bride / bright
16 neat / need

th/s

17 think / sink
18 thick / sick
19 path / pass
20 myth / miss

n/ng

21 sin / sing
22 sun / sung
23 gone / gong
24 thin / thing

w/v

25 worse / verse
26 wine / vine
27 wiper / viper
28 weird / veered

Vowels

29 let / late
30 set / sat
31 run / ran
32 coat / caught
33 seat / sit

Skill 5—Listening for Descriptions

When you listen to a conversation or a lecture, you see in your mind what the speaker is discussing. If the speaker talks about a garden, you will see in your mind some plants, trees, and walkways. As the speaker continues and talks about a fountain in the garden, you will add a fountain in your mind's eye. You might think the fountain is made of cement, but the speaker describes one made of marble. You can change the image easily in your mind.

On the IELTS, you will have to listen to descriptions and match them to a drawing in your test booklet.

Questions 1–3

Look at the following houses. Write a short description of each. See the model answers on page 61.

A

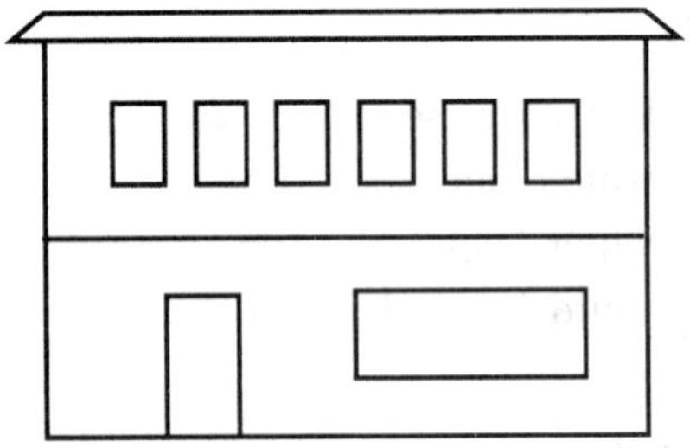

1 ______________________________

____

____

____

B

2 ______________________________

____

____

____

C

3 ______________________________

____

____

____

Track 8

Question 4

Now listen to the conversation. Where does the woman live?

Choose the correct letter, ***A***, ***B***, *or* ***C***.....................

Questions 5–8

Pause audio

5 *Look at the following men. Take notes of their descriptions.*

A **B** **C**

________________ ________________ ________________

________________ ________________ ________________

6 *Now listen to the news bulletin.*
Choose the letter that matches the description, ***A***, ***B***, *or* ***C***. ....

Resume audio

Pause audio

7 *Look at the following women. Take notes of their descriptions.*

A **B** **C**

________________ ________________ ________________

________________ ________________ ________________

8 *Now listen to the conversation.*
Choose the letter that matches the description, ***A***, ***B***, *or* ***C***. ....

Resume audio

Skill 6—Listening for Time

Listening for time is a very important skill. You must know when something happened. You must listen for a date, a day, a month, a year, or a time.

You will hear: The train was almost thirty minutes late. It didn't arrive until five o'clock.

You will see: *Choose the correct letter, A, B, or C.* ....A..........

A

B

C

Useful Words and Phrases for Time		
10:00 A.M. noon 5:00 P.M. midnight	in January in February May 3 November 14	1912 1925 2005 2007
at 4:00 before 6:30 after 7:00 half-past two quarter-past three quarter to four	March 5 of this year April 12 of next year last December 10	in the spring in the summer in the autumn[1] in the winter
Sunday Monday Tuesday	on June 10th on the 5th of July on August 3rd	yesterday tomorrow day after tomorrow
this week this month next week next month next year	on weekday mornings any afternoon from 1:00 during the week every other weekend	two years ago a year from now

[1]AMERICAN: fall and autumn

Track 9

Time—Questions 1–6

Listen for the correct time.

Questions 1 and 2

*Choose the correct letter, **A**, **B**, or **C**.*

1 What time does the class usually begin?

A 2:00
B 2:30
C 4:00

2 What time will the final exam begin?

A 1:45
B 3:15
C 4:05

Questions 3 and 4

*Choose the correct letter, **A**, **B**, or **C**.*

3 What time will the next train leave for Chicago?

A 

B 

C 

4 What time will it arrive in Chicago?

A 

B 

C 

Questions 5 and 6

Complete the schedule with the correct times.

Cindy's Schedule

	Monday
9:00	Spanish class
11:30	haircut
5	lunch with Jeannine
1:30	job interview
6	exercise class

Date—Questions 1–6

Most of the world writes the date as day/month/year (dd/mm/yy). Americans write month/day/year (mm/dd/yy).

American:	May 15, 2014	April 23, 2013
International:	15 May 2014	23 April 2013

Both forms are included in these exercises.

Listen for the correct date.

Track 10

Questions 1 and 2

Complete these notes with the correct date and month.

Notes

City Museum of Art
Opened: August **1** ...., 1898
Opening celebration: **2** 1, 1898

Questions 3 and 4

Complete the form with the correct month and date.

Insurance Application

Applicant name: Priscilla Katz	Date of birth: **3** 22
Spouse: George Katz	Date of birth: July **4** ....

Questions 5 and 6

*Choose the correct letter, **A**, **B**, or **C**.*

5 Which is the most popular time to visit Silver Lake?

A August
B September
C October

6 What day will the man leave for Silver Lake?

A 7 November
B 11 November
C 17 November

Track 11

Day—Questions 1–6

Listen for the correct day.

Questions 1 and 2

Complete the schedule with the correct days.

Class Schedule for		......Jim McDonald......
English:	**1**	......and Wednesday......
History:	**2**	....

Questions 3 and 4

Complete each sentence with the correct day.

There are tennis lessons at the club every **3** .... and Saturday.

The steam room is closed every **4** ....

Questions 5 and 6

*Choose the correct letter, **A**, **B**, or **C**.*

5 When is the final exam?

A Thursday
B Friday
C Saturday

6 When is the essay due?

A Monday
B Tuesday
C Wednesday

Track 12

Year—Questions 1–6

Listen for the correct year.

Questions 1 and 2

Complete the timeline with the correct year.

Life of John James Audubon

1785	**1**	1842	**2** ....
Born in Haiti	Left Haiti for the United States	*Birds of America* published in the United States	Died

Questions 3 and 4

*Choose the correct letter, **A**, **B**, or **C**.*

3 When was Maria Mahoney born?

A 1808
B 1908
C 1928

4 When did she become governor?

A 1867
B 1957
C 1967

Questions 5 and 6

Complete the sentences with the correct years.

5 Library construction was begun in ....

6 The construction was finished in ....

Track 13

Season—Questions 1–6

Listen for the correct season.

Questions 1 and 2

Complete the table with the correct seasons.

Season	**Weather**
1	cool, rainy
2	hot, dry

Questions 3 and 4

*Choose the correct letter, **A**, **B**, or **C**.*

3 When did Josh begin his hiking trip?

A Late winter
B Early spring
C Late spring

4 When did he finish his trip?

A Late summer
B Late autumn[1]
C Early winter

Questions 5 and 6

Complete the sentences with the correct seasons.

5 The busiest time of year at the language school is ....

6 The least busy time of year at the language school is ....

Skill 7—Listening for Frequency

There are certain adverbs that tell you when something might happen. The following two groups of adverbs will help you determine the time.

You will hear: Sam works out at the gym several days a week.

You will see: *Choose the correct letter, A, B, or C.* .....B.....
Sam goes to the gym
A every day.
B often.
C occasionally.

Useful Adverbs of Frequency	Useful Adverbial Time Words or Phrases
always	every day, daily
usually	twice a week
often	every other week
sometimes	once a month
occasionally	every year, yearly
seldom	from time to time
hardly ever	on occasion
rarely	once in a while
never	now and then

[1]AMERICAN: fall or autumn

Track 14

Questions 1–6

Listen to the conversations. Put a check[1] (✓) by the frequency of the action.

	always	often	sometimes	seldom	never
1					
2					
3					
4					
5					
6					

Track 15

Questions 7–12

Listen to the conversations. Put a check (✓) by the frequency of the action.

	daily	twice a week	once a month	every other week	from time to time
7					
8					
9					
10					
11					
12					

Skill 8—Listening for Similar Meanings

The words that you hear are not always the words that you see in your test booklet. You will have to listen for similar meanings. You could hear a synonym or you could hear a paraphrase.

You will hear: The survey participants who wrote answers to the questions are all college graduates.

You will see: *Write the answer.*

Who are the respondents? ....college graduates........

[1]BRITISH: tick

Track 16

Questions 1–6

Look at the underlined words or phrases in the questions below. Listen to the audio. Write the synonym or paraphrase that you hear.

1 How many people are in the group? ....
2 How often does she correct the work? ....
3 How fast is the population increasing? ....
4 What happened to the plants in the region? ....
5 When will the apartment be ready? ....
6 What kind of work does the woman do? ....

Skill 9—Listening for Emotions

Can you tell if someone is excited to do something or is not looking forward to something? While listening, try to determine a speaker's emotion. How is that emotion expressed?

You will hear: Jane: I can't wait to debate the team from Oxford.
Mark: I'm more apprehensive than excited. In fact, I'm not looking forward to it at all.

You will see: *Choose the correct letter, A, B, or C.* .....A.....

What is Mark's attitude toward the debate?

A He's nervous.
B He's looking forward to it.
C He's more excited than Jane.

Useful Words for Expressing Emotion		
afraid	ecstatic	nervous
angry	embarrassed	pleased
annoyed	exhausted	proud
ashamed	frustrated	sad
bored	happy	shocked
confused	jealous	surprised
disappointed	mad	unhappy
disgusted	miserable	upset

Track 17

PRACTICE 1

Questions 1–6

Listen to the conversations and answer the questions about emotions.

1 How did local residents feel about the millionaire's donation?

A angry
B surprised
C excited

2 How does the man feel about his science experiment?

A frustrated
B glad
C eager

3 How do students feel about the equipment?

A pleased
B challenged
C jealous

4 What is the man's attitude toward the contest?

A He's upset.
B He's disappointed.
C He's indifferent.

5 How did people at the school feel about the mayor's visit?

A They were surprised.
B They were bored.
C They were annoyed.

6 How does the woman feel about her research project?

A nervous
B bad
C happy

PRACTICE 2

Listen again. Write the word or phrase that helped you answer the question.

1 ....
2 ....
3 ....
4 ....
5 ....
6 ....

Skill 10—Listening for an Explanation

On the IELTS, a speaker may explain how something is done or made. You will have to listen and remember the steps of the process.

You will hear: How does a toaster brown your toast every morning? Like all household appliances that heat up, a toaster works by converting electrical energy into heat energy. The electrical current runs from the electrical outlet in your kitchen wall, through the toaster plug, to the toaster cord. It travels down the cord to the appliance itself. Inside the toaster are wire loops. The wires are made of a special type of metal. Electricity passes slowly through this metal, creating friction. This friction causes the wires to heat up and glow orange. When the wires have sufficiently heated, your toast pops ready to eat.

You will see: *Match the letter in the diagram with one of these labels.*

1 .....A..... Electrical socket[1]
2 .... Metal loops of wires
3 .... Cord
4 .... Appliance
5 .... Your toast is ready to eat!
6 .... Plug

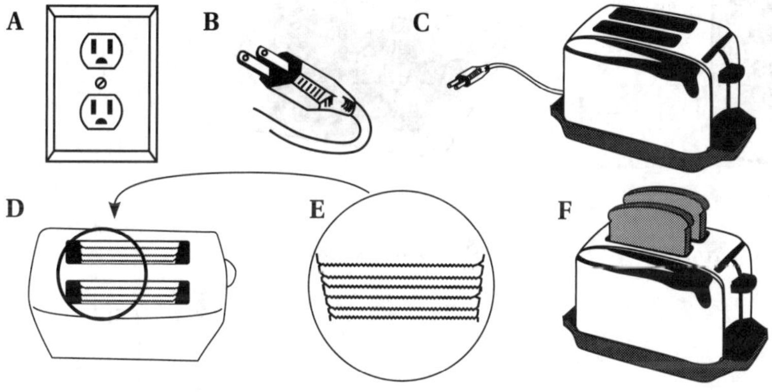

You will see: *Complete these sentences describing the process to make toast. Write* NO MORE THAN THREE WORDS *for each answer.*

7 Electricity runs from ....
8 Electricity runs down ....
9 Electricity runs to ....
10 Electricity is slowed by ....
11 When resistance to metal is high, metal will get ....
12 The wires turn ....
13 The bread ....
14 You eat the ....

[1]AMERICAN: outlet, also socket

Track 18

Questions 1–12

Label the diagram below based on what you hear.

1 ....

2 ....

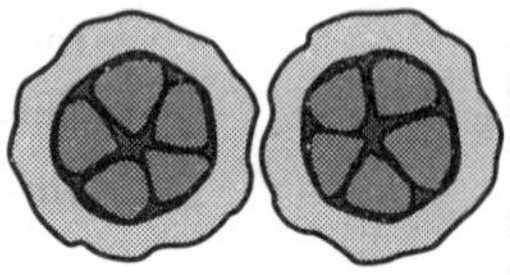

3 ....

4 ....

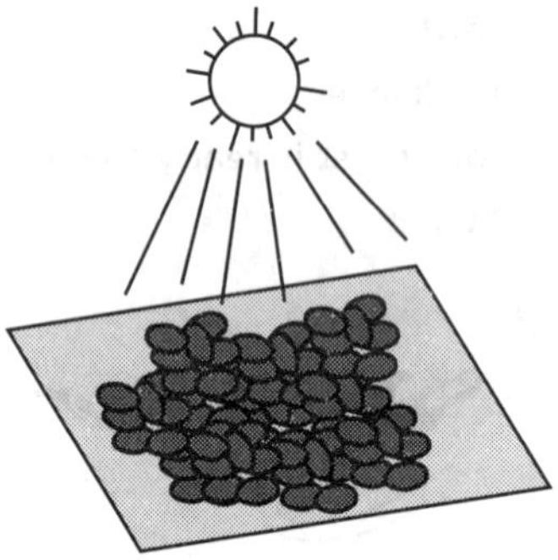

5 ....

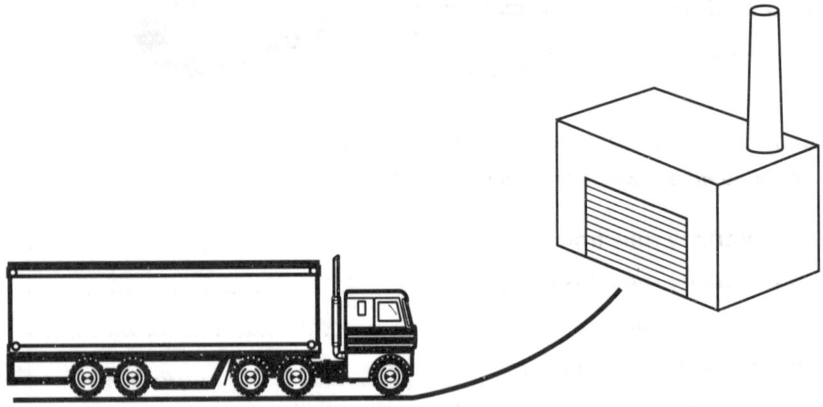

6 ....

Complete the sentences.
Write NO MORE THAN THREE WORDS *for each answer.*

7 When the fruit is ripe, it ....
8 Then the seeds ....
9 The cocoa[1] beans are fermented in vats for ....
10 Then the beans .... in the sun.
11 The cocoa beans .... the factory.
12 At the factory, the cocoa beans are turned into ....

Skill 11—Listening for Classifications

You will have to group similar objects or ideas on the IELTS Listening section. You will have to determine how to classify objects or ideas.

Useful Classification Words and Phrases	
can be divided into	types
can be categorized[6] as	kinds
can fit into this category	ways

You will hear: The school offers two types of courses. One during the day is designed for students who are pursuing their academic degree full time. The night courses are designed for students who work during the day and are taking specific courses for an advanced business certificate.

You will see: *When would these courses most likely be offered? Write them under the appropriate program[2] below.*

Project Management	Literature of the 21st Century
History of Africa	Labor[3] Negotiations
The Art of Negotiating	International Relations
Creativity in the Workplace	Introduction to Philosophy

Course Offerings	
Program 1 ....Academic....	Program 2 ....Business....
When?	When? ....
Introduction to Art	Organizational[4] Behavior[5]
Basic Chemistry	Commerical Law
Beginning Spanish	Compensation and Benefits
....	....
....	....
....	....
....	....

[1]Cacao refers to the tree. Cocoa is the drink. Cocoa is often used for both the tree and the beverage.
[2]BRITISH: programme; [3]BRITISH: Labour; [4]BRITISH: Organisational; [5]BRITISH: Behaviour; [6]BRITISH: categorised

Track 19

Questions 1–5

Complete the classifications below based on what you hear.

1 *Which of the following are offered to first-class passengers only? Choose three letters,* **A–E**.

A pillows and blankets
B snacks
C full meals
D magazines
E free movies

2 *Complete the chart. Write* ONE WORD *for each answer.*

Royal Theater	**Deluxe Theater**
War films	**B** .... films
A .... films	Classic films

3 *Complete the chart. Write* ONE WORD *for each answer.*

	A	**B** ....
Time to fly	Day	Night
Wing position	Folded back	Horizontal
Antennae	Thin	Feathery

4 *Check the things that the woman has already done to get ready for the party.*

To Do List

A ☐ Clean house
B ☐ Cook
C ☐ Go shopping
D ☐ Plan decorations
E ☐ Mail invitations

5 *Complete the chart. Write* NO MORE THAN THREE WORDS *for each answer.*

Tree Type	**Description**
A	Beautiful flowers, interesting leaves
B	Tall, broad leaves
C	Cones, needles

Skill 12—Listening for Comparisons and Contrasts

Speakers often compare or contrast objects or ideas to help describe something. On the IELTS Listening section, you will have to determine what is being compared and what is being contrasted.

You will hear:

Speaker 1: I've been corresponding by letter with a French student.
Speaker 2: In English? You don't speak French, do you?
Speaker 1: No, unfortunately, but she writes English well. We have a lot in common.
Speaker 2: Like what, your age?
Speaker 1: Well, I'm actually about two years older than she is. But we do have the same first name.
Speaker 2: And you're both students.
Speaker 1: Yes, and we both are studying to be doctors, although she wants to be a pediatrician,[1] and I want to be a neurosurgeon.
Speaker 2: It seems the only similarities are your sex and your given name.
Speaker 1: Well, we both like to swim. She likes to dance, too, but you know how little I like dancing.

You will see: *Put a check (✓) to show if these items are alike or different.*

		Alike	Different
A	Nationality		✓
B	Sex	✓	
C	Age		✓
D	Given name	✓	
E	Present occupation	✓	
F	Future occupation		✓
G	Sports	✓	
H	Love of dancing		✓

Useful Words for Comparison		Useful Words for Contrast	
almost the same as	in common	although	more than
also	just as	but	nevertheless
as	like, alike	differ from	on the other hand
at the same time as	neither/nor	different from	otherwise
correspondingly	resemble	even though	still
either/or	similar to	however	unlike
in a like manner	similarly	in contrast to	while
in the same way	than	instead	yet
		less than	

[1]BRITISH: paediatrician

Track 20

Questions 1–4

Complete the chart below based on what you hear.
Put a check (✓) to show if these items are alike or different.

1

Jobs	Alike	Different
A Salary		
B Schedule		
C Responsibilities		
D Location		
E Transportation		

2

Libraries	Alike	Different
A Location		
B Size		
C Parking facilities		
D Number of books		
E Services		

3

Club Memberships	Alike	Different
A Cost		
B Use of club facilities		
C Access to fitness classes		
D Locker room privileges		
E Individual fitness plan		

4

Frogs and Toads	Alike	Different
A Place for babies to live		
B Place for adults to live		
C Type of skin		
D Shape		
E Way to make sounds		

Skill 13—Listening for Negative Meaning

On the IELTS, you may have to determine whether a statement is positive or negative. Listen to the statement carefully to determine whether the sense of the statement is positive or negative.

You will hear: It was a very dense book, but it wasn't impossible to read.

You will see: *Choose the correct letter, A, B, or C.*

What does the woman say about the book? ....B....

A She couldn't read it.

B She was able to read it.

C She enjoyed reading it.

A negative prefix can contradict the word it joins. This usually results in a negative meaning. For example, *unfriendly* contradicts *friendly* and has the negative meaning *not friendly*. But when a negative meaning is added to a negative word, the resulting meaning can be positive. For example, *unselfish* contradicts *selfish* and has the positive meaning *not selfish*.

You can also put a negative word before a verb or clause to change the meaning of the sentence.

Useful Negative Markers

Before verbs/clauses	Before nouns/phrases	Negative prefixes	Positive meanings from negative prefixes
not	no	un-	undone
isn't/can't/won't/ shouldn't/couldn't/ hasn't/mustn't	nowhere	im-	impossible
rarely/only rarely	nothing	il-	illegal
hardly	at no time	in-	indefinite
scarcely	not at this time	non-	nonsense
seldom	in no case		unlimited
never	by no means		unparalleled
barely			invaluable
not since			nonrestrictive
not until			nonviolent
and neither			

Questions 1–6

Put a check (✓) next to the correct paraphrase of each sentence.

1 I can't wait to start the class.

.... **A** I'm looking forward to the class.
.... **B** I'm not looking forward to the class.

2 The teacher is not only my favorite[1] teacher, she's also my neighbor.[2]

.... **A** I like my teacher a lot.
.... **B** I don't like my teacher very much.

3 I can't say that it was a particularly comfortable hotel.

.... **A** The hotel was comfortable.
.... **B** The hotel wasn't comfortable.

4 We'll never find a book as interesting as this.

.... **A** The book is very interesting.
.... **B** The book isn't very interesting.

5 That was not an illegal action.

.... **A** The action was legal.
.... **B** The action wasn't legal.

6 We could scarcely understand him.

.... **A** It was easy to understand him.
.... **B** It wasn't easy to understand him.

[1]British: favourite
[2]British: neighbour

Track 21

Questions 7–12

*Listen to the conversation. Choose the correct letter, **A**, **B**, or **C**.*

7 What describes the weather in the region?

A rainy
B dry
C cloudy

8 When taking the exam, the students can

A take as much time as they need.
B use a dictionary.
C bring several things into the testing room.

9 When will the car be fixed?

A today
B before the end of the week
C on the weekend[1]

10 What is the woman's opinion of the restaurant?

A The food is good.
B The service is bad.
C The wait is too long.

11 Which type of flower is not common in the area?

A violets
B roses
C irises

12 What homework does the man have to do this week?

A write papers and read books
B write papers only
C study for exams

[1]British: at the weekend

Skill 14—Listening for Chronology

Listening for the order in which events occur is an important skill. You will need to listen to what happened first, second, and so on.

You will hear: Before you do your research, we'll have an orientation session in the library so you can become familiar with the various sources of information available there. Each student will give a presentation on his or her research topic after all the papers have been submitted. All of this will have to be completed prior to the date of the final exam.

You will see: *Complete the Class Assignment Sheet, putting the assignments in the correct order. Write* NO MORE THAN THREE WORDS *for each answer.*

Class Assignment Sheet

1 Orientation session

2 Do research

Papers submitted

Student Presentations

3 Final exam

There is more practice on Chronological Order in Writing Skills, Skill 21—Transition Words, pages 176–180 and Speaking, Skill 4—Verb Tenses, pages 246–247.

Useful Words and Phrases That Indicate Chronological Order	
before	at birth, in childhood, in infancy, as an adult,
after	in adulthood, in old age
while	simultaneously, at the same time as
during	former, latter
between ____ and _____	previous
in (year)	previously
on (day)	prior to
at (time)	first, second, third, etc.
since ______	in the first place, second place
later	to begin with
earlier	next, then, subsequently
formerly	in the next place
every (number) (years, months, days)	at last
at the turn of the century (decade)	in conclusion
in the first half of the century	finally
in the 20s, 1980s, ______	

Track 22

Questions 1–5

*Listen to the audio and put these actions in the correct chronological order. Write **1** for the first action, **2** for the second, and so forth.*

1 .... Fill out application
.... Submit application
.... Get references
.... Pay a deposit
.... Receive notification of apartment
.... Sign lease

2 .... Leopold Mozart published a book.
.... Wolfgang Mozart began to compose music.
.... Leopold began taking Wolfgang on tours of Europe.
.... Wolfgang Mozart settled in Vienna.
.... Wolfgang's mother died.

3 .... Left home
.... Had picnic
.... Made sandwiches
.... Went swimming
.... Checked into motel

4 .... Find partner
.... Choose topic
.... Get professor's approval
.... Design research
.... Start research

5 .... Walk through rose garden
.... Show tickets
.... View pond area
.... Visit greenhouse
.... Photograph butterfly garden

ANSWER EXPLANATIONS

COMPLETING THE BLANKS

Number of Words and Spelling (page 18)

2. *the train station.* The word *to* is unnecessary after *near.* The word *station* is misspelled. (BRITISH: mis-spelt)

3. *pay a fine.* The other words are unnecessary and exceed the three-word limit.

4. *the weather* or *the bad weather.* The expression *because of* must be followed by a noun, not by a clause. The words *bad/terrible* are unnecessary.

5. *rose garden.* The word *rose* must be singular because it serves as an adjective to describe *garden.* The words *beautiful, sunny* are not necessary and make the answer exceed the three-word limit.

6. *can choose.* The word *usually* is not necessary. The word *can* is always followed by the base form of the verb, not the infinitive form.

7. *About ten thousand.* Use *about* instead of *more or less* to stay within the three-word limit. The word *thousand* is misspelled. An exact number is not followed by *of.*

8. *ask the professor.* The phrase *have to* cannot correctly follow *should* or any other modal.

9. *going to Alaska* or *traveling to Alaska.* It is not necessary to repeat the word *about.* Using *going to* or *traveling to* instead of *his trip to* keeps the answer within the three-word limit. (BRITISH: travelling)

10. *spend the winter.* The word *long* is not necessary and makes the answer exceed the three-word limit. The word *winter* is misspelled.

Verb, Noun, and Pronoun Agreement (page 20)

1. *build their nests.* The word *their* is misspelled and *nests* must be plural because it refers to many nests belonging to many ducks.

2. *business travelers.* The word *business* is misspelled. The word *travelers* should be plural because *among* implies that there are many. (BRITISH: travellers)

3. *tropical climates.* It isn't necessary to repeat the word *in.* The word *a* is incorrect before a plural noun. The word *tropical* is misspelled.

4. *costs more.* The word *fruit* is a non-count noun and takes a singular verb. The word *more* is misspelled.

5. *her old clothes.* The feminine possessive adjective *her* agrees with the feminine subject *Mrs. Smith.* The word *clothes* is misspelled.

6. *take two exams.* The subject is *students,* so the pronoun *they* is not necessary. Don't use *must* after *have to*—they have the same meaning. The word *exams* must be plural because there are *two.*

7. *a new house.* The singular noun *house* must be preceded by an article.

8. *took their vacation.* The plural adjective *their* agrees with the plural subject. The word *vacation* is singular. (BRITISH: took their holiday)

9. *has a garden.* The verb *has* agrees with the singular subject *Every house.*

10. *lays her eggs* or *lays its eggs.* The words *like to* are unnecessary and make the answer exceed the three-word limit. The possessive adjective must agree with the subject *female dragonfly—her* because the subject is female, or *its* because the subject is an animal.

Articles (page 21)

1. *all the assignments.* The article *the* is required because these are specific assignments—the ones in this class. The word *assignments* is plural because *all* implies that there are more than one.

2. *Moths.* This sentence is a general statement, but the subject must be plural to agree with the plural verb *fly.*

3. *The butterfly. The* is required because this refers to a specific butterfly—the one the professor showed us.

4. *a new library.* A specific library is not referred to here, so the article *a* is used.

5. *Air pollution.* This is a non-count, nonspecific noun.

6. *An animal.* The sentence is a general statement, but the subject must be singular to agree with the singular verb *has.*

7. *the ticket. The* is required because this refers to a specific ticket—*your ticket.*
   Keep your ticket with you at all times. To get a discount at the museum gift shop, show *the ticket* to the gift shop clerk.

8. *The information. The* is required because this refers to the specific information *in this book.*

9. *Gold.* This is a non count, nonspecific noun.

10. *A pet parrot.* The sentence is a general statement, but the subject must be singular to agree with the singular verb *requires.*

Gerunds, Infinitives, and Base Form Verbs (page 23)

1. *reading this novel.* The verb *finish* is followed by a gerund.
2. *plans to arrive.* The verb *plan* is followed by the infinitive.
3. *to go.* The verb *wait* is often followed by the infinitive.
4. *have.* The base form of a verb follows a modal.
5. *Paying a deposit.* In this case, the gerund acts as the subject of the sentence.
6. *to get reservations. Easier* is an adjective that is followed by the infinitive.
7. *giving his report. About* is a preposition followed by a gerund.
8. *miss more than. Cannot* is a modal, so it is followed by base form.

9. *fulfilling the lab*. *About* is a preposition followed by a gerund.

10. *to see alligators*. The verb *hope* is followed by the infinitive.

LISTENING SKILLS

Skill 1—Making Assumptions (page 24)

PRACTICE 1 (PAGE 25)

1. Kingston
2. State
3. 7
4. 721-1127
5. December
6. C
7. D
8. F (Please note that answers for 6–8 can be in any order)
9. month
10. 50 percent

Assumptions

Answers may vary.

Who? James
What? renting an apartment
When? not ready
Where? Woodside Apartments
Why? apartment deposit

A 1
B 2
C 4
D 5
E 6–8
F 9
G 10

PRACTICE 2 (PAGE 27)

11. 15
12. 11
13. Tuesday
14. Modern art
15. City Gallery
16. Portraits
17. East Room
18. art reproductions
19. repairs
20. Second floor

Assumptions

Answers may vary.

Who? visitors to museum
What? information for visitors
When? visiting hours
Where? museum in Jamestown
Why? visit museum

A 11
B 12
C 13
D 16
E 15
F 14
G 17
H 18
I 19
J 20

Skill 2—Understanding Numbers (page 30)

1. 8677532148
2. C
3. 575-3174
4. B
5. XY 538
6. 7036588
7. 7441492
8. 2029983
9. 6714532
10. 8241561
11. 6370550
12. 2651811
13. 2876216
14. 4553021
15. 3058480

Skill 3—Understanding the Alphabet (page 32)

1. Tomas
2. Maine
3. Patti
4. Roberts
5. Springvale
6. Dixson
7. A Miranda
   B 7043218
8. A Bijou
   B 232–5488
9. A Janson
   B 335
10. A String
    B 15 B
11. A Willard
    B 70
12. A 1705
    B Landover

Skill 4—Distinguishing Similar Sounds (page 34)

PRACTICE 2 (PAGE 35)

1. peach
2. back
3. staple
4. cab
5. rain
6. arrive
7. clown
8. light
9. choose
10. sheet
11. dish
12. much
13. tore
14. dyed
15. bright
16. need
17. sink
18. thick
19. path
20. miss
21. sing
22. sun
23. gone
24. thing
25. worse
26. vine
27. viper
28. weird
29. let
30. set
31. ran
32. coat
33. seat

Skill 5—Listening for Descriptions (page 36)

1. It's a house with a flat roof. It's two floors high. On the first floor there is a large window and a door. On the second floor there is a row of windows.
2. It's a small house that's only one floor high. It has a door with a window on each side of it.
3. It's a single-story house for two families. It has two doors and one small window.
4. B
5. A He's a short man with short hair and a mustache. (British: moustache) He's neither fat nor thin.
   B He's a tall, thin man. He has long hair.
   C He's a fat, bald man with a beard. He's neither short nor tall.
6. C
7. A She's a young woman with long hair. She's very thin, and she's wearing earrings.
   B She's a middle-aged woman with long gray hair. She's wearing earrings.
   C She's a young woman with short, curly hair. She's wearing a necklace.
8. A

Skill 6—Listening for Time (page 38)

TIME (PAGE 39)

1. B
2. A
3. C
4. C
5. 12:15
6. 4:00

DAY (PAGE 41)

1. Monday
2. Thursday
3. Thursday
4. Friday
5. B
6. B

SEASON (PAGE 42)

1. winter
2. summer
3. C
4. B
5. fall
6. winter

DATE (PAGE 40)

1. 15
2. December
3. September
4. 7
5. C
6. A

YEAR (PAGE 42)

1. 1803
2. 1851
3. B
4. C
5. 1985
6. 1988

Skill 7—Listening for Frequency (page 43)

1. sometimes
2. seldom
3. always
4. never
5. often
6. always
7. daily
8. once a month
9. twice a week
10. from time to time
11. once a month
12. every other week

Skill 8—Listening for Similar Meanings (page 44)

1. party
2. checks (check)
3. rate
4. vegetation
5. available
6. occupation

Skill 9—Listening for Emotions (page 45)

PRACTICE 1 (PAGE 46)

1. C
2. A
3. B
4. C
5. A
6. C

PRACTICE 2 (PAGE 46)

1. thrilled
2. can't get it, keep trying and trying
3. confused
4. It doesn't really matter.
5. unexpected, have no idea
6. pleased

Skill 10—Listening for an Explanation (page 47)

1. A
2. E
3. C
4. D
5. F
6. B
7. the electrical outlet/socket
8. the cord
9. the appliance
10. (metal) wires
11. hot
12. orange
13. turns brown/toasts/heats up
14. toast

Questions 1–12

1. cacao tree
2. cacao fruit
3. seeds/cocoa beans
4. vat for fermenting/vat
5. drying trays
6. chocolate factory
7. is harvested
8. are removed
9. about a week
10. dry/are dried
11. are shipped to/sent to
12. delicious chocolate treats/chocolate

Skill 11—Listening for Classifications (page 49)

1. Program 1: Academic
   When? Daytime
   History of Africa
   Literature of the 21st Century
   International Relations
   Introduction to Philosophy

2. Program 2: Business
   When? Nighttime
   Project Management
   The Art of Negotiating
   Creativity in the Workplace
   Labor Negotiations

1. A, C, E
2. (A) Horror, (B) Romantic
3. (A) Butterflies, (B) Moths
4. C, D
5. (A) Ornamental, (B) Shade, (C) Evergreen

Skill 12—Listening for Comparisons and Contrasts (page 51)

1. Jobs	2. Libraries	3. Club Memberships	4. Frogs and Toads
A Different	A Alike	A Different	A Alike
B Different	B Different	B Alike	B Different
C Alike	C Different	C Alike	C Different
D Different	D Different	D Different	D Different
E Alike	E Alike	E Different	E Alike

Skill 13—Listening for Negative Meaning (page 53)

1. A
2. A
3. B
4. A
5. A
6. B
7. B
8. A
9. C
10. A
11. C
12. A

Skill 14—Listening for Chronology (page 56)

1. 1, 3, 2, 5, 4, 6
2. 1, 2, 3, 5, 4
3. 2, 3, 1, 5, 4
4. 2, 1, 4, 3, 5
5. 2, 1, 3, 5, 4

4

Reading Module

- **→ QUICK STUDY**
  - **Overview**
  - **Question Types**
  - **Reading Tips**
- **→ READING SKILLS: ACADEMIC**
  - **Skill 1—Using the First Paragraph to Make Predictions**
  - **Skill 2—Using the Topic Sentence to Make Predictions**
  - **Skill 3—Looking for Specific Details**
  - **Skill 4—Analyzing the Questions and Answers**
  - **Skill 5—Identifying the Tasks**
- **→ READING SKILLS: GENERAL TRAINING**
  - **Skill 6—Making Predictions**
  - **Skill 7—Finding the Answers**
  - **Skill 8—Identifying the Tasks**
- **→ ANSWER EXPLANATIONS**

OVERVIEW

The Reading module lasts 60 minutes. The reading passages and the questions will be given to you on a Question Booklet. You can write on the Question Booklet, but you can't take it from the room.

You will write your answers on the answer sheet. Unlike in the Listening module, you will have no time to transfer your answers. You will have only 60 minutes to read the passages, answer the questions, and mark your answers.

The Reading modules on the Academic and the General Training versions of the IELTS are different.

Reading Module: Academic Reading			
Tasks	**Passage Types**	**Topics**	**Sources**
Read 3 passages and answer 40 questions	Narrative, descriptive, and/or argumentative	General interest	Books, magazines, newspapers

Reading Module: General Training Reading			
Section	**Tasks**	**Topics**	**Sources**
Section 1	Read 2–3 short texts and answer 13–14 questions	Basic social English	Advertisements, notices, schedules, brochures, instruction manuals
Section 2	Read 2 texts and answer 13–14 questions	Work-related topics	Job descriptions, employee manuals, training materials
Section 3	Read 1 text and answer 13–14 questions	General interest	Books, magazines, newspapers

QUESTION TYPES

You will see several different question types on the IELTS Reading test. You should become familiar with them. The following question types appear on both the Academic and General Training versions of the test.

MULTIPLE CHOICE

You will see a question with four possible answer choices. You will choose the correct answer from the four choices.

TRUE/FALSE/NOT GIVEN

You will read some statements and identify each one as "True," "False," or "Not Given," based on the information in the passage. "Not Given" means that the passage does not mention this information.

YES/NO/NOT GIVEN

You will read some statements and mark each one "Yes," "No," or "Not Given," based on the opinions expressed by the writer of the passage. "Not Given" means that the passage does not mention this information.

MATCHING INFORMATION

You will locate specific information in the text and identify its location (paragraph or section).

CLASSIFYING INFORMATION

You will match information to the correct category or description, based on the information in the passage.

MATCHING HEADINGS

You will match headings to the correct paragraph or section of the text.

SENTENCE/SUMMARY/NOTE/CHART COMPLETION

You will complete sentences, notes, a chart, or a summary of the text choosing words from the text or from a list of options.

MATCHING SENTENCE ENDINGS

You will see the first part of a sentence and choose the appropriate ending from a list of sentence endings.

DIAGRAM LABEL COMPLETION

You will complete labels on a diagram based on a description given in the text.

SHORT ANSWER

You will write short answers to questions choosing words from the text.

You will practice answering all these question types in the exercises in this chapter.

READING TIPS

Before You Take the Test

1. Read as much as you can in English.
2. Read a variety of topics from a variety of sources, for example, tourist information brochures, government reports, scientific research reports, health and safety brochures, newspapers, news and special interest magazines, information from colleges and universities.
3. Keep a notebook of the words you learn.
4. Try to write these words in a sentence. Try to put these sentences into a paragraph.
5. Learn words in context—not from a word list. Don't be afraid to guess meanings.
6. Know the types of questions found on the IELTS.
7. Know the type of information asked about on the IELTS.
8. Know how to make predictions.
9. Know how to skim and scan—how to look quickly for information.

During the Test

1. Read the title and any headings first. Make predictions about the topic.
2. Look over the questions quickly. Make predictions about content and organization.
3. Read the passage at a normal speed. Don't get stuck on parts or words you don't understand.
4. When you answer the questions, don't spend too much time on the ones you don't feel sure about. Make a guess and go on.
5. After you have answered all the questions, you can go back and check the ones you aren't sure about.
6. Spend no more than 20 minutes on each passage or section.
7. The last passage is longer and more complex than the first two, so remember to save time for it.
8. Be sure to write your answers on the answer sheet before the 60 minutes are up. You will NOT have extra time to transfer your answers.
9. If the instructions ask you to use no more than three words to complete an answer, do not write more than three words. You will lose points.
10. Learn to understand True/False and Yes/No questions. They are the most difficult questions on the test. Practice them often so that you will be confident during the test.

NOTE

If you are studying for the General Training exam, go to Skill 6 (page 90).

In order to understand a reading passage, you need to understand the context of a passage. You need to have an idea about the topic. When you pick up a paper to read, you scan the headlines and choose an article that interests you. The clues in the newspaper (headlines, graphics, photos, captions) catch your eye and give you a context.

A passage on the IELTS is given to you; you did not choose to read it. There are few clues. You do not know what it is about. It may or may not interest you. You need some clues to help you understand the passage. Without the clues, you will not understand it very well. To score well on the IELTS, you should determine *what* you know and *what* you need to know.

When you look at a passage, you must make some predictions about the passage. You want to know *who, what, when, where,* and *why.*

What is the passage about?
What is the main idea?
Who is the passage about?
When are things taking place?
Where is it happening?
Why is it important?

In this section you will learn how the following parts of a passage can give you the answers to *Who? What? When? Where?* and *Why?* questions.

Using the first paragraph
Using topic sentences
Using specific details
Using the questions and answers

Skill 1—Using the First Paragraph to Make Predictions

The first paragraph of a passage can help you make predictions about the context of a passage. The first paragraph often contains:

- the topic sentence (a summary of the main idea of the passage)
- a definition of the topic
- clues to the organization of the passage

Read this first paragraph of a passage on the illness called obsessive-compulsive disorder.

> Obsessive-compulsive disorder (OCD) is clinically diagnosed as an anxiety disorder. This disorder affects up to 4 percent of adults and children. People who suffer from this debilitating disorder have distressing and obsessive thoughts, which usually cause them to perform repetitive behaviors[1] such as counting silently or washing their hands. Though OCD sufferers understand that their obsessions are unrealistic, they find it stressful to put these intrusive thoughts out of their minds. Those who suffer from obsessive-compulsive disorder develop strict behavioral[1] patterns that become extremely time-consuming and begin to interfere with daily routines. Many people with OCD delay seeking treatment because they are ashamed of their own thoughts and behavior.

Now read these predictions about the context.

Topic Sentence	Obsessive-compulsive disorder (OCD) is clinically diagnosed as an anxiety disorder.
Definition of Topic	People who suffer from this debilitating disorder have distressing and obsessive thoughts, which usually cause them to perform repetitive behaviors.
Organizational Clues	The author may discuss (1) obsessive behavior, (2) stress of sufferers, and/or (3) treatment.

[1] British: behaviour/behavioural

PRACTICE

Read these introductory paragraphs of other passages. Make predictions about the context of the passage using the introductions.

1 The spread of wildfire is a natural phenomenon that occurs throughout the world and is especially common in forested areas of North America, Australia, and Europe. Locations that receive plenty of rainfall but also experience periods of intense heat or drought are particularly susceptible to wildfires. As plant matter dries out, it becomes brittle and highly flammable. In this way, many wildfires are seasonal, ignited by natural causes, most specifically lightning. However, human carelessness and vandalism also account for thousands of wildfires around the globe each year. To gain a clear understanding of how wildfires spread, it is necessary to analyze what it takes to both create and control these fires.

Topic Sentence	
Definition of Topic	
Organizational Clues	

2 The term "bird brain" has long been a common means of expressing doubts about a person's intelligence. In reality, birds may actually be a great deal more intelligent than humans have given them credit for. For a long time, scientists considered birds to be of lesser intelligence because the cerebral cortex, the part of the brain that humans and other animals use for intelligence, is relatively small in size. Now scientists understand that birds actually use a different part of their brain, the hyperstriatum, for intelligence. Observations of different species of birds, both in the wild and in captivity, have shown a great deal of evidence of high levels of avian intelligence.

Topic Sentence	
Definition of Topic	
Organizational Clues	

3 In 1834, a little girl was born in New Bedford, Massachusetts. She would grow up to become one of the richest women in the world. Her name was Hetty Green, but she was known to many as the Witch of Wall Street.

Topic Sentence	
Definition of Topic	
Organizational Clues	

Skill 2—Using the Topic Sentence to Make Predictions

Every paragraph has a key sentence called a topic sentence. This topic sentence explains what a paragraph is about. It is the general idea of a paragraph. If you understand the general idea, you can look for the specific details which support the idea.

Read the second paragraph of the passage on OCD below. The first sentence happens to be the topic sentence.

> OCD sufferers experience worries that are both unreasonable and excessive and that act as a constant source of internal stress. Fear of dirt and contamination are very common obsessive thoughts. The obsession with orderliness and symmetry is also common. In other cases, persistent thoughts are centered on doubts, such as whether or not a door is locked or a stove is turned off. Impulses, such as the urge to swear in public or to pull a fire alarm, are other types of OCD symptoms. In order to be diagnosed with OCD, a sufferer must exhibit obsessions and/or compulsions that take up a considerable amount of time (at least one hour per day).

Continue to try to make predictions about the context of the passage using the second paragraph.

Topic Sentence	OCD sufferers experience worries that are both unreasonable and excessive and that act as a constant source of internal stress.
Questions to Ask Yourself	What are unreasonable worries? What are excessive worries?

PRACTICE

Read these paragraphs. Underline the topic sentence. Ask one or two questions about the topic sentence.

1 To combat excessive thoughts and impulses, most OCD sufferers perform certain repetitive rituals that they believe will relieve their anxiety. These compulsions can be either mental or behavioral in nature. Common rituals include excessive checking, washing, counting, and praying. Over time, OCD sufferers attach strict rules to their compulsions. For example, a woman who is obsessed with cleanliness might wash her hands three times before having a meal in order to get the thought of the dirty dishes or silverware out of her mind. However, in many cases, the compulsions aren't related to the obsession at all. A man obsessed with the image of dead animals might count silently up to five hundred or touch a specific chair over and over in order to block the images. Holding onto objects that would normally be discarded, such as newspapers and empty containers, is another common compulsion.

Questions to Ask Yourself

1 ....

2 ....

2 OCD symptoms generally begin between the ages of ten and twenty-four and continue indefinitely until a person seeks treatment. A child's upbringing does not seem to be part of the cause of the disorder, though stress can make the symptoms stronger. The underlying causes of OCD have been researched greatly and point to a number of different genetic factors. While studies show that OCD and its related anxiety disorders are often passed down through families, the specific symptoms for each family member are rarely the same. For example, a mother who is obsessed with order may have a son who can't stop thinking about a single word or number.

Questions to Ask Yourself

1 ....

2 ....

3 Research on OCD sufferers has found certain physiological trends. In particular, many studies show an overactivity of blood circulation in certain areas of the brain. As a result of this increase in blood flow, the serotoninergic system, which regulates emotions, is unable to function effectively. Studies have also shown that OCD sufferers have less serotonin than the average person. This type of abnormality is also observed in Tourette syndrome and attention-deficit hyperactivity disorder. People who developed tics as children are found to be more susceptible to OCD as well. Many reports of OCD point to infections that can trigger the disorder, namely streptococcal infections. It is believed that a case of childhood strep throat can elicit a response from the immune system that produces certain neuropsychiatric disorders, such as OCD.

Questions to Ask Yourself

1 ....

2 ....

Skill 3—Looking for Specific Details

When you read, you first want to know the general idea. Next you read for specific ideas. The author supplies specific details to support his or her ideas. Knowing where to look for these supporting details will help you answer questions on the IELTS.

When you identified the topic sentences in Skill 2, you found the general idea of the paragraph. When you asked your questions about the topic sentence, you expected the specific details would be the answers.

Read the second paragraph of the passage on OCD again. The specific details follow the topic sentence.

> OCD sufferers experience worries that are both unreasonable and excessive and that act as a constant source of internal stress. Fear of dirt and contamination are very common obsessive thoughts. The obsession with orderliness and symmetry is also common. In other cases, persistent thoughts are centered on doubts, such as whether or not a door is locked or a stove is turned off. Impulses, such as the urge to swear in public or to pull a fire alarm, are other types of OCD symptoms. In order to be diagnosed with OCD, a sufferer must exhibit obsessions and/or compulsions that take up a considerable amount of time (at least one hour per day).

See how the supporting details answer the questions to yourself.

Topic Sentence	OCD sufferers experience worries that are both unreasonable and excessive and that act as a constant source of internal stress.
Questions to Ask Yourself	What are unreasonable worries? What are excessive worries?
Supporting Details	Fear of dirt and contamination Obsession with orderliness and symmetry Persistent doubts Impulses

PRACTICE

Read the three paragraphs from Skill 2 again. Pay attention to the topic sentence. Circle the details that answer the questions you ask yourself.

Skill 4—Analyzing the Questions and Answers

You made predictions about the content based on the first paragraph, the topic sentences, and the specific details. Now let's look at how the questions or statements in your Reading test booklet can help you narrow these predictions and choose the correct answer.

To help you answer the questions in your Reading test booklet, take a few seconds to look over the questions or statements. Sometimes the questions are before the passage; sometimes they come after the passage. Ask yourself: *Who? What? When? Where?* and *Why?* questions. By looking for the answers to these general questions, you will discover what you know and what you need to know. When you read the passage, you can test the predictions you made.

As you look at the question or statement and answer options, look for the key words. Key words may give you a clue to the context. They may help you predict what the passage is about.

Look at these typical IELTS comprehension questions below. First identify the key words. (These are circled below to help you.) Then look for these words in the passage. You will know where to look because you have made predictions using topic sentences and specific details.

Notice the words close to the circled words in the passage. Do they help you complete the summary below?

PRACTICE

Questions 1–8

Complete the summary of the reading passage below.

Choose your answers from the box below and write them on lines 1–8. There are more words than spaces so you will not use them all.

checking	inherited	treatment	obsession	diagnosis
doctor	reduce	throw away	uncontrollable	optional
upbringing	cause	unreasonable	compulsive	identity

People who suffer from obsessive-compulsive disorder have **1** .... thoughts, doubts, and fears that are **2** .... OCD sufferers develop certain ways of acting in order to **3** .... their fears. For example, being afraid of dirt is a common **4** ...., which may lead to excessive hand washing. Or, an OCD sufferer who worries about a locked door may engage in excessive **5** .... Some OCD sufferers keep things that other people would **6** .... Research shows that OCD may be a disorder that is **7** ...., though members of the same family don't always show the same symptoms. It is also possible that certain infections may **8** .... the disorder.

READING SKILLS—ACADEMIC

Identify the key words in questions 9–16 on page 77. Circle them in the questions and in the reading passage below. Notice the words close to the circled words in the passage. Do they help you complete the questions?

Questions 9–16

You should spend 20 minutes on questions 9–16, which are based on the reading passage below.

Obsessive-Compulsive Disorder

Obsessive-compulsive disorder (OCD) is clinically diagnosed as an anxiety disorder and affects up to 4 percent of adults and children. People who suffer from this debilitating disorder have distressing and obsessive thoughts, which usually cause them to perform repetitive behaviors such as counting silently or washing their hands. Though OCD sufferers understand that their obsessions are unrealistic, they find it stressful to put these intrusive thoughts out of their minds. Those who suffer from obsessive-compulsive disorder develop strict behavioral patterns that become extremely time-consuming and begin to interfere with daily routines. Many people with OCD delay seeking treatment because they are ashamed of their own thoughts and behavior.

OCD sufferers experience worries that are both unreasonable and excessive and that act as a constant source of internal stress. Fear of dirt and contamination are very common obsessive thoughts. The obsession with orderliness and symmetry is also common. In other cases, persistent thoughts are centered on doubts, such as whether or not a door is locked or a stove is turned off. Impulses, such as the urge to swear in public or to pull a fire alarm, are other types of OCD symptoms. In order to be diagnosed with OCD, a sufferer must exhibit obsessions and/or compulsions that take up a considerable amount of time (at least one hour per day).

To combat excessive thoughts and impulses, most OCD sufferers perform certain repetitive rituals that they believe will relieve their anxiety. These compulsions can be either mental or behavioral in nature. Common rituals include excessive checking, washing, counting, and praying. Over time, OCD sufferers attach strict rules to their compulsions. For example, a woman who is obsessed with cleanliness might wash her hands three times before having a meal in order to get the thought of the dirty dishes or silverware out of her mind. However, in many cases, the compulsions aren't related to the obsession at all. A man obsessed with the image of dead animals might count silently up to 500 or touch a specific chair over and over in order to block the images. Holding onto objects that would normally be discarded, such as newspapers and empty containers, is another common compulsion.

OCD symptoms generally begin between the ages of ten and twenty-four and continue indefinitely until a person seeks treatment. A child's upbringing does not seem to be part of the cause of the disorder, though stress can make the symptoms stronger. The underlying causes of OCD have been researched greatly and point to a number of different genetic factors. While studies show that OCD and its related anxiety disorders are often passed down through families, the specific symptoms for each family member are rarely the same. For example, a mother who is obsessed with order may have a son who can't stop thinking about a single word or number.

Research on OCD sufferers has found certain physiological trends. In particular, many studies show an overactivity of blood circulation in certain areas of the brain. As a result of this increase in blood flow, the serotoninergic system, which regulates emotions, is unable to function effectively. Studies have also shown that OCD sufferers have less serotonin than the average person. This type of abnormality is also observed in Tourette syndrome and attention deficit hyperactivity disorder. People who developed tics as children are found to be more susceptible to OCD as well. Many reports of OCD point to infections that can trigger the disorder, namely streptococcal infections. It is believed that a case of childhood strep throat can elicit a response from the immune system that produces certain neuropsychiatric disorders, such as OCD.

Because OCD sufferers tend to be so secretive about their symptoms, they often put off treatment for many years. The average OCD sufferer waits about seventeen years before receiving medical attention. As with many anxiety disorders, early diagnosis and proper medication can lessen many of the symptoms and allow people to live fairly normal lives. Most treatment plans for OCD involve a combination of medication and psychotherapy. Both cognitive and behavioral therapies are used to teach patients about their disorder and work through the anxiety. Serotonin reuptake inhibitors are prescribed to increase the brain's concentration of serotonin. This medication successfully reduces the symptoms in many OCD sufferers in a short amount of time. For cases when OCD is linked to streptococcal infection, antibiotic therapy is sometimes all that is needed.

> **TIP**
>
> **False/No/Not Given**
>
> **False** or **No** means that the statement contradicts information in the passage.
>
> **Not Given** means that the information in the statement is not mentioned in the passage.

Do the following statements agree with the information in the reading passage?

In the space provided for questions 9–16 write

TRUE	*if the statement is true according to the passage.*
FALSE	*if the statement contradicts the passage.*
NOT GIVEN	*if there is no information about this in the passage.*

9 OCD often results from the way a child is raised. ....

10 Stress can have an effect on OCD. ....

11 OCD sufferers are deficient in serotonin. ....

12 Obsessive-compulsive disorder usually begins after the age of seventeen. ....

13 Many OCD patients prefer psychotherapy to medication. ....

14 OCD is very difficult to treat. ....

15 Many OCD sufferers keep their problem a secret. ....

16 Antibiotics can be used to treat OCD. ....

Skill 5—Identifying the Tasks

On the Reading test, you will see a variety of questions types. (See pages 66–67 in the Quick Study section of this chapter for a complete list of question types and descriptions.) The questions test your ability to identify details and main ideas, find specific information, and understand how facts and ideas are linked. You should become familiar with the different types of questions and how to answer them.

In the following practice exercises, you will read three reading texts and answer questions about them. Note the question types as you answer them.

PRACTICE 1

Before you read the following passage, "Zulu Beadwork," try to make predictions about the context. Use the first paragraph, the topic sentence, specific details, and the questions to help you make predictions.

Complete this chart on the passage "Zulu Beadwork."

Topic Sentence	
Questions to Ask Yourself	
Supporting Details	

Now analyze questions 1–11 on pages 81–82. What are these questions asking?

Questions 1–6

Who? What? When? Where? How many?

1 What? ....

2 ....

3 ....

4 ....

5 ....

6 ....

Questions 7–11

Who? What? When? Where? How many?
What key words might help you answer the question?

7 Who? Where? .... Key Words: ....

8 .... Key Words: ....

9 .... Key Words: ....

10 .... Key Words: ....

11 .... Key Words: ....

Now read the passage and answer the questions.

Zulu Beadwork

The South African province of KwaZulu-Natal, more commonly referred to as the Zulu Kingdom, is named after the Zulu people who have inhabited the area since the late 1400s. KwaZulu translates to mean "Place of Heaven." "Natal" was the name the Portuguese explorers gave this region when they arrived in 1497. At that time, only a few Zulu clans occupied the area. By the late 1700s, the AmaZulu clan, meaning "People of Heaven," constituted a significant nation. Today the Zulu clan represents the largest ethnic group in South Africa, with at least 11 million people in the kingdom. The Zulu people are known around the world for their elaborate glass beadwork, which they wear not only in their traditional costumes but as part of their everyday apparel. It is possible to learn much about the culture of the Zulu clan through their beadwork.

The glass bead trade in the province of KwaZulu-Natal is believed to be a fairly recent industry. In 1824, an Englishman named Henry Francis Fynn brought glass beads to the region to sell to the African people. Though the British are not considered the first to introduce glass beads, they were a main source through which the Zulu people could access the merchandise they needed. Glass beads had already been manufactured by the Egyptians centuries earlier around the same time when glass was discovered. Some research points to the idea that Egyptians tried to fool South Africans with glass by passing it off as jewels similar in value to gold or ivory. Phoenician mariners brought cargoes of these beads to Africa along with other wares. Before the Europeans arrived, many Arab traders brought glass beads down to the southern countries via camelback. During colonization,[1] the Europeans facilitated and monopolized[2] the glass bead market, and the Zulu nation became even more closely tied to this art form.

The Zulu people were not fooled into believing that glass beads were precious stones but, rather, used the beads to establish certain codes and rituals in their society. In the African tradition, kings were known to wear beaded regalia so heavy that they required the help of attendants to get out of their thrones. Zulu beadwork is involved in every realm of society, from religion and politics to family and marriage. Among the Zulu women, the craft of beadwork is used as an educational tool as well as a source of recreation and fashion. Personal adornment items include jewelry, skirts, neckbands, and aprons. Besides clothing and accessories, there are many other beaded objects in the Zulu culture, such as bead-covered gourds, which are carried around by women who are having fertility problems. Most importantly, however, Zulu beadwork is a source of communication. In the Zulu tradition, beads are a part of the language with certain words and symbols that can be easily read. A finished product is considered by many artists and collectors to be extremely poetic.

The code behind Zulu beadwork is relatively basic and extremely resistant to change. A simple triangle is the geometric shape used in almost all beaded items. A triangle with the apex pointing downward signifies an unmarried man, while one with the tip pointing upward is worn by an unmarried woman. Married women wear items with two triangles that form a diamond shape, and married men signify their marital status with two triangles that form an hourglass shape. Colors are also significant, though slightly more complicated since each color can have a negative and a positive meaning. Educated by their older sisters, young Zulu girls quickly learn how to send the appropriate messages to a courting male. Similarly, males learn how to interpret the messages and how to wear certain beads that express their interest in marriage.

The codes of the beads are so strong that cultural analysts fear that the beadwork tradition could prevent the Zulu people from progressing technologically and economically. Socio-economic data shows that the more a culture resists change the more risk there is in a value system falling apart. Though traditional beadwork still holds a serious place in Zulu culture, the decorative art form is often modified for tourists, with popular items such as the beaded fertility doll.

[1] BRITISH: colonisation

[2] BRITISH: monopolised

CLASSIFYING INFORMATION

Questions 1–3

Match each definition in List A with the term it defines in List B.

*Write the correct letter **A–E** in the spaces provided for questions 1–3. There are more terms than definitions, so you will not use them all.*

List A		Definitions
1	....	It means *Place of Heaven.*
2	....	It is the Portuguese name for southern Africa.
3	....	It means *People of Heaven.*

List B	Terms
A	Phoenician
B	Natal
C	AmaZulu
D	Explorer
E	KwaZulu

SHORT ANSWER

Questions 4–6

Answer the questions below. Write NO MORE THAN THREE WORDS *for each answer. Write your answers in the spaces provided for questions 4–6.*

4 Which country does the Zulu clan reside in?

....

5 When did the Portuguese arrive in KwaZulu-Natal?

....

6 How many members of the Zulu kingdom are there?

....

TRUE/FALSE/NOT GIVEN

Questions 7–11

Do the following statements agree with the information given in the passage? In the spaces provided for questions 7–11, write

TRUE	*if the statement is true according to the passage.*
FALSE	*if the statement contradicts the passage.*
NOT GIVEN	*if there is no information about this in the passage.*

7 The British were the first people to sell glass beads in Africa.

....

8 Henry Frances Flynn made a lot of money selling glass beads to the Zulu people.

....

9 The Zulu people believed that glass beads were precious stones.

....

10 The Zulu people use glass beads in many aspects of their daily lives.

....

11 Zulu women believe that bead-covered gourds can help them have babies.

....

DIAGRAM LABEL COMPLETION

Label the diagram below. Choose one or two words from the reading passage for each answer. Write your answers in the spaces provided for questions 12–15.

Zulu Beadwork Code

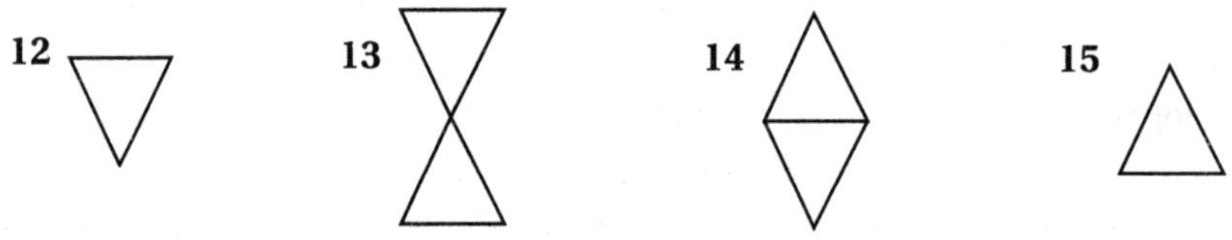

....

PRACTICE 2

Read the passage and answer the questions. Use your predicting skills. Note the type of questions.

MATCHING HEADINGS

Questions 1–5

*The following reading passage has five paragraphs, **A–E**. Choose the correct heading for each paragraph from the list of headings below. Write the correct number **i–viii** in the spaces provided for questions 1–5. There are more headings than paragraphs, so you will not use them all.*

TIP

If the test uses lower case Roman numerals, then you should, too.

List of Headings

i	Colorblindness[1] in Different Countries
ii	Diagnosing Colorblindness
iii	What Is Colorblindness?
iv	Curing Colorblindness
v	Unsolved Myths
vi	Animals and Colorblindness
vii	Developing the Ability to See Color
viii	Colorblindness and the Sexes

1 Paragraph **A** ....

2 Paragraph **B** ....

3 Paragraph **C** ....

4 Paragraph **D** ....

5 Paragraph **E** ....

Colorblindness

A

Myths related to the causes and symptoms of "colorblindness" abound throughout the world. The term itself is misleading, since it is extremely rare for anyone to have a complete lack of color perception. By looking into the myths related to colorblindness, one can learn many facts about the structure and genetics of the human eye. It is a myth that colorblind people see the world as if it were a black and white movie. There are very few cases of complete colorblindness. Those who have a complete lack of color perception are referred to as monochromatics, and usually have a serious problem with their overall vision as well as an inability to see colors. The fact is that in most cases of colorblindness, there are only certain shades that a person cannot distinguish between. These people are said to be dichromatic. They may not be able to tell the difference between red and green, or orange and yellow. A person with normal color vision has what is called trichromatic vision. The difference among the three levels of color perception has to do with the cones in the human eye. A normal human eye has three cones located inside the retina: the red cone, the green cone, and the

[1]British: colour, colourblindness, colourful

READING SKILLS—ACADEMIC

yellow cone. Each cone contains a specific pigment whose function is to absorb the light of these colors and the combinations of them. People with trichromatic vision have all three cones in working order. When one of the three cones does not function properly, dichromatic vision occurs.

B

Some people believe that only men can be colorblind. This is also a myth, though it is not completely untrue. In an average population, 8% of males exhibit some form of colorblindness, while only 0.5% of women do. While there may be some truth to the idea that more men have trouble matching their clothing than women, the reason that color vision deficiency is predominant in males has nothing to do with fashion. The fact is that the gene for colorblindness is located on the X chromosome, which men only have one of. Females have two X chromosomes, and if one carries the defective gene, the other one naturally compensates. Therefore, the only way for a female to inherit colorblindness is for both of her X chromosomes to carry the defective gene. This is why the incidence of color deficiency is sometimes more prevalent in extremely small societies that have a limited gene pool.

C

It is true that all babies are born colorblind. A baby's cones do not begin to differentiate between many different colors until the baby is approximately four months old. This is why many of the modern toys for very young babies consist of black and white patterns or primary colors, rather than traditional soft pastels. However, some current research points to the importance of developing an infant's color visual system. In 2004, Japanese researcher Yoichi Sugita of the Neuroscience Research Institute performed an experiment that would suggest that color vision deficiency isn't entirely genetic. In his experiment, he subjected a group of baby monkeys to monochromatic lighting for one year. He later compared their vision to normal monkeys who had experienced the colorful world outdoors. It was found that the test monkeys were unable to perform the color-matching tasks that the normal monkeys could. Nevertheless, most cases of colorblindness are attributed to genetic factors that are present at birth.

D

Part of the reason there are so many inconsistencies related to colorblindness, or "color vision deficiency" as it is called in the medical world, is that it is difficult to know exactly which colors each human can see. Children are taught from a very young age that an apple is red. Naming colors allows children to associate a certain shade with a certain name, regardless of a color vision deficiency. Someone who never takes a color test can go through life thinking that what they see as red is called *green*. Children are generally tested for colorblindness at about four years of age. The Ishihara Test is the most common, though it is highly criticized[1] because it requires that children have the ability to recognize[2] numerals. In the Ishihara Test, a number made up of colored dots is hidden inside a series of dots of a different shade. Those with normal vision can distinguish the number from the background, while those with color vision deficiency will only see the dots.

[1]British: criticised

[2]British: recognise

E

While many of the myths related to colorblindness have been disproved by modern science, there are still a few remaining beliefs that require more research in order to be labeled as folklore. For example, there is a longstanding belief that colorblindness can aid military soldiers because it gives them the ability to see through camouflage. Another belief is that everyone becomes colorblind in an emergency situation. The basis of this idea is that a catastrophic event can overwhelm the brain, causing it to utilize[3] only those receptors needed to perform vital tasks. In general, identifying color is not considered an essential task in a life or death situation.

MULTIPLE CHOICE

Questions 6–8

*Choose the correct letter, **A**, **B**, **C**, or **D**.*

6 People who see color normally are called

A monochromatic.
B dichromatic.
C trichromatic.
D colorblind.

7 Children usually begin to see a variety of colors by the age of

A one month.
B four months.
C one year.
D four years.

8 Children who take the Ishihara Test must be able to

A distinguish letters.
B write their names.
C read numbers.
D name colors.

[3]BRITISH: utilise

SUMMARY COMPLETION

Questions 9–12

Complete the summary using words from the box below. Write your answers in the spaces provided for questions 9–12. There are more answers than spaces, so you will not use them all.

myth	exactly	defective genes
X chromosomes	more probable	slightly more
fact	a little less	less likely

It is a common **9** .... that only men suffer from colorblindness. On average **10** .... than 10 percent of men have this problem. Women have two **11** .... For this reason it is **12** .... for a woman to suffer from colorblindness.

PRACTICE 3

Read the passage and answer the questions. Use your predicting skills. Note the type of question.

Antarctic Penguins

Though penguins are assumed to be native to the South Pole, only four of the seventeen species have evolved the survival adaptations necessary to live and breed in the Antarctic year round. The physical features of the Adelie, Chinstrap, Gentoo, and Emperor penguins equip them to withstand the harshest living conditions in the world. Besides these four species, there are a number of others, including the yellow feathered Macaroni penguin and the King penguin that visit the Antarctic regularly but migrate to warmer waters to breed. Penguins that live in Antarctica year round have a thermoregulation system and a survival sense that allows them to live comfortably both on the ice and in the water.

In the dark days of winter, when the Antarctic sees virtually no sunlight, the penguins that remain on the ice sheet sleep most of the day. To retain heat, penguins huddle in communities of up to 6,000 of their own species. When it's time to create a nest, most penguins build up a pile of rocks on top of the ice to place their eggs. The Emperor penguin, however, doesn't bother with a nest at all. The female Emperor lays just one egg and gives it to the male to protect while she goes off for weeks to feed. The male balances the egg on top of his feet, covering it with a small fold of skin called a brood patch. In the huddle, the male penguins rotate regularly so that none of the penguins have to stay on the outside of the circle exposed to the wind and cold for long periods of time. When it's time to take a turn on the outer edge of the pack, the penguins tuck their feathers in and shiver. The movement provides enough warmth until they can head back into the inner core and rest in the warmth. In order to reduce the cold of the ice, penguins often put their weight on their heels and tails. Antarctic penguins also have complex nasal passages that prevent 80 percent of their heat from leaving the body. When the sun is out, the black dorsal plumage attracts its rays and penguins can stay warm enough to waddle or slide about alone.

Antarctic penguins spend about 75 percent of their lives in the water. A number of survival adaptations allow them to swim through water as cold as –2 degrees Celsius. In order to stay warm in these temperatures, penguins have to keep moving. Though penguins don't fly in the air, they are often said to fly through water. Instead of stopping each time they come up for air, they use a technique called "porpoising," in which they leap up for a quick breath while swiftly moving forward. Unlike most birds that have hollow bones for flight, penguins have evolved hard solid bones that keep them low in the water. Antarctic penguins also have unique feathers that work similarly to a waterproof diving suit. Tufts of down trap a layer of air within the feathers, preventing the water from penetrating to the penguin's skin. The pressure of a deep dive releases this air, and a penguin has to rearrange the feathers through a process called "preening." Penguins also have an amazing circulatory system, which in extremely cold waters diverts blood from the flippers and legs to the heart.

While the harsh climate of the Antarctic doesn't threaten the survival of Antarctic penguins, overheating can be a concern, and therefore, global warming is a threat to them. Temperate species have certain physical features such as fewer feathers and less blubber to keep them cool on a hot day. African penguins have bald patches on their legs and face where excess heat can be released. The blood vessels in the penguin's skin dilate when the body begins to overheat, and the heat rises to the surface of the body. Penguins who are built for cold winters of the Antarctic have other survival techniques for a warm day, such as moving to shaded areas, or holding their flippers out away from their bodies.

CLASSIFYING INFORMATION

Questions 1–5

Classify the following facts as applying to

A *Antarctic penguins*
B *Temperate-zone penguins*

Write the appropriate letter, **A** *or* **B**, *in the spaces provided for questions 1–5.*

1 stand in large groups to keep warm ....

TIP

Think of alternate ways to represent numbers and symbols (e.g., 75 percent—three-quarters).

2 spend about three-quarters of their time in the water ....

3 have feathers that keep cold water away from their skin ....

4 have areas of skin without feathers ....

5 have less blubber ....

SENTENCE COMPLETION

Questions 6–9

Complete each of the following sentences with information from the reading passage. Write your answers in the spaces provided for questions 6–9. Write **NO MORE THAN THREE WORDS** *for each answer.*

6 Most penguins use .... to build their nests.

7 While the male Emperor penguin takes care of the egg, the female goes away to ....

TIP

Remember to spell correctly. Copy spelling from the passage or questions when possible.

8 A .... is a piece of skin that the male Emperor penguin uses to protect the egg.

9 Penguins protect their feet from the cold of the ice by resting on their ....

MATCHING SENTENCE ENDINGS

Questions 10–12

Complete each sentence with the correct ending, A–E, from the box below. Write the correct letter in the spaces provided for questions 10–12. There are more answers than sentences, so you won't use them all.

Sentence Endings	
A	to hide from their enemies.
B	to breed.
C	to lose their feathers.
D	to cool off on a hot day.
E	to survive in very cold water.

10 Some penguins leave Antarctica for warmer areas ....

11 Antarctic penguins have special adaptations that enable them ....

12 Penguins may seek shady places ....

READING SKILLS—ACADEMIC

Skill 6—Making Predictions

On the General Training Reading test, you will see a variety of text types. Skim each text before you read it to identify the text type and get an idea of the contents. This will help you make predictions about the text and focus your reading.

When you skim, look for general ideas, not details. Look at

- the title
- the headings
- the first sentence of each paragraph
- words in bold or a different font
- words in lists

PRACTICE

Skim the text to answer the questions.

Text A

Parkside Community Pool

SCHEDULE

Time	Activity	Notes
10:00 A.M.–12:00 P.M.	Lap swim	Open to both adults and children.
12:00 P.M.–2:00 P.M.	Children's swim lessons	Parents are requested to remain in the pool area during the entire lesson.
2:00 P.M.–4:00 P.M.	Swim team practice	Practice is mandatory for all team members.
4:00 P.M.–6:00 P.M.	Family swim time	Children under the age of 16 must be accompanied by an adult.
6:00 P.M.–8:00 P.M.	Adult swim	No children under age 18 are permitted in the pool at this time.

INFORMATION

- **The pool is open seven days a week.** The locker rooms are closed every Wednesday afternoon for cleaning and maintenance.
- **One-year and six-month memberships** are available for both individuals and families. Nonmembers may purchase a one-day pass at the reception desk.
- **High school students are eligible for a junior membership** with special privileges. See the receptionist for details.
- **Swim lessons** start the first week of every month. Call the administrative office for more information or to sign up.

1 What type of text is this? (Choose one.)

course descriptions | employee handbook | magazine article
instruction manual | schedule | advertisement

2 What is the topic? ....

3 Which of the following subjects are mentioned? (Choose four.)

swim lessons | pool rules | membership | swim team
pool location | weekly schedule | towel rentals

Text B

Brentwood Institute
Fall Semester

The fall semester runs from September 8 through December 5. Registration begins the week of August 28. Full payment is due at the time of registration. All required texts are available for purchase from your instructor.

Beginning French
This course covers the basics—everyday home, school, and work vocabulary, as well as common useful phrases and the basic verb tenses.
Text: *French for Beginners*
Monday, Tuesday, Thursday 4:00–6:00 P.M.
Instructor: Mme. La Farge

Intermediate French
For those who are ready to move to the next level. We practice everyday conversations and read and discuss a selection of stories and magazine articles, which will be provided by the instructor.
There is no required text for the class.
Monday, Wednesday, 6:00–8:00 P.M.
Instructor: Mme. La Farge

Japanese for Travelers
Are you planning a trip to Japan? Whether your trip is for business or pleasure, this course will prepare you with the basic words and phrases you will need for everyday communication. We will also read a selection of articles and view a few short films to provide an introduction to Japanese culture and history.
Text: *The Basics of the Japanese Language*
Tuesday, Thursday, 6:00–8:00 P.M.
Instructor: Mr. Sato

Advanced Spanish
This class is for students who have successfully completed Beginning and Intermediate Spanish, or who have passed a proficiency test. We will review grammar and vocabulary, read articles, and have in-depth discussions about current events.
Text: *Spanish for Today*
Monday, Wednesday, 4:00–6:00 P.M.
Instructor: Sr. Lopez

4 What type of text is this? (Choose one.)

course descriptions | employee handbook | magazine article
instruction manual | schedule | advertisement

5 What is the topic? ....

6 Which of the following subjects are mentioned? (Choose three.)

classroom locations | class schedules | instructors' names
cost of each class | required texts | homework policy

Text C

A Healthy Lifestyle

Your health is one of your most valuable assets. When you keep your body in good shape, you have the energy you need to keep going all day, both at home and at work. It is worthwhile to take a little time everyday to make sure you have given your body what it needs to stay healthy, and it may be more convenient than you think.

The first step is to start the day with a good breakfast that includes whole grains, protein, and fruit. Diet is one of the most important aspects of a healthy lifestyle, so be sure to have three nutritious meals a day. *If you are concerned about your weight, don't skip meals, but do avoid high-calorie snacks.*

Physical exercise benefits your health in many ways. It keeps your muscles strong and in good condition and helps you avoid injury from strains and falls. It keeps your mind alert and helps you control your weight. *You will see results with as little as 30 minutes a day of physical exercise.*

Stress is one of the biggest factors contributing to poor health. Stress can lead to chronic conditions such as high blood pressure and may also weaken your immune system, making you more susceptible to infections. *It is important to find a way to relax every day.* Turn off the computer and spend some quiet time reading, doing yoga, or even talking with some friends.

Rest is necessary for both your mind and body. Adults need seven to eight hours of sleep every night. To get a goodnight's sleep, create a peaceful environment in your bedroom. Make sure that it is quiet and dark. It is also important to go to bed at around the same time every night. This will ensure that you are prepared for a good rest.

7 What type of text is this? (Choose one.)

course descriptions | employee handbook | magazine article
instruction manual | schedule | advertisements

8 What is the topic? ....

9 What kind of information does the text contain? (Choose one.)

opinion | advice | news | history

Skill 7—Finding the Answers

When you read a question, identify the key words, or the most important words. Then scan the text for information that answers the question.

When you scan, you don't read every word. You run your eyes over the page looking for specific information. When you scan for answers, look for key words. The text may use the same key words as the question, or it may use synonyms or words that are related in meaning.

Look at this example. The key words, synonyms, and related words are underlined.

Question

On what date were repairs to the building completed?

Text

The original City Hall was damaged by a major storm in December, which left holes in the roof as well as numerous broken windows and doors. Funds were quickly raised to restore the historic hall to its original state. The damage to the building was fixed by a local construction company. The work was finished on May 10.

Key Word	Synonym/Related Word/Repeated Key Word
date	May 10
repairs	fixed
building	building
completed	finished

The answer, *May 10*, is related to the key word *date* and is found in the text near other synonyms and key words.

PRACTICE 1

Circle the synonyms and related words for each key word. There may be more than one answer for each key word.

1	**mothers and fathers**	cats and dogs	parents	coaches	guardians
2	**classes**	lessons	bosses	windows	courses
3	**children**	pets	adults	kids	friends
4	**allowed**	given	permitted	needed	obeyed
5	**not open**	closed	shut	cold	quiet
6	**buy**	give	drop	purchase	pay for
7	**teenagers**	high schoolers	babies	elderly	adolescents
8	**qualify**	be eligible	fail	reach	understand
9	**contact**	call	get in touch with	discover	learn
10	**day**	August 28	semester	2015	Monday
11	**sign up**	write	register	enroll	study

READING SKILLS—GENERAL TRAINING

12	**books**	assignments	toys	texts	chapters
13	**news**	fiction	discuss	TV	current events
14	**movies**	films	culture	rooms	magazines
15	**talk about**	read	discuss	watch	enjoy
16	**fit**	good shape	healthy	big	camera
17	**eat**	run	breakfast	diet	meal
18	**move**	weak	control	exercise	turn off
19	**relax**	stress	dine	unwind	weigh
20	**sleep**	rest	dream	swim	work

PRACTICE 2

Read the texts and answer the questions. The key words in the questions have been underlined.

Text A

Parkside Community Pool

SCHEDULE

Time	Activity	Notes
10:00 A.M.–12:00 P.M.	Lap swim	Open to both adults and children.
12:00 P.M.–2:00 P.M.	Children's swim lessons	Parents are requested to remain in the pool area during the entire lesson.
2:00 P.M.–4:00 P.M.	Swim team practice	Practice is mandatory for all team members.
4:00 P.M.–6:00 P.M.	Family swim time	Children under the age of 16 must be accompanied by an adult.
6:00 P.M.–8:00 P.M.	Adult swim	Adults age 18 and over only are permitted in the pool at this time.

INFORMATION

- **The pool is open seven days a week.** The locker rooms are closed every Wednesday afternoon for cleaning and maintenance.
- **One-year and six-month memberships** are available for both individuals and families. Nonmembers may purchase a one-day pass at the reception desk.
- **High school students are eligible for a junior membership** with special privileges. See the receptionist for details.
- **Swim lessons** start the first week of every month. Call the administrative office for more information or to sign up.

Complete the sentences below.

Choose NO MORE THAN TWO WORDS *from the text for each answer.*

1 Mothers and fathers should stay in the .... during their children's swim classes.

2 Children are not allowed in the pool during ....

3 The locker rooms are not open on ....

4 Nonmembers can buy a ....

5 Teenagers qualify for a ....

6 People who would like to register for swim classes should contact the ....

Text B

Brentwood Institute
Fall Semester

The fall semester runs from September 8 through December 5. Registration begins the week of August 28. Full payment is due at the time of registration. All required texts are available for purchase in class from your instructor.

Beginning French

This course covers the basics—everyday home, school, and work vocabulary, as well as common useful phrases and the basic verb tenses.

Text: *French for Beginners*

Monday, Tuesday, Thursday 4:00–6:00 P.M.

Instructor: Mme. La Farge

Intermediate French

For those who are ready to move to the next level. We practice everyday conversations and read and discuss a selection of stories and magazine articles, which will be provided by the instructor.

There is no required text for the class.

Monday, Wednesday, 6:00–8:00 P.M.

Instructor: Mme. La Farge

Japanese for Travelers

Are you planning a trip to Japan? Whether your trip is for business or pleasure, this course will prepare you with the basic words and phrases you will need for everyday communication. We will also read a selection of articles and view a few short films to provide an introduction to Japanese culture and history.

Text: *The Basics of the Japanese Language*

Tuesday, Thursday, 6:00–8:00 P.M.

Instructor: Mr. Sato

Advanced Spanish

This class is for students who have successfully completed Beginning and Intermediate Spanish, or who have passed a proficiency test. We will review grammar and vocabulary, read articles, and have in-depth discussions about current events.

Text: *Spanish for Today*

Monday, Wednesday, 4:00–6:00 P.M.

Instructor: Sr. Lopez

Answer the questions below.
Choose NO MORE THAN THREE WORDS *from the text for each answer.*

7 What is the first day to sign up for classes? ....

8 Where can students buy books for these courses? ....

9 In which course will students talk about the news? ....

10 Which course meets three days a week? ....

11 In which course will students watch movies? ....

12 Which course does not use a book? ....

Text C

A Healthy Lifestyle

A

Your health is one of your most valuable assets. When you keep your body in good shape, you have the energy you need to keep going all day, both at home and at work. It is worthwhile to take a little time everyday to make sure you have given your body what it needs to stay healthy, and it may be more convenient than you think.

B

The first step is to start the day with a good breakfast that includes whole grains, protein, and fruit. Diet is one of the most important aspects of a healthy lifestyle, so be sure to have three nutritious meals a day. If you are concerned about your weight, don't skip meals, but do avoid high-calorie snacks.

C

Physical exercise benefits your health in many ways. It keeps your muscles strong and in good condition and helps you avoid injury from strains and falls. It keeps your mind alert and helps you control your weight. You will see results with as little as 30 minutes a day of physical exercise.

D

Stress is one of the biggest factors contributing to poor health. Stress can lead to chronic conditions such as high blood pressure and may also weaken your immune system, making you more susceptible to infections. It is important to find a way to relax every day. Turn off the computer and spend some quiet time reading, doing yoga, or even talking with some friends.

E

Rest is necessary for both your mind and body. Adults need seven to eight hours of sleep every night. To get a good night's sleep, create a peaceful environment in your bedroom. Make sure that it is quiet and dark. It is also important to go to bed at around the same time every night. This will ensure that you are prepared for a good rest.

The text has five paragraphs, **A–E**.

*Choose the correct heading for paragraphs **A–E** from the list of headings below.*

*Write the correct number, **i–vii**, in the spaces provided for questions 13–17.*

List of Headings

i	Get Moving
ii	Get Enough Sleep
iii	The Importance of Staying Fit
iv	Nutrition and Cooking
v	Relax
vi	A Fitness Schedule
vii	Eat Right

13 Paragraph **A** ....

14 Paragraph **B** ....

15 Paragraph **C** ....

16 Paragraph **D** ....

17 Paragraph **E** ....

READING SKILLS—GENERAL TRAINING

Skill 8—Identifying the Tasks

On the Reading test, you will see a variety of questions types. (See page 66–67 in the Quick Study section of this chapter for a complete list of question types and descriptions.) The questions test your ability to identify details and main ideas, find specific information, and understand how facts and ideas are linked.

You should become familiar with the different types of questions and how to answer them.

PRACTICE

Read the texts and answer the questions. Note the question types.
Read the text below and answer questions 1–8.

MATCHING INFORMATION

Questions 1–8

Look at the five advertisements, ***A–E.***

A

Trout Heaven Lakeside Resort

Relax in our **spacious waterfront cabins**, large enough for Mom, Dad, and the kids.

Each cabin includes a fully equipped kitchen and all linens.

Rent by the week or month.
Enjoy your next vacation with us!

Trout Heaven
110 Quabbish Road
Westminster

413-555-1212
www.troutheaven.com

B

Green Valley Hotel

Come see why people have been staying with us since 1920.

We offer:

- luxury rooms and suites
- boating, swimming, and fishing in our private lake
- three meals daily served in our elegant dining room overseen by our world class chef

Visit us at *www.greenvalleyhotel.com* and find out what everyone is talking about.

C

Shady Porch Hotel and Resort

- Luxuriate in the state-of-the art comfort of our rooms and suites.
- Experience fine dining at its best.
- Enjoy daily sports activities or simply relax in a quiet country setting.
- Improve your tennis, golf, or horse-back riding skills under the guidance of our professional staff instructors.

The Shady Porch
3495 Sunrise Lane
Bolton
340-556-0303
www.shadyporch.com

D

Visit
Mountain Top Resort

The premier vacation resort in the Sky Mountains.

Relax in the clean mountain air.

Enjoy guided hikes and bus tours of the area led by resort staff.

Extended stay packages available.

Reduced off-season prices:

May 1-31, October 1-15.

Book your vacation now.

516-434-3333

www.mountaintopresort.com

E

Sandy Side Lodge

Open for the season May 15–Nov. 1

Experience an unforgettable beach vacation in a spectacular setting.

✔ Picnic on the dunes.
✔ Watch the sun set over the ocean from the balcony of your room.
✔ Enjoy walking through the adjacent salt marsh, observing shore birds and native plants.

All this at a price you can afford!

Make your reservation today.

SandySideLodge.com

Which advertisement mentions the following information?
Write the correct letter, ***A–E****, in the spaces provided for questions 1–8.*
You may use any letter more than once.

1 that arrangements can be made for side trips ....

2 accommodations for families ....

3 opportunities to enjoy water sports ....

4 discounts at certain times of the year ....

5 that the resort has been in existence for a long time ....

6 the beauty of the natural surroundings ....

7 the availability of lessons ....

8 the possibility of cooking ....

Read the text below and answer questions 9–18.

Student Housing Options at Bucktown University

Accommodation Types
Bucktown University students can choose from several housing options, depending on their needs and budget.

The majority of full-time students live in one of the five on-campus dormitories. These offer rooms that can accommodate up to three students. All rooms come with a bed, desk, and chair for each student at no extra charge. Each dorm has a basement cafeteria where breakfast and dinner are served daily. Food charges are extra. Part-time students are not eligible for rooms in student dormitories.

For students who find that the dormitories do not suit their needs, there are two student apartment buildings located near the northern edge of the university campus, close to the athletic center. Each building has 25 unfurnished one-bedroom apartments. These small units are best suited for individuals or married couples. Rental fees include parking space in the garage beneath building. Apartment residents are eligible to purchase meal cards for use in campus cafeterias, if desired.

A small number of university-owned houses are available for rent on Oak Street, two blocks from the south entrance to campus. These two- and three-bedroom houses can accommodate parents with children. They are available to both married students and faculty members.

Applying for Accommodations
Most new students choose to live in a room in one of the on-campus dormitories. Older and married students can apply to live in one of the apartments or houses. To apply, complete the Housing Request Form and submit it to the Student Housing Office no later than six weeks before the beginning of the semester. After receiving his or her living accommodations assignment, the student must submit a check covering the first three months' rent. Upon receiving the check, the Student Housing Office will supply the student with a key, and the student can move in any time during the week prior to the beginning of the semester.

CLASSIFYING INFORMATION

Questions 9–15

Classify the following facts as describing

A *on-campus dormitories*
B *on-campus apartments*
C *university-owned houses*

*Write the correct letter, **A–C**, in the spaces provided for questions 9–15.*
You may use any letter more than once.

9 is suitable for families with children ....

10 is for full-time students only ....

11 serves meals ....

12 is located off campus ....

13 is large enough for only one or two people ....

14 comes with furniture ....

15 has a place to keep a car ....

SUMMARY COMPLETION

Questions 16–18

Complete the summary below.
Choose NO MORE THAN THREE WORDS from the text for each answer.
Write your answers in the spaces provided for questions 16–18.

New students usually live in **16** .... while the apartments and houses are for older and married students. Students should apply for housing **17** ....the semester begins. Before they move in, students must pay **18** ....Students can move in one week before the semester starts.

Read the text below and answer questions 19–26.

Volunteer Opportunities at Apex, Inc.

A

Through its volunteer program, Apex, Inc. supports community involvement by allowing employees paid time off of work to volunteer with an approved organization. Full-time employees (working a minimum of 35 hours a week) who have been with the company for at least six months may take up to one full day a month of paid time for volunteer work. Part-time employees (working a minimum of 20 hours a week) who have been with the company for at least one year may take up to one half day a month of paid time for volunteer work. Volunteer work must be with an approved organization in order to qualify for this program.

B

Employees who are considering participating in the program can request a list of approved organizations from the Human Resources office for review. The list includes a wide variety of community service organizations that receive volunteers from our company. Most do not require any special skills or previous experience, Organizations include local schools, health clinics, recreation centers, libraries, housing programs, and many others.

C

Employees who would like to participate in the program should request an application form from the Human Resources Office. Also available from that office is a list of approved volunteer organizations, including a description of the type of work they do and a list of which Apex, Inc. employees are currently volunteering with each organization. Completed forms should be returned to the Human Resources and should indicate at least three organizations that the employee would like to work with. Once the HR office has approved the form and selected and contacted the volunteer organization, the employee can begin.

D

Georgette Y. Plimpton, our company's founder, devoted many hours of her own free time to volunteer service in our community. A strong believer in community spirit, she started the volunteer program here in order to provide company employees with the opportunity to contribute to the community. For over 25 years, Apex, Inc. employees have been contributing their skills to a long list of local community service organizations through this program.

MATCHING HEADINGS

Questions 19–22

The text has four paragraphs, ***A–D****.*
Choose the correct heading for paragraphs ***A–D*** *from the list of headings below.*
Write the correct number, ***i-vi****, in the spaces provided for questions 19–22.*

List of Headings

i	History of the Program
ii	Popular Volunteer Organizations
iii	Who Can Volunteer
iv	How to Apply
v	Required Skills
vi	Where to Volunteer

19 Paragraph **A** ....

20 Paragraph **B** ....

21 Paragraph **C** ....

22 Paragraph **D** ....

TIP

Read the directions carefully. Some directions give a word limit, for example: "Write no more than three words." You will lose points if you write more words.

SHORT ANSWER

Questions 23–26

Answer the questions below.
Choose NO MORE THAN THREE WORDS AND/OR A NUMBER *from the text for each answer.*
Write your answers in the spaces provided for questions 23–26.

23 When is a full-time employee eligible to participate in the volunteer program?

....

24 Where can an employee get a list of volunteer organizations?

....

25 How many organizations should be listed on the application form?

....

26 How long has the volunteer program been operating?

....

Read the text below and answer questions 27–32.

What is Soil?

You may think of soil as just a pile of dirt. In fact, there is much more to soil than meets the eye. When you dig down into it, you will find that between the surface and the bedrock, soil is made up of several distinct layers. Closer to the surface, soil contains more organic matter, while deeper down there is more rock. At the surface, soil is composed of decaying organic matter, such as fallen leaves and rotting logs. Beneath this top layer you will find what is called topsoil, which is made up of a combination of organic matter and minerals. This is where seeds germinate and plants take root. Between this layer and the subsoil is the eluviation layer, composed mostly of sand and silt. As water drips through this layer, it leaches out most of the mineral content, which accumulates below in the subsoil. The mineral-rich subsoil sits on top of what is called the regolith, which consists mostly of broken up rock and little or no organic matter. Holding up all the other layers is the bedrock, a mass of rock such as granite, limestone, or sandstone.

DIAGRAM LABEL COMPLETION

Questions 27–32

Label the layers of soil in the diagram below. Choose one or two words from the text for each answer. Write your answers in the spaces provided for questions 27–32.

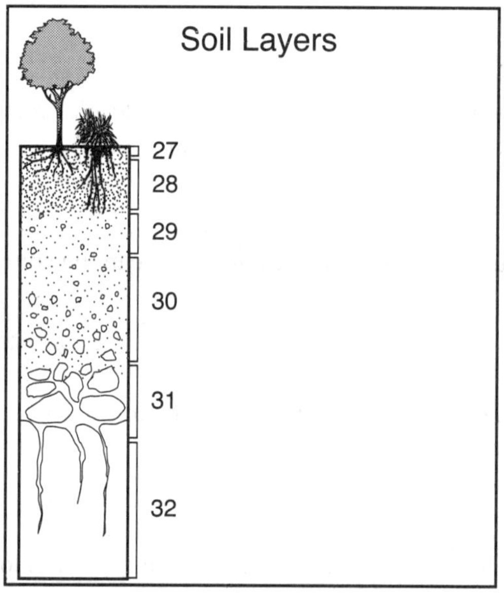

27 ....

28 ....

29 ....

30 ....

31 ....

32 ....

Read the text below and answer questions 33–39.

Ponce de Leon and the Fountain of Youth

People everywhere are interested in finding ways to avoid the effects of aging. Special diets, exercise programs, and beauty treatments that promise to help people look and feel young attract thousands of followers. And this interest is nothing new. Legends of youth-giving waters have been around for centuries. The ancient Greeks wrote about a fountain of youth. Alexander the Great supposedly went in search of one. And there are many more examples. So it is no wonder that the adventures of the Spanish explorer, Ponce de Leon, and his quest for the Fountain of Youth have long captured the public's imagination. It turns out, however, that the story of Ponce de Leon's search may be as imaginary as the fountain itself.

Ponce de Leon was a Spanish explorer who traveled to the Americas with Christopher Columbus. He was also the first European to explore what is now the state of Florida, in 1513. School children learn in history class that his travels through that area were motivated by his search for the Fountain of Youth. According to legend, this was a magical spring that bestowed eternal youth on anyone who bathed in or drank its waters. As Ponce de Leon explored the Florida Keys and journeyed up the west coast of Florida, he hoped at every turn to stumble upon the source of these magical youth-giving waters. Or so the story goes.

Although many people take the story of Ponce de Leon's quest for the Fountain of Youth as historical fact, historians have long debated its truth. What is fact is that Ponce de Leon was the first governor of the island of Puerto Rico, from 1509 to 1511. After he was forced to give up this position in favor of Columbus' son, Diego, the Spanish king offered him the governorship of the island of Bimini in compensation. Ponce de Leon set off in search of Bimini but ended up landing on the coast of Florida instead. He spent some time exploring the area before returning to Puerto Rico. Eight years later, he returned to Florida and attempted to establish a colony. There he met his fate. Instead of finding the waters that would give him eternal youth, he was shot and killed by a native.

In the years following the explorer's death, the story of his expeditions to Florida in search of the Fountain of Youth was recorded by several writers and historians. Despite this, there is no real evidence to back up the idea that Ponce de Leon was really looking for the legendary waters. There is no record of it in any documents from Ponce de Leon's lifetime, and he himself never mentioned it in his correspondence with the king about his journeys. What seems more likely is that at least one of the writers, who was a political friend of Ponce de Leon's rival, Diego Columbus, invented the story in order to make the explorer look foolish. From there, the legend grew.

Public interest in the story did not take off until the early nineteenth century, when Ponce de Leon became the subject of paintings and short stories. Then, the city of St. Augustine, Florida claimed to be the site of the actual Fountain of Youth that Ponce de Leon sought, and tourists began visiting the city to see the famous spring. Even though there is no evidence that Ponce de Leon ever visited this part of Florida, visitors continue to flock to St. Augustine, where they can see statues of the explorer and drink water from the spring. They can also buy specially labeled bottles to fill with the spring water and take home with them. And St. Augustine isn't the only city that says it has a "Fountain of Youth." Several other Florida cities also make the claim. Despite the thousands of tourists that visit these places annually, it appears that no one yet has succeeded in attaining eternal youth.

TRUE/FALSE/NOT GIVEN

Questions 33–37

Do the following statements agree with the information given in the text?
In the spaces provided for questions 33–37, write

TRUE	*if the statement agrees with the information*
FALSE	*if the statement contradicts the information*
NOT GIVEN	*if there is no information on this*

33 Ponce de Leon was the first person in recorded history to seek a fountain of youth. ....

34 Ponce de Leon first went to Florida after Columbus had explored it. ....

35 Ponce de Leon was succeeded by Diego Columbus as governor of Puerto Rico. ....

36 Ponce de Leon never found the island of Bimini. ....

37 Ponce de Leon died in Florida. ....

MULTIPLE CHOICE

Questions 38–39

*Choose the correct letter: **A**, **B**, **C**, or **D**.*

38 Ponce de Leon's letters to the king
A did not refer to a search for the Fountain of Youth.
B ended up making the explorer look foolish.
C described in detail his problems with Diego Columbus.
D were invented by a writer following the explorer's death.

39 St. Augustine, Florida is known as the site of
A Ponce de Leon's grave.
B a spring called the "Fountain of Youth."
C a museum of nineteenth-century art.
D the most visited attraction in Florida.

NOTE

After you have completed this section, study the skills for the Academic Reading test (pages 69–89). Those skills will help you in Section 3 of the General Training Reading test.

ANSWER EXPLANATIONS

READING SKILLS: ACADEMIC

Skill 1—Using the First Paragraph to Make Predictions (page 70)

PRACTICE (PAGE 71)

1. **Topic Sentence.** The spread of wildfire is a natural phenomenon that occurs throughout the world and is especially common in forested areas of North America, Australia, and Europe.

   Definition of Topic. Locations that receive plenty of rainfall but also experience periods of intense heat or drought are particularly susceptible to wildfires.

   Organizational Clues. Author may discuss

   - How wildfires start
   - How to control wildfires
   - Wildfires as a global problem

2. **Topic Sentence.** In reality, birds may actually be a great deal more intelligent than humans have given them credit for.

   Definition of Topic. For a long time, scientists considered birds to be of lesser intelligence because the cerebral cortex, the part of the brain that humans and other animals use for intelligence, is relatively small in size.

   Organizational Clues. Author may discuss

   - Misunderstandings about the intelligence of birds
   - The anatomy of a bird's brain
   - Evidence of avian intelligence

3. **Topic Sentence.** She would grow up to become one of the richest women in the world.

   Definition of Topic. Her name was Hetty Green, but she was known to many as the Witch of Wall Street.

   Organizational Clues. Author may discuss

   - Hetty Green's early years
   - How Hetty Green got rich
   - Why Hetty Green had a nickname

Skill 2—Using the Topic Sentence to Make Predictions (page 72)

PRACTICE (PAGE 72)

1. **Topic Sentence.** To combat excessive thoughts and impulses, most OCD sufferers perform certain repetitive rituals that they believe will relieve their anxiety.

   Questions to Ask Yourself
   What types of rituals do they perform?
   How does this help them?

2. **Topic Sentence.** A child's upbringing does not seem to be part of the cause of the disorder, though stress can make the symptoms stronger.

   Questions to Ask Yourself
   Is the disorder present at birth?
   Are there outside factors involved?
   What leads parents to seek treatment?

3. **Topic Sentence.** Research on OCD sufferers has found certain physiological trends.

   Questions to Ask Yourself
   What part of the body does it affect?
   What are some common trends?
   What can parents look for?

Skill 3—Looking for Specific Details (page 74)

PRACTICE (PAGE 74)

1. **Supporting Details**
   Compulsions can be mental or physical
   Examples include: checking, hand washing, disturbing images
   Compulsions and obsessions may or may not be related

2. **Supporting Details**
   Most cases are genetic
   Stress can add to the problem
   Many members of the family may have OCD

3. **Supporting Details**
   Over activity of blood in the brain
   Less serotonin
   Linked to other disorders such as Tourette syndrome and ADHD

Skill 4—Analyzing the Questions and Answers (page 75)

PRACTICE (PAGE 75)

1. *unreasonable.* Paragraph 1 states that, "OCD sufferers understand that their obsessions are unrealistic."

2. *uncontrollable.* Paragraph 1 states that "they find it stressful to put these intrusive thoughts out of their minds."

3. *reduce.* The first sentence of paragraph 3 states: "To combat excessive thoughts and impulses, most OCD sufferers perform certain repetitive rituals that they believe will relieve their anxiety."

4. *obsession.* Paragraph 2 states that "Fear of dirt and contamination are very common obsessive thoughts."

5. *checking.* Paragraph 3 states that "Common rituals include excessive checking."

6. *throw away.* The last sentence in paragraph 3 states that, "Holding onto objects that would normally be discarded, such as newspapers and containers, is another common compulsion."

7. *inherited.* Paragraph 4 states that "a number of different genetic factors" have been found as underlying causes of the disease.
8. *cause.* Paragraph 5 gives an example of an illness (strep throat) that is thought to be the cause behind some OCD cases.

Key Words in Statements 9–16: (Answers may vary.) child, stress, serotonin, age seventeen, psychotherapy, medication, treat, secret, antibiotics

9. False. Paragraph 4 states: "A child's upbringing does not seem to be part of the cause of the disorder, though stress can make the symptoms stronger. The underlying causes of OCD have been researched greatly, and point to a number of different genetic factors."
10. True. Paragraph 4 states: "A child's upbringing does not seem to be part of the cause of the disorder, though stress can make the symptoms stronger."
11. True. Paragraph 5 states: "Studies have also shown that OCD sufferers have less serotonin than the average person."
12. False. Paragraph 4 states: "OCD symptoms generally begin between the ages of ten and twenty-four and continue indefinitely until a person seeks treatment."
13. Not Given. Paragraph 6 mentions both psychotherapy and medication but does not discuss which one patients prefer.
14. False. Paragraph 6 discusses different treatment options, and states that, "early diagnosis and proper medication can lessen many of the symptoms and allow people to live fairly normal lives."
15. True. Paragraph 6 begins with this sentence: "Because OCD sufferers tend to be so secretive about their symptoms, they often put off treatment for many years."
16. True. The final sentence in Paragraph 6 indicates that antibiotics can be used in special cases of OCD: "For cases when OCD is linked to streptococcal infection, antibiotic therapy is sometimes all that is needed."

Skill 5—Identifying the Tasks (page 78)

PRACTICE 1 (PAGE 78)

Topic Sentence. The South African province of KwaZulu-Natal, more commonly referred to as the Zulu Kingdom, is named after the Zulu people who have inhabited the area since the late 1400s.

Questions to Ask Yourself
Who are the Zulu people?
What is the history behind this clan?
What are they known for?

Supporting Details
Large South African ethnic group
Region explored by Europeans
Zulu wear traditional jewelry/jewelry and clothing
Beadwork is important to the culture

Analyzing (page 79)

1. What?
2. What?
3. What?
4. Where?
5. When?
6. How many?
7. Who? Where? **Key Words:** British
8. What? **Key Words:** Henry Frances Flynn
9. What? **Key Words:** precious stones
10. What? Why? **Key Words:** daily lives
11. What? Why? **Key Words:** gourds

Classifying Information (page 81)

1. (E) Paragraph 1 states: "KwaZulu translates to mean 'Place of Heaven'."
2. (B) Paragraph 1 states: "'Natal' was the name the Portuguese explorers gave this region when they arrived in 1497."
3. (C) Paragraph 1 states: "By the late 1700s, the AmaZulu clan, meaning 'People of Heaven,' constituted a significant nation."

Short Answer (page 81)

4. *South Africa.* The first sentence of Paragraph 1 states that KwaZulu-Natal is a South African province.
5. *1497.* Paragraph 1 states: "Portuguese explorers . . . arrived in 1497."
6. *11 million.* Midway through paragraph 1 the passage states: "Today the Zulu clan represents the largest ethnic group in South Africa, with at least 11 million people in the kingdom."

True/False/Not Given (page 82)

7. *False.* Paragraph 2 talks about how the Egyptians were the first to bring beads to the area, though the British later facilitated the trade.
8. *Not Given.* Paragraph 2 states that Henry Frances Flynn brought glass beads to the region, but it doesn't state anywhere that he earned a lot of money doing this.
9. *False.* Paragraph 3 states: "The Zulu people were not fooled into believing that glass beads were precious stones but, rather, used the beads to establish certain codes and rituals in their society."

10. *True.* Paragraph 3 discusses how beads are used for adornment, education, recreation, and communication.

11. *True.* Paragraph 3 discusses how bead-covered gourds are carried around by women who are having fertility problems. "Fertility problems" means *difficulty becoming and staying pregnant.*

Diagram Label Completion (page 82)

12. *unmarried man.* Paragraph 4 states: "A triangle with the apex pointing downward signifies an unmarried man."

13. *married man.* Paragraph 4 states that "married men signify their marital status with two triangles that form an hourglass shape."

14. *married woman.* Paragraph 4 states: "Married women wear items with two triangles that form a diamond shape."

15. *unmarried woman.* Paragraph 4 states that a triangle "with the tip pointing upward is worn by an unmarried woman."

PRACTICE 2 (PAGE 83)

Note: Alternative spellings: colour blindness, colour, colourful

Matching Headings (page 83)

1. iii. What Is Colorblindness? Paragraph A discusses what people think colorblindness is, and what it really is. In the middle of the paragraph it states, "The fact is that in most cases of colorblindness, there are only certain shades that a person cannot distinguish between. These people are said to be dichromatic."

2. viii. Colorblindness and the Sexes. Paragraph B discusses the fact that men are more prone to colorblindness than women, and states the genetic reasons why this is the case.

3. vii. Developing the Ability to See Color. Paragraph C discusses the fact that babies are all born colorblind and that they do not develop the ability to see colors until they are a few months old. This paragraph also discusses the possibility that infants may require a colorful environment in order to develop proper color vision.

4. ii. Diagnosing Colorblindness. Paragraph D discusses the reasons why colorblindness is difficult to diagnose. It also discusses the Ishihara Test, which distinguishes those who are colorblind from those who have normal color vision.

5. v. Unsolved Myths. Paragraph E mentions two beliefs about colorblindness that haven't been proven: that colorblindness can aid military soldiers and that everyone is colorblind in an emergency.

Multiple Choice (page 85)

6. C. The second to the last sentence of Paragraph A states that: "People with trichromatic vision have all three cones in working order."

7. B. The second sentence in Paragraph C states that: "A baby's cones do not begin to differentiate between many different colors until the baby is approximately four months old."

8. C. Paragraph D states the main downfall of the Ishihara Test: "The Ishihara Test is the most common, though it is highly criticized because it requires that children have the ability to recognize numerals."

Summary Completion (page 86)

9. *myth.* Paragraph B introduces the idea that although color vision deficiency is predominant in males, it is still possible for females to be colorblind.

10. *a little less.* Paragraph B states: "In an average population, 8% of males exhibit some form of colorblindness."

11. *X chromosomes.* Paragraph B states: "Females have two X chromosomes."

12. *less likely.* Paragraph B explains that it is less likely for women to be colorblind, because if one of their X chromosomes "carries the defective gene, the other one naturally compensates."

    "Compensate" means *to make up for another's weakness.*

PRACTICE 3 (PAGE 86)

Classifying Information (page 88)

1. A. Paragraph 2 discusses how Antarctic penguins "huddle in communities" to keep warm.

2. A. The first sentence of Paragraph 3 states: "Antarctic penguins spend about 75 percent of their lives in the water."

3. A. Paragraph 3 discusses the unique feathers of Antarctic penguins that work similarly to a waterproof diving suit: "Tufts of down trap a layer of air within the feathers, preventing the water from penetrating to the penguin's skin."

4. B. Paragraph 4 discusses the bald patches of a temperate species called African penguins.

5. B. Paragraph 4 states: "Temperate species have certain physical features such as fewer feathers and less blubber to keep them cool on a hot day."

Sentence Completion (page 88)

6. rocks. Paragraph 2 states: "When it's time to create a nest, most penguins build up a pile of rocks on top of the ice to place their eggs."

7. feed/eat. Paragraph 2 discusses the Emperor penguin's gender roles: "The female Emperor lays just one egg and gives it to the male to protect while she goes off for weeks to feed."

8. brood patch. Paragraph 2 explains how the male Emperor penguin takes care of the egg: "The male balances the egg on top of his feet, covering it with a small fold of skin called a brood patch."
9. heels and tails. Toward the end of paragraph 2 the text states: "In order to reduce the cold of the ice, penguins often put their weight on their heels and tails."

Matching Sentence Endings (page 89)

10. B. Paragraph 1 states that a number of penguin species "migrate to warmer waters to breed."
11. E. Paragraph 3 describes "a number of survival adaptations" that allow penguins to survive in cold water.
12. D. Paragraph 4 describes how penguins behave in warm weather, including "moving to shaded areas."

READING SKILLS: GENERAL TRAINING

Skill 6—Making Predictions (page 90)

PRACTICE (PAGE 90)

1. schedule
2. swimming pool information
3. swim lessons, membership, swim team, weekly schedule
4. course descriptions
5. language classes
6. class schedules, instructors' names, required texts
7. magazine article
8. how to stay healthy
9. advice

Skill 7—Finding the Answers (page 93)

PRACTICE 1 (PAGE 93)

1. parents, guardians
2. lessons, courses
3. kids
4. permitted
5. closed, shut
6. purchase, pay for
7. high schoolers, adolescents

8. be eligible
9. call, get in touch with
10. August 28, Monday
11. register, enroll
12. texts, chapters
13. current events
14. films
15. discuss
16. good shape, healthy
17. breakfast, diet, meal
18. exercise
19. stress, unwind
20. rest, dream

PRACTICE 2 (PAGE 94)

1. *pool area.* The notes about children's lessons state: "Parents are requested to remain in the pool area during the entire lesson."
2. *adult swim.* The notes about adult swim state: "Adults age 18 and over only are permitted in the pool at this time."
3. *Wednesday afternoon.* Under Information it says: "The locker rooms are closed every Wednesday afternoon."
4. *one-day pass.* Under Information it says: "Nonmembers may purchase a one-day pass."
5. *junior membership.* Under Information it says: High school students are eligible for a junior membership."
6. *administrative office.* Under Information about swim lessons it says: "Call the administrative office for more information or to sign up."
7. *August 28.* Paragraph 1 states: "Registration begins the week of August 28."
8. *In class.* Paragraph 1 states: "All required texts are available for purchase in class from your instructor."
9. *Advanced Spanish.* The description for Advanced Spanish mentions "in-depth discussions about current events."
10. *Beginning French.* According to the description, this class meets Monday, Tuesday, and Thursday.
11. *Japanese for Travelers.* The description for this class mentions that students will "view a few short films."

12. *Intermediate French.* The description for this class states: "There is no required text for the class."
13. iii. Paragraph A explains why good health is important.
14. vii. Paragraph B explains the importance of healthy meals and a good diet.
15. i. Paragraph C is about physical exercise.
16. v. Paragraph D explains why stress is bad and how to avoid it by relaxing.
17. ii. Paragraph E is about rest and sleep.

Skill 8—Identifying the Tasks (page 98)

PRACTICE (PAGE 98)

Matching Information (Page 98)

1. D. This ad mentions "guided hikes and bus tours of the area led by resort staff."
2. A. This ad mentions "cabins, large enough for Mom, Dad, and the kids."
3. B. This ad mentions "boating, swimming, and fishing."
4. D. This ad mentions "Reduced off-season prices."
5. B. This ad states "people have been staying with us since 1920."
6. E. This ad mentions "the sun set over the ocean" and "walking through the adjacent salt marsh, observing shore birds and native plants."
7. C. This ad mentions "our professional staff instructors."
8. A. This ad states "Each cabin includes a fully equipped kitchen."

Classifying Information (Page 101)

9. C. Paragraph 4 states that the houses "can accommodate parents with children."
10. A. Paragraph 2 states: "Part-time students are not eligible for rooms in student dormitories."
11. A. Paragraph 2 states: "Each dorm has a basement cafeteria where breakfast and dinner are served daily."
12. C. Paragraph 4 states that the houses are "two blocks from the south entrance to campus."
13. B. Paragraph 3 states that the apartments are "best suited for individuals or married couples."
14. A. Paragraph 2 states that the dorm rooms "come with a bed, desk, and chair for each student at no extra charge."
15. B. Paragraph 3 states about the apartment buildings: "Rental fees include parking space in the garage beneath building."

Summary Completion (Page 101)

16. *on-campus dormitories.* The first two sentences of Paragraph 5 state: "Most new students choose to live in a room in one of the on-campus dormitories. Older and married students can apply to live in one of the apartments or houses."

17. *six weeks before.* Paragraph 5 states: "To apply, complete the Housing Request Form and submit it to the Student Housing Office no later than six weeks before the beginning of the semester."

18. *three months' rent.* Paragraph 5 states: "After receiving his or her living accommodations assignment, the student must submit a check covering the first three months' rent."

Matching Headings (Page 103)

19. iii. Paragraph A explains that full-time and part-time employees can volunteer.

20. vi. Paragraph B explains that there is a list of approved organizations and gives a general description of what they are.

21. iv. Paragraph C explains the application process.

22. i. Paragraph D explains why and how long ago the company's founder started the volunteer program.

Short Answer (Page 103)

23. *after six months.* Paragraph A states that full-time employees "who have been with the company for at least six months may take up to one full day a month of paid time for volunteer work."

24. *Human Resources office.* Paragraph B states that an employee can "request a list of approved organizations from the Human Resources office."

25. *at least 3.* Paragraph C states that the application form "should indicate at least three organizations that the employee would like to work with."

26. *over 25 years.* Paragraph D states that employees have been contributing their skills "for over 25 years."

Diagram Label Completion (Page 104)

27. *organic matter.* The text states: "At the surface, soil is composed of decaying organic matter."

28. *topsoil.* The text states: "Beneath this top layer you will find what is called topsoil."

29. *eluviation layer.* The text states: "Between this layer and the subsoil is the eluviation layer."

30. *subsoil.* The text states: "As water drips through this layer, it leaches out most of the mineral content, which accumulates below in the subsoil."

31. *regolith.* The text states: "The mineral-rich subsoil sits on top of what is called the regolith."

32. *bedrock.* The text states: "Holding up all the other layers is the bedrock."

True/False/Not Given (Page 106)

33. *False.* Paragraph 1 explains that throughout history people have been interested in finding a fountain of youth.

34. *False.* Paragraph 2 states that Ponce de Leon was "the first European to explore what is now the state of Florida," so he wouldn't have explored after Columbus, another European.

35. *True.* Paragraph 3 states that Ponce de Leon "was forced to give up this position in favor of Columbus' son, Diego." "This position" refers to his position as governor of Puerto Rico.

36. *Not Given.* Paragraph 3 explains that Ponce de Leon landed in Florida while he was looking for Bimini, but it doesn't say whether he did or did not travel to Bimini at some other time.

37. *True.* Paragraph 3 explains that Ponce de Leon was killed by a native when he returned to Florida.

Multiple Choice (Page 106)

38. A. Paragraph 4 states that Ponce de Leon "never mentioned it in his correspondence with the king about his journeys. "It" refers to the Fountain of Youth."

39. B. Paragraph 5 states: "Then, the city of St. Augustine, Florida claimed to be the site of the actual Fountain of Youth that Ponce de Leon sought, and tourists began visiting the city to see the famous spring."

Writing Module 5

QUICK STUDY

OVERVIEW

There are two writing tasks in both the Academic and General Training Writing modules. Task 2 is worth twice as much as Task 1. Consider the importance of Task 2 as you plan and write.

Task	Number of Minutes	Minimum Number of Words
1	20	150
2	40	250

QUESTION TYPES

You should be familiar with the types of tasks in both the Academic and General Training Writing modules.

	Academic Writing Module
Task 1	Write a short report summarizing information presented in one or more charts, graphs, or tables. - OR - Write a short report describing a diagram that illustrates changes over time or steps in a process.
Task 2	Write an essay supporting an opinion with reasons and examples.

	General Training Writing Module
Task 1	Write a letter in response to a situation ■ requesting or giving information ■ making an invitation or an apology ■ explaining a problem
Task 2	Write an essay supporting an opinion with reasons and examples.

ASSESSMENT CRITERIA

Responses to the IELTS writing tasks are assessed according to the following criteria:

TASK ACHIEVEMENT This refers to how completely you respond to all parts of the task.

COHERENCE AND COHESION This refers to how well you organize your writing and connect your ideas.

LEXICAL RESOURCE This refers to the variety of vocabulary words you use and how accurately you use them.

GRAMMATICAL RANGE AND ACCURACY This refers to the variety and accuracy of the grammatical forms and structures you use.

WRITING TIPS

1. Make sure you plan before you begin writing. Use the bottom of page 2 of your test booklet to make an outline or concept map.
2. The examiners judge your writing on its clarity. Make sure you have supported your ideas with specific details.
3. You can write more than 150 words for Task 1 or more than 250 words for Task 2, but you can't write less. You will lose points if you have less than the assigned number of words in your essay.
4. Learn to look at your writing and estimate how many words it is. Don't waste precious time counting words. You can photocopy the Writing Answer Sheet from any one of the practice tests to use when you practice. When you practice your essay, you can judge how many words in your handwriting are on a page.
5. Remember that you will be allowed to use a second sheet of paper if necessary.
6. Paraphrase the question in your introduction.
7. Learn the words and phrases used to link sentences and paragraphs.
8. In Task 2, add personal experiences and details whenever possible.
9. Understand the question before you begin to answer. You must answer the question completely. Make sure you address all parts of the task.
10. Organize your time carefully. Leave time for planning, writing, and revising.
11. Write your essays in the correct place. Task 1 needs to be written on pages 1 and 2 of your writing test booklet. Task 2 needs to be written on pages 3 and 4.
12. Indent each paragraph or leave spaces between paragraphs. Make sure it is clear where each paragraph begins and ends.
13. Write clearly and legibly.
14. Cross out changes neatly or erase thoroughly.
15. Leave some time at the end to check for and correct spelling and grammar mistakes.
16. Read as much and as often as you can so that you become more familiar with the way writing is organized.
17. Study the sample scored responses to the IELTS writing tasks that are available at *www.ielts.org*.
18. Watch your time. You have only 20 minutes for Task 1 and 40 minutes for Task 2.

TASK ACHIEVEMENT SKILLS

TASK 1—ACADEMIC WRITING

NOTE

If you are studying for the General Training exam, go to Skill 8 (page 140).

Skill 1—Determining the Task

In Writing Task 1 on the Academic Test, you will write a report summarizing and comparing the main features of a graphic. The graphic may be a bar graph, line graph, pie chart, table, or diagram. You must recognize the type of graphic and the type of information it shows.

PRACTICE

Look at the following tasks and graphics. Write the letter of each graphic or set of graphics next to the corresponding task.

Tasks

1 ....

The bar graphs on page 123 show information about spending and test grades in the Riverdale Public School system.

Summarize the information by selecting and reporting in the main features and make comparisons where relevant.

2 ....

The diagram on page 124 shows the town of Sanditon Beach before and after an airport was built.

Summarize the information by selecting and reporting in the main features and make comparisons where relevant.

3 ....

The table on page 123 shows the average time and money spent at different types of restaurants.

Summarize the information by selecting and reporting in the main features and make comparisons where relevant.

4 ....

The pie charts on page 123 show professions chosen by female graduates of a certain university.

Summarize the information by selecting and reporting in the main features and make comparisons where relevant.

Graphics

A

Restaurant Types

	Sit-Down Restaurant	Cafeteria	Fast-Food Restaurant
Average cost of lunch	$10.00	$7.00	$4.50
Average time spent eating lunch	45 min.	30 min.	20 min.
Average cost of dinner	$17.00	$9.50	$5.00
Average time spent eating dinner	60 min.	45 min.	20 min.

B

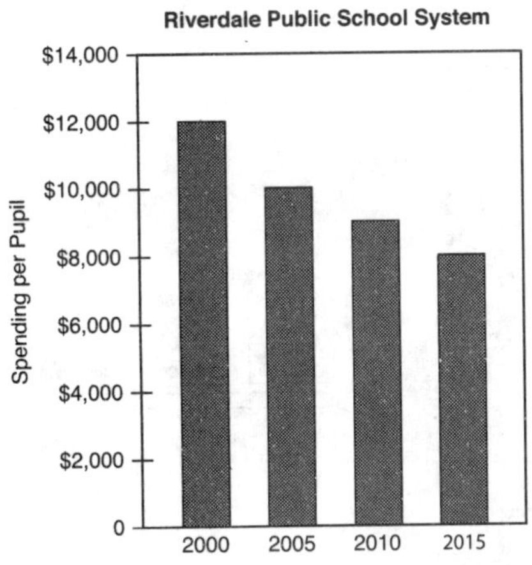

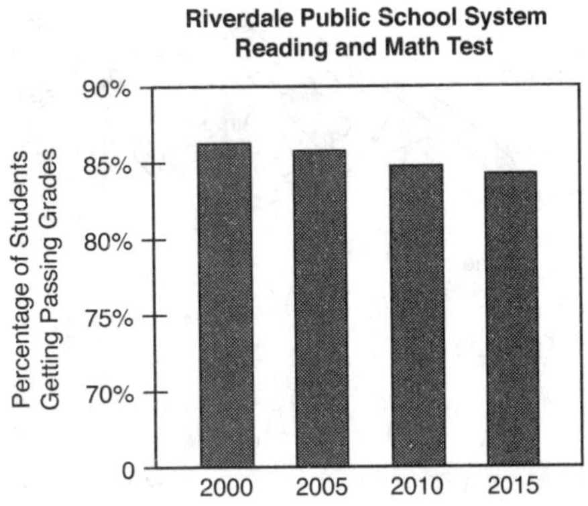

C

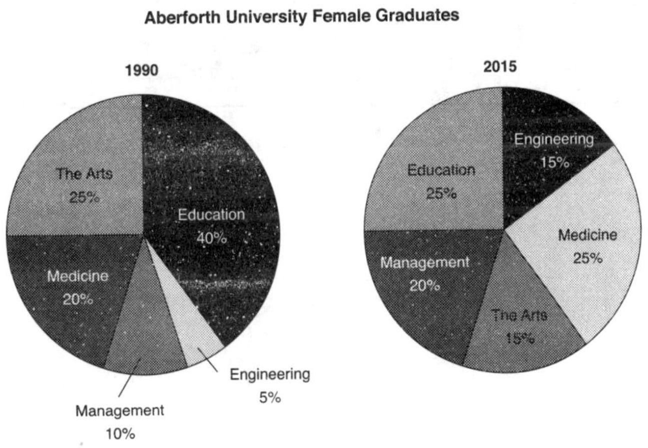

D

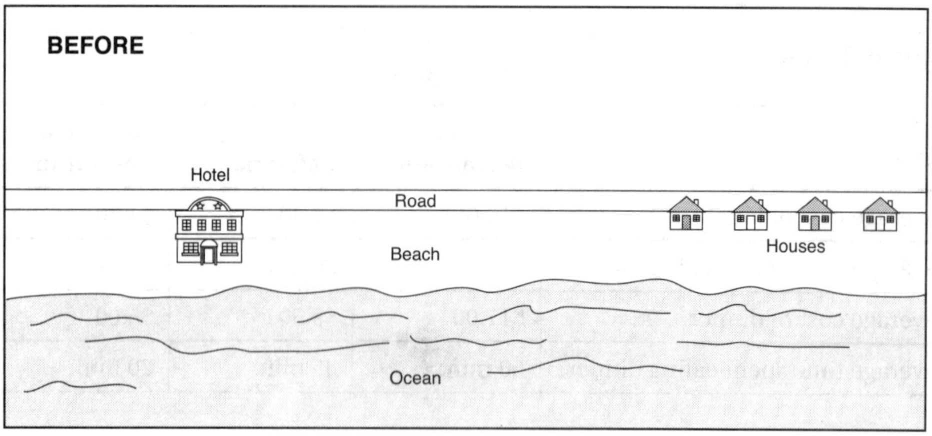
BEFORE
Hotel
Road
Beach
Houses
Ocean

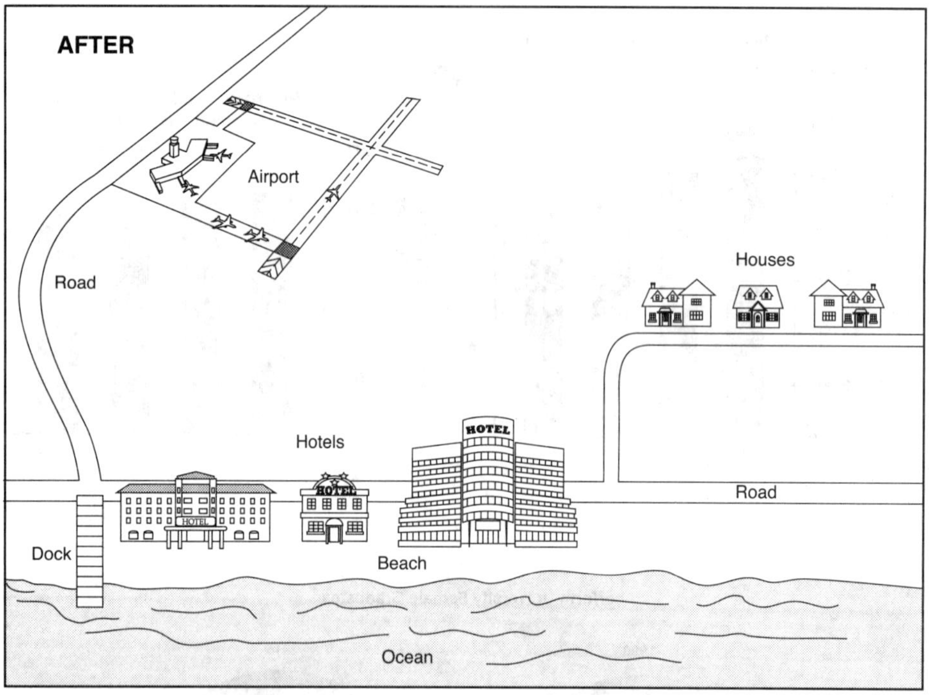
AFTER
Airport
Road
Houses
Hotels
HOTEL
HOTEL
HOTEL
Road
Dock
Beach
Ocean

Skill 2—Determining the Topic

Determine the topic of the graphic by reading the graphic title and description. Later, you will use this information to write the topic sentence of your report.

PRACTICE

Choose the best topic for each of the graphics in Skill 1 (pages 123–124).

1 **Graphic A**

A How much money three types of restaurants earn at lunch and dinner time

B How long it takes to serve lunch and dinner at three types of restaurants

C How much time and money customers spend at three types of restaurants

2 **Graphic B**

A Per pupil spending and test grades in the Riverdale Public School System

B Time spent on giving tests to each pupil in the Riverdale Public School System

C How much pupils spend to study in the Riverdale Public School System

3 **Graphic C**

A Percentage of female graduates of Aberforth University who changed their careers

B Careers chosen by women graduating from Aberforth University

C Percentage of female students who graduated from Aberforth University

4 **Graphic D**

A The appearance of Sanditon Beach before and after the construction of an airport

B Maps of two different areas of the town of Sanditon Beach

C Plans for building a new town on Sanditon Beach

Skill 3—Making Comparisons

In Task 1, you are asked to make comparisons. Look for things you can compare in the graphic. You might see information about places, types of people, types of activities, products, and/or changes over time. Look for similarities and differences among these things.

Look at this sample task and the notes about comparisons.

> *The bar graph below shows the average housing costs in three different regions for two different years.*
>
> *Summarize the information by selecting and reporting in the main features and make comparisons where relevant.*

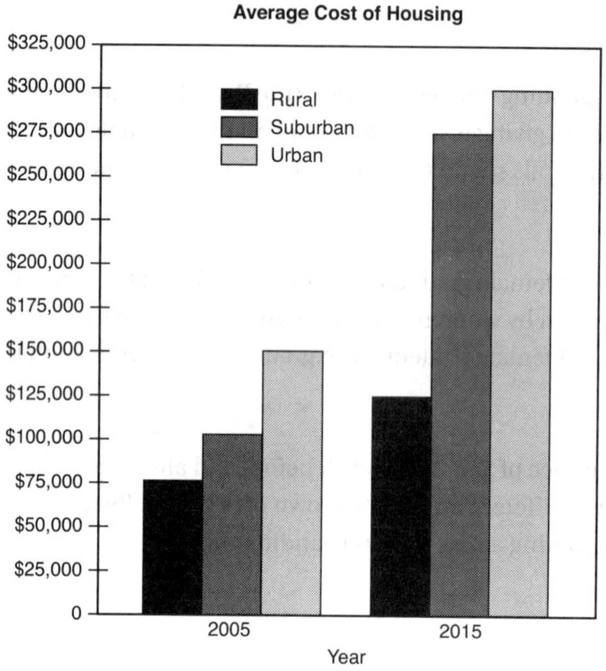

Comparison 1 The average cost of housing in rural, urban, and suburban areas
Comparison 2 The average cost of housing in 2005 and 2015

PRACTICE

Determine two comparisons you can make for each of the graphics in Skill 1 (pages 123–124). The first one has been started for you.

1 **Graphic A**

Comparison 1 The average cost of meals in three types of restaurants ....

Comparison 2 ....

2 **Graphic B**

Comparison 1 ....

Comparison 2 ....

3 **Graphic C**

Comparison 1 ....

Comparison 2 ....

4 **Graphic D**

Comparison 1 ....

Comparison 2 ....

Skill 4—Making an Outline

An outline is a plan for what you will write. Start with the topic you determined and the comparisons you made. Then add supporting details to describe the comparisons.

Look at the graphic for big changes or differences. Look for numbers that go up or down. The changes and differences are the details that support your comparisons.

Read this outline for the sample task in Skill 3 (page 126). Then compare the outline with the report that follows it.

Outline
Introduction
Topic Housing costs in rural, urban, and suburban areas in two different years

Body
Comparison 1 The average cost of housing in rural, urban, and suburban areas
- Supporting Detail 1 Average cost in rural areas
- Supporting Detail 2 Average cost in suburban areas
- Supporting Detail 3 Average cost in urban areas

Comparison 2 The average cost of housing in 2005 and 2015
- Supporting Detail 1 Change in housing cost in rural areas
- Supporting Detail 2 Change in housing cost in urban areas
- Supporting Detail 3 Change in housing cost in suburban areas

The bar graph shows the average cost of housing in rural, urban, and suburban areas in 2005 and 2015. Housing costs were different in each of the areas. However, they rose significantly in all three areas in the time period shown on the graph.

There was a significant difference in housing costs in all three areas in both 2005 and 2015. The average housing cost in rural areas was lowest at $75,000 in 2005 and $125,000 in 2015. The average housing cost in suburban areas was slightly higher than rural areas in 2005 and a good deal higher in 2015. Urban housing costs were the highest and were around twice as high as costs in rural areas in both years.

Housing costs in all three areas rose between 2005 and 2015. Average rural housing costs rose from $75,000 to $125,000. Average urban housing costs doubled, going from $150,000 to $300,000. Average suburban housing costs almost tripled, rising from $100,000 to $275,000.

Overall, average housing costs in urban and suburban areas remained higher than in rural areas, but they rose significantly more in the time period shown on the graph.

PRACTICE 1

Look at the outline and report about Graphic A in Skill 1 (page 123). Complete the missing parts of the outline.

Introduction

Topic How much time and money customers spend at three types of restaurants

Body

Comparison1 The average cost of meals in three types of restaurants

Supporting Detail 1 Average spending at a fast-food restaurant

Supporting Detail 2 (1) ....

Supporting Detail 3 Average spending at a sit-down restaurant

Comparison2 The average time eating in three types of restaurants

Supporting Detail 1 (2) ....

Supporting Detail 2 Average time eating at a cafeteria

Supporting Detail 3 (3) ....

The table shows how much time and money customers spend on average at three different types of restaurants. The cost of a meal in each of the three restaurants is significantly different. There is also a significant difference in the time spent eating.

The average cost of both lunch and dinner is very different in each of the three types of restaurants. A fast-food customer spends on average $4.50 for lunch and $5.00 for dinner. At a cafeteria, on the other hand, the average cost for these meals is $7.00 and $9.50, respectively. Meals at a sit-down restaurant are even more expensive. Lunch there costs more than twice as much as a fast-food lunch, and dinner is more than three times as expensive.

Customers at each of these restaurants also spend different amounts of time eating. Lunch and dinner at a fast-food restaurant take only 20 minutes on average. At a cafeteria they take 30 minutes and 45 minutes, respectively. Meanwhile, a customer at a sit-down restaurant spends 45 minutes eating lunch and 60 minutes eating dinner.

In general, customers who spend less on food also spend less time eating, while those who spend more money on restaurant meals also spend more time eating them.

PRACTICE 2

Complete the outlines for Graphics B, C, and D in Skill 1 (pages 123–124). Use the comparisons you made in the practice for Skill 3 (page 127). Include 2–3 supporting details for each comparison.

Graphic B

Introduction

Topic Spending and test grades in the Riverdale Public School System

Body

Comparison 1 ....

Supporting Detail 1 ....

Supporting Detail 2 ....

Supporting Detail 3 ....

Comparison 2 ....

Supporting Detail 1 ....

Supporting Detail 2 ....

Supporting Detail 3 ....

Graphic C

Introduction

Topic Careers chosen by women graduating from Aberforth University

Body

Comparison 1 ....

Supporting Detail 1 ....

Supporting Detail 2 ....

Supporting Detail 3 ....

Comparison 2 ....

Supporting Detail 1 ....

Supporting Detail 2 ....

Supporting Detail 3 ....

Graphic D

Introduction

Topic The appearance of Sanditon Beach before and after the construction of an airport

Body

Comparison 1 ....

Supporting Detail 1 ....

Supporting Detail 2 ....

Supporting Detail 3 ....

Comparison 2 ....

Supporting Detail 1 ....

Supporting Detail 2 ....

Supporting Detail 3 ....

Skill 5—Writing the Introduction

Begin your report with a brief introduction. The introduction states the topic and summarizes the ideas you will discuss in the report.

The first sentence of your introduction is the topic sentence. It tells what the graphic is about. The next sentences tell what comparisons you will make. Use the topic and comparisons from your outline to write your introduction.

Look at these notes and introduction for the sample task in Skill 3 (page 126).

Notes

Topic Housing costs in rural, urban, and suburban areas in two different years
Comparison 1 The average cost of housing in rural, urban, and suburban areas
Comparison 2 The average cost of housing in 2005 and 2015

Introduction

The bar graph shows the average cost of housing in rural, urban, and suburban areas in 2005 and 2015. Housing costs were different in each of the areas. However, they rose significantly in all three areas in the time period shown on the graph.

- The first sentence of the paragraph is the topic sentence.
- The second sentence, *Housing costs were different in each of the areas*, corresponds to Comparison 1.
- The third sentence, *However, they rose significantly in all three areas in the time period shown on the graph*, corresponds to Comparison 2.

Look at these notes and introduction for Graphic A in Skill 1 (page 123).

Notes

Topic How much time and money customers spend at three types of restaurants
Comparison 1 The average cost of meals in three types of restaurants
Comparison 2 The average time eating in three types of restaurants

Introduction

The table shows how much time and money customers spend on average at three different types of restaurants. The cost of a meal in each of the three restaurants is significantly different. There is also a significant difference in the time spent eating.

- The first sentence of the paragraph is the topic sentence.
- The second sentence, *The cost of a meal in each of the three restaurants is significantly different*, corresponds to Comparison 1.
- The third sentence, *There is also a significant difference in the time spent eating*, corresponds to Comparison 2.

PRACTICE

Look at these notes and introductions for Graphics B, C, and D in Skill 1 (pages 123–124). Choose the correct sentence to complete each introduction.

Graphic B

Topic Per pupil spending and test grades in the Riverdale Public School System

Comparison 1 Spending per pupil in 2000–2015

Comparison 2 Percentage of students passing a reading and math test in 2000–2015

The bar graphs show per pupil spending as well as the percentage of students who passed a test in the Riverdale Public School System in 2000–2015. .... The percentage of students who passed the test also went down.

A Pupils in the school system spent more per year.
B One hundred percent of students in the school system took the test.
C Per pupil spending went down noticeably in that time period.

Graphic C

Topic Careers chosen by women graduating from Aberforth University

Comparison 1 Percentage of female graduates choosing different professions in 1990

Comparison 2 Percentage of female graduates choosing different professions in 2015

The pie charts show the different careers chosen by women graduating from Aberforth University in 1990 and 2015. In 1990, well over half the graduates chose humanities careers. ....

A In 2015, the choices were more evenly distributed among different types of careers.
B Only 30% chose careers in medicine or engineering.
C Fewer women graduated from Aberforth University in 2015.

Graphic D

Topic The appearance of Sanditon Beach before and after the construction of an airport

Comparison 1 Sanditon Beach before airport was built

Comparison 2 Sanditon Beach after airport was built

The diagram illustrates the appearance of Sanditon Beach before and after the construction of an airport. .... After the airport was built, the town looked quite different.

A Before the airport was built, there was high unemployment in the town.
B The airport looked very modern and clean.
C Originally, it looked like a quiet town with few buildings.

Skill 6—Writing the Paragraphs

After you write the introduction, write one paragraph for each of the comparisons. Follow your outline. For the main idea of each paragraph, write one sentence that summarizes the comparison. Then write one or two sentences for each supporting detail.

Look at this part of the outline for Graphic B in Skill 1 (page 123). Then read the paragraph that follows. Notice how it follows the outline.

Outline

Comparison 1 *Spending per pupil in 2000–2015*
- Supporting Detail 1 *spending in 2000*
- Supporting Detail 2 *spending drop in 2005, 2010, 2015*
- Supporting Detail 3 *difference in spending, 2000 and 2015*

Paragraph

There was a significant drop in per pupil spending between 2000 and 2015. The school system spent $12,000 per pupil in 2000. This dropped to $10,000 in 2005. There was a smaller drop in 2010 and another drop in 2015. In that year, per pupil spending was $4,000 less than it had been 15 years earlier.

The first sentence is the main idea and corresponds to Comparison 1. The second sentence corresponds to Supporting Detail 1. The third and fourth sentences correspond to supporting Detail 2, and the fifth sentence corresponds to Supporting Detail 3.

Useful words for writing about graphs

Verbs	Nouns	Adjectives and Adverbs
rose	increase	steady
increased	growth	rapid
grew	rise	sharp
fell	surge	steadily
dropped	decrease	sharply
declined	drop	significantly
decreased	decline	slightly

When you write the paragraphs, use words from the table above to describe trends. Look at this example.

Ticket sales on the Western Railroad rose during the four months shown on the graph. In April, 5,000 tickets were sold. There was a sharp rise in sales between then and May, when 10,000 tickets were sold. Sales remained steady through June, then their sales increased slightly, to just under 12,000 tickets in July.

PRACTICE 1

Use words from the table on page 134 to complete the paragraph below.

Ticket sales on the Norfolk Railroad, on the other hand, (1) .... and fell during the same time period. There was a slight (2) .... between April and May, from just under 8,000 sales to around 9,000. There was another (3) .... in sales between May and June, to 10,000 tickets sold. Then there was a (4) .... drop between June and July, to around 5,000 sales.

PRACTICE 2

Use the outlines to write paragraphs for Graphics C and D in Skill 1 (pages 123–124)

Graphic C

Comparison 1 Percentage of female graduates choosing different professions in 1990

Supporting Detail 1 education and the arts

Supporting Detail 2 science-related careers

Supporting Detail 3 management

....

....

....

Comparison 2 Percentage of female graduates choosing different professions in 2015

Supporting Detail 1 education and the arts

Supporting Detail 2 science-related careers

Supporting Detail 3 management

....

....

....

Graphic D

Comparison 1 *Sanditon Beach before airport was built*

Supporting Detail 1 one hotel

Supporting Detail 2 houses

Supporting Detail 3 one road

....

....

....

Comparison 2 *Sanditon Beach after the airport was built*

Supporting Detail 1 new road

Supporting Detail 2 new hotels and dock

Supporting Detail 3 houses moved

....

....

....

Skill 7—Writing the Conclusion

In the introduction, you state the comparisons that you will discuss in your report. The conclusion is similar. You conclude your report by making a general statement about the comparisons.

Words and Phrases for Generalizing
in general
generally
overall
on the whole
all in all

Look at this introduction and conclusion from the first sample report in Skill 4 (page 128).

Introduction
The bar graph shows the average cost of housing in rural, urban, and suburban areas in 2005 and 2015. Housing costs were different in each of the areas. However, they rose significantly in all three areas in the time period shown on the graph.

Conclusion
Overall, average housing costs in urban and suburban areas remained higher than in rural areas, but they rose significantly more in the time period shown on the graph.

The introduction states the comparisons—housing costs in different areas and housing costs over time.

The conclusion makes a general statement about these comparisons—that costs were higher in some areas and that costs in these areas rose significantly over time.

Look at this introduction and conclusion from the second sample report in Skill 4 (page 129).

Introduction
The table shows how much time and money customers spend on average at three different types of restaurants. The cost of a meal in each of the three restaurants is significantly different. There is also a significant difference in the time spent eating.

Conclusion
In general, customers who spend less on food also spend less time eating, while those who spend more money on restaurant meals also spend more time eating them.

The introduction states the comparisons—the costs of meals and the time spent eating in different restaurants.

The conclusion makes a general statement about these comparisons—that in some restaurants people spend both less time and money, whereas in others they spend both more time and money.

PRACTICE 1

Write a conclusion for each of the following reports about graphics B, C, and D in Skill 1 (pages 123–124).

Graphic B

The bar graphs show per pupil spending as well as the percentage of students who passed a test in the Riverdale Public School System in 2000–2015. Per pupil spending went down noticeably in that time period. The percentage of students who passed the test also went down.

There was a significant drop in per pupil spending between 2000 and 2015. The school system spent $12,000 per pupil in 2000. This dropped to $10,000 in 2005. There was a smaller drop in 2010 and another drop in 2015. In that year, per pupil spending was $4,000 less than it had been 15 years earlier.

In the same time period, there was also a drop in the percentage of students who passed the reading and math test. In 2000, just over 85% percent of students passed the test. This dropped to 85% in 2005 and to just under 85% in 2010. There was another slight drop in 2015, but the percentage was still above 80%.

....

....

....

Graphic C

The pie charts show the different careers chosen by women graduating from Aberforth University in 1990 and 2015. In 1990, well over half the graduates chose humanities careers. In 2015, the choices were more evenly distributed among different types of careers.

In 1990, the majority of female graduates at Aberforth chose careers in the humanities. Forty percent chose education and 25% chose the arts. Thirty percent chose science-related careers (medicine and engineering). Meanwhile, just 10% of female graduates chose careers in management.

In 2015, there was a more even distribution of career types chosen. The number of women choosing careers in the humanities dropped, with 25% choosing education and 15% choosing the arts. At the same time, interest in science-related careers had risen to 40%. Interest in management had doubled, with 20% of female graduates choosing that type of career.

....

....

....

Graphic D

The diagram illustrates the appearance of Sanditon Beach before and after the construction of an airport. Originally, it looked like a quiet town with few buildings. After the airport was built, the town looked quite different.

Before the airport was constructed, the town had few buildings. There was just one hotel on the beach. There were also a few houses further down the shore. There was one road, which ran along the beach behind the buildings.

The town looked very different after the construction of the airport. A new road was built between the airport and the beach. Several new hotels were built along the beach. There was a new dock, too. The houses that had been on the beach were moved to a place away from the beach area.

....

....

....

PRACTICE 2

Make an outline and write a report in response to the following task. Be sure to include a conclusion.

You should spend about 20 minutes on this task.

> ***The charts below show how average middle-income families spent their household budget in two different years.***
>
> ***Summarize the information by selecting and reporting the main features, and make comparisons where relevant.***

Write at least 150 words.

Household Budget Allocation—Middle Income

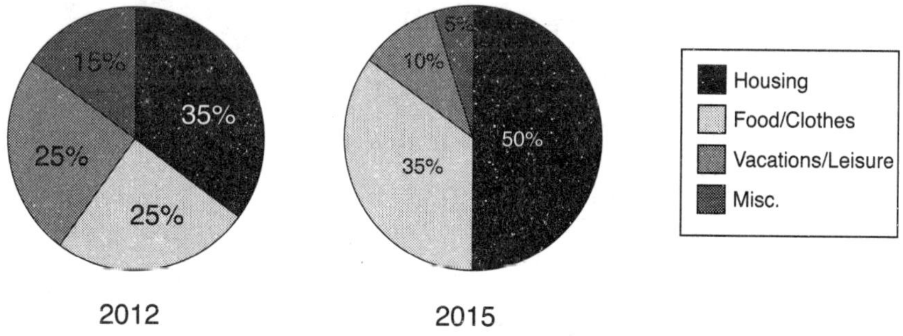

TASK 1—GENERAL TRAINING WRITING

NOTE

If you are studying for the Academic exam, go to Skill 15 (page 158).

Skill 8—Determining the Task

In Writing Task 1 on the General Training exam, you will be asked to write a letter in response to a situation. You will see a description of the situation and three points which you must address in your letter. You may be asked to

- describe a place, a thing, or a problem
- explain a reason
- ask for help or advice
- suggest a solution to a problem
- make a complaint or
- make an invitation

You must do what the task asks you to do.

You recently ordered an item of clothing through a store's website. When you received it, you discovered that it was the wrong size and color.

Write a letter to the store manager. In your letter,

- *describe the item you ordered*
- *explain what was wrong with the item you received*
- *say what you would like the manager to do*

Write at least 150 words.

You do **NOT** need to write any addresses.

Begin your letter as follows:

Dear ....,

PRACTICE

Read the following tasks and determine what each one asks you to do. Choose two actions from the list for each task and write them on the lines. You may use any action more than once.

Describe a place	Describe a problem	Suggest a solution
Describe a thing	Make an invitation	Ask for help

Task A

You are moving to a new city and are looking for a place to live there.
Write a letter to a friend who lives in that city. In your letter,

- *explain why you are moving*
- *describe the kind of place you would like to live in*
- *ask your friend for advice about finding a place to live*

1 ....

Task B

You recently ate at a restaurant. When you got home, you realized you had left your jacket behind.
Write a letter to the restaurant manager. In your letter,

- *explain how and when you lost your jacket*
- *describe your jacket*
- *say what you would like the manager to do to help you find it*

2 ....

Task C

You are bothered by the amount of trash in your local park.
Write a letter to the head of the city parks department. In your letter,

- *describe the problem with the trash*
- *explain why it is a problem*
- *say what you think the city should do*

3 ....

Task D

You are planning a big party to celebrate a special event.
Write a letter to a friend. In your letter,

- *explain why you are giving the party*
- *describe the place where the party will be held*
- *say why you want your friend to come to the party*

4 ....

Skill 9—Determining the Topic

Writing Task 1 begins with a brief description of a situation. This tells you the topic of the letter you will write.

PRACTICE

Choose the correct topic for each of the tasks in Skill 8 (page 141) and write it on the corresponding line below. You will not use all the topics.

Task A ....

Task B ....

Task C ....

Task D ....

Topics
Complaining about trash in the park
Moving to a new city
Buying clothes for a party
Visiting a friend
Planning a party
Recommending a restaurant
Looking for a lost jacket

Skill 10—Brainstorming Ideas

In Writing Task 1, you will be given three points. You must address all three points in your letter. Before you write, take a minute to brainstorm. Think of different ways you could respond to each of the points. Then choose one idea for each point. Remember, there is no one correct way to respond. You just have to address all three of the points in a way that makes sense.

PRACTICE

Look at the tasks in Skill 8 (page 141). Brainstorm a short list of ideas for addressing each point in each of the tasks. The lists have been started for you

1 Task A

A Explain why you are moving.

I want to live closer to my family.

....

....

B Describe the kind of place you would like to live.

near stores and schools

....

....

C Ask your friend for advice about finding a place to live.

suggest some neighborhoods

....

....

2 Task B

A Explain how and when you lost your jacket.

I left it on my chair at dinner last night.

....

....

B Describe your jacket.

dark blue, silk

C Say what you would like the manager to do to help you find it.

look for it in the coat room

3 Task C

A Describe the problem with the trash.

the sidewalks and grass are covered with trash

B Explain why it is a problem.

unsafe, unclean, and unpleasant

C Say what you think the city should do.

have a daily trash pick up

4 **Task D**

A Explain why you are giving the party.

It's my birthday.

....

....

....

B Describe the place where the party will be held.

a country club

....

....

....

C Say why you want your friend to come to the party.

You are a special family friend

....

....

....

Skill 11—Making an Outline

Plan your letter by making an outline. Start with the topic and the ideas you have chosen for each point. Then add supporting details to support your ideas. Write 2–3 supporting details for each idea.

Read this task and outline. Then compare the outline with the letter that follows it.

You recently ordered an item of clothing through a store's website. When you received it, you discovered that it was not the same item that you had ordered.

Write a letter to the store manager. In your letter,

- *describe the item you ordered*
- *explain what was wrong with the item you received*
- *say what you would like the manager to do*

Outline

Introduction
Topic Problem with an order

Body
Point 1 Winter coat

Supporting Detail 1	wool with silk lining
Supporting Detail 2	came in several colors
Supporting Detail 3	dark green/size 12

Point 2 Received wrong coat

Supporting Detail 1	wrong size and color
Supporting Detail 2	bright red/size 8
Supporting Detail 3	can't wear it

Point 3 Want compensation

Supporting Detail 1	another coat
Supporting Detail 2	a large discount

Dear Manager,

I am writing about a problem with an item I recently ordered from your store's website. I ordered a winter coat, but the one I received was the wrong size and color. I think your company should compensate me for the coat as well as for my disappointment.

Last week, I ordered a winter coat from your website. It was a wool coat lined with silk, and it came in several colors. I ordered it in dark green, size 12.

When I received my order, I was disappointed to discover that the size and color were wrong. Your company sent me a bright red coat in size 8. This coat is too small and the color is too bright for me to wear.

I would like your company to compensate me for the coat. Please send me another coat in the right size and color. I think you should also give me a large discount on my next order to make up for my disappointment.

I hope you agree with my solution to this problem. I look forward to receiving my new coat.

Sincerely,
Marcus Wells

PRACTICE 1

Look at the outline for Task A in Skill 8 (page 141) and read the letter that follows it. Complete the missing parts of the outline.

Introduction

Topic Moving to a new city

Body

Point 1 New job

Supporting Detail 1 Looking for a while

Supporting Detail 2 1 ....

Supporting Detail 3 Excited about working at Acme

Point 2 2 ....

Supporting Detail 1 Not large

Supporting Detail 2 Near job

Point 3 Help me find an apartment

Supporting Detail 1 3 ....

Supporting Detail 2 Show me around

Supporting Detail 3 4 ....

Dear Marjorie,

I wanted to let you know that I will be moving to your city soon. I got a new job there. I will need to find a place to live, and I hope you can help me with that.

I got a fantastic job with the Acme Company, located in your city. You know that I have been looking for a new job for a while. I have been unhappy with my job here because the salary is low and the work is boring. So I am excited to be starting at Acme next month.

I need to find an apartment soon. It doesn't have to be large. The important thing is that I want to live close to my job. I would like to be able to walk to work, if possible.

I hope you can help me find an apartment. You know a lot about the city, so maybe you can suggest some nice neighborhoods near Acme. It would be great if you could show me around the area. I will call you soon so we can talk about it.

Thank you in advance for your help. Talk to you soon!

Your friend,
Marty

PRACTICE 2

Complete the outlines for Tasks B, C, and D in Skill 8 (page 141). Use your ideas from the practice for Skill 10 (page 143). Include 2–3 supporting details for each point.

Task B

Introduction

Topic Looking for a lost jacket ....

Body

Point 1 ....

Supporting Detail 1 ....

Supporting Detail 2 ....

Supporting Detail 3 ....

Point 2 ....

Supporting Detail 1 ....

Supporting Detail 2 ....

Supporting Detail 3 ....

Point 3 ....

Supporting Detail 1 ....

Supporting Detail 2 ....

Supporting Detail 3 ....

Task C

Introduction

Topic Complaining about trash in park ....

Body

Point 1 ....

Supporting Detail 1 ....

Supporting Detail 2 ....

Supporting Detail 3 ....

Point 2 ....

Supporting Detail 1 ....

Supporting Detail 2 ....

Supporting Detail 3 ....

Point 3 ....

Supporting Detail 1 ....

Supporting Detail 2 ....

Supporting Detail 3 ....

Task D

Introduction

Topic Planning a party

Body

Point 1 ....

Supporting Detail 1 ....

Supporting Detail 2 ....

Supporting Detail 3 ....

Point 2 ....

Supporting Detail 1 ....

Supporting Detail 2 ....

Supporting Detail 3 ....

Point 3 ....

Supporting Detail 1 ....

Supporting Detail 2 ....

Supporting Detail 3 ....

Skill 12—Writing the Introduction

Begin your letter with a brief introduction. The introduction states the topic and summarizes the ideas you will discuss in the letter.

The first sentence of the introduction is the topic sentence. It tells what the letter is about. Begin the sentence with a phrase such as the following:

I want to let you know . . .
I want to inform you . . .
I thought you should know . . .
I thought you'd be interested . . .
I am writing about . . .
I am writing to request . . .
I would like to ask . . .

Then briefly explain the topic of the letter. Look at these topics and topic sentences from the sample letters in Skill 11 (pages 146–147)

Topic Problem with an order

Topic Sentence I am writing about a problem with an item I recently ordered from your store's website.

Topic Moving to a new city

Topic Sentence I wanted to let you know that I will be moving to your city soon.

PRACTICE 1

Write topic sentences for Tasks B, C, and D in Skill 8 (page 141). The topics are shown below.

Task B

Topic Looking for a lost jacket

Topic Sentence ....

Task C

Topic Complaining about trash in the park

Topic Sentence ....

Task D

Topic Planning a party

Topic Sentence ....

When you write your outline, you choose an idea for addressing each of the three points in the task. In your introduction, you summarize those ideas.

Look at these notes and introduction for the first sample letter in Skill 11 (page 146).

Notes

Topic Problem with an order

Point 1 Winter coat

Point 2 Received wrong coat

Point 3 Want compensation

Introduction

I am writing about a problem with an item I recently ordered from your store's website. I ordered a winter coat, but the one I received was the wrong size and color. I think your company should compensate me for the coat as well as for my disappointment.

- The first sentence of the paragraph is the topic sentence.
- The second sentence, *I ordered a winter coat, but the one I received was the wrong size and color,* corresponds to points 1 and 2 in the notes.
- The third sentence, *I think your company should compensate me for the coat as well as for my disappointment,* corresponds to point 3 in the notes.

Look at these notes and introduction for the second sample letter in Skill 11 (page 147).

Notes

Topic Moving to a new city

Point 1 New job

Point 2 Need to find an apartment

Point 3 Help me find an apartment

Introduction

I wanted to let you know that I will be moving to your city soon. I got a new job there. I will need to find a place to live, and I hope you can help me with that.

- The first sentence of the paragraph is the topic sentence.
- The second sentence, *I got a new job there,* corresponds to point 1 in the notes.
- The third sentence, *I will need to find a place to live, and I hope you can help me with that,* corresponds to points 2 and 3 in the notes.

PRACTICE 2

Look at these notes and introductions for Tasks B, C, and D in Skill 8 (page 141). Choose the correct sentence to complete each introduction.

Task B

Topic Looking for a lost jacket
Point 1 left jacket at restaurant last night
Point 2 light spring jacket
Point 3 let me know if you find it

I am writing about a jacket I lost at your restaurant. ....
It is a light spring jacket, and I would like to ask you to let me know if you find it.

A I always enjoy dinner at your restaurant.
B I left it there last night.
C I paid a lot of money for my jacket.

Task C

Topic Complaining about trash in the park
Point 1 trash cans are overflowing
Point 2 unsafe, unclean, and unpleasant
Point 3 solution: daily trash pick up

I want to inform you about a problem with trash in City Park. The trash cans are always overflowing with trash and this is an unclean, unsafe, and unpleasant situation. ....

A However, I have an idea for a solution to this problem.
B No one wants to use the park anymore.
C There is too much trash in the park.

Task D

Topic Planning a party
Point 1 my 30th birthday
Point 2 country club
Point 3 you are a good friend

I want to let you know about a party I am planning for next month. .... The party will be held at my parent's county club and since you are such a good friend, I hope you will come.

A I really need some help with organizing the party.
B I feel so old.
C I am celebrating because I will turn 30 years old.

Skill 13—Writing the Paragraphs

After you write the introduction, write one paragraph for each of the points in the task. Follow your outline. Write one sentence for your main one idea and one sentence for each supporting detail.

Look at this part of the outline for Task B in Skill 8 (page 141). Then read the paragraph that follows. Notice how it follows the outline.

Outline

Point 1 *left jacket at restaurant last night*
- Supporting Detail 1 *hung on back of chair*
- Supporting Detail 2 *forgot to take it with me*
- Supporting Detail 3 *warm night*

Paragraph

I left my jacket at your restaurant when I was there for dinner last night. I hung it on the back of my chair when I sat down. Then I forgot to take it home with me. The night was warm so I didn't miss it.

The first sentence corresponds to the idea *left jacket at restaurant last night*. The second sentence corresponds to Supporting Detail 1. The third sentence corresponds to Supporting Detail 2, and the fourth sentence corresponds to Supporting Detail 3.

PRACTICE

Use the outlines to write paragraphs for Tasks B and C in Skill 8 (page 141).

Task B

Point 2 light spring jacket
- **Supporting Detail 1** beige with brown trim
- **Supporting Detail 2** cotton
- **Supporting Detail 3** two side pockets

....

....

....

Point 3 let me know if you find it
- **Supporting Detail 1** call me at work
- **Supporting Detail 2** I will pick it up

....

....

....

Task C

Point 1 trash cans are overflowing

Supporting Detail 1 trash spills on grass and sidewalk

Supporting Detail 2 blown around by wind

Point 2 unsafe, unclean, and unpleasant

Supporting Detail 1 attracts rats

Supporting Detail 2 makes sidewalks dirty

Supporting Detail 3 not nice to walk there

Point 3 solution: daily trash pick up

Supporting Detail 1 there is a lot of trash

Supporting Detail 2 things will look nicer

Supporting Detail 3 people will use trash cans

EXTRA PRACTICE

Use the outlines you wrote in Skill 11 Practice 2 (pages 148–149) to write paragraphs for Tasks B, C, and D.

Skill 14—Writing the Conclusion

End your letter with a brief conclusion suggesting an action, conveying a feeling, or thanking the reader, depending on the topic of the letter.

Here are some ways to conclude the letter.

If the letter **asks for advice or help**, you can write

Thank you for your advice.
Thank you in advance for your help.
Let me know if you can help me.

If the letter contains **an invitation**, you can write

I hope you can accept my invitation.
I look forward to seeing you.
Please let me know if you will be able to join us.

If the letter **suggests some solutions** to a problem, you can write

Let me know what you think of my ideas.
I hope we can agree on a solution to these problems.
I hope you are willing to accept my solution.

Then write a signature. If the letter is to a friend, you can sign with *Your friend* or *Best wishes.*

If the letter is to someone you don't know personally, such as a store manager or landlord, sign with *Sincerely*.

PRACTICE 1

Choose the best conclusion for each of the following letters.

Dear Manager,

I am writing about a jacket I lost at your restaurant. I left it there last night. It is a light spring jacket, and I would like to ask you to let me know if you find it.

I left my jacket at your restaurant when I was there for dinner last night. I hung it on the back of my chair when I sat down. Then I forgot to take it home with me. The night was warm so I didn't miss it.

It is a light spring jacket. The color is beige, and it has brown trim on the collar. It is made of cotton. There are two side pockets, and they are probably empty.

Please let me know if you find my jacket. If you do, you can call me at my work number: 555-1212. I will come by the restaurant and pick up the jacket as soon as I hear from you.

1

A Thank you in advance for your help.
B I hope you are willing to accept my solution.
C I look forward to seeing you soon.

Dear Sir or Madam,

I want to inform you about a problem with trash in City Park. The trash cans are always overflowing with trash and this is an unclean, unsafe, and unpleasant situation. However, I have an idea for a solution to this problem.

The trash cans in the park are always overflowing. Trash spills on the grass and sidewalks around the cans. On windy days, it gets blown all around the park, and this makes the problem even worse.

This creates an unsafe, unclean, and unpleasant situation. For one thing, it attracts rats, which carry disease. In addition, things like leftover soda and melted ice cream spill all over the sidewalks, making them very dirty. It is not nice to walk through a park covered with dirty trash.

This is a serious problem, but I think it can be solved by having trash trucks pick up the trash daily. There is a lot of trash in the park, so I think it is enough to justify a daily pick up. If the trash cans are emptied daily, then the park will look nicer. A prettier park will encourage people to use the trash cans instead of throwing their trash on the ground.

2

A Let me know which dates are best for you.
B Let me know what you think of my idea.
C Thank you so much for your help.

Dear Sandy,

I want to let you know about a party I am planning for next month. I am celebrating because I will turn 30 years old. The party will be held at my parent's county club, and since you are such a good friend, I hope you will come.

I am so excited to be celebrating my 30th birthday. I think this is a really important birthday. I really want to have my friends with me to celebrate.

I've decided to hold the party at the Green Valley Country Club. My parents are members, and they suggested it as a good place for a party. I will rent their large party room, which is very nicely furnished. There are also gardens just outside, which we can enjoy if the weather is nice.

I am telling you about this because you are one of my best friends. This party just wouldn't be the same without you. I really hope you can be there to celebrate with me.

3

A Let me know what you think of my idea.
B I hope you can accept my invitation.
C Thank you very much for your advice.

PRACTICE 2

Make an outline and write a complete letter for the following task. Be sure to include a conclusion.

You should spend about 20 minutes on this task.

You live near a university and would like to earn some extra money by renting a room in your apartment to a student. ***Write a letter to the university housing office. In your letter,*** • ***introduce yourself*** • ***explain why your apartment would be a good living place for a student*** • ***describe the room you have for rent***

Write at least 150 words.

You do NOT need to write any addresses.

Begin your letter as follows:

Dear Sir or Madam,

TASK 2: GENERAL TRAINING AND ACADEMIC WRITING

Skill 15—Determining the Task

In Writing Task 2, you will write an essay expressing and supporting an opinion. You will be asked to write about your opinion in one of the following ways:

- agree or disagree
- describe advantages and disadvantages
- discuss two points of view and give your own
- suggest solutions to a problem
- answer two questions

You must do what the task asks you to do.

PRACTICE

Read the following tasks and determine what each one asks you to do. Choose your answers from the list above and write them on the lines.

Task A ....

Some people believe that success means earning a lot of money. Others believe that success is defined by personal happiness.

Discuss both these views and give your own opinion.

Task B ....

Smoking tobacco is becoming increasingly popular among young people, with potentially serious effects on their health.

Explain some reasons for this problem and suggest some possible solutions.

Task C ....

More and more fathers are taking a break from their careers so that they can stay home and take care of their children while their wives work. This is better for the family than having both parents work full time.

To what extent do you agree or disagree with this opinion?

Task D ....

These days, children have easy access to home computers, tablet computers, and smartphones, and many spend a large part of their free time using these devices.

Discuss the advantages and disadvantages of this situation and give your own opinion.

Task E ....

Most schools offer some type of physical education classes to their students.
Why is physical education important? Should physical education classes be required or optional?

Skill 16—Developing a Thesis Statement

A thesis statement states what your essay is about. Begin your planning by writing a thesis statement that presents your ideas and addresses the task. Your thesis statement will help you organize your writing.

Look at these thesis statements for Task A in Skill 15 (page 158).

1 *While there are people whose biggest goal is to become wealthy, there are others who feel that personal happiness is more important and I agree with this point of view.*

2 *Wealth is one way to define success, but I agree more with those people who measure success by their degree of personal happiness.*

3 *I think the most successful people are those who earn a lot of money.*

The task asks the writer to: *Discuss both these views and give your own opinion.*

Statements 1 and 2 both address the task. They mention both the views stated in the task as well as the writer's opinion.

Statement 3 does not address the task. It explains the writer's opinion about success. However, it does not mention *both* of the points of view stated in the task.

PRACTICE

Choose the best thesis statement for Tasks B, C, D, and E in Skill 15 (pages 158–159).

1 **Task B**

A The best way to solve the problem of smoking among youth is to make it illegal for minors.

B Smoking is enjoying widespread popularity among youth for a variety of reasons; however, there are solutions.

C The reasons that young people choose to smoke are not very good ones, and I believe this is a serious problem.

2 **Task C**

A Men who give up their careers in order to care for their children are often very happy.

B Some women earn enough money to support their families, and then their husbands don't have to work.

C Many fathers give up their jobs in order to take care of their homes and families, but I don't agree that this is the best choice they can make.

3 **Task D**

A I think one of the biggest advantages of computers is that they give children access to an infinite amount of information.

B Children who learn to use computers from a very early age will have a lot of advantages in their lives.

C Computers have become an integral part of children's lives, and this situation has both advantages and disadvantages.

4 **Task E**

A Physical education gives children the opportunity to learn different sports and to be physically active, but I think it is up to each family to decide whether or not their child needs to participate in these classes.

B Physical education classes teach children the importance of staying fit as well as giving them a restful break from their academic studies.

C Schools should require students to participate in physical education classes at least two times a week.

Skill 17—Organizing Your Writing

Your thesis statement tells what your essay is about. Now you have to support it with main ideas and details. You should have two or three main ideas to support your thesis and two or three details to support each main idea.

You can use a concept map to organize your ideas. Follow these steps to organize your writing.

1. **READ THE TASK.**

   More and more fathers are taking a break from their careers so that they can stay home and take care of their children while their wives work. This is better for the family than having both parents work full time.

   To what extent do you agree or disagree with this opinion?

2. **DETERMINE THE TASK.** Agree or disagree.

3. **WRITE A THESIS STATEMENT.** Many fathers give up their jobs in order to take care of their homes and families, but I don't agree that this is the best choice they can make.

4. ADD MAIN IDEAS.

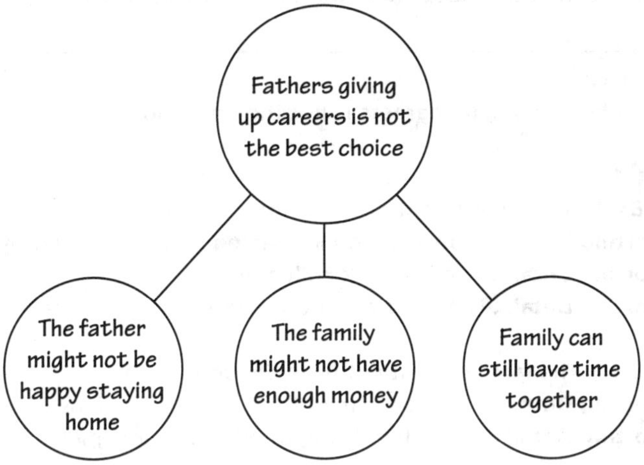

5. ADD SUPPORTING DETAILS

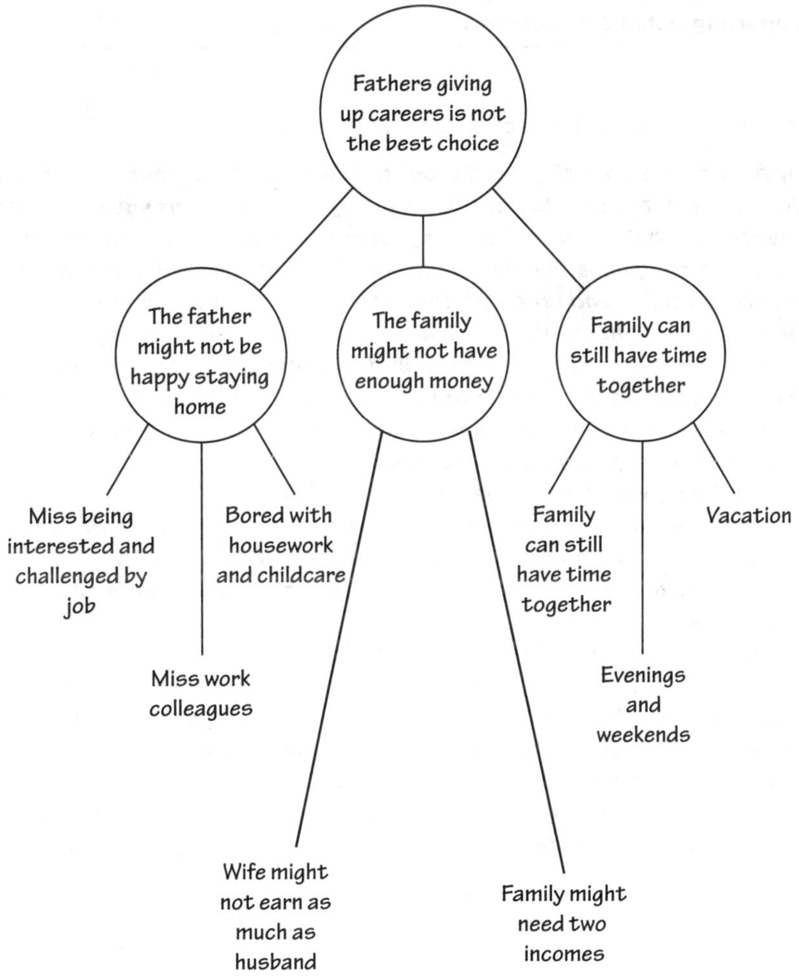

If you prefer, you can use an outline to organize your ideas. An outline contains the same information as a concept map but in a different format.

INTRODUCTION
THESIS Fathers giving up careers is not the best choice

BODY
MAIN IDEA 1 The father might not be happy staying home
- **Supporting Detail 1** miss being interested and challenged by job
- **Supporting Detail 2** miss work colleagues
- **Supporting Detail 3** bored with housework and childcare

MAIN IDEA 2 The family might not have enough money
- **Supporting Detail 1** the wife might not earn as much as husband
- **Supporting Detail 2** the family might need two incomes

MAIN IDEA 3 The family can still have time together
- **Supporting Detail 1** children in school all day
- **Supporting Detail 2** evenings and weekends
- **Supporting Detail 3** vacations

Compare this passage with the concept map and outline.

Many fathers give up their jobs in order to take care of their homes and families, but I don't agree that this is the best choice they can make. This situation might work for some families, but I believe it causes problems for many. A stay-at-home father might end up feeling unhappy, the family could end up not having enough money, and parents can still spend time with their children without staying home all day.

A father who stays home all day could end up feeling very unhappy. If he gave up a job that he enjoyed, then he also gave up doing something that interested and challenged him. In addition, he gave up the opportunity to be with colleagues who shared his professional interests. In exchange for these things, he spends his days doing boring chores such as mopping floors and feeding and dressing his children.

When a father gives up his career, he also gives up his salary. His wife may continue working, but she may not earn as much money as her husband did. In addition, even if the wife earns a good salary, it is still only one salary. When a family goes from two salaries to one, they have to make many changes in their lifestyle that are not always convenient.

Children can still have the benefit of time with their parents even when both parents work. In the first place, children spend most of the day in school, unless they are very young. In addition, parents can spend quality time with their children in the evenings and on weekends. They can also plan family vacations that give them the opportunity to have special experiences together.

A stay-at-home father may seem like a good idea, but families need to consider all sides of the issue, both emotional and financial, before making such a big change in their lifestyle.

PRACTICE 1

This exercise will help you learn the steps to organize your writing. Look at the concept map. Read the essay on page 164. Complete the missing parts of the map.

1. **Read the topic.**

   There should be laws to control the amount and type of violence shown on television programs.

   To what extent do you agree or disagree with this statement?

2. **Determine the task.** Agree or disagree.
3. **Write a thesis statement.** We are free to choose the shows we watch. Laws are not necessary to help us decide what to watch.
4. **Add main ideas.**

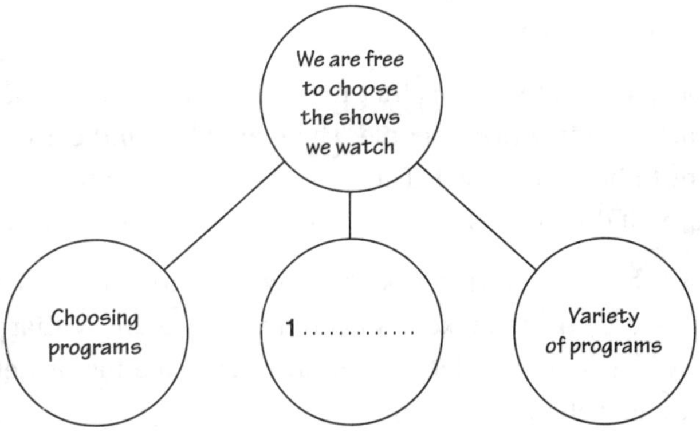

5. **Add supporting details.**

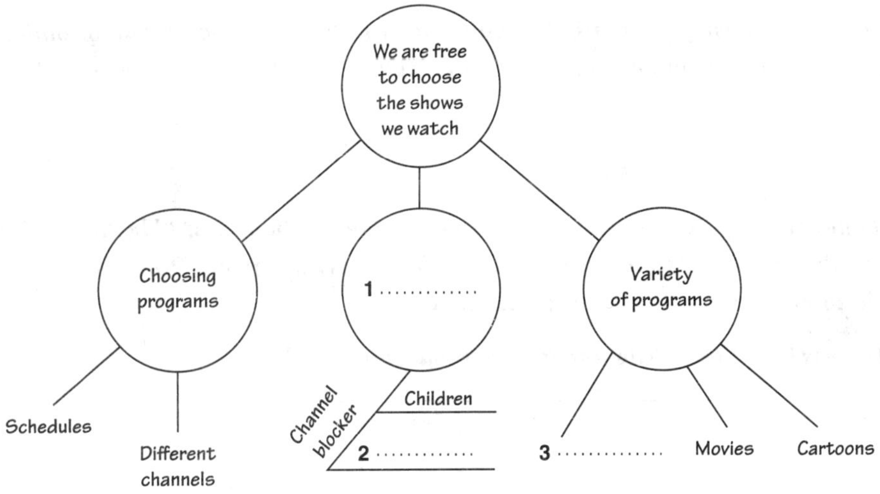

While it is true that there is violence on television, each individual has his or her own idea about how much is too much. Fortunately, we are all free to choose which TV programs we want to watch. Laws are not necessary to help us decide.

It isn't difficult to find out which programs are on TV at any given time. Most newspapers publish a schedule of TV programs every day. Also, anyone who watches TV regularly knows which programs she likes and which she doesn't like. She knows what kinds of programs each different channel tends to have. Because of this, it's easy for everyone to avoid violent programs if they want to.

TIP

You may use *she* for variety (rather than *he*) or you may use *he or she* but be consistent in the essay.

Modern technology has given us a tool for controlling the TV programs we see. Most TVs can be programmed to block certain channels. Thus, parents have a way to protect their children from seeing shows[1] that are too violent. Adults can also use this technology to avoid seeing programs that they don't want to see.

The best thing about TV is that there is a variety of programs. There are news programs for serious people. There are films and cartoons for people who want to be entertained. The variety of TV programs needs to be protected, even if that means allowing some of them to show violence.

We each have our own ideas about what is too violent and what isn't. It would be difficult to make laws about violence on TV that would satisfy everybody. It is better to let each individual make his or her own choice about what to watch.

PRACTICE 2

For each of the following questions, determine the task, create a concept map or outline, then write an essay using the concept map or outline as a guide. Compare your essays with those in the answer key.

1

> ***Some people believe that children's time outside of school should be filled with scheduled activities such as art and music classes and sports. Others feel that children need free time to play and relax.***
>
> ***Discuss both these views and give your own opinion.***

2

> ***In many parts of the world, people are relying more and more on prepared food from grocery stores and restaurants because they are too busy to cook at home. This is a bad idea because home-cooked food is much better for us.***
>
> ***To what extent do you agree or disagree?***

[1]British: programmes

Skill 18—Writing the Introduction

The introduction to your essay guides the reader. It is like a map. It tells the reader how you plan to develop your topic. The topic sentences you develop from the main ideas in your concept map or outline can be summarized in the introduction.

Compare these two introductions:

INTRODUCTION 1

Weak Introduction
In my opinion, physical education is important. It's better for children to have it than not.

Strong Introduction
Physical education is an important part of every child's education. In the first place, children learn better if they spend part of each day getting some physical exercise. Additionally, physical education teaches children important skills such as teamwork. Also, it contributes to their overall physical and mental health.

The first introduction tells us the writer's opinion, but not much about it. Why does the writer feel this way? We need to know the reasons for the opinion so that we can be ready to follow the supporting details in the body of the essay.

The second introduction outlines three specific reasons why the writer thinks physical education is important. We can expect that each paragraph in the body of the essay will explain one of these reasons more thoroughly. We will be able to follow the writer's ideas because we know what to look for as we read. These reasons (or main ideas) provide a focus to the paragraph. They guide the reader.

Thesis	Physical education is important.
Main Idea	It helps children learn better.
Main Idea	It teaches important skills.
Main Idea	It contributes to physical and mental health.

INTRODUCTION 2

Weak Introduction
Art museums are public places and should be funded by the government.

Strong Introduction
I don't agree that art museums should be funded by private instead of public money. It is difficult to raise enough private money to run a museum well. In addition, charging high entrance fees will keep many people away from museums. Most important, art is a valuable part of culture and should receive support from society as a whole through government funding.

With the first introduction, the reader knows what the writer believes, but not why. The second introduction gives detailed reasons to support the writer's opinion, and the reader can expect to read about these reasons in the body of the essay.

Thesis	Art museums should be funded with public money.
Main Idea	It's difficult to raise private money.
Main Idea	High entrance fees keep people away.
Main Idea	Art is a valuable part of culture.

PRACTICE 1

Read the following introductions. Tell the topic of the essay and what the main idea or focus of each paragraph will be.

1 Many modern couples are beginning to recognize that it is better to have a parent at home to take care of the children, rather than relying on a full-time babysitter or preschool. I agree that this is a good idea. First, no one can care for a child as well as his own parents. Parents also have to face the fact that childcare costs are very high. Finally, it is my belief that family life is better when one of the spouses devotes his or her time to maintaining the home and family.

Topic ....

Main Idea ....

Main Idea ....

Main Idea ....

2 These days, people around the world use the Internet to get news and information. There are both advantages and disadvantages to this situation. On the one hand, the Internet has many advantages because it provides instant access to huge amounts of information that might be difficult to get otherwise. On the other hand, the Internet has certain problems, including the fact that much of the information you find there is unreliable.

Topic ....

Main Idea ....

Main Idea ....

3 People complain about the amount of violence on TV these days. While I do not enjoy watching violent TV programs myself, I do not agree that there should be laws regulating violence on TV. In the first place, TV stations should be able to develop the types of programs they want without any legal restrictions. In the second place, we are free to decide which programs we want to watch and can easily choose to avoid any programs we don't like.

Topic ....

Main Idea ....

Main Idea ....

PRACTICE 2

Read these tasks. Determine the task. Write your thesis statement. Make a concept map or outline. Write your topic sentences. (You can have between two and four topic sentences.) Then write the introduction to your essay. Be sure you answer all parts of the task.

1

> ***Some people think that the best way to learn a language is "learning by doing" rather than learning through books and teachers.***
>
> ***To what extent do you agree or disagree with this opinion?***

Task:

....

Thesis Statement:

....

Concept Map or Outline: Use a separate sheet of paper for this if you need more space.

Topic Sentences:

1.1 ....

1.2 ....

1.3 ....

1.4 ....

Introduction:

....

....

....

....

....

....

2

> ***In many parts of the world and throughout history, governments have moved their capitals.***
>
> ***Discuss the advantages and disadvantages of this and say whether you would be in favor of moving your capital?***

Task:

....

Thesis Statement:

....

Concept Map or Outline: Use a separate sheet of paper for this if you need more space.

Topic Sentences:

2.1 ....

2.2 ....

2.3 ....

Introduction:

....

....

....

....

....

Skill 19—Writing the Paragraphs

In Skill 16, you learned to write your thesis statement. The thesis statement is what your essay is about. An essay is made up of paragraphs. Each paragraph has a topic sentence and supporting details.

A topic sentence tells what each paragraph is about. A topic sentence can come at the start of a paragraph, in the middle, or at the end. It can introduce a paragraph or it can summarize a paragraph.

When you made each concept map or outline, you wrote two or three main ideas in words or phrases. Turn those main ideas into a sentence and you have a topic sentence for a paragraph. It is important to write a good topic sentence. It helps the reader follow your line of thinking. It makes your intentions clear. A topic sentence gives your essay clarity.

In your concept maps or outlines, each main idea (topic sentence) is connected to or followed by supporting details. These specific details support your main idea. They help the reader understand your intentions. A topic sentence with supporting details gives your essay clarity.

Look at these examples.

Example 1

A computer is a useful tool for school work. Computers make it very easy to keep notes and write up school projects. Files can be stored and organized on a computer, and the computer's search tool makes finding files later very easy. In addition, the Internet makes research on any subject possible from the comfort of one's own home. Children can do all this work independently, without asking their parents to take them to the library or buy expensive reference books for them.

Topic Sentence	A computer is a useful tool for school work.
Supporting Details	Computers make it very easy to keep notes and write up school projects.
	Files can be stored and organized on a computer, and the computer's search tool makes finding files later very easy.
	In addition, the Internet makes research on any subject possible from the comfort of one's own home.

Example 2

It isn't difficult to find out which programs are on TV at any given time. Most newspapers publish a schedule of TV programs every day. Also, anyone who watches TV regularly knows which programs she likes and which she doesn't like. She knows what kinds of programs each different channel tends to have. It's easy for everyone to avoid violent programs if they want to.

Topic Sentence	It isn't difficult to find out which programs are on TV at any given time.
Supporting Details	Most newspapers publish a schedule of TV programs every day.
	Also, anyone who watches TV regularly knows which programs she likes and which she doesn't like.
	She knows what kinds of programs each different channel tends to have.

When you write your paragraphs, make sure the details support the topic sentence. Look at these examples.

Topic Sentence: Physical education can actually improve children's academic performance.

Supporting Details: It is very hard for growing children to sit at a desk reading and writing all day. They need a break at some time in the day to rest their minds. In addition, it is hard for them to concentrate on their studies when they don't get the physical exercise they need. After being active for an hour or so in a physical education class, children return to their classrooms with renewed energy for their academic work.

The details above support the topic sentence. They explain how physical education can improve academic performance by allowing children to rest their minds, improve their concentration, and renew their energy.

Look at these details for the same topic sentence.

Supporting Details: Many children enjoy physical education classes. They learn how to play different kinds of sports. Some children become very good at certain sports and that improves their self-esteem. Other children just like the opportunity to be physically active during the school day.

These details do not support the topic sentence. They explain why children like physical education, but they say nothing about improving academic performance.

PRACTICE 1

Read the following paragraphs. Write the topic sentence and the supporting details.

1 Modern technology has given us a tool for controlling the TV programs we see. Most TVs can be programmed to block certain channels. Parents use this technology to protect their children from seeing shows that are too violent. Adults can also use this technology to avoid seeing programs that they don't want to see.

Topic Sentence: **1.1** ....

Supporting Details: **1.2** ....

1.3 ....

1.4 ....

2 The best thing about TV is that there is a variety of programs. There are news programs for serious people. There are films and cartoons for people who want to be entertained. The variety of TV programs needs to be protected, even if that means allowing some of them to show violence.

Topic Sentence: **2.1** ....

Supporting Details: **2.2** ....

2.3 ....

2.4 ....

3 Physical education classes teach children important skills that they need in life. They teach children how to work together on a team. They teach children how to set a goal and work to achieve it. They teach children about the importance of looking after their health.

Topic Sentence: **3.1** ....

Supporting Details: **3.2** ....

3.3 ....

3.4 ....

PRACTICE 2

Choose the best supporting details for each topic sentence.

1 **Topic Sentence:** One way to discourage teen smoking is to limit the places where smoking is allowed.

A Teens should not be allowed to smoke at all. It is a bad habit with serious health consequences. High schools need to spend time educating students about the dangers of smoking. That would do a lot to discourage this habit.

B If smoking is banned in school buildings, students will have to go outside to smoke. If it is also banned on school grounds, students will not be able to smoke at all during the school day. Further, if smoking is banned in malls and other places where teens spend time, then it will be very difficult for them to find a place to smoke.

C When I was a teen, a lot of my friends smoked. However, many of them quit later on. Quitting is difficult but not impossible. People who want to quit should not be discouraged. There are many programs that have been successful in helping even long-time smokers stop this bad habit.

2 Topic Sentence: Home-cooked meals are almost always better than prepared meals from a store or restaurant.

A When you cook at home, you can use the best ingredients. You can make sure that all your food is fresh. You can easily avoid high amounts of salt, fat, and sugar. And, of course, you wouldn't add preservatives or other harmful chemicals. Prepared food, on the other hand, usually contains ingredients that are harmful to your health.

B Cooking at home takes time, but some people don't mind that. They enjoy planning meals and preparing the food themselves. They like to serve their families delicious, freshly prepared meals even if that takes more effort than buying something already prepared at a store.

C Many people prefer home-cooked meals, but they don't have time to make them. There are also many people who just don't like cooking. For these people, prepared meals from a store or restaurant are a real convenience. Prepared meals may not taste as good as home-cooked food, but sometimes people just don't have another choice.

3 Topic Sentence: Some families chose to have one parent stay home with the children because childcare costs are so high.

A The most expensive type of childcare is a nanny. When parents hire a nanny to stay home with their children all day, they are responsible for her entire salary. That is a big financial responsibility for one family to take on. That is why many parents chose to send their children to a daycare center.

B Many parents send their children to daycare centers. They need to choose carefully, because not all centers are the same. Parents should make sure that the teachers are trained and experienced and that the building is safe and clean. A better daycare center might cost more than others, but it is worth the extra expense.

C It costs a lot to pay a babysitter or nanny to care for children while the parents are at work. Daycare centers cost less, but they are still expensive. The family may lose the salary of the parent who quits work, but that is partly made up by the savings in childcare costs.

Skill 20—Writing the Conclusion

A good essay has a good conclusion. The conclusion briefly supports your thesis and reminds the reader of your intentions. It returns to the ideas you presented in your introduction and uses them to conclude with a summary, generalization, prediction, question, or recommendation. Look at the following examples, noticing the relationship between the introduction and conclusion:

Restatement

In your conclusion, you can restate your thesis or topic sentence.

Introduction

There are several ingredients to success. Earning a lot of money may be one of them, but money alone doesn't equal success. In order to be considered successful, a person should also develop useful skills and he or she should achieve a level of personal happiness, as well. These are things that money doesn't buy.

Conclusion

Success involves much more than money. Learning skills and having a happy life are equally important parts of a successful life.

Generalization

You can use all the information you provided and make a generalization about it.

Introduction

Many modern couples are beginning to recognize that it is better to have a parent at home to take care of the children rather than relying on a full-time babysitter or preschool. I agree that this is a good idea. First, no one can care for a child as well as his own parents. Parents also have to face the fact that childcare costs are very high. Finally, it is my belief that family life is better when one of the spouses devotes his or her time to maintaining the home and family.

Conclusion

All in all, I would have to say that life is better for families when one parent stays home with the children. Both the parents and the children benefit.

Prediction

You can summarize the information in your essay and use it to suggest what might happen next.

> **Introduction**
>
> These days, people around the world use the Internet to get news and information. There are both advantages and disadvantages to this situation. On the one hand, the Internet has many advantages because it provides instant access to huge amounts of information that might be difficult to get otherwise. On the other hand, the Internet has certain problems, including the fact that much of the information you find there is unreliable.
>
> **Conclusion**
>
> In the future we will rely on the Internet for quick access to all of our news and information. This will bring us many benefits as long as we remain aware of the potential pitfalls.

Recommendation

You can suggest that your readers do something, based on the information you presented in your essay.

> **Introduction**
>
> Providing children with art and music classes as part of their school day means taking time and money away from other areas of their education. Some see this as a disadvantage. On the other hand, art and music classes broaden children's minds and experience and provide support to those who have talents in these areas. These are advantages that far outweigh any disadvantages, in my opinion.
>
> **Conclusion**
>
> While art and music classes cost time and money, they provide children with important experiences. Every school should devote at least some resources to this part of their curriculum.

Question

You can conclude your essay with a question. The question is not really asking for an answer. The answer is contained in the question.

> **Introduction**
>
> Physical education is an important part of every child's education. In the first place, children learn better if they spend part of each day getting some physical exercise. Additionally, physical education teaches children important skills such as teamwork. Also, it contributes to their overall physical and mental health.
>
> **Conclusion**
>
> Physical education is an essential part of any educational program. What would happen to our children's energy level if they didn't get a chance to be active every day? How would they learn to be part of a team if they didn't play sports? How would they stay healthy? Physical education meets all of these needs.

PRACTICE 1

Read each of the following conclusions and decide whether it is a restatement, generalization, prediction, recommendation, or question.

1 We each have our own ideas about what is too violent and what isn't. It would be difficult to make laws about violence on TV that would satisfy everybody. It is better to let each individual make his or her own choice about what to watch.

....

2 Currently, there is a trend toward eating locally grown, organic food, whether at home or in restaurants. If this trend continues, today's children will grow up to be healthier than adults are now and chronic disease may become a thing of the past.

....

3 If art museums are funded by public money, then everyone will have access to them. What would our world be like without any art? What would bring beauty into our lives and give us a greater understanding of who we are? Art museums are a valuable part of our society.

....

4 On the whole, people prefer watching family-oriented TV shows in the evenings. Dramas, mysteries, and police shows are better left for late at night when the children are asleep.

....

5 More and more, computers are becoming a part of daily life and people need to learn how to use them to their advantage. If children don't have enough experience with computers when they are young, they won't learn the skills they will need later in life.

....

PRACTICE 2

Write an essay in response to the following task. Be sure to include a conclusion.

Job satisfaction is more important than earning a high salary.
To what extent do you agree or disagree with this opinion?

COHERENCE AND COHESION

Coherence and cohesion refer to how well you organize your writing and connect your ideas. When you follow the steps described in the Task Achievement section, your writing will be well organized. Your writing will be cohesive when you use transition words, repeating and rephrasing, and pronouns to link your ideas.

TIP

Using transition words will increase your score!

Skill 21—Transition Words

You can use transition words and phrases in your writing to connect your ideas. They help your reader follow your ideas from one sentence to the next or from one paragraph to the next. Transition words can show time, degree, comparison and contrast, and cause and effect. They can also be used to add more information or to refer to previously mentioned subjects.

Read the examples to see how the transition words from the boxes are used to link ideas in the paragraphs.

Time	Degree	Cause and Effect
before	most important	so
after	first	thus
since	primarily	for this reason
next	principally	as a result
then	above all	because
soon	in the first place	since
at the same time	less important	due to
while	second	therefore
meanwhile	in the second place	consequently
simultaneously	to a lesser degree	so that
once		
today		
now		
first, second, third		
in (month, year, century)		
on (day)		
previous		
prior to		
since		
while		

Example 1

After the new highway was built, the village of Palm Grove began to grow. People still worked in the fishing industry. *At the same time*, a few new hotels were built. *Then*, more and more tourists started arriving to spend their vacation time at the beach. *Soon*, the village was crowded with visitors from other places.

Example 2

Family life is better when one of the parents stays home with the children. *Above all*, the children feel secure when they know one of their parents is always available to them. *To a lesser degree*, a parent at home helps the household run more smoothly. But *primarily*, having one parent whose job is to take care of the home and family helps everyone feel safer and happier.

Example 3

I was honored when you offered to lend me your watch *because* I know how much you value it. *Consequently*, I was very careful with it while I had it on. Unfortunately, the buckle seems to have been broken. *As a result*, the watch fell off my wrist while I was at the party.

Comparison	Contrast
similar to	different from
similarly	nevertheless
just as	although/even though
like	unlike
likewise	yet
in the same way	but
at the same time as	in contrast to
also	however
alike	while
just as	difference
	on the other hand

Example 4

Many people believe that art and music classes are just as important as academic classes. *Although* there is validity to this point of view, I disagree with it. Art and music are important, *but* academics are even more important. Academic classes give children knowledge that they will need in their future professions. *Likewise*, academics teach children important cognitive skills. Art and music classes, *on the other hand*, do not help children develop professional skills unless they are planning to become artists or musicians.

Explanation	Adding More Information
in other words	in addition
such as	moreover
to clarify	besides
like	furthermore
for instance	also
for example	as well as
that is	what's more
to illustrate	additionally
namely	likewise

Example 5

The first step in the process is tapping the trees, *that is*, making holes in them so the sap can come out. There are different ways to collect the sap, *for example*, using old-fashioned buckets or using modern plastic tubing. Using buckets is more time consuming, so most people nowadays use plastic tubing. *In other words*, people prefer using the more efficient method.

Example 6

Home-cooked meals are generally more nutritious than store-bought or restaurant meals. They *also* tend to be tastier. *Furthermore*, preparing meals at home contributes to the improvement of family relationships.

PRACTICE 1

Put these sentences into chronological order.

1 .... In the future, the town hopes to build an art museum next to the old factory.

2 .... Once the factory opened, river traffic increased, bringing raw materials to the factories and taking munitions downstream to the major river port at the mouth of the river.

3 .... In the early 1900s, Winston on Hudson was just a small town on the Hudson River.

4 .... Soon, Winston on Hudson became a tourist destination.

5 .... Today, the town's munitions factory has been turned into artist studios.

6 .... Nothing happened in the town until after the start of the First World War when a munitions factory opened.

7 .... Within ten years, cargo boats were followed by passenger boats bringing weekend sightseers.

PRACTICE 2

Complete the blanks with words that show comparison or contrast. Use the words in the boxes below. Some words may be used more than once. Don't forget to add capitals where necessary.

in contrast to	while	difference	however

A

Landline phones and cell phones are devices used for communicating with people in other places. The biggest **1** .... between a landline phone and a mobile phone is that a landline phone stays in one place **2** .... a mobile phone can go everywhere. A landline phone always stays in your home or office. A mobile[1] phone, **3** ...., can go wherever you go. There is a disadvantage to this. You always know where your landline phone is—on your desk, on the kitchen wall, by the bed, or wherever you keep it. **4** .... a landline phone, a mobile phone is easily misplaced.[2]

both	alike	similar to	just as

B

A restaurant is a place where you order food and it is brought to your table. A cafeteria is **5** .... a restaurant, except that in a cafeteria you serve yourself. There are several ways in which a restaurant and a cafeteria are **6** .... In **7** .... places you can eat a good meal without cooking it yourself. In a restaurant you select your meal from a menu. In a cafeteria you can also choose your meal from among several different possibilities, **8** .... in a restaurant. Finally, in **9** .... a restaurant and a cafeteria, you have to pay for what you eat.

[1]AMERICAN: cell or mobile; [2]BRITISH: mis-placed

PRACTICE 3

Read the following paragraphs. Choose the appropriate transition word or expression to complete each sentence. Add capital letters where necessary.

likewise	furthermore	as a result	in other words

By the year 2000, the population distribution had shifted a great deal. Many more people had moved to urban and suburban areas and **1** ...., the rural population was much smaller. **2** ...., the suburban population had grown since 1950. The urban population had **3** .... increased. **4** ...., there were now fewer people living in the countryside and more living in the cities and suburbs.

TIP

Try using a range of vocabulary instead of repeating the same words and phrases.

then	unlike	such as	What's more

I know you will have a good time at the party. **5** .... most parties we go to, at this one I plan to have live music. **6** ...., the band I have hired plays your favorite kind of music. My sister-in-law is planning to prepare some really good dishes **7** .... seafood soup and roast beef. Come early so that you can enjoy the food, and **8** .... you can dance all night!

in addition	but	above all	in other words

Physical education classes help children develop in numerous ways. Academics strengthen children's minds, **9** .... physical education strengthens their bodies. **10** ...., it contributes to their good health. **11** ...., physical education classes help children learn about winning and losing. This is an important life skill. **12** ...., in physical education classes, children have the opportunity to learn about teamwork. This might be one of life's most important skills.

Skill 22—Repeating and Rephrasing

Repeating words and rephrasing ideas are two ways to provide coherence to an essay.

Repeating

Repeating words and phrases adds rhythm to a paragraph and links similar ideas. In the paragraph below, notice how the phrase *It gives* is used several times.

Example

Physical education teaches children much more than the rules to a few sports. *It gives* children the opportunity to learn some important life skills. *It gives* them experience with teamwork. *It gives* them the chance to know how it feels to win and to lose. These are things that have importance in all areas in life, not just on a sports field.

TIP

Repeating and rephrasing will increase your score!

Rephrasing

When you rephrase an idea, you say it again in a different way. This gives the reader a second chance to understand your idea and helps connect one idea to the next. Using synonyms is one way to rephrase.

Example

One problem that *older people face is isolation*. Many of them are widowed, and their children are no longer living with them. Serious physical and mental health problems can arise when *people feel lonely*.

Notice how the two italicized phrases in the paragraph above essentially mean the same thing. Now look at another example, noticing the meaning of the two italicized phrases.

Example

Family members can provide much-needed *companionship*. Even if an elderly parent does not live with his or her grown children, they can all *spend important time together*.

PRACTICE

Choose which phrase or sentence best completes the paragraph and makes it cohesive. Use the italicized phrases to guide you in your choices.

The best thing about TV is that there is a variety of programs. *There are news programs for serious people. There are films and cartoons for people who want to be entertained.* **1** .... The variety of TV programs needs to be protected even if it means allowing some of them to show violence.

A People also enjoy watching baseball and soccer games.
B There are baseball and soccer games for people who enjoy sports.
C We can see baseball and soccer games, too.

I am responsible about my finances. Your records will show that I have always paid my credit card bills *on time.* My **2** .... makes me a desirable customer, and I am sure you wouldn't want to lose my business.

A punctuality
B financial know-how
C honesty

By the year 2050, the suburban population will have *increased* to almost 60% of the population of the entire region. This **3** .... will put heavy *demands* on public services. The regional government will have to start making adjustments now in order to meet the **4** .... of the future.

A area
B number
C growth

A people
B needs
C services

Art brings beauty into our lives. It enriches us in many ways. *It nourishes our minds. It nourishes our spirits.* **5** .... Without access to art, our lives would be greatly impoverished.

A It is good for our bodies, too.
B It also contributes to our physical health.
C You could even say it nourishes our bodies.

Skill 23—Pronouns

Pronouns are used to replace or refer to nouns. Pronouns allow you to link ideas without repeating the same word over and over.

Pronouns				
Subject	he this	she that	it these	they those
Object	his this	her/hers that	it these	them those
Possessive	his	her/hers	its	their/theirs

PRACTICE

Choose the correct pronoun to complete each sentence. Add capital letters where necessary.

her	they	them	their	this	it

I feel that your evening TV programs are not very interesting, and I am sure that few people watch **1** .... For example, last night I watched a drama program on your channel. **2** .... was one of the most boring programs I have ever seen. The leading actress was not very inspiring, and **3** .... voice made me want to fall asleep. If you continue to show programs like **4** .... , you will probably lose most of your viewers. **5** .... will choose to watch channels with more interesting programs instead. Then your advertisers may well decide that **6** .... advertising money would be better spent on channels that have a larger audience.

Skill 24—Stating Your Opinion

For Writing Task 2 on both the Academic and General Training tests, you will probably be asked for your opinion. The introduction to your essay should tell the reader what your opinion is. There is no right or wrong opinion. Whatever your opinion is, the reader will look to see how you express it. You can use certain phrases, verbs, adjectives, and adverbs to express your opinion.

TIP

Prepositional phrases and most adverbs are followed by a comma at the beginning of a sentence.

Phrases	Verbs	Adjectives	Adverbs
In my opinion	agree	certain	definitely
From my point of view	believe	positive	doubtless
In my view	think	convinced	certainly
To my way of thinking	understand	sure	probably
To my mind	suppose	persuaded	conceivably
It seems to me that	guess	confident	maybe
To me	hope		perhaps
It is my opinion that	imagine		possibly
			seemingly

Examples

It seems to me that fathers can take care of children just as well as mothers can.
I suppose that some children could benefit from art and music education.
I am certain that over-reliance on cars has led to many problems in our society.
Parents should definitely put limits on their children's television viewing.
People are probably less polite now than they used to be.

PRACTICE

Give your opinion about these topics. Use the words and phrases suggested.

1 Violence on television (is/is not) very harmful for children.
It is my opinion that ....

2 Parents (should/should not) monitor their children's computer use.
In my view, ...

3 Home-cooked food (is/is not) better for the health of the family.
I understand that ....

4 Dependence on private automobiles (causes/doesn't cause) many problems in our daily lives.
I think that ....

5 Learning about art (is/is not) a good way to spend part of the school day.
I am sure that ....

6 Children (learn/don't learn) better when they have friendly relationships with their teachers.
I am convinced that ....

7 People (spend/do not spend) too much money on stylish clothes.
Perhaps ....

8 Taking a train (is/is not) as convenient as driving a car.
Certainly, ...

Skill 25—Generalizing and Qualifying

Certain phrases can be used to make a general statement about how you feel about something. Others can be used to qualify your opinion, showing that what you state is not completely true.

Generalizing	Qualifying
all in all as a rule basically by and large for the most part generally in general on the whole	in a way more or less so to speak for all intents and purposes to some extent up to a point

Examples

All in all, children learn better when they have a more formal relationship with their teacher.

Generally, people pay too much attention to fashion.

Up to a point, parents should let their children choose their own television programs.

For all intents and purposes, the Internet is a valid educational tool.

PRACTICE

Give your opinion about these topics. Use the phrases suggested to make a general statement or qualify your opinion.

1 Children (learn/don't always learn) better when they spend part of each day getting physical exercise.

As a rule, ...

2 Job security (is/is not) a thing of the past.

On the whole, ...

3 Family ties (are/are not) weaker now than they were in the past.

For the most part, ...

4 Art and music classes (equal/do not equal) academic classes in importance.

To some extent, ...

5 A train (is/is not) as convenient a form of transportation as a private car.

In a way, ...

Skill 26—Synonyms

Using a variety of vocabulary in your essay rather than repeating the same words over and over helps to hold the reader's attention. You can do this by using synonyms—words that are similar in meaning. Synonyms help to keep your writing interesting, and they provide coherence by connecting ideas that are closely related.

Read the paragraph below. Look for synonyms of *choose* and *choice*.

Synonyms of the verb *choose*	Synonyms of the noun *choice*
select	selection
opt	option
pick	alternative

Example

There is a wide variety of television programs to *choose* from. I don't believe that television programming should be regulated, but that individuals should be allowed to *select* for themselves what they want to watch. However, in the case of children, the issue is a bit different. In my opinion, parents should be the ones to *pick* which programs their children see. Children may be attracted to programs that aren't appropriate for them. It is the parents' responsibility to guide their children toward *alternatives* that are more suitable to their age. Television channels have many *options* that actually offer positive contributions to a child's development.

TIP

Using synonyms can increase your score!

PRACTICE

In each of the following groups of sentences, the underlined words are used twice. Choose a synonym from the list in place of the second mention of each underlined word.

curious	alone	easy	supervision
regulate	engaged	ration	plan

Children like to feel that they can do things independently. They gain self-confidence when they know they can complete their homework assignments independently, without asking their parents for help every step of the way.

1 independently synonym: ....

Parents should pay attention to what their children do on the computer, and they should control which websites their children visit. Children have a safer experience on the Internet when their parents control their computer use.

2 control synonym: ....

Children are naturally interested in many things. The Internet provides interested children with a wide range of information to satisfy their hungry minds.

3 interested synonym: ....

It is not necessary for parents to limit the amount of time their children spend on the computer. When parents limit computer time too much, children don't have the chance to learn to manage their own time.

4 limit synonym: ....

A computer can be a good way to keep children gainfully occupied for long periods of time. There are many worthwhile things children can do on the computer. They can spend hours occupied in educational activities.

5 occupied synonym: ....

Children need a certain amount of guidance from their parents. With parental guidance, children can learn to choose computer activities that educate as well as entertain.

6 guidance synonym: ....

A computer is a useful tool for school work. Computers make it very convenient to keep notes and write up school projects. Reference books on computer CDs make it convenient for children to research their school projects.

7 convenient synonym: ....

Skill 27—Plural Nouns

English nouns are either count or noncount. Count nouns are things that can be counted. You can put numbers in front of them. They have both singular and plural forms. Noncount nouns don't have plural forms.

I read one book last week. (singular count noun)
I read 25 books last month. (plural count noun)
I drank some milk. (noncount noun)

When a count noun refers to one thing, use the singular form. When it refers to more than one thing, use the plural form. Follow the rules for correct spelling of plural nouns.

Forming the Plural

Add *-s*

The plural of most nouns is formed by adding *-s* to the end of the noun.

chair/chairs
idea/ideas
profession/professions

Nouns ending in *-y*

For nouns ending in a consonant + *y*, there is a spelling change. Change the *y* to *ie* and then add *s*.

country/countries
supply/supplies
library/libraries

For nouns that end in a vowel + *y*, there is no spelling change. Simply add *-s* to form the plural.

toy/toys
delay/delays
valley/valleys

Nouns ending in *-s, -ch, -sh, -x*

For nouns ending in these ways, the plural is formed by adding an extra *-es*.

cross/crosses
arch/arches
crash/crashes
box/boxes

Nouns ending in a consonant + *o*

Many nouns that end in this way form the plural by adding *-es*

echo/echoes
hero/heroes
potato/potatoes

Nouns ending in *-f* or *-fe*

For most nouns ending in this way, the plural is formed by changing the *-f* or *-fe* to *-ve* and adding *-s*.

life/lives
knife/knives
loaf/loaves

Be careful. Nouns that end in *-ff* form the plural simply by adding *-s*.

cuff/cuffs
sniff/sniffs

Spelling Change

For some nouns, the plural is formed by changing the spelling of the word. There are no patterns for these irregular plural forms. You just have to learn them. Here are some of the most common ones:

child/children	person/people	mouse/mice
woman/women	foot/feet	goose/geese
man/men	tooth/teeth	ox/oxen

These words don't change. The singular and plural forms are the same.

sheep	fish (*fishes* is also used in some cases)
deer	series
moose	species

Nationalities

Like other count nouns, words that refer to nationalities have singular and plural forms. In most cases, the plural is formed by adding *-s* to the end of the word. However, the plural form of nationality words that end with *-ese* is the same as the singular form.

Canadian – Canadians	Greek – Greeks
German – Germans	Japanese – Japanese

PRACTICE

Write the plural form of each word.

1 shelf ....
2 zero ....
3 museum ....
4 tourist ....
5 person ....
6 dictionary ....
7 bus ....
8 knife ....
9 passenger ....
10 tomato ....
11 tax ....
12 play ....
13 thief ....
14 Chinese ....
15 Mexican ....

Skill 28—Commonly Misspelled Words

It is important to use correct spelling in the writing section of the IELTS. Study this list of commonly misspelled words, and be sure you know how to spell them correctly.

Commonly Misspelled Words	
acceptable	library
accommodate	occasionally
argument	people
believe	permission
budget	possession
calendar	roommate
common	uncomfortable
equipment	unfortunately
grateful	until
immediately	

PRACTICE

Correct the spelling mistakes in the following letter.

Dear Housing Office,

I am writing about my accomodations in the university dormitory. The room I have been assigned is not acceptible. I would like to be assigned a new room inmediately.

The main problem with my room is my roomate, Sarah. Unfortunatly, we don't get along well. We have nothing in comon, and we have arguements all the time. In addition, she doesn't respect my possesions and borrows things without asking permmission. I don't mind lending my things occassionally, but Sarah uses them all the time. I especially don't like her using my expensive electronic equiptment. Finally, Sarah is very noisy. She likes to stay up untill late at night talking with her friends. There are always poeple visiting in our room, and that means I can't study there. I spend a lot of time in the libary.

I would be very greateful if you would give me a new room assignment because my current situation is very unconfortable. According to the university calender, the last date to change rooms is next week, as long as there are available rooms. I beleive there is an empty room on the floor above my current room. I would be happy to live in it if it costs the same as the room I am in now. Because of my buget, I can't afford a more expensive room.

Thank you for your help. I hope you can give me a new room soon.

Sincerely,
Sylvia Struthers

GRAMMATICAL RANGE AND ACCURACY

Good writing has well-written sentences. It has variety in sentence structure and sentence length that makes the writing interesting and the ideas clear. Naturally, correct grammatical structures are used.

Skill 29—Parallel Structures

Parallel structures are structures that follow the same pattern. When you write with parallel structures, your writing has a rhythm that is easy to follow. It helps make your ideas easier to understand.

Subjects

Parallel

Play and study are two ways children can use a computer.

Playing and studying are two ways children can use a computer.

In both of the above examples the subjects are parallel. In the first example, they are two simple nouns. In the second example, they are two gerunds.

Not parallel

Playing and study are two things children can use a computer for.

In this example, one word is a gerund and the other is not. The words are not parallel, and the sentence is awkward.

Verbs

Parallel

I reached out my hand, grabbed a glass, and noticed that my watch was gone.

The verbs are parallel because they are all in the same tense.

Not parallel

The village has grown and becoming more prosperous.

The two verbs connected by *and* should be the same tense, *is growing and becoming*. It is not necessary to repeat an auxiliary verb (such as the verb *be* in a continuous tense).

Adjectives

Parallel

Maple syrup is a popular and tasty treat.

This example is parallel because it uses two similar words, that is, two adjectives, to describe maple syrup.

Not parallel

Maple syrup is a popular treat and also tastes good.

This example is grammatically correct, but it is not parallel. It uses two words that are not similar—an adjective, *popular*, and a verb, *tastes*—to describe maple syrup.

Voice

Parallel voice	The house <u>was painted</u> and the roof <u>was repaired</u>.
	This example is parallel because it uses passive voice in both clauses.
Not parallel	The house <u>was painted</u> and we <u>repaired</u> the roof.
	This example is grammatically correct, but it is not parallel. It uses passive voice in the first clause and active voice in the second clause.

PRACTICE

Look at the two underlined words and phrases in each sentence below. Change the second one to make it parallel with the first.

1 Many children like <u>looking</u> for information on the Internet and <u>to play</u> online games.

2 People watch TV for <u>entertainment</u> and <u>to be informed</u>.

3 I <u>will be</u> in your neighborhood tomorrow and <u>am going to bring</u> you the check then.

4 A life that is all <u>work</u> and no <u>playing</u> is a very dull life indeed.

5 The TV programs I am recommending <u>are very amusing</u> and <u>also educate</u>.

6 Now, the citizens of Palm Grove <u>can earn</u> a good living from tourism, but they <u>are no longer able to enjoy</u> the simple, peaceful life they once had.

7 <u>Home-cooked meals are</u> more nutritious, and <u>I like the taste</u> better, too.

8 The hotel district <u>was expanded</u>, and <u>people removed the fishing docks</u>.

Skill 30—Sentence Types

Using variety in your sentences keeps your writing lively and interesting. It also shows the range of your writing ability. One way you can vary your sentences is by using a variety of sentence types. There are four types of sentences: simple, compound, complex, and compound-complex.

Simple Sentence

A simple sentence has one subject and one verb.

Television offers a variety of programs.
subject verb

Compound Sentence

A compound sentence has two or more simple sentences linked by the conjunctions *and*, *or*, and *but*.

Some people are not bothered by violent TV programs, but others avoid them.
simple sentence 1 simple sentence 2

Complex Sentence

A complex sentence is made up of a simple sentence (an independent clause) and one or more subordinate clauses.

If we don't like a particular TV program, we can easily change the channel.
subordinate clause simple sentence

Compound-Complex Sentence

A compound-complex sentence has two or more simple sentences and one or more subordinate clauses.

While many people avoid watching violent TV programs, others don't mind them
subordinate clause simple sentence 1

and they watch them frequently.
simple sentence 2

PRACTICE 1

Combine the sentences using the conjunction provided. Don't change the order of the sentences.

Compound Sentence

1 I like home-cooked food.
I also enjoy eating at restaurants.
(and)

....

2 I think art appreciation is important.
I don't believe valuable school time should be spent on art classes.
(but)

....

Complex Sentence

3 Children should learn to use computers.
They will need computer skills later in life.
(because)

....

4 I don't think there should be laws against violence on TV.
I don't enjoy watching violent programs.
(even though)

....

5 Some people are willing to spend a lot of money on stylish clothes.
Others prefer to dress less expensively.
(while)

....

6 Children don't have opportunities to visit art museums.
They will never learn to appreciate art.
(if)

....

Compound-Complex Sentence

7 I own a TV.
I rarely watch it.
I don't have time.
(but; because)

....

PRACTICE 2

Choose a conjunction from the list for each number and use it to combine the sentences. Don't change the order of the sentences.

1 Everyone arrives.
We will serve dinner.
(as soon as, while, because)

....

2 I don't have a lot of money.
I generally buy expensive clothes.
(because, although, and)

....

3 I know a lot about music.
I took music lessons as a child.
(but, if, because)

....

4 I own a car.
My husband has a motorcycle.
(while, before, and)

....

5 I enjoy watching television.
I don't watch it every day.
(but, and, as soon as)

....

6 Some of the restaurants in my neighborhood serve delicious healthful meals.
Others serve only tasteless junk.
(because, while, if)

....

7 Riding the bus is convenient.
You live close to a bus stop.
(although, if, but)

....

Skill 31—Punctuation

As well as spelling correctly, you will also be expected to use correct punctuation. You must use capital letters in the correct places and use punctuation marks such as periods, commas, and question marks correctly. It is also important to indent each paragraph.

Indent: This is done at the beginning of each paragraph.

Capital letters: These are used at the beginning of each sentence and for proper nouns.

Period, question mark, exclamation point: One of these is always used at the end of a sentence.

Commas are used in the middle of sentences in certain situations:

- In a list of three or more things

  Home-cooked food is nutritious, tasty, and inexpensive.
  I reached out my hand, grabbed a glass, and noticed that the watch was gone.

- To separate transition words from the rest of the sentence

  Additionally, physical education teaches children important skills such as teamwork.
  Children, however, should not be exposed to these violent television programs.

- Between two independent clauses

  I watch television every evening, and I know what kinds of programs are being shown.
  Art and music classes are important, but academic classes are even more important.

- To separate a non-restrictive clause

  Parents, who are responsible for the well being of their children, should carefully monitor their children's computer time.
  Maple syrup, which is made from the sap of the sugar maple tree, is an expensive but tasty treat.

- After a subordinate clause at the beginning of a sentence

  If I had been more careful, I wouldn't have lost the watch.
  Although one can find information about almost anything on the Internet, the information isn't always reliable.

PRACTICE

Read the following paragraphs and check for punctuation errors. Then copy each paragraph on a separate piece of paper, correcting the punctuation as follows: indent, add capital letters and commas, and change periods to question marks where necessary.

1 many families enjoy watching television together during the early evening hours. therefore programs shown during this time should be suitable for children. do you really think it is appropriate for children to see programs that involve shooting fistfights and other forms of violence. most parents do not and they change the channel when such programs are shown.

2 it is important for children to know how to use computers but it is also important for them to spend time on other activities. when children spend a lot of time at the computer they spend less time playing outside. they spend less time interacting with other people. they miss out on activities that are important for their physical and emotional development.

3 i have a lot of fun activities planned for your visit. john who is my next-door neighbor has promised to take us white-water rafting. have you ever done that before. it's a lot of fun and you will surely enjoy it. however there are plenty of other things we can do if you don't want to go rafting. we can ride bikes go to the movies or just relax at home.

4 tourism which brings a lot of money to the town of palm grove is an important part of the local economy. tourist dollars pay the salaries of hotel employees restaurant servers and airport workers. all of these people earn a lot more money from tourism than they ever did from fishing. in addition they now have steady jobs with a steady income.

TIP

Don't forget to indent at the beginning of each paragraph.

REVISION

Skill 32—Using a Revision Checklist

When you respond to the writing tasks, you need to leave a few minutes at the end of each task to revise your writing. You need to check that you responded to all parts of the task. You need to make sure that your ideas are well organized and that you used correct language and punctuation. Here is a checklist that you can use to guide your revision.

REVISION CHECKLIST

Responding to the Task
- ☐ Did I complete the task?
- ☐ Did I write enough words?

Coherence and Cohesion
- ☐ Did I write a thesis statement/topic sentence?
- ☐ Did I include a main idea in each paragraph?
- ☐ Did I write supporting details in each paragraph?
- ☐ Did I write a conclusion?
- ☐ Did I use transition words?

Lexical Resource
- ☐ Did I use a variety of vocabulary?
- ☐ Did I use correct spelling?

Grammatical Range and Accuracy
- ☐ Did I use a variety of sentence structures?
- ☐ Did I use correct grammar?
- ☐ Did I use correct punctuation?

Look at the following model writing task and response. Notice how the response can be checked against the revision checklist.

Academic Task 2

You should spend about 40 minutes on this task.

> ***There should be laws to control the amount and type of violence shown on television programs.***
>
> ***To what extent do you agree or disagree with this statement?***

Give reasons for your answer and include any relevant examples from your own knowledge or experience.

Write at least 250 words.

While it is true that there is violence on television, each individual has his or her own idea about how much is too much. Fortunately, we are all free to choose which TV programs we want to watch. Laws are not necessary to help us decide.

It isn't difficult to find out which programs are on TV at any given time. Most newspapers publish a schedule of TV programs every day. Also, anyone who watches TV regularly knows which programs she likes and which she doesn't like. She knows what kinds of programs each different channel tends to have. Because of this, it's easy for everyone to avoid violent programs if they want to.

Modern technology has given us a tool for controlling the TV programs we see. Most TVs can be programmed to block certain channels. Thus, parents have a way to protect their children from seeing shows that are too violent. Adults can also use this technology to avoid seeing programs that they don't want to see.

The best thing about TV is that there is a variety of programs. There are news programs for serious people. There are movies and cartoons for people who want to be entertained. The variety of TV programs needs to be protected, even if that means allowing some of them to show violence.

We each have our own ideas about what is too violent and what isn't. It would be difficult to make laws about violence on TV that would satisfy everybody. It is better to let each individual make his or her own choice about what to watch.

RESPONDING TO THE TASK

REVISION CHECKLIST

Responding to the Task

- ☑ Did I complete the task?
- ☑ Did I write enough words?

Did I Complete the Task?

The task asks the writer to agree or disagree with the statement. The last sentence of the first paragraph, *Laws are not necessary to help us decide*, states the writer's disagreement. The task also asks for reasons and examples. The second, third, and fourth paragraphs each explain a reason for the writer's opinion, and they include examples to explain and support the reasons.

Did I Write Enough Words?

This passage is 262 words, 12 more than the minimum required.

COHERENCE AND COHESION

REVISION CHECKLIST

Coherence and Cohesion

- ☑ Did I write a thesis statement/topic sentence?
- ☑ Did I include a main idea in each paragraph?
- ☑ Did I write supporting details in each paragraph?
- ☑ Did I write a conclusion?
- ☑ Did I use transition words?

Did I Write a Thesis Statement?

The last two sentences of the first paragraph, *Fortunately, we are all free to choose which TV programs we want to watch. Laws are not necessary to help us decide,* are the thesis statement. They state the writer's opinion, which is explained and supported in the body of the essay.

Did I Include a Main Idea in Each Paragraph?

The first sentence of each paragraph in the body of the essay (paragraphs 2, 3, and 4) is the topic sentence.

Did I Write Supporting Details in Each Paragraph?

Each topic sentence is followed by details that support it.

Did I Write a Conclusion?

The last paragraph is the conclusion. In this paragraph the reader is reminded of the thesis, that laws about violence on television are not necessary, and there is a recommendation: *It is better to let each individual make his or her own choice about what to watch.*

Did I Use Transition Words?

This passage uses appropriate transition words, for example:

Paragraph 2: *also*—adds information
because of—shows cause and effect

Paragraph 3: *thus*—shows cause and effect
also—adds information

LEXICAL RESOURCE

REVISION CHECKLIST

Lexical Resource

☑ Did I use a variety of vocabulary?

☑ Did I use correct spelling?

Did I Use a Variety of Vocabulary?

This passage does not have too many repetitions of words. It uses a variety of ways to state similar ideas, for example, *block*, *protect*, and *avoid* are used to convey the idea of *not watching* certain programs.

Did I Use Correct Spelling?

This passage has no spelling errors.

GRAMMATICAL RANGE AND ACCURACY

REVISION CHECKLIST

Grammatical Range and Accuracy

☑ Did I use a variety of sentence structures?

☑ Did I use correct grammar?

☑ Did I use correct punctuation?

Did I Use a Variety of Sentence Structures?

This passage uses a variety of sentence structures, for example:

Complex:	*While it is true that there is violence on television, each individual has his or her own idea about how much is too much.* *There are movies and cartoons for people who want to be entertained.*
Simple:	*Most newspapers publish a schedule of TV programs every day.* *There are news programs for serious people.*
Compound-complex:	*We each have our own ideas about what is too violent and what isn't.*

Did I Use Correct Grammar?

This passage has no grammatical errors.

Did I Use Correct Punctuation?

This passage has no punctuation errors.

PRACTICE 1

Complete the essays by answering the questions that follow each one.

General Training Task 1

You should spend about 20 minutes on this task.

> *You live near a university and would like to earn some extra money by renting a room in your apartment to a student.*
> *Write a letter to the university housing office. In your letter*
> - *introduce yourself*
> - *explain why your apartment would be a good living place for a student*
> - *describe the room you have for rent*

Write at least 150 words.

You do NOT need to write any addresses.

Begin your letter as follows:
Dear Sir or Madam,

Dear Sir or Madam,

1 .... I am a resident of the university neighborhood. My apartment is very close to campus, and I have a room that would be very nice for a student.

2 .... I work as a paralegal at a law firm downtown.

I have an extra room in my apartment that I would like to rent to a university student.

My apartment is the perfect place for a student. It is just five blocks from the university. A student living here would not have to own a car or even pay bus fare to get to classes. Also, the rent I am charging is not high. **3** ...., it is very quiet here, so it is a good place to study undisturbed.

The room is very cozy. It isn't a large room. However, it is very comfortable. **4** .... Kitchen privileges are included in the rent.

I am ready to show the room to anyone who is interested. Please have them call me at 123-4567. Thank you for your help.

Sincerely,
Rosa Davies

1 Choose the best topic sentence for the letter.

A I need money so that is why I am renting a room in my apartment.
B I think you know that a lot of students are looking for housing at this time of year.
C I want to let you know about a housing opportunity I have available for students.

2 Choose the best main idea for this paragraph.

A My name is Rosa Davies and I have lived in this neighborhood for ten years.
B I am a responsible, honest, and hardworking person.
C I live in a small building that is very safe and quiet.

3 Choose the best transition word for this sentence.

A Nevertheless
B However
C Furthermore

4 Choose the missing supporting detail.

A The bus stop is right across the street.
B It has a bed, desk with a chair, and a dresser.
C I have two cats and a dog, so I am looking for a tenant who likes animals.

Academic Training Task 1

You should spend about 20 minutes on this task.

> *The charts below show how average middle-income families spent their household budget in two different years.*
>
> *Summarize the information by selecting and reporting the main features, and make comparisons where relevant.*

Write at least 150 words.

Household Budget Allocation—Middle Income

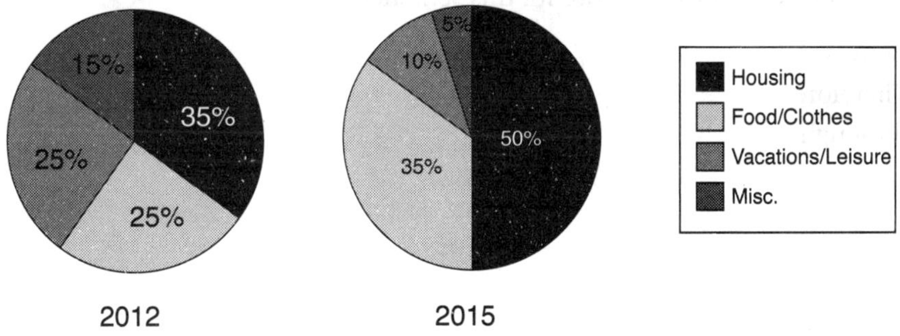

5 .... In 2010, spending was more or less evenly distributed among the different categories. In 2015, half of the budget went to housing alone.

In 2010, middle-income families spread their budget more or less evenly among the four categories shown. The largest amount—35%—went to housing. Spending on food/clothes and vacations/leisure was not far behind, with 25% of the budget going to each of these things. **6** ....

7 .... Fully 50% of spending was on housing. Spending on food/clothes had also risen, to 35%. **8** ...., there was much less left for the other two categories. Spending on vacations/leisure dropped to 10%, and spending on miscellaneous expenses fell to just 5% of the budget.

Overall, housing was the largest part of the budget in both years, but it was significantly higher in 2015, and this affected the rest of the budget.

5 Choose the best topic sentence for the report.

A The pie charts show how two different families spent money.
B The pie charts show how middle-income families spent their household budget in 2010 and 2015.
C The pie charts show the cost of living for a middle-income family in 2010 and 2015.

6 Choose the missing supporting detail.

A Finally, the smallest portion of the budget—15%—went to miscellaneous expenses.
B Additionally, families generally allocate a certain percentage of the budget for miscellaneous expenses.
C Miscellaneous expenses commonly take up the smallest portion of the budget.

7 Choose the best main idea for this paragraph.

A In 2015, middle-income families had a smaller budget for household expenses.
B In 2015, the budget included the same four categories.
C In 2015, housing took up a much larger portion of the budget.

8 Choose the best transition word for this sentence.

A Because
B Therefore
C Although

Academic/General Training Task 2

In many parts of the world, people are relying more and more on prepared food from grocery stores or restaurants because they are too busy to cook at home. This is a bad idea because home-cooked food is much better for us.

To what extent do you agree or disagree?

9 .... In the first place, it is more nutritious than store-bought or restaurant food. It is also less expensive. In addition, preparing and eating home-cooked food helps strengthen family bonds.

Home-cooked food has higher nutritional value than prepared food. A lot of prepared food is high in sugar and fat. It is also not very fresh, so it has lost nutritional value while sitting on the shelf waiting to be bought. **10** .... , it often contains highly refined products, such as white flour, which are not as good for our health as whole grain products are.

11 .... A restaurant meal, even at a fast-food restaurant, is more expensive than a meal at home. Additionally, you have to tip the server and pay for transportation to and from the restaurant. Buying a pre-packaged meal at a grocery store is not any better. It costs a lot more than buying the ingredients and preparing the meal yourself.

Family ties grow stronger when family members cook and eat meals together. When family members prepare a meal together, they spend time together. They have the chance to share ideas and discuss problems. **12** .... They have fun as a family. Their relationships are stronger.

Home-cooked food is good for our health, our wallets, and our family relationships. There is no reason to eat prepared food on a regular basis.

9 Choose the best thesis statement.

A Home-cooked food is better for us than prepared food in several ways.
B Home-cooked food takes time to prepare, but it tastes very good.
C Home-cooked food requires following several steps.

10 Choose the best transition word for this sentence.

A However
B In addition
C For instance

11 Choose the best main idea for this paragraph.

A Eating at a restaurant is not as simple as it looks.
B Many people enjoy eating at restaurants.
C It costs a lot of money to buy prepared food.

12 Choose the missing supporting detail.

A They prepare healthy meals.
B They learn to communicate with each other.
C They may have a large or small family.

PRACTICE 2

Read the following essay and use the revision checklist below to identify what is missing or incorrect. Then rewrite the essay, adding the missing parts and correcting the errors.

REVISION CHECKLIST

Responding to the Task
- ☐ Did I complete the task?
- ☐ Did I write enough words?

Coherence and Cohesion
- ☐ Did I write a thesis statement/topic sentence?
- ☐ Did I include a main idea in each paragraph?
- ☐ Did I write supporting details in each paragraph?
- ☐ Did I write a conclusion?
- ☐ Did I use transition words?

Lexical Resource
- ☐ Did I use a variety of vocabulary?
- ☐ Did I use correct spelling?

Grammatical Range and Accuracy
- ☐ Did I use a variety of sentence structures?
- ☐ Did I use correct grammar?
- ☐ Did I use correct punctuation?

Academic/General Training Task 3

A successful person is one who has earned a lot of money.

To what extent do you agree or disagree?

To a large extent. Having money can be one part of success. Having good relationships is another very important part of success. So is feeling fulfilled.

Everybody needs money, but the amount of money necessary depend on each person's goals. For example, one person may want a lot of material things, like fancy cars and big houses. For this person, a lot of money is important.

Everybody needs to have good relationships. Even a multi-millionaire is not successful if he or she does not have close connections with other people. If a woman always fights with her husband, if a man's children refuse to speak to him, when adult children might never see their parents, they cannot be considered successful people.

It is important to develop skills and talents and pursue interests. It is important to spend time doing things that are enjoyable or meaningful. A person who is unhappy at work, in addition, cannot be considered successful no matter how big his salary is. A person who spends evenings and weekends just sitting in front of the TV cannot be considered successful, either.

Money and the material things it can by may be one part of success, but non-material things like relationships and self-fulfillment are just as important.

Missing items

Paragraph 1: ....

Paragraph 2: ....

Paragraph 3: ....

Paragraph 4: ....

Paragraph 5: ....

Grammar and vocabulary errors

Paragraph 1: ....

Paragraph 2: ....

Paragraph 3: ....

Paragraph 4: ....

Paragraph 5: ....

Writing Samples

Sample responses to the IELTS writing tasks with scores can be found on *www.ielts.org*. Click Test Takers, then How do I prepare, then Sample questions online, then Writing, then Sample script.

ANSWER EXPLANATIONS

Skill 1—Determining the Task (page 122)

PRACTICE (PAGE 122)

1. B
2. D
3. A
4. C

Skill 2—Determining the Topic (page 125)

PRACTICE (PAGE 125)

1. C
2. A
3. B
4. A

Skill 3—Making Comparisons (page 126)

PRACTICE (PAGE 127)

1.	Comparison 2	The average time spent eating in three types of restaurants
2.	Comparison 1	Spending per pupil in 2000–2015
	Comparison 2	Percentage of students passing a reading and math test in 2000–2015
3.	Comparison 1	Percentage of female graduates choosing different professions in 1990
	Comparison 2	Percentage of female graduates choosing different professions in 2015
4.	Comparison 1	Sanditon before airport was built
	Comparison 2	Sanditon after airport was built

Skill 4—Making an Outline (page 128)

PRACTICE 1 (PAGE 129)

1. Average spending at a cafeteria
2. Average time eating at a fast-food restaurant
3. Average time eating at a sit-down restaurant

PRACTICE 2 (PAGE 130)

Sample answers. Wording may vary.

Graphic B

Comparison 1 *Spending per pupil in 2000–2015*

- Supporting Detail 1 *spending in 2000*
- Supporting Detail 2 *spending drop in 2005, 2010, 2015*
- Supporting Detail 3 *difference in spending, 2000 and 2015*

Comparison 2 *Percentage of students passing a reading and math test in 2000–2015*

Supporting Detail 1 *percentage passing in 2000*
Supporting Detail 2 *percentage drop in 2005 and 2010*
Supporting Detail 3 *percentage drop in 2015*

Graphic C

Comparison 1 *Percentage of female graduates choosing different professions in 1990*

Supporting Detail 1 *education and the arts*
Supporting Detail 2 *science-related careers*
Supporting Detail 3 *management*

Comparison 2 *Percentage of female graduates choosing different professions in 2015*

Supporting Detail 1 *education and the arts*
Supporting Detail 2 *science-related careers*
Supporting Detail 3 *management*

Graphic D

Comparison 1 *Sanditon Beach before airport was built*

Supporting Detail 1 *one hotel*
Supporting Detail 2 *houses*
Supporting Detail 3 *one road*

Comparison 2 *Sanditon Beach after the airport was built*

Supporting Detail 1 *new road*
Supporting Detail 2 *new hotels and dock*
Supporting Detail 3 *houses moved*

Skill 5—Writing the Introduction (page 132)

PRACTICE (PAGE 133)

Graphic B C
Graphic C A
Graphic D C

Skill 6—Writing the Paragraphs (page 134)

PRACTICE 1 (PAGE 135)

1. rose/increased
2. rise/increase
3. rise/increase
4. sharp/significant

PRACTICE 2 (PAGE 135)

Sample answers. Wording may vary.

Graphic C

Comparison 1

In 1990, the majority of female graduates at Aberforth chose careers in the humanities. Forty percent chose education, and 25% chose the arts. Thirty percent chose science-related careers (medicine and engineering). Meanwhile, just 10% of female graduates chose careers in management.

Comparison 2

In 2015, there was a more even distribution of career types chosen. The number of women choosing careers in the humanities dropped, with 25% choosing education and 15% choosing the arts. At the same time, interest in science-related careers had risen to 40%. Interest in management had doubled, with 20% of female graduates choosing that type of career.

Graphic D

Comparison 1

Before the airport was constructed, the town had few buildings. There was just one hotel on the beach. There were also a few houses further down the shore. There was one road, which ran along the beach behind the buildings.

Comparison 2

The town looked very different after the construction of the airport. A new road was built between the airport and the beach. Several new hotels were built along the beach. There was a new dock, too. The houses that had been on the beach were moved to a place away from the beach area.

Skill 7—Writing the Conclusion (page 137)

PRACTICE 1 (PAGE 138)

Sample answers. Answers will vary.

Graphic B

Overall, in the time period shown, both per pupil spending and the percentage of passing grades dropped. However, the drop in passing grades was very small and may be insignificant.

Graphic C

On the whole, female graduates in 2015 chose more science and business careers than they had in 1990.

Graphic D

All in all, the airport changed the town from a quiet to a busy place. It looked like it had become a good spot for tourists.

PRACTICE 2 (PAGE 139)

Answers will vary.

Skill 8—Determining the Task (page 140)

PRACTICE (PAGE 141)

1. Describe a place, ask for help
2. Describe a thing, ask for help
3. Describe a problem, suggest a solution
4. Describe a place, make an invitation

Skill 9—Determining the Topic (page 142)

PRACTICE (PAGE 142)

Task A	Moving to a new city
Task B	Looking for a lost jacket
Task C	Complaining about trash in the park
Task D	Planning a party

Skill 10—Brainstorming Ideas (page 143)

PRACTICE (PAGE 143)

Sample answers. Answers will vary.

1. A. I got a new job.
   My husband got a new job.
   There are more job opportunities there.
   B. a quiet neighborhood
   near my job
   near downtown
   C. give names of real estate agents
   suggest places to find real estate ads
   show me around the city

2. A. I put it in the coat room last week at lunchtime.
   I may have dropped it on the floor while I was here for breakfast yesterday.
   It was warm last night so I forgot to put it on when I left.
   B. wool blazer with my initials on the front pocket
   red with black trim
   green plaid
   C. look for it in the dining room
   let me know if you see it
   ask your staff to keep an eye out for it

3. A. There is trash all over the park.
   The trash cans are never emptied.
   B. No one wants to go to the park.
   There is no place for the children to play.
   It attracts crime.
   C. fine people for throwing trash on the ground
   put more trash cans in the park
   have more police officers patrol the park

4. A. my daughter's graduation
   my parents' wedding anniversary
   my wife's job promotion
   B. the party room in my apartment building
   a hotel
   a friend's mansion
   C. You've known my parents for a long time.
   You are my best friend.
   You are like a member of the family.

Skill 11—Making an Outline (page 146)

PRACTICE (PAGE 147)

1. unhappy at old job
2. need to find an apartment
3. suggest neighborhoods
4. I will call you.

PRACTICE 2 (PAGE 148)

Sample answers. Answers will vary.

Task B

Point 1 *left jacket at restaurant last night*

Supporting Detail 1	*hung on back of chair*
Supporting Detail 2	*forgot to take it with me*
Supporting Detail 3	*warm night*

Point 2 *light spring jacket*

Supporting Detail 1	*beige with brown trim*
Supporting Detail 2	*cotton*
Supporting Detail 3	*two side pockets*

Point 3 *let me know if you find it*

Supporting Detail 1	*call me at work*
Supporting Detail 2	*I will pick it up*

Task C

Point 1 *trash cans are overflowing*

Supporting Detail 1	*trash spills on grass and sidewalk*
Supporting Detail 2	*blown around by wind*

Point 2 *unsafe, unclean, and unpleasant*

Supporting Detail 1	*attracts rats*
Supporting Detail 2	*makes sidewalks dirty*
Supporting Detail 3	*not nice to walk there*

Point 3 *solution: daily trash pick up*

Supporting Detail 1	*there is a lot of trash*
Supporting Detail 2	*things will look nicer*
Supporting Detail 3	*people will use trash cans*

Task D

Point 1 *my 30th birthday*

Supporting Detail 1	*an important birthday*
Supporting Detail 2	*want to celebrate with friends*

Point 2 *country club*

Supporting Detail 1	*my parents are members*
Supporting Detail 2	*large room with nice furniture*
Supporting Detail 3	*nice gardens*

Point 3 *you are a good friend*

Supporting Detail 1	*party wouldn't be the same without you*
Supporting Detail 2	*I hope you will come*

Skill 12—Writing the Introduction (page 150)

PRACTICE (PAGE 150)

Sample answers. Answers will vary.

Task B	I am writing about a jacket that I lost at your restaurant.
Task C	I want to inform you about a problem with trash in City Park.
Task D	I want to let you know about a party I am planning for next month.

PRACTICE 2 (PAGE 152)

Task B	B
Task C	A
Task D	C

Skill 13—Writing the Paragraphs (page 153)

PRACTICE (PAGE 153)

Sample answers. Wording may vary.

Task B

Point 2

It is a light spring jacket. The color is beige, and it has brown trim on the collar. It is made of cotton. There are two side pockets, and they are probably empty.

Point 3

Please let me know if you find my jacket. If you do, you can call me at my work number: 555-1212. I will come by the restaurant and pick up the jacket as soon as I hear from you.

Task C

Point 1

The trash cans in the park are always overflowing. Trash spills on the grass and sidewalks around the cans. On windy days, it gets blown all around the park, and this makes the problem even worse.

Point 2

This creates an unsafe, unclean, and unpleasant situation. For one thing, it attracts rats, which carry disease. In addition, things like leftover soda and melted ice cream spill all over the sidewalks, making them very dirty. It is not nice to walk through a park, covered with dirty trash.

Point 3

This is a serious problem, but I think it can be solved by having trash trucks pick up the trash daily. There is a lot of trash in the park, so I think it is enough to justify a daily pick up. If the trash cans are emptied daily, then the park will look nicer. A prettier park will encourage people to use the trash cans instead of throwing their trash on the ground.

Skill 14—Writing the Conclusion (page 155)

PRACTICE (PAGE 155)

1. A
2. B
3. B

PRACTICE 2 (PAGE 157)

Answers will vary.

Skill 15—Determining the Task (page 158)

PRACTICE (PAGE 158)

A. discuss two points of view and give your own
B. suggest solutions to a problem
C. agree or disagree
D. describe advantages and disadvantages
E. answer two questions

Skill 16—Developing a Thesis Statement (page 159)

PRACTICE (PAGE 159)

1. B
2. C
3. C
4. A

Skill 17—Organizing Your Writing (page 160)

PRACTICE 1 (PAGE 163)

4. **Add main ideas.** The top circle shows the idea from paragraph 1, the introduction. The bottom three circles contain the ideas in the body paragraphs. The second body paragraph mentions "Modern technology."
   1. Technology

5. **Add supporting details.** These lines show the supporting details for each paragraph. Each line matches one of the body paragraphs. There are three body paragraphs in this essay. The answer "for adults" is expressed in the line, "Adults can also use this technology to avoid seeing programs that they don't want to see." The answer "news" is found in the statement: "There are news programs for serious people."
   1. Technology
   2. Channel blocker for children (for adults)
   3. News

PRACTICE 2 (PAGE 164)

Sample answers. Answers will vary.

1. **Task:** Discuss two views

INTRODUCTION
THESIS The best way is to do a little bit of both.

BODY
MAIN IDEA 1 Parents want children to use time productively.
Supporting Detail 1 expose children to a variety of experiences
Supporting Detail 2 children discover things they enjoy
Supporting Detail 3 parents too busy

MAIN IDEA 2 Other families value freedom.
Supporting Detail 1 children develop creativity
Supporting Detail 2 children learn independence and responsibility
Supporting Detail 3 children need time to relax

MAIN IDEA 3 Children need structured and unstructured time.

Supporting Detail 1	chance to discover interests and talents
Supporting Detail 2	chance to be independent
Supporting Detail 3	chance to relax

Many parents feel it is important to schedule their children's free time with different types of organized activities. Other parents want their children to be able to use their free time as they please. In my opinion, the best way is to do a little bit of both.

Many parents want to make sure their children use all their time productively, so they sign them up for sports teams and enroll them in art, music, and language classes. They may do this for any of several reasons. Some may want to expose their children to a variety of experiences so they can discover what they enjoy doing. Others may want their children to have the chance to develop a range of skills at an early age. And others may simply need to have a place to send their children because they are busy with work or other obligations.

In other families, parents place more value on freedom. They believe that unstructured time allows children the chance to develop their creativity. It can also help children learn a sense of independence and responsibility. Some parents understand, too, that after a long day at school, children need some time to just relax.

I believe that children need both structured and unstructured time. I think participation in classes and sports teams gives children a chance to discover and develop their interests and talents. But I also think that children need some time to be independent and choose their own activities. And of course, they need some rest time, just like adults do.

Special opportunities to learn things outside of school can be very good for children, but free time is just as important. The best way is to create a balance between scheduled and unscheduled time.

2. **Task:** Agree or disagree

INTRODUCTION

THESIS Don't agree that it is better to eat home-cooked food

BODY

MAIN IDEA 1 Not all prepared food is bad for you.

Supporting Detail 1	some is unhealthful
Supporting Detail 2	healthful meals in restaurants and grocery stores
Supporting Detail 3	anybody can choose healthful food

MAIN IDEA 2 Prepared food helps people eat healthfully.

Supporting Detail 1	people are too busy too cook
Supporting Detail 2	skip meals or eat snacks
Supporting Detail 3	prepared food means eating good meals

These days people eat a lot of prepared food instead of cooking at home. Some people think this is a bad idea because it isn't healthful, but I do not agree with this point of view. There are a lot of healthful food choices available, and they make it easier for busy people to eat instead of skipping meals.

Not all prepared food is bad for you. Some of it, of course, is high in sugar, fat, and salt. That is the kind of food you will get if you make certain choices, such as eating at fast-food restaurants. But there are plenty of other options. Many restaurants serve fresh, healthfully prepared meals. Fresh and organic food is also available in grocery stores. Anybody who wants to eat delicious, nutritious meals can do so, even people who buy prepared meals instead of eating at home.

Prepared food can actually help people to eat more healthfully. Some people are just too busy to cook. These people could choose to skip meals, or they could choose to fill up on snacks such as potato chips and cookies. But if they buy prepared food from a grocery store or restaurant, then they are actually eating a complete meal. This much better than eating snacks or, worse, nothing.

Whether you cook your meals yourself or buy them already prepared, you have both healthful and unhealthful choices. The type of food you choose to eat is more important than whether or not you cook it yourself.

Skill 18—Writing the Introduction (page 165)

PRACTICE 1 (PAGE 166)

1. Topic — Parents stay at home to take care of children
   Main Idea — Parents are the best caretakers
   Main Idea — High cost of child care
   Main Idea — Better family life

2. Topic — Advantages and disadvantages of the Internet
   Main Idea — Advantages of the Internet
   Main Idea — Disadvantages of the Internet

3. Topic — Disagree with laws about violence on TV
   Main Idea — TV stations should not have legal restrictions on programs.
   Main Idea — We are free to choose what we want to watch.

PRACTICE 2 (PAGE 167)

1.

Task: Agree or disagree.

Thesis Statement: "Learning by doing" is a better way to learn a language.

Concept Map:

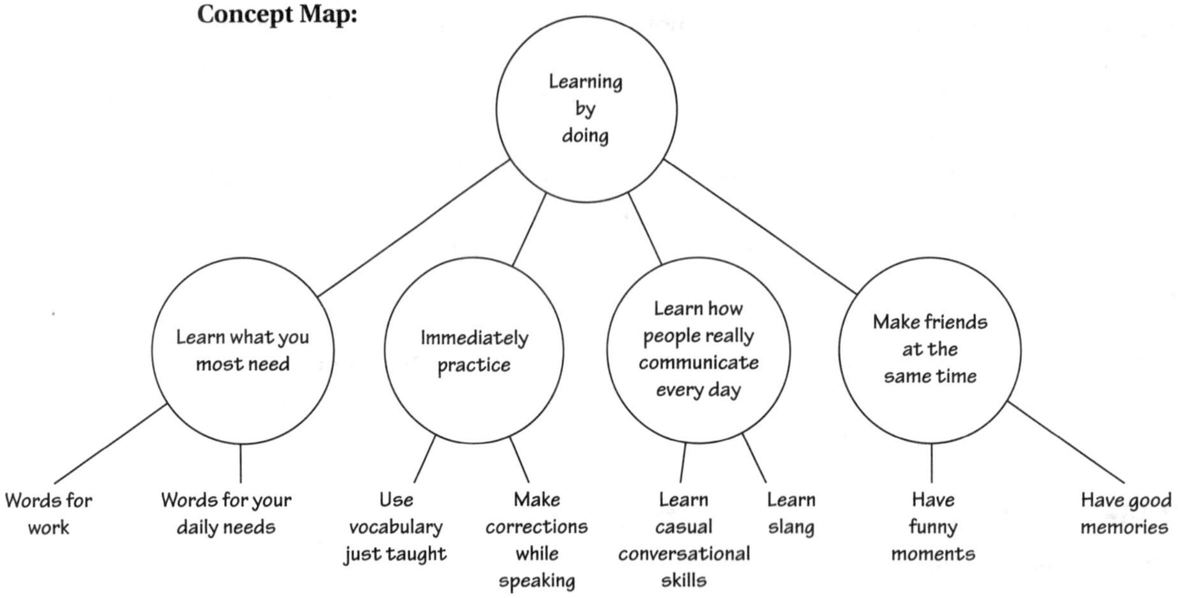

Topic Sentences:

1.1 You learn the most important words, the ones that you most need in order to communicate.

1.2 You immediately practice what you have learned.

1.3 You learn how people really communicate every day, instead of formal language that may only be used at school.

1.4 You make friends and learn a language at the same time.

Introduction: People often discuss what the best way is to learn languages: "learning by doing" or from books and teachers. In "learning by doing," you learn the most important words that you need. You immediately practice what you have learned. You learn how people really communicate every day, instead of formal language that may only be used at school. You make friends and learn a language at the same time. "Learning by doing" is a better way to learn a language.

2.

Task: Discuss advantages and disadvantages.

Thesis Statement: Because of the tremendous challenges caused by this change, I would vote against moving my capital.

Concept Map:

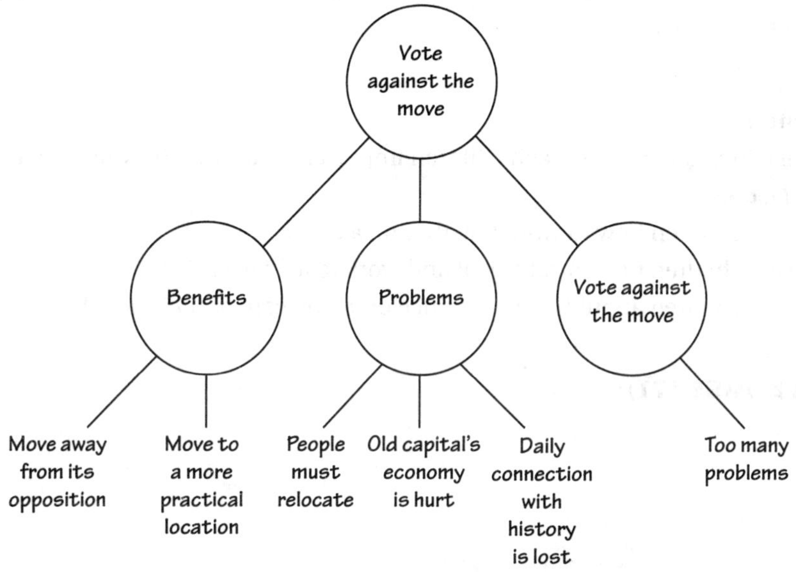

Topic Sentences:

2.1 A government may move its capital because of the benefits.

2.2 However, there are also some problems to consider.

2.3 If I were asked to move my capital, I would definitely vote against it.

Introduction: Perhaps you have never thought about moving your government's capital. However, it has happened worldwide and for hundreds of years. A government may move its capital because of the benefits. However, there are also some problems to consider. Because of the tremendous challenges caused by this change, I would vote against moving my capital.

Skill 19—Writing the Paragraphs (page 169)

PRACTICE (PAGE 170)

1.

Topic Sentence:

1.1 Modern technology has given us a tool for controlling the TV programs[1] we see.

Supporting Details:

1.2 Most TVs can be programmed to block certain channels.

1.3 Parents use this technology to protect their children from seeing shows that are too violent.

1.4 Adults can also use this technology to avoid seeing programs that they don't want to see.

[1]BRITISH: programmes

2.

Topic Sentence:

2.1 The best thing about TV is that there is a variety of programs.

Supporting Details:

2.2 There are news programs for serious people.

2.3 There are movies and cartoons for people who want to be entertained.

2.4 The variety of TV programs needs to be protected, even if that means allowing some of them to show violence.

3.

Topic Sentence:

3.1 Physical education classes teach children important skills that they need in life.

Supporting Details:

3.2 They teach children how to work together on a team.

3.3 They teach children how to set a goal and work to achieve it.

3.4 They teach children about the importance of taking care of their health.

PRACTICE 2 (PAGE 171)

1. B
2. A
3. C

Skill 20—Writing the Conclusion (page 173)

PRACTICE 1 (PAGE 175)

1. recommendation
2. prediction
3. question
4. generalization
5. restatement

PRACTICE 2 (PAGE 175)

Answers will vary.

Skill 21—Transition Words (page 176)

PRACTICE 1 (PAGE 178)

1. 7
2. 3
3. 1
4. 5
5. 6
6. 2
7. 4

PRACTICE 2 (PAGE 179)

A

1. difference
2. while
3. however
4. In contrast to

B

5. similar to
6. alike
7. both
8. just as
9. both

PRACTICE 3 (PAGE 180)

1. as a result
2. Furthermore
3. likewise
4. In other words
5. Unlike
6. What's more
7. such as
8. then
9. but
10. In other words
11. In addition
12. Above all

Skill 22—Repeating and Paraphrasing (page 181)

PRACTICE (PAGE 182)

1. B
2. A
3. C
4. B
5. C

Skill 23—Pronouns (page 183)

PRACTICE (PAGE 183)

1. them
2. It
3. her
4. this
5. They
6. their

Skill 24—Stating Your Opinion (page 184)

PRACTICE (PAGE 185)

1. It is my opinion that violence on television is (is not) very harmful for children.
2. In my view, parents should (should not) monitor their children's computer use.
3. I understand that home-cooked food is (is not) better for the health of the family.
4. I think that dependence on private automobiles causes (doesn't cause) many problems in our daily lives.
5. I am sure that learning about art is (is not) a good way to spend part of the school day.
6. I am convinced that children learn (don't learn) better when they have friendly relationships with their teachers.
7. Perhaps people spend (do not spend) too much money on stylish clothes.
8. Certainly, taking a train is (is not) just as convenient as driving a car.

Skill 25—Generalizing and Qualifying (page 186)

PRACTICE (PAGE 186)

1. As a rule, children learn (don't always learn) better when they spend part of each day getting physical exercise.
2. On the whole, job security is (is not) a thing of the past.
3. For the most part, family ties are (are not) weaker now than they were in the past.
4. To some extent, art and music classes equal (do not equal) academic classes in importance.
5. In a way, a train is (is not) as convenient a form of transportation as a private car.

Skill 26—Synonyms (page 187)

PRACTICE (PAGE 187)

1. alone
2. regulate
3. curious
4. ration
5. engaged
6. supervision
7. easy

Skill 27—Plural Nouns (page 189)

PRACTICE (PAGE 191)

1. shelves
2. zeroes
3. museums
4. tourists
5. people
6. dictionaries
7. buses
8. knives
9. passengers
10. tomatoes
11. taxes
12. plays
13. thieves
14. Chinese
15. Mexicans

Skill 28—Commonly Misspelled Words (page 192)

PRACTICE (PAGE 192)

accommodations
acceptable
immediately
roommate
unfortunately
common
arguments
possessions
permission
occasionally
equipment
until
people
library
grateful
uncomfortable
calendar
believe
budget

Skill 29—Parallel Structures (page 193)

PRACTICE (PAGE 194)

1. playing
2. information
3. will bring
4. play
5. educational
6. can no longer enjoy
7. they taste
8. the fishing docks were removed

Skill 30—Sentence Types (page 195)

PRACTICE 1 (PAGE 196)

1. I like home-cooked food, and I also enjoy eating at restaurants.
2. I think art appreciation is important, but I don't believe valuable school time should be spent on art classes.
3. Children should learn to use computers because they will need computer skills later in life.
4. I don't think there should be laws against violence on TV even though I don't enjoy watching violent programs.
5. While some people are willing to spend a lot of money on stylish clothes, others prefer to dress less expensively.
6. If children don't have opportunities to visit art museums, they will never learn to appreciate art.
7. I own a TV, but I rarely watch it because I don't have time.

PRACTICE 2 (PAGE 197)

1. As soon as everyone arrives, we will serve dinner.
2. Although I don't have a lot of money, I generally buy expensive clothes.
3. I know a lot about music because I took music lessons as a child.
4. I own a car, and my husband has a motorcycle.
5. I enjoy watching television, but I don't watch it every day.
6. While some of the restaurants in my neighborhood serve delicious healthful meals, others serve only tasteless junk.
7. Riding the bus is convenient if you live close to a bus stop.

Skill 31—Punctuation (page 198)

PRACTICE (PAGE 199)

Corrections are underlined. Each paragraph has been indented.

1.

Many families enjoy watching television together during the early evening hours. Therefore, programs shown during this time should be suitable for children. Do you really think it is appropriate for children to see programs that involve shooting, fistfights, and other forms of violence? Most parents do not, and they change the channel when such programs are shown.

2.

It is important for children to know how to use computers, but it is also important for them to spend time on other activities. When children spend a lot of time at the computer, they spend less time playing outside. They spend less time interacting with other people. They miss out on activities that are important for their physical and emotional development.

3.

I have a lot of fun activities planned for your visit. John, who is my next-door neighbor, has promised to take us white-water rafting. Have you ever done that before? It's a lot of fun, and you will surely enjoy it. However, there are plenty of other things we can do if you don't want to go rafting. We can ride bikes, go to the movies, or just relax at home.

4.

Tourism, which brings a lot of money to the town of Palm Grove, is an important part of the local economy. Tourist dollars pay the salaries of hotel employees, restaurant servers, and airport workers. All of these people earn a lot more money from tourism than they ever did from fishing. In addition, they now have steady jobs with a steady income.

Skill 32—Using a Revision Checklist (page 200)

PRACTICE 1 (PAGE 204)

1. B	4. B	7. C	10. B
2. A	5. B	8. B	11. C
3. C	6. A	9. A	12. B

PRACTICE 2 (PAGE 208)

Missing items:

Paragraph 1: thesis statement
Paragraph 2: supporting ideas
Paragraph 3: none
Paragraph 4: topic sentence
Paragraph 5: none

Grammar and vocabulary errors:

Paragraph 1: none
Paragraph 2: the amount of money necessary depends
Paragraph 3: if adult children never see (parallel structures)
Paragraph 4: unhappy at work, for example
Paragraph 5: it can buy

Revised Essay

Added and corrected parts are underlined.

I believe that success has many facets. Having money can be one part of success. Having good relationships is another very important part of success. So is feeling fulfilled.

Everybody needs money, but the amount of money necessary depends on each person's goals. For example, one person may want a lot of material things, like fancy cars and big houses. For this person, a lot of money is important. Another person may need money to pay for food and shelter so that she is then free to do the things she enjoys doing. For this person, the amount of money required is much less.

Everybody needs to have good relationships. Even a multi-millionaire is not successful if he or she does not have close connections with other people. If a woman always fights with her husband, if a man's children refuse to speak to him, if adult children never see their parents, they cannot be considered successful people.

Everybody needs to feel fulfilled. It is important to develop skills and talents and pursue interests. It is important to spend time doing things that are enjoyable or meaningful. A person who is unhappy at work, for example, cannot be considered successful no matter how big his salary is. A person who spends evenings and weekends just sitting in front of the TV cannot be considered successful, either.

Money and the material things it can buy may be one part of success, but non-material things like relationships and self-fulfillment are just as important.

Speaking Module 6

→ **QUICK STUDY**
- **Overview**
- **Question Types**
- **Speaking Tips**

→ **SPEAKING SKILLS**

Part 1: Introduction and Interview
- **Skill 1—Talking About Yourself**

Part 2: Long Turn
- **Skill 2—Organizing a Topic**
- **Skill 3—Discussing a Topic**
- **Skill 4—Verb Tenses**
- **Skill 5—Sequence**
- **Skill 6—Comparing and Contrasting**
- **Skill 7—Explaining**
- **Skill 8—Describing**
- **Skill 9—Responding to Follow-up Questions**

Part 3: Discussion
- **Skill 10—Explaining an Issue in Depth**
- **Skill 11—Describing an Issue in Depth**
- **Skill 12—Comparing and Contrasting an Issue in Depth**
- **Skill 13—Giving an In-Depth Opinion**

General Speaking Skills
- **Skill 14—Asking for Clarification**
- **Skill 15—Delay Tactics**
- **Skill 16—Avoiding Short Answers**
- **Skill 17—Word Families and Stress**
- **Skill 18—Sentence Stress**
- **Skill 19—Transition Words and Intonation**
- **Skill 20—Lists and Intonation**

→ **ANSWER EXPLANATIONS**

OVERVIEW

There are three parts to the Speaking module, which lasts between 11 and 14 minutes. You will be alone in a room with one examiner, who will ask you questions and ask you to talk on certain topics. The interview will be recorded. You will be able to make notes in Part 2 only.

The Speaking modules are the same for both the Academic and the General Training versions of the IELTS. Topics include discussions about you, your family, and topics of everyday interest.

Speaking Module		
Sections	**Time**	**Tasks**
1	4-5 minutes	Answer questions about yourself and your activities
2	3-4 minutes: 1 minute, preparation 1-2 minutes speaking 1 minute follow-up questions	Talk on a topic presented on a task card
3	4-5 minutes	Discuss with examiner issues related to the topic in Part 2

QUESTION TYPES

There are a variety of questions and prompts the examiner will use to get you to talk during the IELTS Speaking module. You should be familiar with these types.

Part 1 *Wh-* questions
Yes/No questions

Part 2 Describe and explain
Wh- questions
Yes/No questions

Part 3 *Wh-* questions
Yes/No questions

The following activities will help you become familiar with these question types.

Part 1

PRACTICE A

Write the answers to the examiner's questions for Part 1.

1 Let's talk about where you live. Can you describe your neighborhood?

....

2 What is an advantage of living there?

....

3 What is a disadvantage of living there?

....

4 Let's talk about jobs. What kind of job do you have?

....

5 What is the best thing about your job?

....

6 What kind of training or experience did you need to get this job?

....

7 Let's talk about free time. What is one activity you enjoy doing in your free time?

....

8 How did you become interested in this activity?

....

PRACTICE B

Pretend you are taking the Speaking module. The examiner asked you the questions in Practice A. Now give your answers out loud to the examiner's questions for Part 1.

Part 2

PRACTICE C

Make notes to answer the questions on the Task Card for Part 2. Try to do this in one minute.

> **Task Card**
>
> Describe a place that you like to go.
>
> You should say:
> where the place is
> how you get there
> what it looks like
>
> and explain why you like this place.

Notes:

Place ....

Location ....

Transportation ....

Appearance ....

Why I like it

....

....

PRACTICE D

Pretend you are taking the Speaking module. The examiner gave you the Task Card in Practice C. Now give your answers out loud to the examiner's questions for Part 2.

PRACTICE E

Write the answers to the examiner's follow-up questions for Part 2.

1 Do you go alone to this place?

....

2 Are there similar places you like to go?

....

PRACTICE F

Pretend you are taking the Speaking module. The examiner asked you the questions in Practice E. Now give your answers out loud to the examiner's questions for Part 2 follow-up.

Part 3

PRACTICE G

Write the answers to the examiner's questions for Part 3. Note that these questions are related to the theme of Part 2.

1 Let's consider why people need to vary their surroundings.

- What kinds of vacations[1] do most people take?
- Are these different from the places that people used to go to in the past?

....

....

....

2 Finally, let's talk about leisure time.

- Why is leisure time important?

....

....

....

[1]BRITISH: holidays

SPEAKING TIPS

Tips to Help You While Taking the Test

1. **Focus on the task.** Think what the examiner is asking you. Respond precisely to the question or topic.
2. **Speak clearly.** Sit up straight. Talk directly to the examiner. Do not be afraid to make eye contact.
3. **Speak loudly.** Make sure you are heard, but do not yell.
4. **Make notes.** Don't waste preparation time writing out full sentences. Write just your key ideas.
5. **Laugh.** Do this before you meet the examiner. On your way to the speaking test, tell yourself a joke or think of something funny. Start to laugh. Laugh harder. Laugh louder. Laughter will make you feel better and more relaxed. It will also push air into your lungs and help you speak better. People around you may think you're crazy,[1] but you're there to do well on the IELTS, not to impress people with your sanity.
6. **Smile.** Smile at the examiner. This will put both of you at ease and make you both more comfortable.
7. **Don't rehearse.** Don't try to memorize answers in advance.
8. **Pay attention to verb tenses.** You may need to talk about the past, present, and future in the same topic.
9. **Make sure you understand the task.** Ask the examiner to repeat or explain a question if the task is unclear.

Tips to Help You Study for the Speaking Test

1. **Talk to yourself.** When you walk down the street, pay attention to the things around you. What do the buildings look like? Is there a lot of traffic? How is the weather? Is this a typical day and scene in your city? In your mind, describe the scene to someone in English. Imagine a person who has never visited your city, and describe the scene to that person.

   You can do the same thing at school, at work, or anywhere you go. Imagine describing the scene to a person from another country. Explain the customs of people in your country: how they dress, act, and talk in the different situations that you describe.
2. **Make up stories.** Use your imagination. Look around on the street, on the bus, on the elevator, wherever you are. Who are those people? Where are they going and why? What are they carrying? What will they do with what they are carrying? Imagine yourself in the story. What would you say to these people?

   Ask yourself questions about everything and everyone you see. How did it get here? Why is it here? What will happen to it next?
3. **Make your daily plans.** Do you talk to yourself about your plans for the day when you get up in the morning? Do this in English. If you have to decide what clothes to wear, what to have for breakfast, if you will walk or take the bus, think about these

[1]British: mad

decisions in English. If you make a shopping list or a reading list or a list of chores, you can do this in English too.

4. **Think about your job.** Imagine you are at a job interview. Talk about your educational and work background. What kind of training and experience do you have? What can you do well? How do you see your future? In your mind, try to sell yourself to a future employer by talking about your strengths and good qualities.
5. **Explain your interests.** Choose a hobby or free time interest that you have. Imagine that you are teaching another person how to do it. Explain everything step by step. Describe any equipment or tools that are needed. Then pick another hobby and do it again.
6. **Read books, watch movies and TV shows, and listen to the radio.** Think about a book, film, show, or program that you really enjoy. In your mind, tell another person what it is about and why you like it. Think about a book, film, show, or program that you dislike. Explain why you don't like it.
7. **Read about the news.** When you read the newspaper or watch the news on TV, think about it in English. How could you explain it to another person in English? How could you explain your own opinions or feelings about particular news events?
8. **Talk to everyone you meet.** Talk to cashiers, bus drivers, neighbors—everyone!
9. **Introduce yourself.** Practice introducing yourself and answering typical "getting-to-know-you" questions.
10. **Make notes.** Practice making notes about different topics and turning those notes into a short speech.
11. **Explain your opinions.** Practice giving opinions and explaining them with examples and details.
12. **Remember.** You are being marked on your speaking abilities, not on your knowledge.

What the Examiner Measures

FLUENCY AND COHERENCE

When you answer the examiner's questions or talk about a topic, your speech must be fluent and cohesive. This means the words you use must fit the situation, and these words must come quickly. You must address the topic fully, and your ideas must be tied together.

It is important to speak for a least one full minute during Part 2. You can speak up to two minutes if you can. The examiner will tell you to stop and will then ask a question related to the topic.

ACCURACY

Accuracy is very important. An examiner will listen to your vocabulary, your grammar, and your pronunciation. She or he will want to make sure that you have a large enough vocabulary to express yourself easily and be understood completely.

The examiner will want to make sure that the grammar you use is varied and appropriate to what you want to say.

The examiner will, of course, be paying close attention to your pronunciation. Your speech must be comprehensible. You can have an accent, but the words must be intelligible.

PART 1: INTRODUCTION AND INTERVIEW

Skill 1—Talking About Yourself

In Part 1 of the Speaking Test, you will be asked questions about yourself and your everyday life. You may be asked to talk about things such as the place where you live, your job or your studies, or your free time activities.

Your Home and Hometown

You may be asked to talk about your home, your neighborhood, or your hometown. You can talk generally about these, or you can talk more personally. Try to have a lot of specific details prepared. This will help your answers be more cohesive and fluent.

Home

We live in a flat[1] in the old section of the city. It was once a large home that was converted to several flats. Now, five families live in this home. We have two bedrooms: one for me and one for my parents. There is a large living room and a kitchen with a small balcony overlooking the street. The streets are very narrow, and there are no trees.

Neighborhood[2]

I was born in Beijing. Even though it is a very large city and the capital, we live in a part that is like a small village. We know everyone here. On the corner of my street, there is a small grocery store. Across from that, there is a dry cleaner. Next to the dry cleaner is a big clothing store. On the corner opposite the grocery store, there is a bus stop so we can easily go anywhere in the city.

Useful Words

Type	Relation	Description
balcony	across from	large/small
one-bedroom	along	spacious
kitchen	behind	airy
section/area	beside	narrow
grocery store	corner	old/new
park	end	lots of
post office	facing	a lot of
department store	in back/front/middle of	big
taxi stand/rank	left-hand/right-hand side	
clothing store	near	
dry cleaner	next to	
park	overlooking	

[1]American: apartment; [2]British neighbourhood

SPEAKING SKILLS—ACADEMIC/GENERAL TRAINING

PRACTICE 1

Complete these forms about your home and neighborhood. This will help you organize your personal information.

Home Information Form

Size ....

Age ....

Number of bedrooms ....

Other rooms ....

Garden/yard ....

Special features ....

My bedroom

Size ....

Furniture ....

Colors[1] ....

Art ....

Other ....

Neighborhood[2] Information Form

Name ....

Style of houses ....

Shops/businesses ....

....

Schools ....

Religious buildings ....

Other buildings ....

Transportation ....

Parks/gardens ....

Special characteristics ....

[1]British: colour; [2]British: neighbourhood

Write four sentences about your home. Use the examples as models. Then, without looking at the form or sentences, describe your home and hometown out loud. Record your description and listen to it. Record it over and over until you are satisfied with your presentation.

Home

1 ....

2 ....

3 ....

4 ....

Neighborhood

1 ....

2 ....

3 ....

4 ....

Your Occupation or School

You may be asked to discuss how you spend your day. Do you work or do you study? Be prepared with specific details about your occupation or your school life.

Occupation
I'm an engineer. I've worked for the same company for three years. My specific job is working with the senior engineer and helping her prepare presentations for contractors and their clients. I'd like to get an advanced[1] degree. That's why I'm applying to study at an engineering school in Australia.

School
I'm a third-year student at National University. I'm studying psychology. I'm in class most of the day, and when I'm not in class I have to spend a lot of time working on my assignments. My goal is to become a research psychologist, so I'll have to get a doctorate degree. I have a lot of years of studying ahead of me.

[1]British: higher degree

Useful Words		
boss	duties	qualified
co-workers	assignments	goal
clients	position	advanced degree
classmates	schedule	bachelor's degree
instructors	salary	master's degree
manager	hourly	doctorate degree

PRACTICE 2

Complete this form about your occupation or studies. This will help you organize your personal information.

Job Information Form

Company name ....

Job title ....

Length of time at this job ....

Duties ....

Training required for this job ....

....

Skills required for this job ....

....

Things I like about this job ....

Things I don't like about this job ....

....

Future career goals ....

Education Information Form

Name of college/university ....

Major/subject[1] ....

Classes I am taking now ....

Hours per week in class ....

Years to complete degree/certificate ....

Educational goals ....

Future career goals ....

[1]BRITISH: doing a degree in

Write four sentences about your occupation or your studies. Use the examples as models. Then, without looking at the form or sentences, describe your job or school out loud. Record your discussion and listen to it. Record it over and over until you are satisfied with your presentation.

My occupation: .... **or My studies:** ....

1 ....

2 ....

3 ....

4 ....

Your Hobbies

The examiner may ask you how you spend your free time. Do you like to read, go to the cinema, play sports? Do you have any hobbies like collecting stamps, bird watching, photography?

Example 1

I enjoy bird watching. I often go to a park near my house in the early morning to watch the birds. I also belong to a bird watching club. Several times a year we take trips to other places. We try to find birds that we've never seen before. You don't need much equipment for bird watching, just a pair of binoculars and a pair of strong legs for walking. I enjoy this hobby because I like to be outside, and I'm fascinated by the natural world.

Example 2

I like to play the guitar. I took lessons when I was a child. Some friends and I had a rock band once, a long time ago. We played at parties. Now I mostly play on my own at home, and sometimes I get together with friends to play. I'm thinking about taking lessons again. I'd like to learn how to play jazz guitar. I have a large collection of jazz CDs.

Useful Words		
interested in	club	equipment
enjoy	get together	collect/collection
join	learn how	passion
belong to	lessons	fascinate/fascinated by

PRACTICE 3

Complete this form about your hobbies or general interests. This will help you organize your personal information.

Hobby/Free-Time Activity Information Form

Hobby/Activity #1 ....

How often do you do this hobby or activity? ....

Do you do it on your own or with other people? ....

Do you belong to a club related to this hobby/activity? ....

How did you learn how to do this hobby/activity?

....

Do you need special equipment for it?

....

What do you like most about it?

....

Hobby/Activity #2 ....

How often do you do this hobby or activity? ....

Do you do it on your own or with other people? ....

Do you belong to a club related to this hobby/activity? ....

How did you learn how to do this hobby/activity?

....

Do you need special equipment for it?

....

What do you like most about it?

....

Write four sentences about how you spend your free time. Use the examples as models. Then, without looking at the form or sentences, describe your hobbies and general interests out loud. Record your description and listen to it. Record it over and over until you are satisfied with your presentation.

Hobby/Activity ....

1 ....

2 ....

3 ....

4 ....

PART 2: LONG TURN

Skill 2—Organizing a Topic

The examiner will give you a task card. The card will have a topic and some questions to guide your discussion of the topic. You will have one minute to prepare your answer. The questions are very important. They will guide your organization. You must answer ALL the questions on the task card. You can make notes on paper provided by the examiner. Your discussion will be more cohesive if you can provide a sequence of events or actions for your topic.

Example

> Describe a museum that you have visited.
>
> You should say:
>
> where it is located and what kind of museum it is
> what specific things you can see there
> when and why you last visited it
>
> and discuss how it compares to other museums you have visited.

Notes

Museum	Greenport Ship Museum
Location and type of museum	Greenport, a beach resort in Massachusetts; a museum about old whaling ships
Specific things seen	Parts of old ships, items used by sailors, explanations of shipbuilding methods, information about whaling, whale bone products
When and why visited	Last summer with niece and nephew to pass the time on a rainy day
Compare to other museums	Not like a city museum, smaller, simpler exhibits, but friendlier staff

TIP

Answer the questions on the task card. Don't talk about a different topic.

PRACTICE

Make notes about these topics. Then, without looking at your notes, discuss the topics out loud. Be sure to address every question on each task card. Record your discussion and listen to it. Record your discussion over and over until you are satisfied with your presentation.

Make notes about these topics. Give short answers to the question. Pay attention to the tense.

Topic 1

> Talk about a pet that you or someone you know once had.
>
> You should say:
> what kind of animal it was
> what kind of care it needed
> what you liked/didn't like about it
>
> and explain why this is or is not a popular type of pet to own.

Pet ....

Kind of animal ....

Kind of care ....

Liked/didn't like ....

Why it is/isn't popular ....

Topic 2

> Describe a birthday celebration that you attended recently.
>
> You should say:
> whose birthday it was and that person's age
> who attended the party
> where the party took place
>
> and describe some activities that happened at the party.

Birthday ....

Name and age of celebrant ....

Who attended ....

Location ....

Activities ....

Topic 3

Talk about a friend you had as a child or teenager. You should say: when and how you first met this friend what things you liked to do together what things you had in common and explain why this friendship was important to you.

Friend ....

When and how met ....

Things did together ....

Things in common ....

Why important ....

Topic 4

Describe a trip you have taken recently. You should say: where you went who went with you why you went there and describe some things you saw and did on your trip.

Trip ....

Where ....

Who ....

Why ....

Activities ....

Skill 3—Discussing a Topic

When you write, you state a general idea and then add supporting details. The same is true in speaking.

Topic A museum you have visited

Question Discuss how this museum compares to other museums you have visited.

Ideas for Response

Main Idea The Greenport Ship Museum is different from a museum in the city.

Supporting Detail 1 It is smaller.
Supporting Detail 2 The exhibits are simpler.
Supporting Detail 3 The staff is friendlier.

TIP

Your notes can be full sentences or phrases.

PRACTICE

For each question, write one main idea followed by three supporting details. Then, without looking at your notes, answer the questions out loud. Record your answers and listen to them. Record your answers over and over until you are satisfied with your presentation.

1 Topic A TV program you enjoy
Question Explain why this is or is not a popular TV show.

Main Idea ....

Supporting Detail 1 ....

Supporting Detail 2 ....

Supporting Detail 3 ....

2 Topic A trip you have taken recently
Question Describe some things you saw and did on your trip.

Main Idea ....

Supporting Detail 1 ....

Supporting Detail 2 ....

Supporting Detail 3 ....

3 Topic A close friend you have now
Question Tell about some things you have in common with this friend.

Main Idea ....

Supporting Detail 1 ....

Supporting Detail 2 ....

Supporting Detail 3 ....

4 Topic — A book you have read recently
Question — Tell what the book is about.

Main Idea ....

Supporting Detail 1 ....

Supporting Detail 2 ....

Supporting Detail 3 ....

TIP

Pay attention to the intonation for lists. See the practice exercises in the General Speaking Skills section.

Skill 4—Verb Tenses

You may be asked to talk about something that you experienced in the past, or about something that is still true now. Be careful to use the correct verb tense.

Past Tenses

Simple past	Last summer, we went to the Greenport Ship Museum.
Past continuous	When we left the house, it was raining.
Past perfect	By the time we got there, the demonstration had already begun.

Present Tenses

Simple present	This program appears on TV once a week.
Present continuous	TV stations are still showing the program even though it was originally made over ten years ago.
Present perfect	I have enjoyed this program since I was a child.

PRACTICE

For each question, circle the verb tense you will mostly use in your answer. Then write three main ideas to answer the question. Then, without looking at your notes, answer the questions out loud. Record your answers and listen to them. Record your answers over and over until you are satisfied with your presentation.

1 Topic — A popular tourist destination in your country
Question — Explain why this is a popular place for tourists to visit.
Verb Tense — Past Present

Main Idea ....

Main Idea ....

Main Idea ....

2 Topic — Your favorite year in either primary or secondary school
Question — Explain why you liked this year in school so much.
Verb Tense — Past Present

Main Idea ....

Main Idea ....

Main Idea ....

3 Topic — A time your plane/train/bus was delayed
Question — What did you do while you were waiting for the plane/train/bus to leave?
Verb Tense — Past Present

Main Idea ....

Main Idea ....

Main Idea ....

4 Topic — A popular place to go shopping in your city
Question — Describe the things you can see and do there.
Verb Tense — Past Present

Main Idea ....

Main Idea ....

Main Idea ....

Skill 5—Sequence

When you describe something that happened in the past, you can use certain words to show the sequence of events.

Useful Words		
first/second	next	then
after	before	until
by the time	finally	at last
as soon as	when	later

Example

After we watched the shipbuilding demonstration, we looked at some of the exhibits. *Then* we had a snack in the café. We stayed at the museum *until* it closed.

PRACTICE

Choose the correct sequence words to complete each paragraph. Add capital letters where necessary.

until	finally	then	as soon as

I arrived at the train station at 10:00. **1** .... I got there, I checked my luggage. **2** .... I heard the announcement: the train was delayed. I sat in the café and drank coffee **3** .... I heard the boarding announcement. I boarded the train at 12:30. **4** ...., the train left the station at 12:50.

by the time	before	first	then

Our last day in Vancouver was very busy. **5** ...., we spent several hours at the anthropology museum. **6** .... we had seen all the exhibits, we were very hungry. We had a quick snack in the cafeteria, and **7** .... we took the bus to Chinatown for lunch. We studied the menu carefully **8** .... ordering lunch and chose a variety of delicious Chinese dishes. It was a very good restaurant, and we really enjoyed our meal.

Skill 6—Comparing and Contrasting

You may be asked to compare the person, place, or event of your topic to another one.

Useful Words		
same	different from	alike
like	unlike	more
less	similar to	as . . . as

Comparative and superlative adjectives are also used to compare and contrast.

Example

The Greenport Ship Museum is not <u>like</u> city museums.
It is <u>smaller</u> and the exhibits are <u>simpler</u>.
But it is just <u>as</u> interesting <u>as</u> some of the <u>bigger</u> museums.

PRACTICE

Answer the following questions. First, write three main ideas for each answer. Use compare *and* contrast *words. Then, without looking at your notes, answer the questions out loud. Record your answers and listen to them. Record your answers over and over until you are satisfied with your presentation.*

1 Topic A teacher you remember
Question Compare this teacher to other teachers you have had.

Main Idea ....

Main Idea ....

Main Idea ....

2 Topic A party you attended
Question Compare this party to other parties you have attended.

Main Idea ....

Main Idea ....

Main Idea ....

3 Topic A popular tourist destination in your country
Question Compare this place to other tourist destinations you have visited.

Main Idea ....

Main Idea ....

Main Idea ....

4 Topic A TV program you enjoy watching
Question Compare this program to other popular TV programs.

Main Idea ....

Main Idea ....

Main Idea ....

Skill 7—Explaining

You may be asked to explain *why*. For example, you may be asked why you like something or why something is important.

Useful Words	
because (of)	since
for this reason	another reason
that's why	so

Example

It's important to visit museums *because* they teach us about a lot of things. *Since* museums show us things, they can help us understand concepts and facts better than books can. *Another reason* is that museums are a representation of our culture.

PRACTICE

Answer the following questions. First, write three main ideas for each answer. Use explaining *words. Then, without looking at your notes, answer the questions out loud. Record your answers and listen to them. Record your answers over and over until you are satisfied with your presentation.*

1 Topic: A book you have read recently
Question: Explain why you liked this book.

Main Idea ....

Main Idea ....

Main Idea ....

2 Topic: Your favorite year in primary or secondary school
Question: Explain why this was your favorite year.

Main Idea ....

Main Idea ....

Main Idea ....

3 Topic: A popular tourist destination in your country
Question: Explain why this is a popular place to visit.

Main Idea ....

Main Idea ....

Main Idea ....

4 Topic A movie you have seen
Question Explain why you remember this movie.

Main Idea ....

Main Idea ....

Main Idea ....

Skill 8—Describing

You may be asked to describe some activities or events. Don't just list activities. Think of something interesting to say about each one. For example, talk about how long it took, say why you liked it, give some details about what it involved, or use some adjectives to describe it.

Example

Topic	A museum you visited recently
Question	Describe some things you did there.
Activities	(1) looked at exhibits, (2) watched a movie, (3) had a snack
Description	We spent about an hour looking at exhibits about ships and whaling. Then we watched a short but interesting movie that showed how ships were built. After that, we were tired, so we had some snacks in the museum café and looked at the view of the harbor.

PRACTICE

For each question, choose three activities to describe. Write one sentence about each one. Then, without looking at your notes, answer the questions out loud. Record your answers and listen to them. Record your answers over and over until you are satisfied with your presentation.

1 Topic A trip you took recently
Question Describe some things you did on your trip.
Activities ....
Description ....
....
....

2 Topic A party you attended recently
Question Describe some activities that took place at the party.
Activities ....
Description ....
....
....

TIP

Answer the questions thoroughly and in detail to make sure your answers are long enough.

3 Topic — A holiday you enjoy

Question — Describe some things you do to celebrate this holiday.

Activities ....

Description ....

....

....

Skill 9—Responding to Follow-up Questions

The examiner may ask you specific questions about your discussion of a topic.

Follow-up questions for the example task card in Skill 2:

How often do you go to museums?
What kinds of museums do you generally prefer to visit? Why?
Is it important to take children to visit different kinds of museums?

Useful Words		
According to my point of view	I believe	I'm in favor of .... because ....
As far as I'm concerned	I don't know if	It seems to me
I agree with/disagree with	I don't know whether	Personally, I think
I'm certain/positive/sure	I think it's a good idea because	The advantage of .... is that
I assume	I'm against	The disadvantage of .... is that

PRACTICE

Look at these follow-up questions for the task cards from the practice exercise in Skill 2, page 243. Make notes for your response. Then, without looking at your notes, answer the questions out loud. Record your answers and listen to them. Record your answers over and over until you are satisfied with your presentation.

Topic 1

What are some of the most popular pets in your country?
What animal do you think makes the best pet?
What animal do you think would not make a good pet?
What are some advantages to owning pets?

1 ....

2 ....

3 ....

4 ....

TIP

If your two minutes are up, the examiner will immediately say, "Thank you. So, you've been talking about . . . , and now I'd like to discuss . . . ."

Topic 2

How do you like to celebrate your birthday?
In your country, what kinds of gifts are common to give for birthdays?
Do you think it is important to celebrate birthdays? Why or why not?
What other kinds of celebrations are important for you?

1 ....

2 ....

3 ....

4 ....

Topic 3

Are you still friends with this person? Why or why not?
How do you make new friends?
What are some things you like to do with your friends now?
Do you think it's better to have a lot of friends, or just a few good friends?

1 ....

2 ....

3 ....

4 ....

Topic 4

Would you visit this place again? Why or why not?
Where would you like to go on your next vacation?
When you travel, what kinds of places do you usually visit?
Do you like to travel? Why or why not?

1 ....

2 ....

3 ....

4 ....

PART 3: DISCUSSION

In the last part of the Speaking section of the test, the examiner will ask you some more questions and give you an opportunity to discuss in depth some of the issues related to the topic in Part 2.

Skill 10—Explaining an Issue in Depth

You may be asked to explain more about your ideas on a topic.

Topic	A museum you visited recently (See Skill 2 example for task card questions.)
Related Questions	What role do museums play in a society? Why do people visit museums? What can we learn from museums? Is learning about art important? Why or why not?

Useful Words	
for example	for instance
in other words	such as
to illustrate	that is

You can organize your ideas in terms of a main idea with supporting details.

Question

What role do museums play in a society?

Ideas for Response

Main Idea Different roles

Supporting Detail 1 Education

Supporting Detail 2 Entertainment

Supporting Detail 3 Represent culture

Response

Museums have several different roles in society. They educate us about a wide range of things such as art, science, and history. They also provide us with entertainment, as going to a museum is a pleasant and interesting way to spend a day. Most of all, they are a representation of our culture. In other words, they reflect back to us the things that are considered to be valuable or important in our culture.

PRACTICE

Look at these questions on issues related to the topic on a task card from the practice exercise in Skill 2. Make notes for your response.

Issues from Topic 2

1. Are birthday celebrations important in your country? Why or why not?
2. How do people in your culture generally feel about their birthdays?
3. How are older people treated in your culture?
4. What other types of anniversaries are celebrated in your culture? Why are they important?

Notes

1 Main Idea ....

Supporting Detail 1 ....

Supporting Detail 2 ....

Supporting Detail 3 ....

2 Main Idea ....

Supporting Detail 1 ....

Supporting Detail 2 ....

Supporting Detail 3 ....

3 Main Idea ....

Supporting Detail 1 ....

Supporting Detail 2 ....

Supporting Detail 3 ....

4 Main Idea ....

Supporting Detail 1 ....

Supporting Detail 2 ....

Supporting Detail 3 ....

Without looking at your notes, discuss the issues out loud. Record your discussion and listen to it. Record your discussion over and over until you are satisfied with your presentation.

Skill 11—Describing an Issue in Depth

You may be asked to describe more details about your topic.

Topic A museum you visited recently

Related Questions What does a museum near you look like?
What kinds of objects are in a museum near you?
What are some different ways museums present information?
What are some ways that museums use technology?

Useful Words		
also	usually	first
additionally	generally	similarly
in addition	typically	likewise
another	ordinarily	otherwise

Organize your response beginning with a main idea followed by supporting details.

Question

What are some different ways museums present information?

Ideas for Response

Main Idea Exhibits, films, and hands-on
Supporting Detail 1 Different kinds of displays to see
Supporting Detail 2 Films related to the exhibits
Supporting Detail 3 Exhibits you can touch and workshops to make things

Response

Museums present information through exhibits, films, and different hands-on activities. Museums exhibit things in different ways. Art might hang on the wall, or a scene from history may be shown in a diorama. In addition, museums usually show films that are specially made to accompany the exhibits. Many museums also have hands-on activities. For example, they have exhibits that can be touched. They also often offer workshops where participants can learn to make things that are similar or related to the items in the museum's exhibits.

PRACTICE

Look at each question below. Write your ideas on the lines. Not all lines may be used.

TIP

Contractions will make your speech sound more natural.

1 What are some different kinds of places people visit on their vacations?

....

....

....

....

2 In your country, how much annual vacation time do people generally get? Is this enough?

....

....

....

....

3 Describe your ideal vacation.

....

....

....

....

4 What are some transportation problems in your country?

....

....

....

....

Without looking at your notes, discuss the issues out loud. Record your discussion and listen to it. Record your discussion over and over until you are satisfied with your presentation.

Skill 12—Comparing and Contrasting an Issue in Depth

You may be asked to compare and contrast issues related to your topic.

Topic A museum you visited recently.

Related Questions How are small town museums different from museums in big cities?
What do museums offer in terms of education that books or other sources don't?
Which are more interesting, art museums or history museums? Why?
How will museums be different in the future?

Useful Words	
Comparison	**Contrast**
similar to	different from
also	although/even though
like	but
the same as	on the other hand
both	less/more
as...as	however

Organize your ideas by thinking about similarities and differences.

Question

How will museums be different in the future?

Ideas for Response

Similarities
A. similar type of content
B. some similar exhibits

Differences
A. more use of computers
B. many exhibits online

Response

In the future, I think that museums will be both similar to and different from museums now. I think they will have similar content. There will still be art museums that show paintings and sculpture and natural history museums that show dinosaurs, for example. And I think some of the exhibits will be set up in similar ways, too. But I also think that museums in the future will make more use of technology. Computers will be used to make the exhibits more interactive. Most museums will probably also have exhibits online. Then it won't be necessary to actually visit the museums, at least in some cases.

PRACTICE

Look at each question below. Write your ideas on the lines. Not all lines may be used.

1 How have your friendships changed as you've grown older?

....

....

....

....

2 What differences are there between men's and women's friendships?

....

....

....

....

3 Do you think friendships have changed because of technology?

....

....

....

....

4 What is the difference between a friend and a friendship?

....

....

....

....

Without looking at your notes, discuss the issues out loud. Record your discussion and listen to it. Record your discussion over and over until you are satisfied with your presentation.

Skill 13—Giving an In-Depth Opinion

You may be asked to give your opinion on issues related to your topic.

Topic	A museum you have visited recently
Related Questions	What type of museum do you prefer to visit? Why? How important is it for parents to take their children to museums? Discuss whether museums should be allowed to charge high admission fees. Discuss whether schools should include museum visits as part of their program.

Useful Words		
I believe that	I tend to think	I agree that
To my mind	From my point of view	If I had to choose
I would prefer to	To my way of thinking	In my opinion

Organize your ideas by thinking about your opinion and details to support it.

Question

Do you agree or disagree: Museums should not be allowed to charge high admission fees.

Ideas for Response

Opinion	Agree—no high admission fees
Supporting Detail 1	High fees keep people away.
Supporting Detail 2	Even high fees don't provide funds.
Supporting Detail 3	Government should fund museums.

Response

I agree that museums should not be allowed to charge high admission fees. In my opinion, museums should not charge any fees at all. Many people, especially families with children, cannot afford to pay to go to a museum, so admission fees just keep people away. In any case, admission fees provide only a very small part of the funds a museum needs, so no one really benefits from them. To my way of thinking, museums benefit the public, so the government should provide most or all of the funds for museums.

PRACTICE

Look at each question below. Write your ideas on the lines. Not all lines may be used.

1 Do you agree or disagree: Some people spend too much money on their pets.

....

....

....

....

2 What kind of animal makes the best pet?

....

....

....

....

3 Do you prefer to have a pet or not? Why?

....

....

....

....

4 Is it important for children to have pets? Why or why not?

....

....

....

....

Without looking at your notes, discuss the issues out loud. Record your discussion and listen to it. Record your discussion over and over until you are satisfied with your presentation.

Skill 14—Asking for Clarification

If you don't understand a question, ask for clarification. This will give you time to think a bit.

Examples

Do you mean the house I live in or my hometown?
Would you like me to describe the house generally or in great detail?

Useful Words	
do you mean	would you like me to
do you want me to	generally or in great detail
could you explain what you mean by	should I
I'm not sure what you mean by	can I

PRACTICE

Read each question. Then complete the sentence asking for clarification.

1 Describe a friend who is important to you.

.... a friend I have now or a friend from the past?

2 Explain why you liked this movie.

.... explain it generally or in great detail?

3 In your opinion, what kinds of people make the best friends?

.... close friends or friends in general?

4 How will the role of older people change in the future?

.... older people?

5 In what different ways have animals been useful to people throughout history?

.... just pets or animals in general?

Skill 15—Delay Tactics

You sometimes need time to think about what you are going to say. A short silence is okay, but a long one is not. You have only a short amount of time to show how well you speak English.

While you think, you can paraphrase the question.

Question: What kinds of books do you prefer to read?
Paraphrase: What are my favorite books?

You can also use certain phrases to provide transition and fill the silence.

Useful Phrases	
That's an interesting question.	I've never heard that one before.
I've never thought about that before.	That's a complicated issue.
There are a lot of different reasons.	There are many ways to answer that.

Example

What are my favorite books? That's an interesting question.

PRACTICE

First, paraphrase these questions to keep the conversation moving. Then, add a filler expression. Say the sentences out loud.

1 Tell some things that you have in common with this friend.

....

2 Explain why this is a popular place for people to visit.

....

3 Describe some things you do to celebrate this holiday.

....

4 What kind of animal makes the best pet?

....

5 What kind of training did you need to get this kind of job?

....

Skill 16—Avoiding Short Answers

The more you say, the more you can show your ability to use a variety of grammar and vocabulary. Try not to answer a question with a simple *yes* or *no*. Use a full sentence.

Example

Question:	Do you live in Mumbai?
Avoid:	No.
Say:	No, I don't live in Mumbai. I live in a suburb outside of Mumbai.

PRACTICE

Answer these yes/no questions with long answers.

1 Do you live with your parents?

....

2 Are you a student?

....

3 Do you like living in an apartment?

....

4 Is your family large?

....

5 Do you like your job?

....

Skill 17—Word Families and Stress

Using word families shows your fluency in English. Be careful to pronounce the words correctly. Depending on what suffixes you add to a root word, the stress may or may not shift.

Some suffixes cause no change in stress.

-able	comfort—comfortable
-ive	support—supportive
-ful	meaning—meaningful
-ment	govern—government
-ize	special—specialize
-ly	happy—happily

Some suffixes cause the stress to shift to the syllable immediately preceding the suffix.

-ity	uniform—uniformity
-ic	alcohol—alcoholic
-ify	solid—solidify
-ical	history—historical
-ian	library—librarian

Some suffixes cause the stress to shift to the first syllable of the suffix.

-ation/-ition/-ution	combine—combination

PRACTICE

Look at these word families. Read the words out loud. Underline the stressed syllable in each word. Read the words out loud again.

	Root Word	Noun	Verb	Adjective	Adverb
1	politics	politician	politicize	political	politically
2	imagine	imagination	imagine	imaginative	imaginatively
3	beauty	beauty	beautify	beautiful	beautifully
4	agree	agreement	agree	agreeable	agreeably
5	acid	acid/acidity	acidify	acidic	acidly
6	quote	quotation	quote	quotable	
7	act	activity	act	active	actively
8	energy	energy	energize	energetic	energetically
9	civil	civility	civilize	civil	civilly
10	rare	rarity	rarify	rare	rarely

Skill 18—Sentence Stress

In a sentence there are words that carry meaning and words that are function words. The words that carry meaning are usually stressed.

Meaning	Function
nouns	articles
verbs	prepositions
adjectives	conjunctions
question words	pronouns
	relative pronouns
	auxiliaries

Examples

The **large museums** in **town** were **built** in the **late 1900s.**
People who **buy expensive things** for their **pets** are **wasting** their **money.**
It's a **romance novel** that **takes place** in the **1800s.**

PRACTICE

Read each sentence out loud. Underline the stressed words. Then read the sentence out loud again.

1 I live in one of the newer neighborhoods in my city.

2 I've been working at the same company for twelve years.

3 I generally don't like parties because I'm a quiet person.

4 There is an excellent view of the ships in the harbor.

5 A statue of the first president of our country stands in the center of the park.

Skill 19—Transition Words and Intonation

A transition word has a rising intonation. The end of the sentence or clause has a falling intonation.

First, a museum is a fun place to visit.

However, not everyone likes paintings.

I have lived in the same house since I was born.

PRACTICE

Read each sentence out loud. Mark the intonation patterns for transition words. Then read the sentence out loud again.

1 Nevertheless, it's a pleasant place to live.

2 We took a boat ride after we finished at the museum.

3 Next, the birthday cake was served.

4 It's a position that pays well, unlike many jobs in my field.

5 A good friend also helps you when you are in need.

Skill 20—Lists and Intonation

When you have a list of words in a sentence, there is a specific stress pattern.

The first words of a list have a rising intonation. The last word of a list has a falling intonation.

I always eat three vegetables a day: corn ↗, carrots ↗, and peas ↘.

Near my home you can find a bakery ↗, a bank ↗, a laundry ↗, and a restaurant ↘.

PRACTICE

Read each sentence out loud. Mark the intonation pattern. Then read the sentence out loud again.

1 Cats are affectionate, clean, and smart.

2 In addition to English and my native language, I speak Chinese, Korean, and French.

3 I read a variety of things, such as novels, newspapers, magazines, and journals.

4 This TV program is well-written, well-acted, and funny.

5 We had a very active vacation and played tennis, golf, and volleyball.

ANSWER EXPLANATIONS

QUICK STUDY—QUESTION TYPES (PAGE 230)

Part 1

PRACTICE A (PAGE 231)

Answers will vary. Possible answers are given.

1. *Let's talk about where you live. Can you describe your neighborhood/neighbourhood?*
   My neighborhood/neighbourhood has lots of apartment buildings. We have a school and a playground. There is also a park in my neighborhood/neighbourhood.
2. *What is an advantage of living there?*
   It's a quiet neighborhood/neighbourhood. That's an advantage.
3. *What is a disadvantage of living there?*
   It is not close to the bus stop or to the train station.
4. *Let's talk about jobs. What kind of job do you have?*
   My job is an office job. I work as a secretary.
5. *What is the best thing about your job?*
   I like the people at my office. They're very friendly.
6. *What kind of training or experience did you need to get this job?*
   I took a course at a secretarial school. Also, I worked for two years at a different company before I got my current job.
7. *Let's talk about free time. What is one activity you enjoy doing in your free time?*
   I enjoy cooking in my free time.
8. *How did you become interested in this activity?*
   My mother taught me how to cook. I have loved it since I was a little girl.

PRACTICE B (PAGE 231)

Answers will vary.

Part 2

PRACTICE C (PAGE 232)

Possible answers:

Place:	the park
Location:	in my neighborhood, 2 blocks away/2 streets away
Transportation:	walking or riding my bike
Appearance:	green grass and playground equipment
Why I like it:	It's peaceful. I like watching the children playing and families having fun.

PRACTICE D (PAGE 232)

Answers will vary.

PRACTICE E (PAGE 232)

Possible answers:

1. *Do you go alone to this place?*
   Yes, usually I go alone/on my own. Sometimes a friend comes with me.

2. *Are there similar places you like to go?*
   There is a park in another neighborhood. Sometimes I go there, too.

PRACTICE F (PAGE 232)

Answers will vary.

Part 3

PRACTICE G (PAGE 233)

Possible answers:

1. Most people take vacations to the beach/take holidays by the seaside, a famous city, or a unique location. Many of the places are the same. But now people can travel far away with less trouble. In the past, this was more difficult or impossible.

2. Leisure time is important. It gives people the chance to relax. It refreshes them. It helps people to be ready to do more work in the future.

Skill 1—Talking About Yourself (page 236)

PRACTICE 1 (PAGE 237)

Home Information Form

Size	medium
Age	fifty years
Number of bedrooms	four
Other rooms	kitchen, living room, dining room, 2 bathrooms
Garden/yard	large size, lots of flowers
Special features	attic
My bedroom	
Size	medium
Furniture	wood, painted brown, have a desk and a bed
Colors	white/cream paint on the walls
Art	poster of favorite musicians
Other	computer

Neighborhood Information Form

Name	Flower Valley
Style of houses	older, family homes
Shops/businesses	restaurant, small grocery store/shop, dry cleaner, gas/petrol station
Schools	one school for children
Religious buildings	church and a mosque
Other buildings	none
Transportation	bus stop, train stop
Parks/gardens	one park with a playground
Special characteristics	friendly neighborhood, very comfortable

Home

1. Our home is medium-sized. It is about fifty years old.
2. We have four bedrooms, two bathrooms, and some other rooms.
3. Our yard is large, with lots of flowers.
4. We have an attic that we use for storage.

Neighborhood

1. We live in a neighborhood called Flower Valley.
2. The neighborhood's homes are older.
3. Many of the homes are large and usually families live in them.
4. We have some stores in the neighborhood, so shopping is convenient.

PRACTICE 2 (PAGE 239)

Answers will vary.

Job Information Form

Company name: Translational International
Job title: Japanese translator
Length of time at this job: 2 years
Duties: translate technical materials
Training required for this job: computer training, using software, training in technical language
Skills required for this job: language skills in English and Japanese, computer skills
Things I like about this job: using language
Things I don't like about this job: can be tiring; requires a lot of concentration
Future career goals: manage a large translation project

Education Information Form

Name of college/university: City University
Major/subject: English literature
Classes I am taking now: Structure of English, World Literature
Hours per week in class: 8
Years to complete degree/certificate: 2
Educational goals: master's degree
Future career goals: teach English and write a book

My occupation: Japanese translator

1. I work as a Japanese translator at Translational International.
2. I have worked there for two years.
3. My main duty is translating technical materials.
4. I like using language skills for my work, but sometimes it can be very tiring. Working as a translator requires a lot of concentration.

PRACTICE 3 (PAGE 241)

Answers will vary.

Hobby/Free-Time Activity Information Form

Hobby/Activity#1 playing computer games

How often do you do this hobby or activity? almost every day

Do you do it on your own or with other people? both

Do you belong to a club related to this hobby/activity? no

How did you learn how to do this hobby/activity?
from friends and from the instructions that come with games

Do you need special equipment for it?
yes, a computer and an Internet connection

What do you like most about it?
fun and I can do it any time of the day or night

Hobby/Activity#2 cooking

How often do you do this hobby or activity? twice a week

Do you do it on your own or with other people? alone/on my own

Do you belong to a club related to this hobby/activity? no

How did you learn how to do this hobby/activity?
watching other people, including TV shows/programs

Do you need special equipment for it?
yes, some cooking equipment

What do you like most about it?
I like trying a new recipe and eating the food.

Hobby/Activity: playing computer games

1. I like playing computer games almost every day.
2. I can play games by myself, or I can go online and play against people who live all over the world.
3. I started playing computer games when I was ten years old.
4. I like being able to play any time. The computer graphics improve every year, and that makes the games more fun.

Skill 2—Organizing a Topic (page 242)

PRACTICE (PAGE 243)

Answers will vary. You should create your own shorthand to write notes quickly.

Topic 1

Pet	Parrot
Kind of animal	An African grey parrot named Sammy
Kind of care	Needed a lot of companionship, twice daily feeding, frequent baths, daily cage cleaning
Liked/didn't like	Liked—he was funny and smart and could talk, and he was affectionate. Didn't like—he was noisy and messy.
Why it is/isn't popular	Not popular—hard to care for and expensive to buy, noisy and messy

Topic 2

Birthday	Maria's party last month
Name and age of celebrant	Maria Montalvo, 23 years old
Who attended	Maria's brothers and cousins, some of our old high school friends, some of Maria's work colleagues
Location	Maria's parents' house because they have a pool and a large garden and patio
Activities	Swimming and water games, dancing, eating, jokes and funny speeches, opening presents

Topic 3

Friend	Karl
When and how met	First day of preschool, we were classmates.
Things did together	Played childhood games, as we grew up did school work together, played soccer, hiking, some traveling
Things in common	Being outdoors, science classes, traveling, grew up together and went to school together
Why important	Friends since early childhood, we know each other very well, know each other's families, rely on each other for support.

Topic 4

Trip	Vancouver last June
Where	Vancouver, BC, Canada, a major Canadian city with many interesting tourist activities
Who	Husband and kids
Why	To visit sister and her family; we visit them every year
Activities	Relaxed and talked together; cooked some big meals; bike riding in the park; walked around Chinatown and Gas Town; anthropology museum

Skill 3—Discussing a Topic (page 245)

PRACTICE (PAGE 245)

Answers will vary.

1. Main Idea — TV show is funny
   - Supporting Detail 1 — The actors are excellent comedians.
   - Supporting Detail 2 — The actors are good at physical comedy.
   - Supporting Detail 3 — The story lines make everyone laugh.

2. Main Idea — We went camping in the woods.
   - Supporting Detail 1 — We slept in tents.
   - Supporting Detail 2 — We cooked over a fire.
   - Supporting Detail 3 — We saw beautiful views and lots of wildlife.

3. Main Idea — We grew up in the same place, and we enjoy the same activities.
   - Supporting Detail 1 — We went to all the same schools.
   - Supporting Detail 2 — We have many of the same friends.
   - Supporting Detail 3 — We like the same music, books, and movies.

4. Main Idea — It's a romance novel that takes place in the 1800s.
   - Supporting Detail 1 — A wealthy woman and a poor man fall in love.
   - Supporting Detail 2 — Their families keep them apart.
   - Supporting Detail 3 — In the end they get married.

Skill 4—Verb Tenses (page 246)

PRACTICE (PAGE 246)

Answers will vary.

1. Present
   People like to visit the house where our first president grew up because it is important to the history of our country.
   The style of architecture is also very interesting.
   People also enjoy learning about daily life 300 years ago.

2. Past
   My first year of secondary school was my favorite because I felt grown up.
   I studied a lot of interesting subjects that year that were new to me.
   I participated in several activities such as the chess club and the student government.

3. Past
   I really hate waiting, so I tried to forget about the delay.
   I went to a nearby café and ordered a big meal.
   I bought a newspaper and read almost every article in it.

4. Present
   Since Center City Mall is one of the biggest malls in the country, you can see hundreds of stores there.
   It also has a fountain on each level, and each fountain is surrounded by pretty plants.
   Besides shopping, you can eat a meal, go to the movies, and even visit a doctor or dentist.

Skill 5—Sequence (page 247)

PRACTICE (PAGE 248)

1. As soon as
2. Then
3. until
4. Finally
5. First
6. By the time
7. then
8. before

Skill 6—Comparing and Contrasting (page 248)

PRACTICE (PAGE 249)

Answers will vary.

1. I think she was the nicest teacher I have ever had.
   She had a lot more patience than many teachers have.
   She also had a more interesting way of explaining things.

2. This party was the same as most parties I go to with my friends.
   The food was similar to the food that is served at most parties.
   The music was exactly the same music my friends and I listen to all the time at home or at school.

3. Unlike many other tourist destinations, this one has no admission charge.
   That's what makes it one of the most popular places to visit.
   But it's also one of the most crowded.

4. I think this program is a lot funnier than most other programs you can see on TV.
   The actors are more talented, and the jokes are better.
   It also has a different style of humor from other programs.

Skill 7—Explaining (page 250)

PRACTICE (PAGE 250)

Answers will vary.

1. I liked this book because I enjoy romance stories. They help me escape from the stresses of everyday life. This was a particularly good book because of the strong characters and the romantic setting in the African jungle.

2. This was my favorite year in school because it was the year I learned to read. Since all my older brothers and sisters could already read, I wanted to read, too. For this reason, I was very proud the day I came home from school and read an entire book (a very short one) to my parents.

3. This area has some of the most beautiful beaches in the world, so people come from all over to enjoy them. They enjoy the beaches because of the warm, calm water and the beautiful tropical scenery. Another reason tourists visit this area is the exciting nightlife.

4. I remember this movie because it's one of the scariest I have ever seen. I couldn't sleep well for several nights because of the nightmares the movie gave me. I don't like being scared, so I don't think I will see another movie like this one.

Skill 8—Describing (page 251)

PRACTICE (PAGE 251)

Answers will vary.

1. Activities: relaxed on the beach, took walks, ate great meals

   Description: Most days, we spent the whole morning relaxing on the beach. In the afternoons, we walked around the town and enjoyed looking at the houses and the boats in the harbor. We ate lots of tasty meals, including fresh fish and different kinds of tropical fruit.

2. Activities: danced, ate, talked to friends

   Description: There was good music, and we danced all night. We ate a big birthday cake with chocolate frosting all over it, and there were five or six kinds of ice cream. We had fun talking with friends we hadn't seen in a long time.

3. Activities: cook, clean house, visit with relatives

   Description: Usually I help my mother cook a kind of spicy soup, which is a traditional food for this holiday. Then we spend all morning cleaning the house and decorating it with special holiday decorations. In the afternoon, our relatives come over for a visit, and we talk about everything we've done since the last time we got together.

Skill 9—Responding to Follow-up Questions (page 252)

PRACTICE (PAGE 252)

Answers will vary.

Notes

Topic 1

1. Dogs and cats—good companions—familiar to everyone
2. Fish—easy to care for—not demanding
3. Rabbit—makes a mess—not friendly
4. Advantage—children have responsibility.
   Disadvantage—parents do work if children don't

Topic 2

1. Celebrate with family and friends, at home or go out
2. flowers, cards, clothes
3. Yes—share with people you love—more important for children
4. Celebrating the new year

Topic 3

1. No—different cities—different lives
2. School, with other friends, sports
3. Fix our cars, eat, watch sports
4. A few good friends, so we're closer

Topic 4

1. Yes—more to see there—yearly visit to family
2. beach—relax, be in warm climate
3. Warm weather, different from where I live
4. Yes, so I can experience new things. Meet people, learn language and culture

Skill 10—Explaining an Issue in Depth (page 254)

PRACTICE (PAGE 255)

Answers will vary.

Topic 2

Notes

1. Main Idea Important for children

Supporting Detail 1	They feel special.
Supporting Detail 2	Helps them grow up
Supporting Detail 3	Encourages them to act older.

2. Main Idea Birthdays are for children.

Supporting Detail 1	Children want to grow up.
Supporting Detail 2	Adults don't want to get old.
Supporting Detail 3	Landmark birthdays

3. Main Idea Loved but not always respected

Supporting Detail 1	Families
Supporting Detail 2	Work
Supporting Detail 3	TV and movies

4. Main Idea Wedding anniversaries; graduations

Supporting Detail 1	Marriage central to society
Supporting Detail 2	Graduation = rite of passage, like birthdays

Sample Discussions

1. In my country, we believe that birthdays are important for children. A child's birthday is the day he gets to feel special and be the center of attention. Birthdays also help children feel like they are growing up and encourage them to act older.

2. Generally, we feel birthdays are for children but not for adults. Children want to grow up. In other words, they want to feel older. Adults, on the other hand, don't want to get old, and a birthday is just a reminder that they are getting older and older. Adults sometimes celebrate landmark birthdays, such as their 30th, 40th, or 50th birthdays. For some adults, those are important birthdays.

3. In my country, older adults may be loved, but they are not always respected. Within a family, for example, the parents and grandparents are loved and cared for. Outside of the family, it is different. At work, people may feel that older people can't do the job as well because their minds are old or because they can't keep up with new technology and work methods. Also, the images we see on TV and in the movies show us that youth is valued over old age.

4. It is common to celebrate wedding anniversaries and school graduations in my country. I think wedding anniversaries are important because marriage is an institution that is central to our society. Graduations from high school and university are not really anniversaries, but they are a celebration of an individual, like birthdays are. And like birthdays, they are a rite of passage into the next phase of life.

Skill 11—Describing an Issue in Depth (page 256)

PRACTICE (PAGE 257)

Answers will vary.

Notes

1. Main Idea Beautiful or interesting places

Supporting Detail 1	Beautiful places—beach, lake
Supporting Detail 2	Interesting places—cities, old towns

2. Main Idea Two weeks—not enough

Supporting Detail 1	Need time to rest
Supporting Detail 2	Need time for self and family

3. Main Idea Camping

Supporting Detail 1	Far from city
Supporting Detail 2	Enjoy nature
Supporting Detail 3	Hiking

4. Main Idea Too many cars

Supporting Detail 1	Crowded roads
Supporting Detail 2	Pollution
Supporting Detail 3	Need public transportation

Sample Discussions

1. I think people generally choose either beautiful or interesting places to visit on their vacations. Some people like to go to beaches or lakes because they are pretty and pleasant places to spend time. Other people like to visit interesting places like cities, where there are a lot of different things to do. They might also visit old towns, where they can see interesting things from the past and learn about history.
2. In my country it is customary to give employees two weeks of vacation time a year, and I think this is not enough. First, people need more than just two weeks out of the whole year to rest and relax. Additionally, people need time away from work when they are not thinking about their jobs and can focus on themselves and their families. Two weeks is a very short amount of time for this.
3. I would spend my ideal vacation camping. The most important reason is that it would take me far away from the city. Also, I like to be in the middle of nature and feel wildlife all around me. I enjoy hiking, too, and I could do a lot of hiking on a camping trip.
4. The major transportation problem in my country is that there are too many cars. One result of this is that the roads are usually very crowded. The traffic moves slowly, and it takes a long time to get anywhere. In addition, the large number of cars causes pollution, which contributes to global warming. This is a very serious problem. One big reason we have this problem with cars is that we don't have adequate public transportation. If we had a better public transportation system, people wouldn't have to drive cars.

Skill 12—Comparing and Contrasting an Issue in Depth (page 258)

PRACTICE (PAGE 259)

Answers will vary.

1. **Similarities**

   A. Still have lots of friends

   Differences

   A. Spend less time with them

   B. Not as close

   C. Mostly about our children

2. **Similarities**
   A. Friendships—important

   Differences:
   A. Women—talk
   B. Men—do

3. **Similarities**
   A. Friendships—always important
   B. Support
   C. Companionship

   Differences
   A. Less face-to-face time
   B. More communication through technology

4. **Similarities**
   (none)

   Differences
   A. Circumstances vs. choice
   B. Common interests
   C. Depth of conversation

Sample Discussions

1. Just the same as when I was younger, I still have lots of friends now. However, my friendships are different. I spend less time with my friends now than I did in the past. Also, the friendships of my youth were closer than they are now. Now my friendships center mostly on our children. My friends and I plan activities that we can do together with the children.

2. I think that for both men and women friendships are important. However, men's and women's friendships are about different things. Women's friendships are about talking, sharing problems and experiences. Men's friendships, on the other hand, are about doing things together.

3. In some ways, friendships are still the same as they have always been. It is still important to have friends. We still rely on our friends for companionship. We still need their support. But, the way we interact with our friends is different. Now we spend less face-to-face time with our friends. We communicate with them more through technological means such as cell phones and the Internet.

4. An acquaintance and a friend are two completely different kinds of people. An acquaintance is someone you know through circumstance—you go to the same school or work for the same company or something like that. A friend, on the other hand, is someone you choose to know because you like that person. The interests you have in common with an acquaintance are superficial, but with a friend you share much more important and meaningful interests. Also, the conversations you have with an acquaintance are never as deep as the conversations you have with a friend.

Skill 13—Giving an In-Depth Opinion (page 260)

PRACTICE (PAGE 261)

Answers will vary.

1. Opinion Disagree—pets are important
   Supporting Detail 1 Deserve nice things
   Supporting Detail 2 Deserve good medical care

2. Opinion Best pet is cat
   Supporting Detail 1 Affectionate
   Supporting Detail 2 Easy to care for

3. Opinion I prefer to have a pet
   Supporting Detail 1 Companionship
   Supporting Detail 2 Good for children
   Supporting Detail 3 Help us with certain things

4. Opinion Children should not have pets
   Supporting Detail 1 Too much responsibility for child
   Supporting Detail 2 Lose interest quickly
   Supporting Detail 3 Might be dangerous

Sample Discussions

1. I disagree that some people spend too much money on their pets. Pets are important, and it is impossible to spend too much on them. To my mind, pets are like another member of the family. They deserve to have nice things and to eat good food, just like anybody else in the family. They also deserve good medical care. It might be expensive to take a pet to the vet, but I believe that if we love our pets, it's worth the money.

2. If I had to choose the best pet, I would choose a cat. The first reason is that cats are very affectionate. They like to sit in your lap and be petted. Additionally, cats are the easiest pets to take care of in my opinion. You only have to feed them once a day and maybe brush them once in a while. They don't require a lot of attention like some other pets do.

3. I prefer to have a pet. To my way of thinking, pets are very important because they provide us with companionship. I also believe that pets are good for children. They help children learn about responsibility and compassion. In addition, pets can help us with certain things. For example, cats chase mice and dogs warn us of danger.

4. In my opinion, children should not have pets, in most cases. In the first place, caring for a pet is too big a responsibility for most young children. In the second place, as much as a child may beg for a pet, it is quite likely that he or she will lose interest in it before too long. This is the nature of children. Additionally, some pets can be dangerous for children. Dogs bite and cats scratch and children don't always understand when they should get out of an irritated animal's way.

Skill 14—Asking for Clarification (page 262)

PRACTICE (PAGE 262)

Answers will vary.

1. Do you mean a friend I have now or a friend from the past?
2. Should I explain it generally or in great detail?
3. Do you want me to talk about close friends or friends in general?
4. Could you explain what you mean by older people?
5. Would you like me to discuss just pets or animals in general?

Skill 15—Delay Tactics (page 263)

PRACTICE (PAGE 263)

Answers will vary.

1. How are my friend and I alike? I've never thought about that before.
2. Why do people like to go there? There are a lot of different reasons.
3. What special things do we do on this day? There are a lot of different ways to answer that.
4. What's a good kind of pet? That's a complicated issue.
5. How did I learn my profession? That's an interesting question.

Skill 16—Avoiding Short Answers (page 264)

PRACTICE (PAGE 264)

Answers will vary.

1. Yes, I do because I'm still a student. When I finish school and get a job, I will look for my own apartment.
2. No, I finished school last year and now I work for an engineering firm.
3. Yes. I think it's a lot easier to maintain than a house, and the location is very convenient.
4. No, not really. I just have one brother and one sister.
5. Yes. I'm learning a lot from my work, but in another year or so I would like to get a job with more responsibilities.

Skill 17—Word Families and Stress (page 265)

PRACTICE (PAGE 265)

1.	politics	politician	politicize	political	politically
2.	imagine	imagination	imagine	imaginative	imaginatively
3.	beauty	beauty	beautify	beautiful	beautifully
4.	agree	agreement	agree	agreeable	agreeably
5.	acid	acid/acidity	acidify	acidic	acidly
6.	quote	quotation	quote	quotable	
7.	act	activity	act	active	actively
8.	energy	energy	energize	energetic	energetically
9.	civil	civility	civilize	civil	civilly
10.	rare	rarity	rarify	rare	rarely

Skill 18—Sentence Stress (page 266)

PRACTICE (PAGE 266)

1. I live in one of the newer neighborhoods in my city.
2. I've been working at the same company for twelve years.
3. I generally don't like parties because I'm a quiet person.
4. There is an excellent view of the ships in the harbor.
5. A statue of the first president of our country stands in the center of the park.

Skill 19—Transition Words and Intonation (page 267)

PRACTICE (PAGE 267)

1. Nevertheless, it's a pleasant place to live.
2. We took a boat ride after we finished at the museum.
3. Next, the birthday cake was served.
4. It's a position that pays well, unlike many jobs in my field.
5. A good friend also helps you when you are in need.

Skill 20—Lists and Intonation (page 268)

PRACTICE (PAGE 268)

1. Cats are affectionate, clean, and smart.
2. In addition to English and my native language, I speak Chinese, Korean, and French.
3. I read a variety of things, such as novels, newspapers, magazines, and journals.
4. This TV program is well-written, well-acted, and funny.
5. We had a very active vacation and played tennis, golf, and volleyball.

7 IELTS Model Tests

ACADEMIC

- → **Model Test 1**
- → **Model Test 2**
- → **Model Test 3**
- → **Model Test 4**

GENERAL TRAINING: Reading and Writing

- → **Model Test 1**
- → **Model Test 2**

Academic
MODEL TEST 1

ANSWER SHEET
Academic Model Test 1

IELTS Listening Answer Sheet

1		✓ 1 ✗	21		✓ 21 ✗
2		2	22		22
3		3	23		23
4		4	24		24
5		5	25		25
6		6	26		26
7		7	27		27
8		8	28		28
9		9	29		29
10		10	30		30
11		11	31		31
12		12	32		32
13		13	33		33
14		14	34		34
15		15	35		35
16		16	36		36
17		17	37		37
18		18	38		38
19		19	39		39
20		20	40		40
				Listening Total	

MODEL TEST 1

Candidate Name ____

International English Language Testing System

LISTENING

Time: Approx. 30 minutes

INSTRUCTIONS TO CANDIDATES

Do not open this booklet until you are told to do so.

Write your name and candidate number in the space at the top of this page.

You should answer all questions.

All the recordings will be played ONCE only.

Write all your answers on the Question Paper.

At the end of the test, you will be given ten minutes to transfer your answers to an Answer Sheet.

Do not remove this booklet from the examination room.

INFORMATION FOR CANDIDATES

There are **40** questions on this question paper.

The test is divided as follows:

Section 1	Questions 1–10
Section 2	Questions 11–20
Section 3	Questions 21–30
Section 4	Questions 31–40

SECTION 1

Track 23

Question 1

Match the time with the event. Write the correct number next to the letter.

Example

A ...2... Today

B .... Next week

C .... Next summer

1 Winston will go to Japan

2 Winston will register at the World Language Academy

3 Winston will study Japanese

Questions 2 and 3

*Choose two letters, **A–F**.*

2 What TWO classes are offered at the World Language Academy?

A Japanese for University Professors
B Japanese for Business Travelers
C Japanese for Tour Guides
D Japanese for Tourists
E Japanese for Language Teachers
F Japanese for Restaurant Workers

*Choose two letters, **A–F**.*

3 In Japan, Mark Winston says he will probably

A go shopping.
B climb mountains.
C attend a business meeting.
D try Japanese cuisine.
E take a university course.
F study with a tutor.

Track 24

Questions 4–8

Complete the schedule below.

Write NO MORE THAN TWO WORDS AND/OR A NUMBER *for each answer.*

Japanese Class Schedule

Morning	Days: Monday–Friday Time: **4** .... Level: Beginner
Afternoon	Days: Monday, Wednesday, Thursday Time: 1:00–3:00 Level: **5** ....
Evening	Days: Monday, Wednesday, Thursday Time: 5:30–7:30 Level: **6** .... Days: **7** .... Time: 7:30–9:30 Level: Advanced
Weekend	Days: Saturday Time: **8** .... Level: Beginner

Questions 9 and 10

*Choose the correct letter, **A, B,** or **C**.*

9 Which class will Mark take?

A

C

B

10 How will he pay?

A

B

C

SECTION 2

Questions 11–13

Sumner Mansion

Notice to Visitors

The following activities are prohibited inside the mansion:

- Talking on cell phones
- **11** ....
- **12** ....
- **13** ....

Thank you, and enjoy your visit!

Questions 14–18

Fill in the missing information on the map of Sumner Mansion. Write NO MORE THAN THREE WORDS *for each answer.*

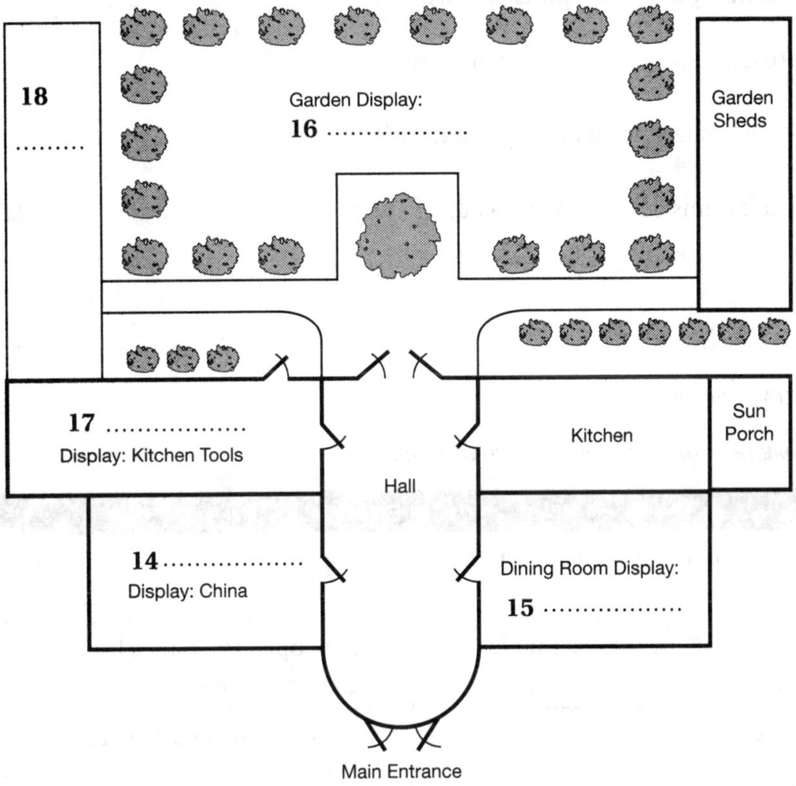

Questions 19–20

Complete the schedule below. Write NO MORE THAN THREE WORDS AND/OR A NUMBER *for each answer.*

Sumner Mansion Hours

Spring:	10 AM to **19** ....
Summer:	10 AM to **20** ....
Autumn:	10 AM to 3 PM.

Closed winters.

SECTION 3

Questions 21–23

Complete the sentences below.

Write NO MORE THAN THREE WORDS *for each answer.*

21 There are high-speed trains in Japan and ....

22 The first high-speed train began operating in ....

23 High-speed trains can travel at speeds of at least .... kilometers an hour.

Questions 24–26

Complete the table below.

Write NO MORE THAN THREE WORDS *for each answer.*

Cause	Effect
We have better roads now than in the past.	More people **24** ....
Now we have plane service that is more **25**	More people use planes for long-distance travel.
There is a lot of **26**	We need to consider new forms of transportation.

Questions 27–30

Choose FOUR *letters,* ***A–G****.*

What are the advantages of trains over other types of transportation according to the people on the panel?

A They are less expensive than cars.

B They are more relaxing than cars.

C They are less polluting than cars.

D They don't cause traffic jams.

E They have better security systems than planes.

F They have a greater capacity for passengers than planes.

G They offer more frequent service than planes.

SECTION 4

Questions 31–40

Complete the timeline below.

Write NO MORE THAN THREE WORDS AND/OR ONE NUMBER *for each answer.*

1879	Einstein was born in **31** ....
At age 12	Einstein began **32** ....
33	Einstein's family moved to Italy
34	Einstein graduated from high school
35	Einstein met Mileva Maric
1900	Einstein received **36** ....
1901	Einstein became **37** ....
1902	Einstein began work at the Swiss Patent Office
	Einstein **38** ....
39	Einstein and Mileva Maric got married
40	Einstein's first son was born

ACADEMIC MODEL TEST 1

ANSWER SHEET
Academic Model Test 1

IELTS Reading Answer Sheet

		✓		✗
1			1	
2			2	
3			3	
4			4	
5			5	
6			6	
7			7	
8			8	
9			9	
10			10	
11			11	
12			12	
13			13	
14			14	
15			15	
16			16	
17			17	
18			18	
19			19	
20			20	

		✓		✗
21			21	
22			22	
23			23	
24			24	
25			25	
26			26	
27			27	
28			28	
29			29	
30			30	
31			31	
32			32	
33			33	
34			34	
35			35	
36			36	
37			37	
38			38	
39			39	
40			40	
	Reading Total			

MODEL TEST 1

Candidate Name ______________________________

International English Language Testing System

ACADEMIC READING

Time: 1 hour

INSTRUCTIONS TO CANDIDATES

Do not open this booklet until you are told to do so.

Write your name and candidate number in the space at the top of this page.

Start at the beginning of the test and work through it.

You should answer all questions.

If you cannot do a particular question, leave it and go on to the next. You can return to it later.

All answers must be written on the Answer Sheet.

Do not remove this booklet from the examination room.

INFORMATION FOR CANDIDATES

There are **40** questions on this question paper.

The test is divided as follows:

Reading Passage 1	Questions 1–13
Reading Passage 2	Questions 14–26
Reading Passage 3	Questions 27–40

Reading Passage 1

You should spend about 20 minutes on questions 1–13, which are based on Reading Passage 1 below.

Alternative Transportation

A Transportation is a major issue in urban areas around the world. Rising fuel costs, environmental problems, and traffic-clogged roads are some of the concerns that have led people to consider alternative forms of transportation.

B Fuel-efficient cars and cars that run on alternative sources of energy are receiving increasing interest as people become more concerned about the costs of using gasoline. These costs include not only the ever increasing price of filling up a car's fuel tank but also the environmental costs of emitting huge amounts of car exhaust into the atmosphere. Climate change is an issue of global concern. Closer to home, cities have to consider the effects on the health of their citizens. Car emissions have been linked to a range of health problems, particularly respiratory problems. For example, studies have linked childhood asthma and stunted lung growth to exposure to car exhaust in the air. Research has also made connections between car emissions and heart disease, certain cancers, and immune system problems.

C The popularity of smaller, more fuel efficient cars is on the rise. Hybrid vehicles are also becoming more common. These cars have two engines—one that is battery powered and one that is gasoline powered. The battery-powered engine gets the car moving from a standstill. Once the car reaches a certain speed, the gasoline engine, which is more efficient at higher speeds, takes over to keep the car moving. There is also a growing interest in cars that are completely battery powered. These are cars that would be plugged into an electric outlet to recharge when not in use. Many consider such vehicles to be the car of the future. However, as long as the electricity is generated by coal-burning plants, as is often the case, these cars cannot be considered as using clean energy. Solar cars and hydrogen cars are other "clean" technologies that are receiving attention and hopes for the future.

D Car emissions are the most serious source of concern, but the sheer number of vehicles on the road—over 250 million in the United States alone and over one billion worldwide—has other repercussions, as well. The roads and highways that are built to accommodate the growing number of cars in use are a source of pollution themselves. Ground that is covered with pavement cannot absorb rainwater, thus motor oil and other pollutants are washed off the roads and into lakes, rivers, and the ocean. Chemicals, herbicides, concrete, asphalt, paint, and other materials that are used during road construction also contribute to environmental pollution.

E Personal convenience and health are also affected. While private cars are seen as a convenient way to get from place to place, crowded roads mean traffic moves much more slowly, making it difficult to travel, especially during "rush hour" periods. And people who spend hours each day sitting in cars stuck in traffic are not standing up, moving around, or getting any sort of exercise, a situation that can lead to a variety of health problems.

F Thus, in addition to developing passenger cars that run on alternative sources of fuel, we also need to look at alternative forms of transportation. These would include walking, bicycle riding, car pooling, and various types of public transportation. The benefits of walking and cycling are obvious. They cause no pollution and improve physical health. Car pools—several people sharing a ride in a private car—mean fewer cars on the road and allow the riders to share the expenses involved. Public transportation—buses, subways, commuter trains—has many benefits, as well. For one, it may provide users with opportunities for physical exercise as people have to get from their homes to the bus stops and train stations, and this is often done on foot. There are also mental health benefits, as relaxing on a train or bus while reading the newspaper or listening to music is a good deal less stressful than driving one's own car through rush hour traffic. All of these forms of transportation decrease the number of cars on the roads and greatly reduce emissions. Looking toward the future, cities need to pay as much attention, or more, to public transportation and to accommodating walkers and cyclists as they do to building roads and accommodating drivers of passenger cars.

Questions 1–5

*Reading Passage 1 has six paragraphs labeled **A–F**.*
Which paragraphs contain the following information?

*Write the correct letter **A–F** in boxes 1–5 on your Answer Sheet.*

You may use any letter more than once.

1 problems caused to individuals by traffic-clogged roads

2 environmental effects of highways

3 how hybrid cars work

4 how public transportation contributes to improved physical and mental health

5 environmental and health problems resulting from car exhaust

Questions 6–13

Do the following statements agree with the views of the writer in the passage? In boxes 6–13 on your Answer Sheet, write

YES *if the statement agrees with the views of the writer.*
NO *if the statement contradicts the views of the writer.*
NOT GIVEN *if it is impossible to say what the writer thinks about this.*

6 Car emissions can contribute to illnesses of the respiratory system.

7 Cars are the largest source of environmental pollution in the modern world.

8 People are becoming more interested in hybrid cars.

9 Electric cars don't pollute the environment.

10 Solar-powered cars are currently too expensive for the average person to own.

11 Roads and highways contribute to water pollution.

12 Bicycle riding has health benefits.

13 Car pools can reduce individuals' transportation costs.

Reading Passage 2

You should spend about 20 minutes on questions 14–26, which are based on Reading Passage 2 below.

Less Television, Less Violence and Aggression

Cutting back on television, videos, and video games reduces acts of aggression among schoolchildren, according to a study by Dr. Thomas Robinson and others from the Stanford University School of Medicine.

The study, published in the January 2001 issue of the *Archives of Pediatric and Adolescent Medicine,* found that third- and fourth-grade students who took part in a curriculum to reduce their TV, video, and video game use engaged in fewer acts of verbal and physical aggression than their peers.

The study took place in two similar San Jose, California, elementary schools. Students in one school underwent an 18-lesson, 6-month program designed to limit their media usage, while the others did not.

Both groups of students had similar reports of aggressive behavior at the beginning of the study. After the six-month program, however, the two groups had very real differences.

The students who cut back on their TV time engaged in six fewer acts of verbal aggression per hour and rated 2.4 percent fewer of their classmates as aggressive after the program.

Physical acts of violence, parental reports of aggressive behavior, and perceptions of a mean and scary world also decreased, but the authors suggest further study to solidify these results.

Although many studies have shown that children who watch a lot of TV are more likely to act violently, this report further verifies that television, videos, and video games actually cause the violent behavior, and it is among the first to evaluate a solution to the problem.

Teachers at the intervention school included the program in their existing curriculum. Early lessons encouraged students to keep track of and report on the time they spent watching TV or videos, or playing video games, to motivate them to limit those activities on their own.

The initial lessons were followed by TV-Turnoff, an organization that encourages less TV viewing. For ten days, students were challenged to go without television, videos, or video games. After that, teachers encouraged the students to stay within a media allowance of seven hours per week. Almost all students participated in the Turnoff, and most stayed under their budget for the following weeks.

Additional lessons encouraged children to use their time more selectively, and many of the final lessons had students themselves advocate reducing screen activities.

This study is by no means the first to find a link between television and violence. Virtually all of 3,500 research studies on the subject in the past 40 years have shown the same relationship, according to the American Academy of Pediatrics.

Among the most noteworthy studies is Dr. Leonard D. Eron's, which found that exposure to television violence in childhood is the strongest predictor of aggressive behavior later in life—stronger even than violent behavior as children.

The more violent television the subjects watched at age eight, the more serious was their aggressive behavior even 22 years later.

Another study by Dr. Brandon S. Centerwall found that murder rates climb after the introduction of television. In the United States and Canada, murder rates doubled 10 to 15 years after the introduction of television, after the first TV generation grew up.

Centerwall tested this pattern in South Africa, where television broadcasts were banned until 1975.

Murder rates in South Africa remained relatively steady from the mid-1940s through the mid-1970s. By 1987, however, the murder rate had increased 130 percent from its 1974 level. The murder rates in the United States and Canada had leveled[1] off in the meantime.

Centerwall's study implies that the medium of television, not just the content, promotes violence, and the current study by Dr. Robinson supports that conclusion.

The Turnoff did not specifically target violent television, nor did the following allowance period. Reducing television in general reduces aggressive behavior.

Even television that is not "violent" is more violent than real life and may lead viewers to believe that violence is funny, inconsequential, and a viable solution to problems. Also, watching television of any content robs us of the time to interact with real people.

Watching too much TV may inhibit the skills and patience we need to get along with others without resorting to aggression. TV, as a medium, promotes aggression and violence. The best solution is to turn it off.

Questions 14–20

Complete the summary using words from the box below.

Write your answers in boxes 14–20 on your Answer Sheet.

parents	scared	time of day
teachers	less TV	number of hours
six months	eighteen days	avoided TV
violently	classmates	favorite[2] programs
watched TV	nonviolent programs	

A study that was published in January 2001 found that when children **14** .... less, they behaved less **15** .... Students in a California elementary school participated in the study, which lasted **16** .... By the end of the study, the children's behavior had changed. For example, the children's **17** .... reported that the children were acting less violently than before. During the study, the children kept a record of the **18** .... they watched TV. Then, for ten days, they **19** .... Near the end of the study, the students began to suggest watching **20** ....

[1]BRITISH: levelled

[2]BRITISH: favourite

Questions 21–24

Do the following statements agree with the information in Reading Passage 2?

In boxes 21–24 on your Answer Sheet, write

TRUE	*if the statement is true according to the passage.*
FALSE	*if the statement contradicts the passage.*
NOT GIVEN	*if there is no information about this in the passage.*

21 Only one study has found a connection between TV and violent behavior.

22 There were more murders in Canada after people began watching TV.

23 The United States has more violence on TV than other countries.

24 TV was introduced in South Africa in the 1940s.

Questions 25 and 26

For each question, choose the correct letter ***A–D*** *and write it in boxes 25 and 26 on your Answer Sheet.*

25 According to the passage,

A only children are affected by violence on TV.
B only violent TV programs cause violent behavior.
C children who watch too much TV get poor grades in school.
D watching a lot of TV may keep us from learning important social skills.

26 The authors of this passage believe that

A some violent TV programs are funny.
B the best plan is to stop watching TV completely.
C it's better to watch TV with other people than on your own.
D seven hours a week of TV watching is acceptable.

Reading Passage 3

You should spend about 20 minutes on questions 27–40, which are based on Reading Passage 3 below.

Questions 27–30

*Reading Passage 3 has four sections (**A–D**). Choose the most suitable heading for each section from the list of headings below.*

*Write the appropriate numbers (**i–vii**) in boxes 27–30 on your Answer Sheet. There are more headings than sections, so you will not use all of them.*

List of Headings

i Top Ocean Predators
ii Toxic Exposure
iii Declining Fish Populations
iv Pleasure Boating in the San Juan Islands
v Underwater Noise
vi Smog in Large Cities
vii Impact of Boat Traffic

27 Section A

28 Section B

29 Section C

30 Section D

Issues Affecting the Southern Resident Orcas

A

Orcas, also known as killer whales, are opportunistic feeders, which means they will take a variety of different prey species. J, K, and L pods (specific groups of orcas found in the region) are almost exclusively fish eaters. Some studies show that up to 90 percent of their diet is salmon, with chinook salmon being far and away their favorite. During the last 50 years, hundreds of wild runs of salmon have become extinct due to habitat loss and overfishing of wild stocks. Many of the extinct salmon stocks are the winter runs of chinook and coho. Although the surviving stocks have probably been sufficient to sustain the resident pods, many of the runs that have been lost were undoubtedly traditional resources favored by the resident orcas. This may be affecting the whales' nutrition in the winter and may require them to change their patterns of movement in order to search for food.

Other studies with tagged whales have shown that they regularly dive up to 800 feet in this area. Researchers tend to think that during these deep dives the whales may be feeding on bottomfish. Bottomfish species in this area would include halibut, rockfish, lingcod, and greenling. Scientists estimate that today's lingcod population in northern Puget Sound and the Strait of Georgia is only 2 percent of what it was in 1950. The average size of rockfish in the recreational catch has also declined by several inches since the 1970s, which is indicative of overfishing. In some locations, certain rockfish species have disappeared entirely. So even if bottomfish are not a major food resource for the whales, the present low numbers of available fish increases the pressure on orcas and all marine animals to find food. (For more information on bottomfish see the San Juan County Bottomfish Recovery Program.)

B

Toxic substances accumulate in higher concentrations as they move up the food chain. Because orcas are the top predator in the ocean and are at the top of several different food chains in the environment, they tend to be more affected by pollutants than other sea creatures. Examinations of stranded killer whales have shown some extremely high levels of lead, mercury, and polychlorinated hydrocarbons. Abandoned marine toxic waste dumps and present levels of industrial and human refuse pollution of the inland waters probably presents the most serious threat to the continued existence of this orca population. Unfortunately, the total remedy to this huge problem would be broad societal changes on many fronts. But because of the fact that orcas are so popular, they may be the best species to use as a focal point in bringing about the many changes that need to be made in order to protect the marine environment as a whole from further toxic poisoning.

C

The waters around the San Juan Islands are extremely busy due to international commercial shipping, fishing, whale watching, and pleasure boating. On a busy weekend day in the summer, it is not uncommon to see numerous boats in the vicinity of the whales as they travel through the area. The potential impacts from all this vessel traffic with regard to the whales and other marine animals in the area could be tremendous.

The surfacing and breathing space of marine birds and mammals is a critical aspect of their habitat, which the animals must consciously deal with on a moment-to-moment basis throughout their lifetimes. With all the boating activity in the vicinity, there are three ways in which surface impacts are most likely to affect marine animals: (a) collision, (b) collision avoidance, and (c) exhaust emissions in breathing pockets.

The first two impacts are very obvious and don't just apply to vessels with motors. Kayakers even present a problem here because they're so quiet. Marine animals, busy hunting and feeding under the surface of the water, may not be aware that there is a kayak above them and actually hit the bottom of it as they surface to breathe.

The third impact is one most people don't even think of. When there are numerous boats in the area, especially idling boats, there are a lot of exhaust fumes being spewed out on the surface of the water. When the whale comes up to take a nice big breath of "fresh" air, it instead gets a nice big breath of exhaust fumes. It's hard to say how greatly this affects the animals, but think how breathing polluted air affects us (i.e., smog in large cities like Los Angeles, breathing the foul air while sitting in traffic jams, etc.).

D

Similar to surface impacts, a primary source of acoustic pollution for this population of orcas would also be derived from the cumulative underwater noise of vessel traffic. For cetaceans, the underwater sound environment is perhaps the most critical component of their sensory and behavioral lives. Orcas communicate with each other over short and long distances with a variety of clicks, chirps, squeaks, and whistles, along with using echolocation to locate prey and to navigate. They may also rely on passive listening as a primary sensory source. The long-term impacts from noise pollution would not likely show up as noticeable behavioral changes in habitat use, but rather as sensory damage or gradual reduction in population health. A new study at The Whale Museum called the SeaSound Remote Sensing Network has begun studying underwater acoustics and its relationship to orca communication.

Questions 31–32

For each question, choose the appropriate letter ***A–D*** *and write it in boxes 31 and 32 on your Answer Sheet.*

31 Killer whales (orcas) in the J, K, and L pods prefer to eat

- **A** halibut.
- **B** a type of salmon.
- **C** a variety of animals.
- **D** fish living at the bottom of the sea.

32 Some groups of salmon have become extinct because

- **A** they have lost places to live.
- **B** whales have eaten them.
- **C** they don't get good nutrition.
- **D** the winters in the area are too cold.

Questions 33–40

Complete the table below.
Choose NO MORE THAN THREE WORDS *from the passage for each answer.*

Write your answers in boxes 33–40 on your Answer Sheet.

Cause	Effect
Scientists believe some whales feed **33**	These whales dive very deep.
Scientists believe that the area is being overfished.	The size of rockfish caught today **34** .... since the 1970s.
Orcas are at the top of the ocean food chain.	**35** .... affect orcas more than they affect other sea animals.
Orcas are a **36** .... species.	We can use orcas to make society aware of the problem of marine pollution.
People enjoy boating, fishing, and whale watching in the San Juan Islands.	On weekends there are **37** .... near the whales.
Kayaks are **38**	Marine animals hit them when they come up for air.
A lot of boats keep their motors running.	Whales breathe **39** ....
Boats are noisy.	It is difficult for orcas to **40** ....

ANSWER SHEET
Academic Model Test 1

Writing Answer Sheet

TASK 1

ANSWER SHEET
Academic Model Test 1

-2-

ANSWER SHEET
Academic Model Test 1

-3-

TASK 2

ANSWER SHEET
Academic Model Test 1

-4-

MODEL TEST 1

Candidate Name ____________________

International English Language Testing System

ACADEMIC WRITING

Time: 1 hour

INSTRUCTIONS TO CANDIDATES

Do not open this booklet until you are told to do so.

Write your name and candidate number in the space at the top of this page.

All answers must be written on the separate answer booklet provided.

Do not remove this booklet from the examination room.

INFORMATION FOR CANDIDATES

There are **2** tasks on this question paper.

You must do **both** tasks.

Underlength answers will be penalized.

Writing Task 1

You should spend about 20 minutes on this task.

> ***The table below shows the sales at a small restaurant in a downtown business district.***
>
> ***Summarize the information by selecting and reporting the main features, and make comparisons where relevant.***

Write at least 150 words.

Sales: Week of October 7–13

	Mon.	Tues.	Wed.	Thurs.	Fri.	Sat.	Sun.
Lunch	$2,400	$2,450	$2,595	$2,375	$2,500	$1,950	$1,550
Dinner	$3,623	$3,850	$3,445	$3,800	$4,350	$2,900	$2,450

Writing Task 2

You should spend about 40 minutes on this task.

Write about the following topic:

> ***As the world becomes technologically advanced, computers are replacing people at more and more jobs.***
>
> ***What are some job positions that may be lost because of computers? What are some problems that may result from this situation?***

Give reasons for your answer and include any relevant examples from your own knowledge or experience.

Write at least 250 words.

SPEAKING

Examiner questions:

Part 1 (4–5 minutes)

Sports

Tell about a sport that is interesting to you. What is it? Do you like to play this sport yourself? Do you follow professional teams?

Why do you like this sport?

Do you enjoy playing sports or doing other outdoor activities? Why or why not?

In your city or town, what kinds of places are available for sports and other outdoor activities?

What kinds of things do you enjoy doing on weekends?

Do you generally prefer to spend a day off from work or school at home, or do you like to go out to other places? Why?

Who do you like to spend time with on your days off?

Part 2 (3–5 minutes)

You will be given a topic. You will have one to two minutes to talk about this topic. You will have one minute to prepare what you are going to say. You may take some notes if you wish. Here is your topic:

> Describe a relative who you are like.
>
> You should say:
>
> who the relative is and how close you are to them
>
> what makes you and your relative alike
>
> why you think you and your relative have these shared qualities
>
> and describe what you enjoy about your relationship with your relative

Part 3 (4–5 minutes)

Spending Time with Relatives

Do you enjoy spending time with relatives? Why or why not?

What types of traditions do you and your relatives have?

The Importance of Family

Do you think family members are more important than friends? Why or why not?

Do you think having a good relationship with relatives is important to most people? Why or why not?

How do family members help each other?

The Changing Family

Do you think that families are as important as they used to be?

How are families now different from families in the past?

How do you think families will change in the future?

ACADEMIC MODEL TEST 1—ANSWER EXPLANATIONS

LISTENING

1. (A)—2 In Winston's first full exchange, he says he would like to *sign up now*, which means he would like to *register for a class today*.
(B)—3 In the same exchange, he says he wants to register for the classes that begin *next week*.
(C)—1 Winston says, "I'm planning to take a vacation/holiday in Japan next summer. . . ."
2. (B) and (D) either order. The receptionist mentions only three types of courses offered at World Language Academy—Japanese for Tourists, Japanese for Business Travelers, and Japanese for University Students. Two of these courses are included in the answer possibilities (B) and (D). Choice (A) is incorrect because a course is for university students, not professors. Choice (C) is incorrect because the course is for tourists, not tour guides. Choice (E) is incorrect because the speaker talks about native teachers of Japanese as teachers. Choice (F) is incorrect because this type of course is not offered, and Mark is planning on eating, not working, in Japanese restaurants.
3. (A) and (D) either order. The student's reasons for learning Japanese are to order food in a restaurant and go shopping. Winston says, "I just want to learn enough to order food in restaurants and go shopping and things like that." Choice (B) *climbing mountains* is mentioned by the receptionist about what she had done in Japan and is therefore incorrect. Choices (C) and (E) confuse *business meeting* and *university course* with the topics of classes offered at the academy. Choice (F) is incorrect because the student does not want to learn with a tutor. Studying with a tutor is mentioned only as a possibility of how he can achieve his goal of learning basic Japanese.

4–8. The schedule for Japanese classes is as follows:
Beginner: Monday, Tuesday, Wednesday, Thursday, Friday 9:00–10:00 A.M.
Beginner: Monday, Wednesday, Thursday 5:30–7:30
Beginner: Saturday 9:00–2:00
Intermediate: Monday, Wednesday, Thursday 1:00–3:00
Advanced: Tuesday, Thursday 7:30–9:30

4. 9:00–10:00 A.M.
5. Intermediate
6. Beginner
7. Tuesday, Thursday
8. 9:00–2:00
9. (B) Choice (B) is the correct answer because the student decided to take the Saturday class. It meets from 9:00 to 2:00, and the receptionist says it will have only four or five people in it. Choice (A) is incorrect because the student only has evenings and weekends free, but the student cannot take the night classes they offer because the level is too advanced. Choice (C) is incorrect because the student says that a private class is too expensive for him.
10. (A) Choice (A) is correct because the student asks if he can pay by check, and the receptionist says he can. Choice (B) is incorrect because the student decides to pay by check. The receptionist does say that payment *can* be made by credit card or check.

11–13. *Taking photographs. Eating. Drinking.* The tour guide says: "...we ask that you not take photographs inside the building, and please turn off your cell phones during the tour. Also we request that you refrain from eating as well as drinking inside the mansion."

14. *Living room* or *Main living room.* The tour guide says: "To the left of the entrance is the main living room. . . . Here you can see on display the elegant chinaware used for their parties."
15. *Art.* The Sumner art collection is displayed in the dining room, to the right of the main entrance.
16. *Roses.* The tour guide explains: "Right now you can see a spectacular display of roses."
17. *Café.* The café is behind the living room and contains a display of kitchen tools.
18. *Parking area.* The tour guide explains: "Remember that the parking area is just beyond the café."

19. *5 P.M.* "The grounds close at five PM as we are still on our spring schedule."
20. *8 P.M.* "If you come back next week, the summer schedule will have started and we'll be open a full ten hours a day from ten in the morning until eight in the evening."
21. *several European countries/Europe.* These trains are having a great deal of success in Japan and in several European countries, as well.
22. *1964.* "They've actually been around for a while—since 1964, in fact."
23. *200.* "We usually call a train high speed if it's capable of traveling at 200 kilometers/kilometres an hour or faster."
24. *drive (cars).* "Cars and highways were improved, so more and more people started driving cars."
25. *frequent and affordable.* "Plane service is more frequent and affordable now than it was in the past, so planes, like cars, have become more convenient for people."
26. *congestion.* "But with everybody driving cars and taking planes, we have a lot of congestion."

27–30. (B), (D), (F), and (G) are correct.

(B) "But, a train trip is much more relaxing than a car trip. You can read, sleep, eat, whatever, while the train carries you to your destination."

(D) "And of course you're never delayed by traffic jams."

(F) "Also trains can carry more passengers than planes."

(G) "They can also offer more frequent service."

(A) is incorrect because the speaker says that train trips are sometimes more expensive than car trips. (C) is incorrect because the speaker does not discuss pollution from trains or other forms of transportation. (E) confuses security systems on trains with going through security at the airport.

31. *Germany.* Paragraph 2: "Albert Einstein was born in Germany in 1879."
32. *to study* or *studying math(s)/mathematics.* Paragraph 3: "He didn't even begin to study mathematics until he was 12."
33. *at age 15.* Paragraph 5: "When Einstein was 15, his family moved to Italy."
34. *1896.* Paragraph 5: " Soon after that, his parents sent him to Switzerland, where in 1896 he finished high school."
35. *1898.* Paragraph 5: "In 1898, he met and fell in love with a young Serbian woman, Mileva Maric."
36. *a teaching diploma.* Paragraph 5: "After graduating from high school, he enrolled in a Swiss technological institute. He received a teaching diploma from the institute in 1900."
37. *a Swiss citizen.* Paragraph 5: "He remained in Switzerland and eventually became a Swiss citizen, in 1901."
38. *had a daughter.* Paragraph 7: ". . . he and Mileva had their first child, a daughter. . . ."
39. *1903.* Paragraph 7: ". . . they didn't actually get married until 1903."
40. *1904.* Paragraph 7: ". . . they didn't actually get married until 1903. Their son was born the following year."

READING

Passage 1—Alternative Transportation

1. E. Paragraph E explains how "personal convenience and health" are affected by crowded roads.
2. D. Paragraph D explains how highways are a source of pollution.
3. C. Paragraph C discusses both hybrid and electric cars.
4. F. Paragraph F describes how public transportation provides opportunities for physical exercise and relaxation.
5. B. Paragraph B discusses environmental pollution and diseases caused by car exhaust.
6. Y. Paragraph 2: "Car emissions have been linked to a range of health problems, particularly respiratory problems. For example, studies have linked childhood asthma and stunted lung growth to exposure to car exhaust in the air."

7. Not Given. The author mentions pollution caused by cars but doesn't compare this to other sources of pollution.
8. Yes. Paragraph 3: "Hybrid vehicles are also becoming more common."
9. No. Paragraph 3: "However, as long as the electricity is generated by coal-burning plants, as is often the case, these cars cannot be considered as using clean energy."
10. Not Given. Solar-powered cars are mentioned in paragraph 3, but there is no mention of their cost.
11. Yes. Paragraph 4: "The roads and highways that are built to accommodate the growing number of cars in use are a source of pollution themselves."
12. Yes. Paragraph 6: "The benefits of walking and cycling are obvious. They cause no pollution and improve physical health."
13. Yes. Paragraph 6: "Car pools—several people sharing a ride in a private car—means fewer cars on the road and allows the riders to share the expenses involved."

Passage 2—Less Television, Less Violence and Aggression

14. *watched TV.* Paragraph 2: The study found that the third- and fourth-grade students "engaged in fewer acts of verbal and physical aggression than their peers" when they watched less TV.
15. *violently.* Paragraph 2: The study found that the third- and fourth-grade students "engaged in fewer acts of verbal and physical aggression than their peers" when they watched less TV.
16. *6/six months.* Paragraph 3: "18-lesson, 6-month program"
17. *parents.* Paragraph 6: "parental reports of aggressive behavior, and perceptions of a mean and scary world also decreased"
18. *number of hours.* Paragraph 8: "Early lessons encouraged students to keep track of and report on the time they spent watching TV or videos, or playing video games, to motivate them to limit those activities on their own."
19. *avoided TV.* Paragraph 9: "For ten days, students were challenged to go without television, videos, or video games."
20. *less TV.* Paragraph 10 states that "students themselves [began to] advocate reducing screen activities."
21. False. Paragraph 11 states that "This study is by no means the first to find a link."
22. True. Paragraph 14 states that "In the United States and Canada, murder rates doubled."
23. Not Given. Paragraph 14 discusses TV and violence in the United States and Canada, but there is no discussion about which country has more, or if the United States has more than other countries.
24. Not Given. Regarding South Africa, we are given information about how long TV was banned—until 1975 (Paragraph 15)—and that murder rates were steady in the 1940s, but the text does not say when TV was introduced in South Africa.
25. (D) In the second to last paragraph, the text states that "watching television of any content robs us of the time to interact with real people," which can be seen as learning an important social skill. (A), (B), and (C) are incorrect because the text does not address the role of TV for adults (A), does not suggest that TV is the *only* cause of violence (B), and does not make any comparisons between the United States and other countries (C).
26. (B) In the last line, the authors suggest that "[t]he best solution is to turn it [the TV] off." Choice (A) is incorrect because the authors do not discuss humor[1] in TV programs. Choice (C) is incorrect because they do not talk about watching TV alone or with company. Choice (D) is incorrect because the text says in paragraph 9 that the children were encouraged to keep their TV watching time to under seven hours, but that is not suggested as an ideal amount for the reader.

[1]British: humour

Passage 3—Issues Affecting the Southern Resident Orcas

27. iii—Declining Fish Populations is the correct answer. Section A discusses the decrease of fish populations, which affect the diet of the orcas. In the last line of the first paragraph, "This may be affecting . . .," *this* refers to declining fish populations. In addition, there is no other heading listed that can describe the idea of Section A.
28. ii—Toxic Exposure is the correct answer. The first line of Section B starts with "Toxic substances accumulate . . . ," which indicates that the section is about toxic substances. Further reading of the section shows supporting evidence for the topic sentence. Heading (i) is mentioned in the section, but it is not the central idea of the section.
29. vii—Impact of Boat Traffic is the correct answer. Again, the first line of Section C states: "waters around the San Juan Islands are extremely busy due to international commercial shipping, fishing, whale watching, and pleasure boating," and the section goes on to talk about the dangers of various types of boats. The fourth paragraph in Section C mentions "smog" as being similar to the exhaust of idle boat traffic. Also, heading (iv) describes *one* type of boating mentioned in the section.
30. v—Underwater Noise is the correct answer. The first line introduces the idea of "acoustic pollution," suggesting the theme of noise. In the section, there are five additional mentions of "noise," or synonyms of noise: noise, sound, listening, noise, acoustics. Choice (v) is the only logical heading for this section.
31. (B) In section A the text states "90 percent of their [orcas'] diet is salmon." (A) and (D) are both secondary choices for the orcas if there are no salmon, and the orcas must eat from the bottom of the ocean and (C) is true for all orcas, but not for the pods specified in the question—J, K, and L—who eat mostly fish, and the fish they prefer is salmon.
32. (A) Section A states that "salmon have become extinct due to habitat loss." Whales only eat the surviving stocks of salmon after they have already decreased in numbers, so (B) is incorrect; it is *whales* and not the *salmon* that have poor nutrition, making (C) incorrect. Choice (D) assumes that the "winter" is a temperature indicator when it is actually a seasonal adjective and does not describe temperature as being cold.
33. *on bottomfish.* Section A, paragraph 2: "whales may be feeding on bottomfish" becomes "they believe the whales *feed* on bottomfish."
34. *has declined.* Section A states: "The average size of rockfish . . . has also declined . . . . Since the 1970s, which is indicative of overfishing."
35. *Pollutants* or *toxic substances.* Section B states that orcas are affected more by pollutants than other creatures because they are at the top of the food chain.
36. *popular.* The last sentence of section B says: "because orcas are so popular."
37. *numerous boats.* Paragraph 1 in section C states that: "On a busy weekend day in the summer, it is not uncommon to see numerous boats in the vicinity of the whales as they travel through the area."
38. *(so) quiet.* Paragraph 3 of section C says: "Kayakers even present a problem here because they're so quiet."
39. *exhaust fumes.* Paragraph 4 of section C says that whales "get a nice big breath of exhaust fumes."
40. *communicate with each other.* Section D discusses how noise pollution contributes to orca communication.

WRITING

Sample Responses

Writing Task 1

The chart shows the sales at a small restaurant during the week of October 7 to 13. As can be seen, sales followed a fairly set pattern from Monday to Friday and then showed a notable shift on the weekend. Weekday lunch and dinner sales peaked on Friday, then dipped down on the weekend.

Lunch sales during this week averaged approximately $2,400. The highest lunch sales occurred on Friday and the lowest on Sunday. Sunday's lunch sales were approximately $1,000 less than the weekday average.

Dinner sales, which averaged at least $1,000 to $1,500 higher than lunch sales, also remained steady during the week, peaked on Friday, and dipped down on the weekend.

Excluding Wednesday and Thursday, lunch and dinner sales rose gradually until the end of the work week. Midweek they were slightly lower than they were on Tuesday.

The most profitable day during the week shown was Friday and the least profitable was Sunday. Sunday's lunch and dinner sales combined were less than Friday's dinner sales only.

Writing Task 2

People have welcomed computers as a means of making work easier. At the same time however, computers have also eliminated many jobs by making the human worker obsolete. On the other hand, the job performance of computers is often less than adequate.

A number of jobs have been lost as a direct result of computer technology. Human ticket agents, for example, are virtually nonexistent these days. The number of bank tellers has also been greatly reduced due to automated bank machines. Customer service help lines are almost entirely automated. A few years ago, I worked as an assistant at a library. Today that position doesn't exist because the library has installed computers that do most of the same work I did. The number of positions lost to computers continues to grow, along with unemployment.

While computers can easily carry out routine tasks, they often fall short when a customer has a unique request or problem. An automated ticket agent doesn't have insight about an entertainment district and can't offer friendly directions to a tourist. An automated teller machine can't provide assistance and reassurance when a customer's bank card has been stolen. And, more often than not, automated telephone operators can't answer the one question we have, and we end up waiting on line to speak to a real person anyway.

In the future, I believe a new business trend will evolve. As computers eliminate jobs, new positions will have to be invented. More and more people will go into business for themselves and, I hope, put the personal touch back into business. I believe that the human workforce will demonstrate that it is more valuable than computers.

SPEAKING

Sample Responses

Part 1

Tell about a sport that is interesting to you. What is it? Do you like to play this sport yourself? Do you follow professional teams?

Figure skating is a sport that's interesting to me. I don't do it myself, it's much too hard, but I enjoy watching professional skaters. I often watch the national and regional competitions.

Why do you like this sport?
I like it because it takes a lot of skill and grace. It's beautiful to see. And I really admire the skaters. It takes a lot of discipline to be a champion skater.

Do you enjoy playing sports or doing other outdoor activities? Why or why not?
I don't play sports much. I like watching skating, but I don't skate myself. I'm not really interested in soccer or other ball sports. I like to go bike riding, though. I guess that's my sport. Whenever the weather is nice, I try to get outside on my bike. It feels good to be outside and get some exercise. It makes me feel relaxed and healthy.

In your city or town, what kinds of places are available for sports and other outdoor activities?
We have a lot of parks and most of them have a soccer field or a baseball diamond or a basketball court, or something like that. They also have walking trails and biking trails. The city also runs a few public swimming pools, though they can get very crowded. If you take a short trip outside of the city, you can find lots of opportunities for hiking and biking.

What kinds of things do you enjoy doing on weekends?
I'm so busy during the week that on weekends I just want to relax. I like to have a lot of unscheduled time to just rest, maybe read, take a walk, talk to friends, just little things like that.

Do you generally prefer to spend a day off from work or school at home, or do you like to go out to other places? Why?
Generally, I prefer to spend my days off at home. It's easier to relax that way. But I like to go out, too, to see my friends. Sometimes we meet at a café or at the movies. If I can relax at home all day, then it's fun to go out in the evening with my friends.

Who do you like to spend time with on your days off?
I like to spend time with some of my close friends. I'm not married and my family isn't nearby, but I have some close friends that I enjoy spending time with. We have a favorite restaurant that we like to go to. We usually eat there on Saturdays.

Part 2

Everyone says I'm a lot like my dad, because we look a lot alike. But, truthfully, I'm a lot more like my mom. Part of the reason my mom and I are so similar is that we spend so much time together. Besides spending one year abroad, I've lived with my mom for my whole life. My parents split up ten years ago, and ever since then my mom and I have become very close.

My mom and I have the same taste in a lot of things, such as food, fashion, and literature. We both love to eat spicy food, and we both love to bake sweets. Oh, and neither of us ever start the day without our morning cup of green tea. It was weird when I first realized/realised that I could borrow my mom's clothes. I guess she's always just kept up with modern fashion unlike some of my friends' mothers. We both like long skirts and warm sweaters and neither of us ever wear jeans. My mom and I both like to read as well. Ever since I was little my mother always read to me before bed. Sometimes she still reads out loud to me just for fun.

I guess its natural for a person to share some of the same qualities as one or both of their parents. But I also think that part of the reason we are so alike is just that we became dependent on each other. I'm an only child, so my mom always had lots of time to spend with me.

Part 3

Do you enjoy spending time with relatives? Why or why not?
Yes, I love getting together for family functions because it's nice to catch up on each other's lives and see how people have changed.

What types of traditions do you and your relatives have?
We used to have a lot more traditions when we were kids. For example, every New Year, we would have a big party at my grandfather's house, and all of the kids would collect a lot of money. We also used to have a big summer picnic for all of the birthdays that happened in the summer. I miss those traditions.

Do you think family members are more important than friends? Why or why not?
I think it depends on where you are at in life. At some points in my life, my mom has been the most important person, and at other times I have been closer to one of my friends.

Do you think that having a good relationship with relatives is important to most people? Why or why not?
I think that depends on the individual person. I know some people who are very close to their cousins or their siblings or their parents. I know other people who always fight with their relatives and don't like to spend time with them. Some of my friends see their grandparents or uncles and aunts often, and others don't. But even though people have different kinds of relationships with their relatives, I think everybody feels that it's important to know that you have a family who cares about you. You may spend a lot or a little time with your relatives, but it's important to know that they are there.

How do family members help each other?
Family members can help each other in many ways, both emotionally and materially. Older family members serve as role models for younger family members. Parents, older siblings, and family members can provide guidance and advice to their younger relatives. Family members provide each other with companionship. They can also help each other with material things, like lending money or offering a place to stay, or helping to find a job. Grandparents sometimes help take care of their grandchildren. There are a lot of different ways that family members help each other.

Do you think that families are as important as they used to be?
I think families are more important now than ever. These days we have so many choices and so many decisions to make. We have to decide what to study and where. We might have to think about moving to another city or country to take a good job. These are hard decisions and if you don't have the support of your family, who will help you? We might make the decision to go to another country, for example, and that would be far away from the family, but still, it's important to know that your family cares about you and will help you.

How are families now different from families in the past?
Families don't always live close together now, and that makes a big difference. I think in the past, the members of an extended family were always around each other and they always helped each other with daily things. If someone didn't have enough money or a place to live or needed help with the children, there was always a relative who could help out. Now that people often go to other places to live, it's harder for family members to help each other because they are farther apart. They still care for each other and provide support, but it has to be in a different way. For example, maybe they can give advice, but it's harder to help care for a sick relative. Also they spend less time together so they don't know each other as well.

How do you think families will change in the future?
I think families will be even farther apart in the future. Kids growing up today don't know their extended family very well because they live apart from them. By the time they are adults, they might not know their cousins and aunts and uncles at all. They won't have family members that they can ask for support. People will depend even more on the nuclear family, on their spouses and children, because that will be all the family they have.

Academic

MODEL TEST 2

ANSWER SHEET
Academic Model Test 2

IELTS Listening Answer Sheet

		✓ ✗
1		1
2		2
3		3
4		4
5		5
6		6
7		7
8		8
9		9
10		10
11		11
12		12
13		13
14		14
15		15
16		16
17		17
18		18
19		19
20		20

		✓ ✗
21		21
22		22
23		23
24		24
25		25
26		26
27		27
28		28
29		29
30		30
31		31
32		32
33		33
34		34
35		35
36		36
37		37
38		38
39		39
40		40
	Listening Total	

MODEL TEST 2

Candidate Name ______________________________

International English Language Testing System

LISTENING

Time: Approx. 30 minutes

INSTRUCTIONS TO CANDIDATES

Do not open this booklet until you are told to do so.

Write your name and candidate number in the space at the top of this page.

You should answer all questions.

All the recordings will be played ONCE only.

Write all your answers on the Question Paper.

At the end of the test, you will be given ten minutes to transfer your answers to an Answer Sheet.

Do not remove this booklet from the examination room.

INFORMATION FOR CANDIDATES

There are **40** questions on this question paper.

The test is divided as follows:

Section 1	Questions 1–10
Section 2	Questions 11–20
Section 3	Questions 21–30
Section 4	Questions 31–40

Track 24

SECTION 1

Questions 1–7

*Choose the correct letters, **A**, **B**, or **C**.*

Example

What is the man doing?

A Shopping at the mall

(B) Asking shoppers questions

C Looking for a certain shop

1 The interviewer wants to find out about

A when the mall is open.

B people's shopping habits.

C the best stores[1] in the shopping center[2].

2 The interviewer wants to speak with

A married women.

B any shopper.

C children.

3 What is the respondent's age?

A 18–25

B 26–35

C 36–45

4 How often does the respondent shop at the mall?

A Less than once a month

B Once a week

C Two or more times a week

5 What does the respondent usually shop for?

A Clothes

B Books

C Groceries

6 How much time does the respondent usually spend at the mall?

A One hour or less

B Between one and two hours

C More than two hours

7 What method of transportation does the respondent use to get to the mall?

A Car

B Bus

C Subway

[1]British: shops, shoppes

[2]British: shopping centre

Questions 8–10

Complete the sentences below.

Write NO MORE THAN THREE WORDS *for each answer.*

8 Why does the respondent like the shoe store?

....

9 Why doesn't the respondent like the food court?

....

10 What improvement does the respondent suggest?

....

SECTION 2

Question 11

Choose the correct letters, ***A****,* ***B****, or* ***C****.*

11 The tour of the health club is for

A people who want to become members of the club.
B people who are already members of the club.
C people who work at the club.

Questions 12–14

Choose THREE *letters,* ***A–F****.*

What are three things that members can do at the club?

A Learn to play tennis
B Buy exercise equipment
C Consult a nutrition expert
D Exercise on a machine
E Run on a track
F Swim competitively

Questions 15–17

Choose THREE *letters,* ***A–F****.*

What three things should club members bring with them to the locker room?

A Towels
B Soap
C Shampoo
D Hair dryers
E Rubber sandals
F Locks

Questions 18–20

Complete the notice below.

Write NO MORE THAN THREE WORDS *for each answer.*

Swimming Pool Rules

No children allowed without **18** ....

Be safe! Please **19** .... near the pool because the floor is wet.

Be clean! Use **20** .... before getting into the pool.

SECTION 3

Questions 21–22

Write NO MORE THAN THREE WORDS *for each answer.*

21 How often will the students have to write essays?

....

22 How long should each essay be?

....

Questions 23–26

Complete the chart below.

Write NO MORE THAN THREE WORDS *for each answer.*

Essay Type	Sample Topic
23	How to change the oil in a car
24	Three kinds of friends
25	Student cafeteria food and restaurant food
Argumentative	The necessity of **26** ....

Questions 27–30

Choose the correct letters, ***A***, ***B***, *or* ***C***.

27 How will the students get their essay topics?

A The professor will assign them.
B Students will choose them.
C They will come from books.

28 When are the essays due?

- **A** Every Monday
- **B** Every Wednesday
- **C** Every Friday

29 What percentage of the final grade[1] comes from the essays?

- **A** 15 percent
- **B** 20 percent
- **C** 65 percent

30 The professor wants

- **A** computer-written essays.
- **B** handwritten essays.
- **C** photocopied essays.

SECTION 4

Questions 31–32

Answer the questions.

Write NO MORE THAN THREE WORDS *for each answer.*

31 What is the name of the class?

....

32 What day does the class meet?

....

Questions 33–36

Complete the notes below.

Write NO MORE THAN THREE WORDS *for each answer.*

In hunter-gatherer societies, gathering is done by **33** ....

All humans lived in hunter-gatherer societies until **34** .... ago.

Today we can find hunter-gatherer societies in the Arctic, **35** .... ,

and **36** ....

[1]BRITISH: mark

Questions 37–40

The following are characteristics of which types of society?

Check column A if it is a characteristic of hunter-gatherer societies.
Check column B if it is a characteristic of farming societies.

Characteristic	A	B
37 They usually remain in one area.		
38 They move around.		
39 They live in larger groups.		
40 They have an egalitarian social structure.		

ANSWER SHEET
Academic Model Test 2

IELTS Reading Answer Sheet

1		✓ 1 ✗
2		2
3		3
4		4
5		5
6		6
7		7
8		8
9		9
10		10
11		11
12		12
13		13
14		14
15		15
16		16
17		17
18		18
19		19
20		20

21		✓ 21 ✗
22		22
23		23
24		24
25		25
26		26
27		27
28		28
29		29
30		30
31		31
32		32
33		33
34		34
35		35
36		36
37		37
38		38
39		39
40		40
	Reading Total	

MODEL TEST 2

Candidate Name ____

International English Language Testing System

ACADEMIC READING

Time: 1 hour

INSTRUCTIONS TO CANDIDATES

Do not open this booklet until you are told to do so.

Write your name and candidate number in the space at the top of this page.

Start at the beginning of the test and work through it.

You should answer all questions.

If you cannot do a particular question, leave it and go on to the next. You can return to it later.

All answers must be written on the Answer Sheet.

Do not remove this booklet from the examination room.

INFORMATION FOR CANDIDATES

There are **40** questions on this question paper.

The test is divided as follows:

Reading Passage 1	Questions 1-15
Reading Passage 2	Questions 16-28
Reading Passage 3	Questions 29-40

Reading Passage 1

You should spend about 20 minutes on questions 1–15, which are based on Reading Passage 1 on page 341.

Questions 1–5

Reading Passage 1 has five paragraphs, ***A–E****. Choose the most suitable heading for each paragraph from the list of headings below. Write the appropriate numbers* ***(i–viii)*** *on your Answer Sheet. There are more headings than paragraphs, so you will not use them all.*

List of Headings	
i	Glacial Continents
ii	Formation and Growth of Glaciers
iii	Glacial Movement
iv	Glaciers in the Last Ice Age
v	Glaciers Through the Years
vi	Types of Glaciers
vii	Glacial Effects on Landscape
viii	Glaciers in National Parks

1 Paragraph A

2 Paragraph B

3 Paragraph C

4 Paragraph D

5 Paragraph E

Glaciers

A

Besides the earth's oceans, glacier ice is the largest source of water on earth. A glacier is a massive stream or sheet of ice that moves underneath itself under the influence of gravity. Some glaciers travel down mountains or valleys, while others spread across a large expanse of land. Heavily glaciated regions such as Greenland and Antarctica are called *continental glaciers.* These two ice sheets encompass more than 95 percent of the earth's glacial ice. The Greenland ice sheet is almost 10,000 feet thick in some areas, and the weight of this glacier is so heavy that much of the region has been depressed below sea level. Smaller glaciers that occur at higher elevations are called *alpine* or *valley glaciers.* Another way of classifying glaciers is in terms of their internal temperature. In *temperate glaciers,* the ice within the glacier is near its melting point. *Polar glaciers,* in contrast, always maintain temperatures far below melting.

B

The majority of the earth's glaciers are located near the poles, though glaciers exist on all continents, including Africa and Oceania. The reason glaciers are generally formed in high alpine regions is that they require cold temperatures throughout the year. In these areas where there is little opportunity for summer *ablation* (loss of mass), snow changes to compacted *firn* and then crystallized ice. During periods in which melting and evaporation exceed the amount of snowfall, glaciers will retreat rather than progress. While glaciers rely heavily on snowfall, other climactic conditions including freezing rain, avalanches, and wind, contribute to their growth. One year of below average precipitation can stunt the growth of a glacier tremendously. With the rare exception of *surging glaciers,* a common glacier flows about 10 inches per day in the summer and 5 inches per day in the winter. The fastest glacial surge on record occurred in 1953, when the Kutiah Glacier in Pakistan grew more than 12 kilometers in three months.

C

The weight and pressure of ice accumulation causes glacier movement. Glaciers move out from under themselves, via *plastic deformation* and *basal slippage.* First, the internal flow of ice crystals begins to spread outward and downward from the thickened snow pack also known as the *zone of accumulation.* Next, the ice along the ground surface begins to slip in the same direction. Seasonal thawing at the base of the glacier helps to facilitate this slippage. The middle of a glacier moves faster than the sides and bottom because there is no rock to cause friction. The upper part of a glacier rides on the ice below. As a glacier moves it carves out a U-shaped valley similar to a riverbed, but with much steeper walls and a flatter bottom.

D

Besides the extraordinary rivers of ice, glacial erosion creates other unique physical features in the landscape such as horns, fjords, hanging valleys, and cirques. Most of these landforms do not become visible until after a glacier has receded. Many are created by moraines, which occur at the sides and front of a glacier. Moraines are formed when material is picked up along the way and deposited in a new location. When many alpine glaciers occur on the same mountain, these moraines can create a *horn*. The Matterhorn, in the Swiss Alps, is one of the most famous horns. *Fjords*, which are very common in Norway, are coastal valleys that fill with ocean water during a glacial retreat. *Hanging valleys* occur when two or more glacial valleys intersect at varying elevations. It is common for waterfalls to connect the higher and lower hanging valleys, such as in Yosemite National Park. A *cirque* is a large bowl-shaped valley that forms at the front of a glacier. Cirques often have a lip on their down slope that is deep enough to hold small lakes when the ice melts away.

E

Glacier movement and shape shifting typically occur over hundreds of years. While presently about 10 percent of the earth's land is covered with glaciers, it is believed that during the last Ice Age glaciers covered approximately 32 percent of the earth's surface. In the past century, most glaciers have been retreating rather than flowing forward. It is unknown whether this glacial activity is due to human impact or natural causes, but by studying glacier movement, and comparing climate and agricultural profiles over hundreds of years, glaciologists can begin to understand environmental issues such as global warming.

Questions 6–10

Do the following statements agree with the information in the passage? In boxes 6–10 on your Answer Sheet, write

TRUE	*if the statement is true according to the passage.*
FALSE	*if the statement contradicts the passage.*
NOT GIVEN	*if there is no information about this in the passage.*

6 Glaciers exist only near the north and south poles.

7 Glaciers are formed by a combination of snow and other weather conditions.

8 Glaciers normally move at a rate of about 5 to 10 inches a day.

9 All parts of the glacier move at the same speed.

10 During the last Ice Age, average temperatures were much lower than they were during previous Ice Ages.

Questions 11–15

Match each definition below with the term it defines.

*Write the letter of the term, **A–H**, on your Answer Sheet. There are more terms than definitions, so you will not use them all.*

Terms	
A	fjord
B	alpine glacier
C	horn
D	polar glacier
E	temperate glacier
F	hanging valley
G	cirque
H	surging glacier

11 a glacier formed on a mountain

12 a glacier with temperatures well below freezing

13 a glacier that moves very quickly

14 a glacial valley formed near the ocean

15 a glacial valley that looks like a bowl

Reading Passage 2

You should spend about 20 minutes on questions 16–28, which are based on Reading Passage 2 below.

Irish Potato Famine

A

In the ten years following the Irish potato famine of 1845, over 750,000 Irish people died, including many of those who attempted to immigrate to countries such as the United States and Canada. Prior to the potato blight, one of the main concerns in Ireland was overpopulation. In the early 1500s, the country's population was estimated at less than three million, but by 1840 this number had nearly tripled. The bountiful potato crop, which contains almost all of the nutrients that a person needs for survival, was largely to blame for the population growth. However, within five years of the failed crop of 1845, the population of Ireland was reduced by a quarter. A number of factors contributed to the plummet of the Irish population, namely the Irish dependency on the potato crop, the British tenure system, and the inadequate relief efforts of the English.

B

It is not known exactly how or when the potato was first introduced to Europe; however, the general assumption is that it arrived on a Spanish ship sometime in the 1600s. For more than one hundred years, Europeans believed that potatoes belonged to a botanical family of a poisonous breed. It was not until Marie Antoinette wore potato blossoms in her hair in the mid-eighteenth century that potatoes became a novelty. By the late 1700s, the dietary value of the potato had been discovered, and the monarchs of Europe ordered the vegetable to be widely planted.

C

By 1800, the vast majority of the Irish population had become dependent on the potato as its primary staple. It wasn't uncommon for an Irish potato farmer to consume more than six pounds of potatoes a day. Families stored potatoes for the winter and even fed potatoes to their livestock. Because of this dependency, the unexpected potato blight of 1845 devastated the Irish. Investigators at first suggested that the blight was caused by static energy, smoke from railroad trains, or vapors from underground volcanoes; however, the root cause was later discovered as an airborne fungus that traveled from Mexico. Not only did the disease destroy the potato crops, it also infected all of the potatoes in storage at the time. Their families were dying from famine, but weakened farmers had retained little of their agricultural skills to harvest other crops. Those who did manage to grow things such as oats, wheat, and barley relied on earnings from these exported crops to keep their rented homes.

D

While the potato blight generated mass starvation among the Irish, the people were held captive to their poverty by the British tenure system. Following the Napoleonic Wars of 1815, the English had turned their focus to their colonial land holdings. British landowners realized that the best way to profit from these holdings was to extract the resources and exports and charge expensive rents and taxes for people to live on the land. Under the tenure system, Protestant landlords owned 95 percent of the Irish land, which was divided up into five-acre plots for the people to live and farm on. As the population of Ireland grew, however, the plots were continuously subdivided into smaller parcels. Living conditions declined dramatically, and families were forced to move to less fertile land where almost nothing but the potato would grow.

E

During this same period of colonization, the Penal Laws were also instituted as a means of weakening the Irish spirit. Under the Penal Laws, Irish peasants were denied basic human rights, such as the right to speak their own native language, seek certain kinds of employment, practice their faith, receive education, and own land. Despite the famine that was devastating Ireland, the landlords had little compassion or sympathy for tenants unable to pay their rent. Approximately 500,000 Irish tenants were evicted by their landlords between 1845 and 1847. Many of these people also had their homes burned down and were put in jail for overdue rent.

F

The majority of the British officials in the 1840s adopted the laissez-faire philosophy, which supported a policy of nonintervention in the Irish plight. Prime Minister Sir Robert Peel was an exception. He showed compassion toward the Irish by making a move to repeal the Corn Laws, which had been put in place to protect British grain producers from the competition of foreign markets. For this hasty decision, Peel quickly lost the support of the British people and was forced to resign. The new Prime Minister, Lord John Russell, allowed assistant Charles Trevelyan to take complete control over all of the relief efforts in Ireland. Trevelyan believed that the Irish situation should be left to Providence. Claiming that it would be dangerous to let the Irish become dependent on other countries, he even took steps to close food depots that were selling corn and to redirect shipments of corn that were already on their way to Ireland. A few relief programs were eventually implemented, such as soup kitchens and workhouses; however, these were poorly run institutions that facilitated the spread of disease, tore apart families, and offered inadequate food supplies considering the extent of Ireland's shortages.

G

Many of the effects of the Irish potato famine are still evident today. Descendants of those who fled Ireland during the 1840s are dispersed all over the world. Some of the homes that were evacuated by absentee landlords still sit abandoned in the Irish hills. A number of Irish descendents still carry animosity toward the British for not putting people before politics. The potato blight itself still plagues the Irish people during certain growing seasons when weather conditions are favorable for the fungus to thrive.

Questions 16–20

*The passage has seven paragraphs, **A–G**.*

Which paragraph contains the following information?

Write the correct letter in boxes 16–20 on your Answer Sheet.

16 the position of the British government toward the potato famine

17 a description of the system of land ownership in Ireland

18 early European attitudes toward the potato

19 explanation of the lack of legal protection for Irish peasants

20 the importance of the potato in Irish society

Questions 21–28

Complete each sentence with the correct ending, ***A–L****, from the box below.*

Write the correct letter in boxes 21–28 on your Answer Sheet. There are more endings than sentences, so you won't use them all.

Sentence Endings	
A	because they couldn't pay the rent on their farms.
B	because railroad trains caused air pollution.
C	because potatoes were their main source of food.
D	because Charles Trevelyan took over relief efforts.
E	because they needed the profits to pay the rent.
F	because they weren't well-managed.
G	because there wasn't enough land for the increasing population.
H	because his efforts to help the Irish were unpopular among the British.
I	because they believed that potatoes were poisonous.
J	because the British instituted penal laws.
K	because it was discovered that potatoes are full of nutrients.
L	because Marie Antoinette used potato blossoms as decoration.

21 At first Europeans didn't eat potatoes

22 European monarchs encouraged potato growing

23 The potato blight was devastating to the Irish

24 Farmers who grew oats, wheat, and barley didn't eat these crops

25 Many Irish farmers lived on infertile plots

26 Many Irish farmers were arrested

27 Sir Robert Peel lost his position as prime minister

28 Soup kitchens and workhouses didn't relieve the suffering

Reading Passage 3

You should spend about 20 minutes on questions 29–40, which are based on Reading Passage 3 below.

Anesthesiology

Since the beginning of time, man has sought natural remedies for pain. Between 40 and 60 A.D., Greek physician, Dioscorides traveled with the Roman armies, studying the medicinal properties of plants and minerals. His book, *De materia medica,* written in five volumes and translated into at least seven languages, was the primary reference source for physicians for over sixteen centuries. The field of anesthesiology,[1] which was once nothing more than a list of medicinal plants and makeshift remedies, has grown into one of the most important fields in medicine.

Many of the early pain relievers were based on myth and did little to relieve the suffering of an ill or injured person. The mandragora (now known as the mandrake plant) was one of the first plants to be used as an anesthetic.[1] Due to the apparent screaming that the plant made as it was pulled from the ground, people in the Middle Ages believed that the person who removed the mandrake from the earth would either die or go insane. This superstition may have resulted because the split root of the mandrake resembled the human form. In order to pull the root from the ground, the plant collector would loosen it and tie the stem to an animal. It was believed that the safest time to uproot a mandrake was in the moonlight, and the best animal to use was a black dog. In his manual, Dioscorides suggested boiling the root with wine and having a man drink the potion to remove sensation before cutting his flesh or burning his skin. Opium and Indian hemp were later used to induce sleep before a painful procedure or to relieve the pain of an illness. Other remedies such as cocaine did more harm to the patient than good as people died from their addictions. President Ulysses S. Grant became addicted to cocaine before he died of throat cancer in 1885.

The modern field of anesthetics dates to the incident when nitrous oxide (more commonly known as laughing gas) was accidentally discovered. Humphrey Davy, the inventor of the miner's lamp, discovered that inhaling the toxic compound caused a strange euphoria, followed by fits of laughter, tears, and sometimes unconsciousness. U.S. dentist, Horace Wells, was the first on record to experiment with laughing gas, which he used in 1844 to relieve pain during a tooth extraction. Two years later, Dr. William Morton created the first anesthetic machine. This apparatus was a simple glass globe containing an ether-soaked sponge. Morton considered ether a good alternative to nitrous oxide because the numbing effect lasted considerably

[1]BRITISH: anaesthesiology/an anaesthetic

longer. His apparatus allowed the patient to inhale vapors[1] whenever the pain became unbearable. In 1846, during a trial experiment in Boston, a tumor[2] was successfully removed from a man's jaw area while he was anesthetized with Morton's machine.

The first use of anesthesia in the obstetric field occurred in Scotland by Dr. James Simpson. Instead of ether, which he considered irritating to the eyes, Simpson administered chloroform to reduce the pain of childbirth. Simpson sprinkled chloroform on a handkerchief and allowed laboring[3] women to inhale the fumes at their own discretion. In 1853, Queen Victoria agreed to use chloroform during the birth of her eighth child. Soon the use of chloroform during childbirth was both acceptable and fashionable. However, as chloroform became a more popular anesthetic, knowledge of its toxicity surfaced, and it was soon obsolete.

After World War II, numerous developments were made in the field of anesthetics. Surgical procedures that had been unthinkable were being performed with little or no pain felt by the patient. Rather than physicians or nurses who administered pain relief as part of their profession, anesthesiologists became specialists in suppressing consciousness and alleviating pain. Anesthesiologists today are classified as perioperative physicians, meaning they take care of a patient before, during, and after surgical procedures. It takes over eight years of schooling and four years of residency until an anesthesiologist is prepared to practice in the United States. These experts are trained to administer three different types of anesthetics: general, local, and regional. General anesthetic is used to put a patient into a temporary state of unconsciousness. Local anesthetic is used only at the affected site and causes a loss of sensation. Regional anesthetic is used to block the sensation and possibly the movement of a larger portion of the body. As well as controlling the levels of pain for the patient before and throughout an operation, anesthesiologists are responsible for monitoring and controlling the patient's vital functions during the procedure and assessing the medical needs in the post-operative room.

The number of anesthesiologists in the United States has more than doubled since the 1970s, as has the improvement and success of operative care. In addition, complications from anesthesiology have declined dramatically. Over 40 million anesthetics are administered in the United States each year, with only 1 in 250,000 causing death.

[1]British: vapours
[2]British: tumour
[3]British: labouring

Questions 29–34

Do the following statements agree with the information in Passage 3? In boxes 29–34 on your Answer Sheet, write

TRUE	*if the statement is true according to the passage.*
FALSE	*if the statement contradicts the passage.*
NOT GIVEN	*if there is no information about this in the passage.*

29 Dioscorides' book, *De materia medica,* fell out of use after 60 A.D.

30 Mandragora was used as an anesthetic during the Middle Ages.

31 Nitrous oxide can cause the user to both laugh and cry.

32 During the second half of the 19th century, most dentists used anesthesia.

33 Anesthesiologists in the United States are required to have 12 years of education and training.

34 There are fewer anesthesiologists in the United States now than there were 40 years ago.

Questions 35–40

*Match each fact about anesthesia with the type of anesthetic that it refers to. There are more types of anesthetics listed than facts, so you won't use them all. Write the correct letter, **A–H**, in boxes 35–40 on your Answer Sheet.*

Types of Anesthetic

A	general anesthetic
B	local anesthetic
C	regional anesthetic
D	chloroform
E	ether
F	nitrous oxide
G	opium
H	mandrake

35 used by sprinkling on a handkerchief

36 used on only one specific part of the body

37 used by boiling with wine

38 used first during a dental procedure

39 used to stop feeling over a larger area of the body

40 used in the first anesthetic machine

ANSWER SHEET
Academic Model Test 2

Writing Answer Sheet

TASK 1

ANSWER SHEET
Academic Model Test 2

-2-

ANSWER SHEET
Academic Model Test 2

-3-

TASK 2

ANSWER SHEET
Academic Model Test 2

-4-

MODEL TEST 2

Candidate Name ________________________________

International English Language Testing System

ACADEMIC WRITING

Time: 1 hour

INSTRUCTIONS TO CANDIDATES

Do not open this booklet until you are told to do so.

Write your name and candidate number in the space at the top of this page.

All answers must be written on the separate answer booklet provided.

Do not remove this booklet from the examination room.

INFORMATION FOR CANDIDATES

There are **2** tasks on this question paper.

You must do **both** tasks.

Underlength answers will be penalized.

Writing Task 1

You should spend no more than 20 minutes on this task.

> ***The diagram below shows the steps in the process of manufacturing yogurt.***
>
> ***Summarize the information by selecting and reporting the main features, and make comparisons where relevant.***

Write at least 150 words.

Manufacturing Yogurt

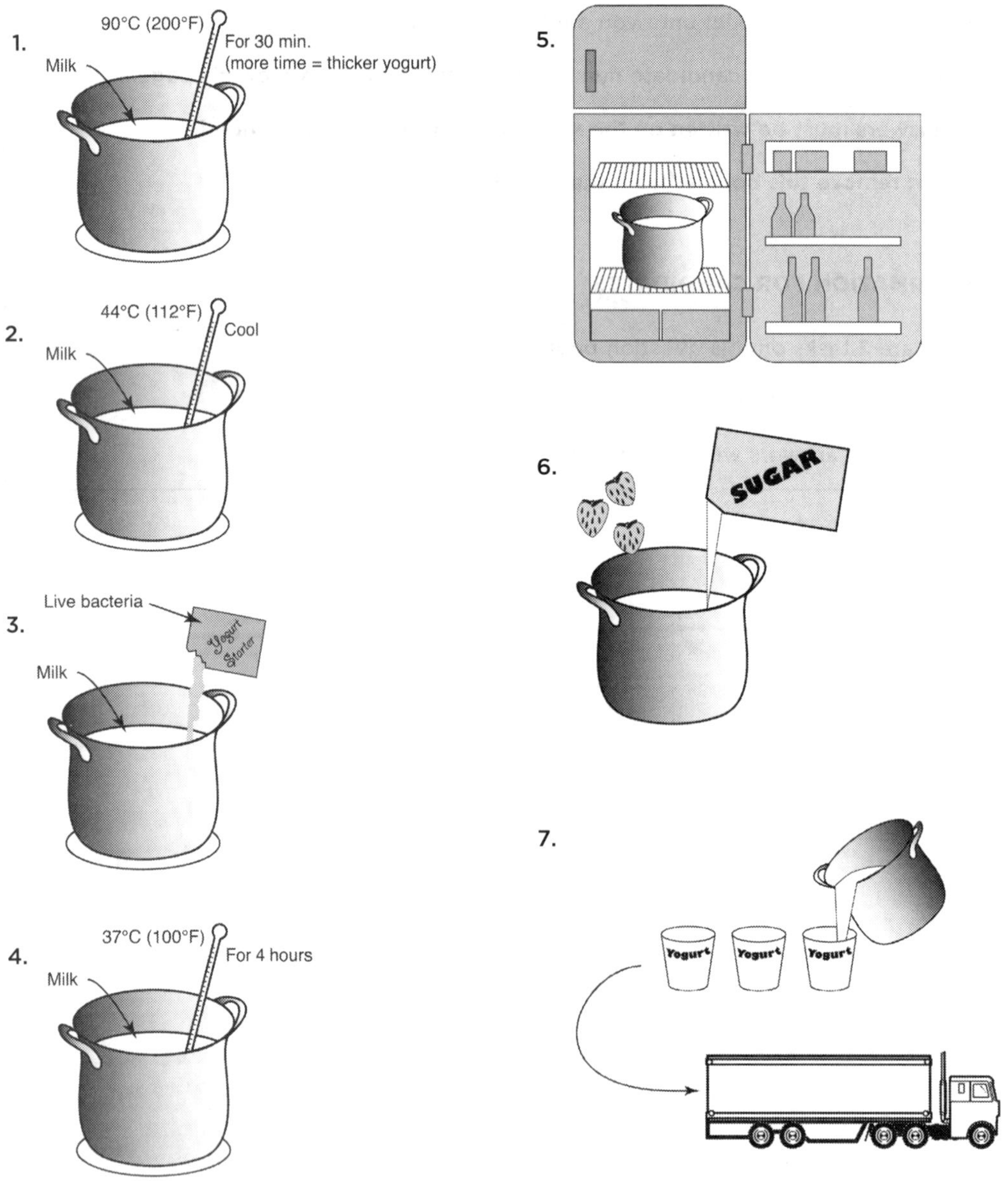

Writing Task 2

You should spend no more than 40 minutes on this task.

Write about the following topic:

> ***Families who do not send their children to government-financed schools should not be required to pay taxes that support universal education.***

To what extent do you agree or disagree with this statement? Give reasons for your answer, and include any relevant examples from your own knowledge or experience.

You should write at least 250 words.

SPEAKING

Examiner Questions:

Part 1 (4–5 minutes)

Jobs

Do you have a job? Do you like it? Why or why not?
Why did you choose this job?
What kind of education or training did you need to get this job?

Free Time

Describe an activity you enjoy doing in your free time.
How long have you been doing this activity? How did you learn it?
In your free time, do you prefer activities you can do with other people, or activities you can do alone? Why?
Is having a lot of free time important to you? Why or why not?

Part 2 (4–5 minutes)

You will be given a topic. You will have one to two minutes to talk about this topic. You will have one minute to prepare what you are going to say. You may take some notes if you wish. Here is your topic:

> Describe a holiday[1] that you have celebrated recently.
>
> You should say:
>
> what the purpose of the holiday is
> who you celebrated with
> why this holiday is important to you
>
> and describe some activities that you did as part of the celebration

You will have one to two minutes to talk about this topic.
You will have one minute to prepare what you are going to say.

Part 3 (4–5 minutes)

The Importance of Holidays

What are some important holidays in your country?
Why do people celebrate holidays?

Changes in Holidays

Do you think holiday celebrations have changed over the years? Why or why not?
Do you think the importance of holiday celebrations has changed over the years? Why or why not?
How will holidays be different in the future?

[1]AMERICAN and BRITISH: A special day commemorating a religious, historical, social, or political event.

ACADEMIC MODEL TEST 2—ANSWER EXPLANATIONS

LISTENING

Example. (B) Choice (B) is correct because the man is "conducting a survey of shoppers at this mall." He also wants to learn about "people's habits when they shop at the mall." Choice (A) is incorrect because the man is not shopping at the mall; he is conducting a survey. Choice (C) is incorrect because he is not looking for a shop.

1. (B) The man wants to learn about "people's habits when they shop at the mall." The other choices—(A) and (C)—are not mentioned during their conversation.
2. (A) Choice (A) is correct because the man is "interviewing married women, that is women with husbands and children who shop for their families." Choice (B) is incorrect because the man won't talk to "any shopper." Choice (C) is incorrect because the man does not want to speak to children.
3. (B) Choice (B)—26–35—is correct because she says, "I'm 34," which fits into that range. Choices (A) and (C) give numeric ranges that do not match her age.
4. (C) Choice (C) is correct because she says, "I'm here at least twice a week." This statement is the equivalent of choice (C)—two or more times a week. Choice (A)—less than once a month—is incorrect because it is a time period that the man mentions, but the woman does not select that time period. Choice (B)—once a week—is incorrect. It is never mentioned during their conversation.
5. (C) Choice (C) is correct because she says, "The reason I come here so often is for food. I told you I have a large family. I buy all our food at the supermarket here." Choice (A) is incorrect because the woman says, "The clothing stores are quite nice," but she doesn't say that she usually shops for clothes. Choice (B) is incorrect because she says, "I like the bookstore," but she doesn't say that she usually shops for books.
6. (B) Choice (B) is correct because she spends "about an hour and a half or so." Choice (A)—one hour or less—is incorrect because she doesn't say that she ever spends that amount of time at the mall. Choice (C)—more than two hours—is incorrect because she says, "I'm hardly ever here for more than two hours." So, she is not usually at the mall for that amount of time . . . and the question asks for her usual length of time.
7. (A) Choice (A) is correct because the woman says, "I always drive." Choice (B)—bus—is provided by the man as an option, which she doesn't select. Choice (C)—subway—is incorrect. It is never mentioned.
8. Multiple possible answers:
   (a) Employees are polite
   (b) Give good service
   (c) Very good service
   (d) Polite employees
   The woman likes the shoe store because, "the employees there are so polite. They give very good service."
9. The correct answer is "it's very expensive." The woman says, "[the food] is very expensive. It shouldn't cost so much."
10. Multiple possible answers
    (a) add more parking
    (b) more parking spaces/places
    (c) add parking spaces/places
    (d) add parking
    The woman says, "You should add more parking spaces."
11. (A) Choice (A) is correct because the purpose of the tour is to let people "become familiar with the different activities available at the club." The goal of the tour is to have everyone "decide to become

ACADEMIC MODEL TEST 2

members." Choice (B) is incorrect because the club members already have a membership. They don't need to be convinced to join again. Choice (C) is incorrect because the people who work at the club already know about all of the club's activities.

12–14. Choices (A), (D), and (F) are correct.

Choice (A)—learn to play tennis—is correct because the club does "offer tennis lessons." Choice (D) is correct because the club has "the most modern exercise machines." Choice (F) is correct because club members "have the opportunity to swim competitively."

Choice (B) is incorrect because their club store offers only "snacks or drinks." Choice (C) is incorrect because the only expert mentioned is a fitness and technology expert, but not a nutrition expert. Choice (E) is incorrect because "run on a track" is never mentioned.

15–17. Choices (C), (E), and (F) are correct.

Choice (C) is correct because they are told to "supply your own shampoo." Choice (E) is correct because people are told that everyone must "wear rubber sandals in the changing rooms" and since they aren't told where to get the sandals, it is understood that you need to bring your own. Choice (F) is correct because people are told "to supply your own lock."

Choices (A) and (B) are incorrect because the club's locker/changing rooms are kept "well-stocked with basic necessities such as towels and soap." Choice (D) is incorrect because "There are plenty of . . . hair dryers."

18. *an adult.* "Children must be accompanied by an adult at all times."
19. *don't run.* "No running near the pool."
20. *the shower.* People are told, "we ask everyone to shower before entering the pool."
21. *weekly/once a week/every week.* The professor says, "You'll have to write one essay each week." Also, she says, "Every week I'll assign a different type of essay."
22. *350–400 words.*

Essay Type	Sample Topic
23. Process	How to change the oil in a car
24. Classification	Three kinds of friends
25. Compare and contrast	Student cafeteria food and restaurant food
Argumentative	The necessity of 26. homework

27. (B) Choice (B) is correct because the professor tells the students that she wants them to "pick your own topics." Choices (A) and (C) are incorrect because the professor says that students will pick their own topics. The professor mentions books, but only when telling students that the topics must be original: "I want them [the topics] to come out of your own heads, not out of any book on essay writing."
28. (C) Choice (C)—Friday—is correct because the professor says each student will "hand [it] in to me the following Friday." Choice (A) is incorrect—Monday—because that is the day that the essay assignment is given, not when it is due. Choice (B)—Wednesday—is incorrect because that day is never mentioned.
29. (C) Choice (C) is correct because the professor says that "your essays will count for 65 percent of your final grade.[1]" Choice (A) is incorrect because it doesn't refer to essays: "Other class work will count for 15 percent." Choice (B) is incorrect because it doesn't refer to essays: "Your tests will be 20 percent of the final grade."
30. (A) Choice (A) is correct because the professor tells them, "Please type your essays on a computer." Choice (B) is incorrect because the professor says, "Handwritten essays are not acceptable." Choice (C) is incorrect because the professor says, "I don't want to receive any photocopied work."

[1]BRITISH: mark

31. *Introduction to Anthropology.* "This class is Introduction to Anthropology."
32. *Tuesday.* "This class meets every Tuesday evening."
33. *women.* "The men's job is to hunt . . . while the women gather plants . . . ."
34. *twelve thousand years.* "Before 12,000 years ago, all humans lived as hunter-gathers."
35. *some desert areas/deserts.* "Today hunter-gatherer societies still exist in the Arctic, in some desert areas, and in tropical rainforests."
36. *rainforests/tropical rainforests.* (see #35).

Characteristic	A	B
37. They usually remain in one area.		XX
38. They move around.	XX	
39. They live in larger groups.		XX
40. They have an egalitarian social structure.	XX	

37. (B) Choice (B) is correct because the professor says that farmers are more likely to be sedentary. They can't move often because they need to plant their crops. Choice (A) is incorrect because the hunter-gatherers "travel from place to place."
38. (A) Choice (A) is correct because the professor says that they tend to be nomadic. Choice (B) is incorrect because farmers can't move often because they need to plant their crops.
39. (B) Choice (B) is correct because "Farming can support much higher population densities than hunting and gathering can because farming results in a larger food supply." Choice (A) is incorrect because "hunter-gatherer societies generally have lower population densities." Also, the farming society's population density is higher than theirs.
40. (A) Choice (A) is correct because hunter-gatherer societies "tend not to have hierarchical social structures." Choice (B) is incorrect because farming societies had "hierarchical social structures begin to develop."

READING

Passage 1—Glaciers

1. vi—Types of Glaciers is the correct answer. Paragraph A defines the term *glacier* and describes four specific types of glaciers.
2. ii—Formation and Growth of Glaciers is the correct answer. Paragraph B describes the reason why glaciers generally form in the high alpine regions—because "they require cold temperatures throughout the year." The paragraph also describes the retreat of glaciers during periods when melting and evaporation exceed the amount of snowfall.
3. iii—Glacial Movement is the correct answer. Paragraph C begins with a clear topic sentence: "The weight and pressure of ice accumulation causes glacier movement." The rest of the paragraph then provides details about this movement.
4. vii—Glacial Effects on Landscape is the correct answer. Like the previous paragraph, paragraph D begins with a clear topic sentence directly related to the topic: "glacial erosion creates other unique physical features in the landscape such as horns" and so on. Each feature is described in the following sentences.
5. v—Glaciers Through the Years is the correct answer. Paragraph E refers to the glaciers from the Ice Age, the past century, and even looks into the future by referring to studies that glaciologists can conduct now and in the future.
6. False. Paragraph B, first sentence states: "glaciers exist on all continents," and paragraph B, last sentence states: "The fastest glacial surge on record occurred in . . . the Kutiah Glacier in Pakistan," which is not at the poles.

7. True. Paragraph B, middle sentence states: "While glaciers rely heavily on snowfall, other climatic conditions including freezing rain, avalanches, and wind, contribute to their growth."
8. True. Paragraph B, second to the last sentence states: "With the rare exception of *surging glaciers,* a common glacier flows about 10 inches per day in the summer and 5 inches per day in the winter." This fits the 5–10 inch range.
9. False. Paragraph C states: "The middle of a glacier moves faster than the sides and bottom because there is no rock to cause friction."
10. Not Given. Paragraph E refers to the last Ice Age and the percentage of glaciers that covered the earth's surface. However, no mention is made of the temperatures then.
11. (B) Paragraph A explains: "Smaller glaciers that occur at higher elevations are called *alpine* or *valley glaciers.*" Paragraph D refers to "alpine glaciers [occurring] on the same mountain."
12. (D) Paragraph A states: "*Polar glaciers* . . . always maintain temperatures far below melting." Therefore, these temperatures are freezing, and D is the correct answer.
13. (H) Paragraph B says: "With the rare exception of *surging glaciers,* a common glacier flows about 10 inches per day in the summer and 5 inches per day in the winter. The fastest glacial surge on record occurred in 1953." So the reader can infer that the term surging glacier is related to the speed of the glacier's movement.
14. (A) Paragraph D explains: "*Fjords* . . . are coastal valleys that fill with ocean water." Therefore, the reader assumes that fjords form near the ocean and term A (fjord) is selected as the correct answer.
15. (G) Paragraph D states: "A *cirque* is a large bowl-shaped valley that forms at the front of a glacier."

Passage 2—Irish Potato Famine

16. (F) Paragraph F begins by stating the British government's political policy toward Ireland during the famine: "The majority of the British officials in the 1840s adopted the laissez-faire philosophy." The rest of the paragraph provides details about the British government's action (or lack of action) to help Ireland and the impact that had on Ireland.
17. (D) Paragraph D describes the British tenure system, including how British landowners charged rent and people lived on smaller and smaller parcels of land.
18. (B) Paragraph B describes how Europeans changed their attitude about potatoes, from saying it "belonged to a botanical family of a poisonous breed" to having the European monarchs order the wide planting of the vegetable.
19. (E) Paragraph E examines the Penal Laws and the many rights those laws denied the Irish peasants.
20. (C) Paragraph C describes Ireland's dependence on the potato—as a crop and as a stored food item.
21. (I) Paragraph B states: "Europeans believed that potatoes belonged to a botanical family of a poisonous breed."
22. (K) Paragraph B states: "By the late 1700s, the dietary value of the potato had been discovered, and the monarchs of Europe ordered the vegetable to be widely planted."
23. (C) Paragraph C states: "By 1800, the vast majority of the Irish population had become dependent on the potato as its primary staple."
24. (E) Paragraph C states: "Those who did manage to grow things such as oats, wheat, and barley relied on earnings from these exported crops to keep their rented homes."
25. (G) Paragraph D states: "As the population of Ireland grew, however, the plots were continuously subdivided . . . families were forced to move to less fertile land where almost nothing but the potato would grow."
26. (A) Paragraph E states: "Approximately 500,000 Irish tenants were evicted . . . . Many of these people . . . were put in jail for overdue rent."

27. (H) Paragraph F states: "Sir Robert Peel . . . showed compassion toward the Irish by making a move to repeal the Corn Laws . . . . For this hasty decision, Peel quickly lost the support of the British people and was forced to resign."
28. (F) Paragraph F states: "A few relief programs were eventually implemented, such as soup kitchens and workhouses; [but] these were poorly run institutions."

Passage 3—Anesthesiology

29. False. Paragraph 1 states that his book "was the primary reference source for physicians for over sixteen centuries," so it did not fall out of use after 60 A.D.
30. True. Paragraph 2 states: "The mandragora . . . was one of the first plants to be used as an anesthetic." Then the paragraph refers to its use in the Middle Ages.
31. True. Paragraph 3 explains nitrous oxide caused "a strange euphoria, followed by fits of laughter, tears, and sometimes unconsciousness."
32. Not Given. Paragraph 3 refers to laughing gas being used in 1844 to relieve pain during a tooth extraction. However, no details are given about anesthesia/anaesthesia being used for the remainder of the century.
33. True. Paragraph 5 states: "It takes over eight years of schooling and four years of residency until an anesthesiologist is prepared to practice in the United States."
34. False. Paragraph 6 states: "The number of anesthesiologists in the United States has more than doubled since the 1970s."
35. (D) Paragraph 4 states: "Simpson sprinkled chloroform on a handkerchief."
36. (B) Paragraph 5 states: "Local anesthetic is used only at the affected site."
37. (H) Paragraph 2 states: "Dioscorides suggested boiling the root [of mandrake] with wine."
38. (F) Paragraph 3 states: "laughing gas [also known as nitrous oxide], which he used in 1844 to relieve pain during a tooth extraction."
39. (C) Paragraph 5 states: "Regional anesthetic is used to block the sensation and possibly the movement of a larger portion of the body."
40. (E) Paragraph 3 states that the first anesthetic machine contained an ether-soaked sponge.

WRITING

Sample Responses

Writing Task 1

The diagram shows the steps involved in the process of manufacturing yogurt and preparing it for sale.

First, milk has to be heated to the proper temperature, which is 90° Celsius, or 200° Fahrenheit. The milk is kept at this temperature for at least ten minutes. The longer this temperature is maintained, the thicker the yogurt will be. Thirty minutes is generally the maximum time.

Next, the milk is cooled to 44° Celsius, or 112° Fahrenheit. Yogurt starter, or live bacteria, is added. The yogurt is kept at a temperature of 37° Celsius, or 100° Fahrenheit, while it incubates for four hours. After four hours, incubation is stopped by putting the yogurt in a cool place.

Now the yogurt is ready to have things added to it, usually fruit, sweetener, and different flavorings. Then it is put into containers. The containers are labeled and packed for shipping. Soon, the yogurt will show up in your neighborhood grocery store.

Writing Task 2—Agree

Families who do not send their children to government-financed schools should not be required to pay taxes that support universal education.

When families send their children to private school, they must pay tuition and other school expenses. Spending additional money to pay taxes creates an even greater financial hardship for these families. For example, my friend Amalia is a single mother with an eight-year-old son, Andrew. Because they survive solely on her income, money is tight. Amalia works at least 10 hours of overtime each week to cover Andrew's school expenses. This gives Amalia and Andrew less time to spend together, and she is always so tired that she is impatient with him when they do have family time.

While some people may consider private school to be a luxury, for many families it is essential because their community's public schools fail to meet their children's needs. Unfortunately, due to shrinking budgets, many schools lack well-qualified, experienced educators. Children may be taught by someone who is not a certified teacher or who knows little about the subject matter. Some problems are even more serious. For example, the public high school in my old neighborhood/neighbourhood had serious safety problems, due to students bringing guns, drugs, and alcohol to school.

Unfortunately, even when families prefer public schools, sometimes they can't send their children to one. These families are burdened not only by paying expenses at another school, but also by being forced to pay taxes to support a public school that they do not use.

Writing Task 2—Disagree

Families who do not send their children to public school should be required to pay taxes that support public education.

Every child in my country is required to attend school, and every child is welcome to enroll at his/her local public school. Some families choose to send their children to other schools, and it is their prerogative to do so. However, the public schools are used by the majority of our children and must remain open for everyone. For example, my uncle sent his two children to a private academy for primary school. Then he lost a huge amount of money through some poor investments and he could no longer afford the private school's tuition. The public schools supported their family when they had no money to educate their children.

Because the public schools educate so many citizens, everyone in my country—whether a parent or not—should pay taxes to support our educational system. We all benefit from the education that students receive in public school. Our future doctors, firefighters, and teachers—people whom we rely on every day—are educated in local public schools. Providing an excellent education in the public school system is vital to the strength of our community and our country.

Our government must offer the best education available, but it can only do so with the financial assistance of all its citizens. Therefore, everyone—including families who do not send their children to public school—should support public education by paying taxes.

SPEAKING

Sample Responses

Part 1

Do you have a job? Do you like it? Why or why not?

Yes, I have a job. I work as an enrollment manager for a university. I recruit new students into the program. I like it a lot because I can help people, and I get to meet a lot of new and interesting people. Also I have the opportunity to travel a lot.

Why did you choose this job?
I chose this job because I enjoy traveling, and I like meeting people. I have to travel at least 25 percent of the time for my job. I am always talking to people, e-mailing them, or writing articles about our university. It's really interesting.

What kind of education or training did you need to get this job?
I have my MBA (Masters in Business Administration) and that's the same program that I recruit students into. So, having that education really helped me to get this job, because I know what the students need to succeed in our program. Also, I've taken courses in public speaking so I'm comfortable giving presentations about our university.

Describe an activity you enjoy doing in your free time.
One of my favorite free-time activities is painting with watercolors. I especially like to paint outdoor scenes, so when the weather is nice, I go outside and paint.

How long have you been doing this activity? How did you learn it?
I've been painting since I was in high school. I learned how to use watercolors in one of my classes and I really liked it and I've been painting ever since. Sometimes I take a painting class at the local community center, but mostly I learn by doing.

In your free time, do you prefer activities you can do with other people, or activities you can do alone? Why?
It really depends on the activity. Painting is something I usually do alone, although sometimes I go to a park or other pretty place with some other painters I know and we paint together. But if I want to go to the movies or go shopping, those things are always much more fun when you do them with other people.

Is having a lot of free time important to you? Why or why not?
I like having a lot of free time because I always have so much to do. I have my painting and then I want to spend time with my family, of course. I think family is really the most important reason to have free time. It's important to do things with your family.

Part 2

I recently celebrated New Year's Day. The purpose of this day is to welcome the New Year. I think people celebrate it just about everywhere in the world. I celebrated with my cousins. We try to get together every year to celebrate this holiday, even though some of us live far away now. They're like my brothers and sisters; we grew up together. And that's the reason why this holiday is important to me, because I know I will see my cousins then. We're still young, so we did what young people do. We went to some clubs and stayed out all night dancing. We also met up with some old school friends, so it was like a reunion. We stayed out really late, until about 5:00 in the morning. The next day we went to my aunt's house and had a big family dinner with all the aunts and uncles and cousins, everyone in the family of all ages. We ate/had my country's traditional food and told stories and played games. It was a traditional family party. We do it every year.

Part 3

What are some important holidays in your country?
Some important holidays in my country are New Year's Day, National Day, and Children's Day.

Why do people celebrate holidays?
Holidays are a time to remember important dates and people from our past and to practice our traditions. They're also a time to be with our families, and to relax and enjoy good food.

Do you think holiday celebrations have changed over the years? Why or why not?
Holiday celebrations haven't changed much over the years. The dates are the same, and the reason for each day hasn't changed. Families and friends still meet and spend time together.

Do you think the importance of holiday celebrations has changed over the years? Why or why not?
No, I don't think that the importance of holiday celebrations has changed. These days are still special for everyone. But sometimes it's difficult for people to have time to really enjoy the holiday.

How will holidays be different in the future?
In the future, we may have some new holidays. Also, with so many busy families, some of the holiday traditions may change. Instead of eating home-cooked food on holidays, I think that more and more families will go to restaurants. Then they can do less work and still enjoy the holiday together.

Academic
MODEL TEST 3

ANSWER SHEET
Academic Model Test 3

IELTS Listening Answer Sheet

1		✓ 1 ✗
2		2
3		3
4		4
5		5
6		6
7		7
8		8
9		9
10		10
11		11
12		12
13		13
14		14
15		15
16		16
17		17
18		18
19		19
20		20

21		✓ 21 ✗
22		22
23		23
24		24
25		25
26		26
27		27
28		28
29		29
30		30
31		31
32		32
33		33
34		34
35		35
36		36
37		37
38		38
39		39
40		40
	Listening Total	

MODEL TEST 3

Candidate Name ______________________________

International English Language Testing System

LISTENING

Time: Approx. 30 minutes

INSTRUCTIONS TO CANDIDATES

Do not open this booklet until you are told to do so.

Write your name and candidate number in the space at the top of this page.

You should answer all questions.

All the recordings will be played ONCE only.

Write all your answers on the Question Paper.

At the end of the test, you will be given ten minutes to transfer your answers to an Answer Sheet.

Do not remove this booklet from the examination room.

INFORMATION FOR CANDIDATES

There are 40 questions on this question paper.

The test is divided as follows:

Section 1	Questions 1–10
Section 2	Questions 11–20
Section 3	Questions 21–30
Section 4	Questions 31–40

Track 25

SECTION 1

Questions 1–4

Complete the form below. Write NO MORE THAN ONE WORD AND/OR A NUMBER *for each answer.*

Lost Item Report

Example

Day item was lost: ...Monday...

Reported by:

Last Name ...Brown... First name **1** ....

Address **2** .... High Street, **3** .... #5

City ...Riverdale...

Phones: Home ...(not given)... Office ...(not given)... **4** 305–5938

Questions 5–10

*Choose the correct letter, **A**, **B**, or **C**.*

5 What do the woman's glasses look like?

A

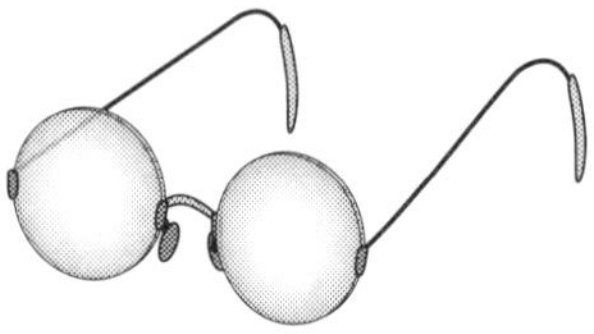

B

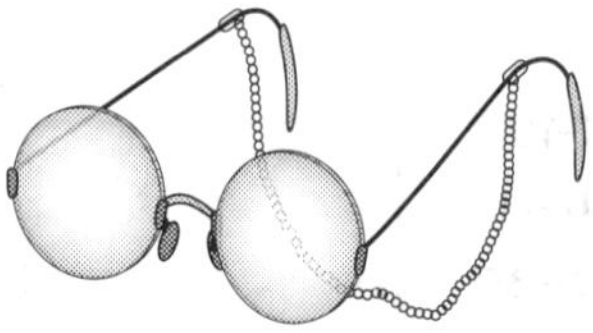

C

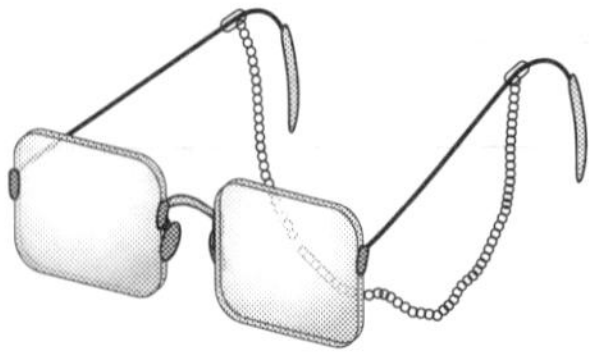

6 Where was the woman sitting when she lost her glasses?

A By the window

B Next to the door

C In the train station

7 What was the woman reading?

- **A** A book
- **B** A newspaper
- **C** A magazine

8 Where was the woman going on the train?

- **A** Home
- **B** To work
- **C** To visit her aunt

9 What time did the train arrive?

- **A** 5:00
- **B** 10:00
- **C** 10:30

10 Where did the woman find her glasses?

A

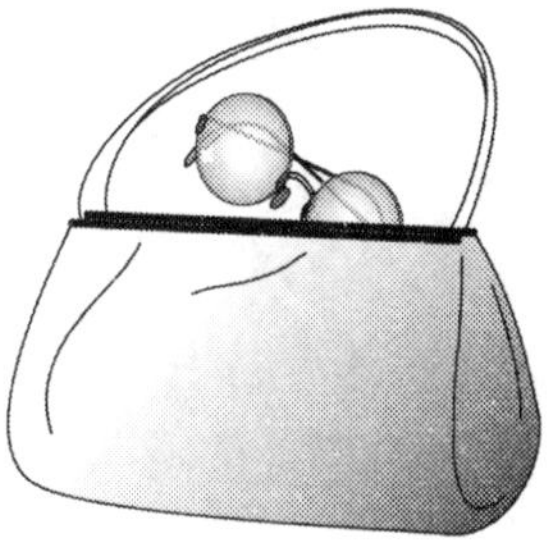

B

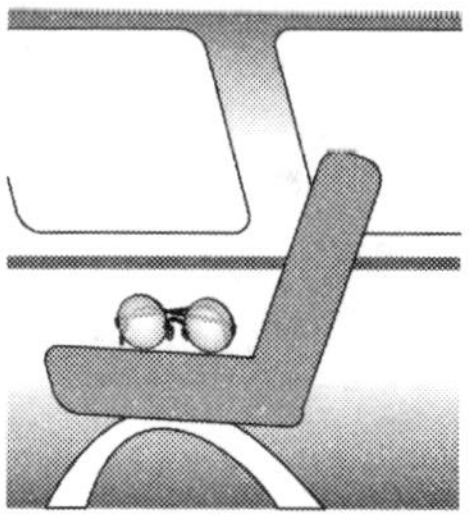

C

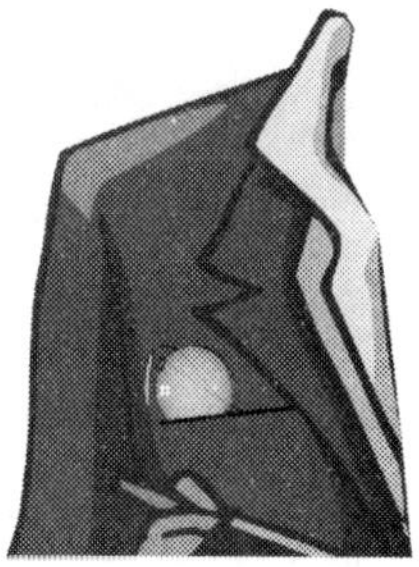

SECTION 2

Questions 11–20

Complete the notes. Write NO MORE THAN THREE WORDS *for each answer.*

Places to look for housing

Not recommended:

Near university — too expensive

Downtown[1] — **11** ....

12 .... from the university

Recommended:

Uptown[2] — **13** ....

a lot of buses go there

Greenfield Park — closer to the university

you need **14** ....

Places to look for ads[3]

15 ....

University newspaper

16 ....

Internet

Available at the Student Counseling Center[4]

city maps

city **17** ....

18 .... service

list of **19** ....

information about **20** .... plans

[1]British: city centre
[2]British: area north of city centre
[3]British: advertisements/adverts
[4]British: Centre

SECTION 3

Questions 21–25

*Choose FIVE letters, **A–I**.*

What five advantages and disadvantages of bicycles do the students mention?

A They help you stay healthy.

B They are simple to maintain.

C They are easy to store.

D They are less expensive than other types of transportation.

E They are nonpolluting.

F They are not comfortable to use in the rain and cold.

G They are easily stolen.

H They are not convenient for long trips.

I They are dangerous to ride on busy highways.

Questions 26–30

Complete the notes below. Write NO MORE THAN THREE WORDS for each answer.

Encouraging Bicycle Riding

Cities can:

26 .... on roads

make places to **27** .... at subway stations

provide **28** ....

Bicycling Equipment

Safety: wear a **29** ....

reflective tape

Comfort: light clothes

30 ....

SECTION 4

Questions 31–40

Complete the outline. Write NO MORE THAN THREE WORDS *for each answer.*

Writing a Research Paper

I. Choose a topic

- **A** Look at **31** ....
- **B** Make topic more specific
- **C** Get **32** ....

II. **33** ....

- A. Library
    1. Reference and other types of books
    2. Journals, **34** ....
    3. Atlases and other similar sources
- B. Internet
    1. Online journals and newspapers
    2. Online **35** ....

III. Write a thesis statement

IV. **36** ....

- A. Introduction
- B. **37** ....
- C. **38** ....

V. **39** ....

VI. Write first draft

VII. **40** ....

VIII. Type final draft

ANSWER SHEET
Academic Model Test 3

IELTS Reading Answer Sheet

		✓		✗
1			1	
2			2	
3			3	
4			4	
5			5	
6			6	
7			7	
8			8	
9			9	
10			10	
11			11	
12			12	
13			13	
14			14	
15			15	
16			16	
17			17	
18			18	
19			19	
20			20	

		✓		✗
21			21	
22			22	
23			23	
24			24	
25			25	
26			26	
27			27	
28			28	
29			29	
30			30	
31			31	
32			32	
33			33	
34			34	
35			35	
36			36	
37			37	
38			38	
39			39	
40			40	
	Reading Total			

MODEL TEST 3

Candidate Name ____________________

INTERNATIONAL ENGLISH LANGUAGE TESTING SYSTEM

ACADEMIC READING

Time: 1 hour

INSTRUCTIONS TO CANDIDATES

Do not open this booklet until you are told to do so.

Write your name and candidate number in the space at the top of this page.

Start at the beginning of the test and work through it.

You should answer all questions.

If you cannot do a particular question, leave it and go on to the next. You can return to it later.

All answers must be written on the Answer Sheet.

Do not remove this booklet from the examination room.

INFORMATION FOR CANDIDATES

There are **40** questions on this question paper.

The test is divided as follows:

Reading Passage 1	Questions 1-14
Reading Passage 2	Questions 15-27
Reading Passage 3	Questions 28-40

Reading Passage 1

You should spend about 20 minutes on questions 1–14, which are based on Reading Passage 1 below.

Allergy Testing

Allergic reactions are triggered by the contact, inhalation, or ingestion of a number of different allergens. Some of the most common allergens are made up of proteins found in plants, mold, food, venom, animal skin, and medication. Symptoms of allergic reactions range from mild irritation such as itching, wheezing, and coughing to life-threatening conditions related to the respiratory and gastrointestinal organs. Serious allergic reactions are more likely to result from food, drugs, and stinging insects. A person does not become allergic to a particular substance until after the first exposure. However, in some cases, even trace amounts of a substance, such as peanuts or seafood in a mother's breast milk, can cause an allergic reaction in a subsequent exposure.

A variety of allergy tests are available for determining specific substances that trigger allergic reactions in individuals. Allergists, also known as immunologists, are trained in selecting the types of tests that are both safe and appropriate, depending on the suspected allergies. By using allergen extracts, tiny amounts of commonly bothersome allergens (usually in the form of purified liquid drops), immunologists are often able to isolate which substances cause reactions in allergy sufferers.

One of the most common types of environmental allergy tests is the skin-prick test. This technique involves placing small drops of potential allergen onto the skin of the forearm about one to two inches apart. After the drops are placed on the arm, a needle is used to puncture the skin at the site of each drop. (Though the procedure is virtually painless, this test is often done on the upper back of children to prevent them from seeing the needle.) If an allergy is present, an allergic antibody called *immunoglobulin* E (IgE) will activate a special cell called a *mast* cell. Mast cells release chemicals (also known as *mediators*) that cause itching and swelling. The most common mediator is *histamine*. Histamine is what causes the controlled hive known as a *wheal and flare*. The white wheal is the small raised surface, while the flare is the redness that spreads out from it. In an uncontrolled allergic reaction, wheals and flares can get much bigger and spread all over a person's body. Results from a skin test can usually be obtained within 20 to 30 minutes, while the reaction usually fades within a few hours.

Another test that is very similar to the skin-prick test is the intradermal allergy test. This involves placing the allergen sample under the skin with a syringe. The intradermal test involves more risk and is usually saved for use if the allergy persists even after a skin-prick test comes back negative. People who have experienced serious allergic reactions called anaphylactic reactions are not advised to have these types of tests. These allergy sufferers may be hypersensitive to even trace amounts of the allergens when they are introduced into the blood. Anaphylaxis is an allergic reaction that affects the whole body and is potentially life-threatening. Hives on the lips and throat can become severe enough to block air passage. Anaphylactic shock occurs when enough histamine is released to cause the blood vessels to dilate and release fluid into the tissues. This lowers blood volume and can result in heart failure.

A blood test can be performed to safely isolate over 400 different allergies, including dangerous food and environmental allergens. The Radio Allergo Sorbant Test (RAST) measures specific IgE antibodies using a blood sample. IgE is normally found in very small amounts in the blood; it is created as a defense[1] mechanism when it senses an intruder. Separate tests are done for each potential allergen, and IgE results are graded from 0 to 6. For example, canine serum IgE will be high if a person has an allergy to dogs. The RAST is used if patients have pre-existing skin conditions or if patients cannot stop taking certain medications such as antidepressants or antihistamines for even a short period of time. (People must stop taking antihistamines several days prior to taking a skin allergy test because the medication can interfere with the results.) The RAST is a more expensive test that does not provide immediate results.

A number of other allergy tests are available, though many are considered unreliable according to The Academy of Allergy, Asthma, and Immunology. Applied kinesiology is a test that analyzes[2] the loss of muscle strength in the presence of potential allergens. Provocation and neutralization[3] testing involves injecting food allergens into the skin in different quantities, with the goal of determining the smallest dose needed to neutralize the symptoms. Sublingual provocation and neutralization is a similar test, except that the allergens are injected underneath the tongue. Cytotoxity testing involves watching for the reaction of blood cells after placing allergens on a slide next to a person's blood samples.

After using a reliable testing method, the cause of an allergic reaction is often identified, and a physician is able to help a patient develop a treatment plan with the goal of controlling or eliminating the allergic symptoms. Those who are allergic to furry pets, pollen, and plants are prescribed mild medication or taught how to control their reactions with simple lifestyle changes, while those with food allergies learn to safely remove certain foods from their diets. Allergy sufferers who are prone to anaphylactic reactions are educated about life-saving techniques such as carrying the drug epinephrine and wearing medical alert bracelets. As soon as people understand their allergies, they can begin to experience an improved quality of life.

[1]BRITISH: defence
[2]BRITISH: analyses
[3]BRITISH: neutralisation/neutralise

Questions 1–7

The passage describes three different types of allergy tests. Which of the characteristics below belongs to which type of test? In boxes 1–7 on your Answer Sheet, write

A if it is a characteristic of the skin-prick test.
B if it is a characteristic of the intradermal test.
C if it is a characteristic of the blood test.

1 A substance is inserted beneath the skin with a needle.

2 It is often done on a patient's back.

3 It is advisable for patients who have skin problems.

4 It is not advisable for patients who have had serious allergic reactions in the past.

5 It shows results within half an hour.

6 It can cause red and white bumps on the patient's skin.

7 It has a higher cost than other tests.

Questions 8–14

Complete the summary of the reading passage below. Choose your answers from the box below, and write them in boxes 8–14 on your Answer Sheet. There are more words than spaces so you will not use them all.

mold	smelling	identify	allergens
avoiding	medicines	eating	treat
antihistamine	anaphylaxis	causes	signs

Allergic reactions result from touching, breathing, or **8** .... certain substances called **9** .... Coughing or itching are two possible **10** .... of an allergic reaction. More serious allergic reactions may result from certain insect bites, foods, or **11** .... A severe allergic reaction is known as **12** .... It can result in loss of blood volume and heart failure. Doctors can use a variety of tests to **13** .... the source of an allergy. Treatment may include taking medication or **14** .... the substances that cause the allergic reaction.

Reading Passage 2

You should spend about 20 minutes on questions 15–27, which are based on Reading Passage 2 below.

The Sacred Pipe

The sacred pipe was one of the most important artifacts of the indigenous people of North America. In almost every culture, the sacred pipe was considered a gift from The Great Spirit. The Cree believed that the pipe, the tobacco, and the fire were given as parting gifts from the Creator, while the Iowa Black Bear clan believed that the pipe bowl and later the pipe stem emerged from the earth as gifts to the earth's first bears. In most cases, the sacred pipe was considered a medium through which humans could pray to The Great Spirit, asking for guidance, health, and the necessities of life. In order for the prayers to reach the Great Spirit, they had to travel in the plumes of smoke from the sacred pipe. Because of its connection to the spiritual world, the pipe was treated with more respect than any human being, especially when the pipe bowl was joined to the stem.

Unlike the common pipe, which was used by average tribesmen for casual smoking purposes, the sacred pipe was built with precise craftsmanship. Before a pipe was carved, the catlinite (pipestone) was blessed and prayed over. The bowl of the traditional sacred pipe was made of red pipestone to represent the Earth. The wooden stem represented all that grew upon the Earth. In the Lakota Society, as in many Native American tribes, the people believed that the pipe bowl also represented a woman while the pipe stem represented a man. Joined together, the pipe symbolized the circle of love between a man and woman. The sacred pipe was the only object that was built by both genders; men carved the bowl and stem while women decorated the pipe with porcupine quills. In many tribes the man and woman held onto the sacred pipe during the marriage ceremony.

Cultivating the tobacco was the responsibility of certain members of the tribe. Generally, tobacco was mixed with herbs, bark, and roots, such as bayberry, mugwort, and wild cherry bark. These mixtures varied depending on the plants that were indigenous to the tribal area. Ceremonial tobacco was much stronger than the type that was used for everyday smoking. Rather than being inhaled, the smoke from the sacred pipe was puffed out the mouth in four directions.

In a typical pipe ceremony, the pipe holder stood up and held the pipe bowl in his left hand, with the stem held toward the East in his right hand. Before adding the first pinch of tobacco to the pipe bowl, he sprinkled some on the ground as an offering to both Mother Earth and the East. The East was acknowledged as the place where the morning star rose. Tribes believed that peace would evolve from wisdom if they prayed to the morning star.

Before offering a prayer to the South, the pipe holder again offered Mother Earth a sprinkling of tobacco and added another pinch into the bowl. The South was believed to bring strength, growth, and healing. While facing west the pipe holder acknowledged Mother Earth and prepared to thank the area where the sun sets. West was where the tribe believed the Spirit Helpers lived. At this time, they prayed for guidance from the spiritual world. The ceremony then proceeded to the North, which was thanked for blanketing Mother Earth with white snow, and for providing health and endurance.

After these four prayers, the pipe holder held the stem to the ground again and the tribe promised to respect and protect Mother Earth. Next, the stem was held up at an angle so that Father Sky could be thanked for the energy and heat he gave to the human body. Finally, the stem was held straight up and the tribe acknowledged The Great Spirit, thanking him for being the creator of Mother Earth, Father Sky, and the four directions.

After the pipe holder had worked his way around the four directions, he lit the pipe and passed it around the sacred circle in the same direction as the ceremonial prayers, starting from the East. Each member took a puff of smoke and offered another prayer. When the pipe had made a full circle, it was capped with bark, and the stem was removed. It was important for the stem and bowl to be stored in separate pockets in a pipe pouch. These pieces were not allowed to touch each other, except during a sacred pipe ceremony.

Pipestone, Minnesota, is considered hallowed ground for North American tribes. Regardless of their conflicts, tribes put their weapons down and gathered in peace in these quarries. According to the Dakota tribe, The Great Spirit once called all Indian nations to this location. Here the Spirit stood on the red pipestone and broke a piece away from the rock to make a giant pipe. He told his people that the red stone was their flesh and that it should be used to make a sacred pipe. He also said that the pipestone belonged to all native tribesmen and that the quarries must be considered a sacred place. Thus, people who had sacred pipes in their possession were considered caretakers, not owners.

Questions 15–19

*Choose the correct letters, **A–C**, and write them in boxes 15–19 on your Answer Sheet.*

15 The sacred pipe was important in native American cultures because

A it was part of their spiritual practice.
B it was used in gift exchanges between tribes.
C it represented traditional handicrafts.

16 The pipe was made of

A stone and wood.
B bark and roots.
C red clay from the Earth.

17 The pipe was sometimes used at

A funerals.
B births.
C weddings.

18 During the pipe ceremony, tribe members smoked

A plain tobacco.
B a combination of plants.
C only bark.

19 Pipestone, Minnesota, is an important place because it is

A the site of a major battle.
B the origin of the Dakota tribe.
C the source of stone for pipes.

Questions 20–27

Complete the flowchart about the pipe ceremony. Write NO MORE THAN THREE WORDS *from the passage for each answer.*

The pipe holder takes the **20** .... in his left hand and the **21** .... in his other hand.
↓
The pipe holder offers tobacco to Mother Earth and **22** .... , the place where the morning star rises, and then puts some in the pipe.
↓
The pipe holder prays to **23** .... to bring strength, growth, and healing and then prays to the remaining directions.
↓
The pipe holder points the pipe stem down and then up and prays to The Great Spirit, in appreciation for **24** .... , Father Sky, and **25** ....
↓
The pipe holder passes the pipe around the sacred circle, and all members of the circle **26** .... and pray.
↓
The bowl and stem are stored **27** .... because they can only touch each other during the ceremony.

Reading Passage 3

You should spend about 20 minutes on questions 28–40, which are based on Reading Passage 3 below.

Bathymetry

The ocean floor is often considered the last frontier on earth, as it is a domain that remains greatly unexplored. Bathymetry, also known as sea-floor topography, involves measuring and mapping the depths of the underwater world. Today much of the ocean floor still remains unmapped because collecting bathymetry data in waters of great depth is a time consuming and complex endeavor[1].

Two hundred years ago most people assumed that the ocean floor was similar to the beaches and coastlines. During the nineteenth century, attempts to produce maps of the seafloor involved lowering weighted lines from a boat and waiting for the tension of the line to change. When the handline hit the ocean floor, the depth of the water was determined by measuring the amount of slack. Each of these measurements was called a sounding, and thousands of soundings had to be done just to get a rough measurement of a small portion of the ocean floor. Besides estimating the depth, these surveys helped in identifying large shipping hazards, especially near the shoreline. A naval officer published the first evidence of underwater mountains in a bathymetric chart in 1855.

During World War I, scientists developed the technology for measuring sound waves in the ocean. Anti-Submarine Detection Investigation Committee (ASDICs) was the original name for these underwater sound projectors, but by World War II the term *sonar* was adopted in the United States and many other nations. Sonar, which stands for Sound, Navigation, and Ranging, was first used to detect submarines and icebergs. By calculating the amount of time it took for a sound signal to reflect back to its original source, sonar could measure the depth of the ocean as well as the depth of any objects found within it. The first sonar devices were passive systems that could only receive sound waves. By the 1930s, single-beam sonar was being used to transmit sound waves in a vertical line from a ship to the seafloor. The sound waves were recorded as they returned from the surface to the ship. However, this type of sonar was more useful in detecting submerged objects than mapping the seafloor. Throughout World War II, technology improved, and active sonar systems that both received and produced sound waves were being used. It was the invention of the acoustic transducer and the acoustic projector that made way for this modern sonar. The newer systems made it possible to identify certain material, such as rock or mud. Since mud absorbed a good portion of a sound signal, it provided a much weaker echo than rocks, which reflected much of the sound wave.

[1] British: endeavour

The multi-beam sonar, which could be attached to a ship's hull, was developed in the 1960s. With this type of sonar, multiple beams could be adjusted to a number of different positions, and a larger area of the ocean could be surveyed. Maps created with the aid of multi-beam sonar helped to explain the formation of ridges and trenches, including the Ring of Fire and the Mid-Ocean Ridge. The Ring of Fire is a zone that circles the Pacific Ocean and is famous for its seismic activity. This area, which extends from the coast of New Zealand to the coast of North and South America, also accounts for more than 75 percent of the world's active and dormant volcanoes. The Mid-Ocean Ridge is a section of undersea mountains that extends over 12,000 feet high and 1,200 miles wide. These mountains, which zigzag around the continents, are generally considered the most outstanding topographical features on earth.

The invention of the side-scan sonar was another modern breakthrough for the field of bathymetry. This type of sonar is towed on cables, making it possible to send and receive sound waves over a broad section of the seafloor at much lower angles than the multi-beam sonar. The benefit of the side-scan sonar system is that it can detect very specific features over a large area. The most modern form of bathymetry, which is also the least accurate, is done with data collected by satellite altimetry. This method began to be used in the 1970s. This type of mapping relies on radar altimeters that receive echoes from the sea surface. These signals measure the distance between the satellite and the ocean floor. Unfortunately, due to water vapor[1] and ionization, electromagnetic waves are often decelerated as they move through the atmosphere; therefore, the satellite receives inaccurate measurements. The benefit of using satellites to map the ocean is that it can take pictures of the entire globe, including areas that have not yet been measured by sonar. At this time, satellite altimetry is mainly used to locate areas where detailed sonar measurements need to be conducted.

Due to a constant flux of plate activity, the topography of the seafloor is ever-changing. Scientists expect bathymetry to become one of the most important sciences as humans search for new energy sources and seek alternate routes for telecommunication. Preserving the ocean's biosphere for the future will also rely on an accurate mapping of the seafloor.

[1] British: vapour

Questions 28–33

Complete the table below. Write **NO MORE THAN THREE WORDS** *from the passage for each answer. Write your answers in boxes 28–33 on your Answer Sheet.*

Mapping the Ocean Floor

Method	First Used . . .	Used for . . .	How It Works
weighted line	**28**	determining **29**	drop a line until it hits the bottom
30	1930s	detecting objects underwater	send **31** .... to ocean floor
multi-beam sonar	**32**	mapping larger areas of the different directions	send multiple sound waves in
satellite altimetry	1970s	taking pictures of **33**	send signals from satellite

Questions 34–37

Match each description below with the ocean region that it describes.

In boxes 34–37 on your Answer Sheet, write

A if it describes the Ring of Fire.
B if it describes the Mid-Ocean Ridge.

34 It is known for the earthquakes that occur there.

35 It is over one thousand miles wide.

36 It is a mountain range.

37 It contains the majority of the earth's volcanoes.

Questions 38–40

Do the following statements agree with the information in Reading Passage 3?
In boxes 38–40 on your Answer Sheet, write

TRUE *if the statement is true according to the passage.*
FALSE *if the statement contradicts the passage.*
NOT GIVEN *if there is no information about this in the passage.*

38 The shape of the ocean floor remains fairly constant over time.

39 Bathymetry provides information important for protecting ocean life.

40 Maps of the ocean floor have led to improved methods for predicting earthquakes.

ANSWER SHEET
Academic Model Test 3

Writing Answer Sheet

TASK 1

ANSWER SHEET
Academic Model Test 3

-2-

ANSWER SHEET
Academic Model Test 3

-3-

TASK 2

ANSWER SHEET
Academic Model Test 3

-4-

MODEL TEST 3

Candidate Name ____________________

International English Language Testing System

ACADEMIC WRITING

Time: 1 hour

INSTRUCTIONS TO CANDIDATES

Do not open this booklet until you are told to do so.

Write your name and candidate number in the space at the top of this page.

All answers must be written on the separate answer booklet provided.

Do not remove this booklet from the examination room.

INFORMATION FOR CANDIDATES

There are **2** tasks on this question paper.

You must do **both** tasks.

Underlength answers will be penalized.

WRITING TASK 1

You should spend no more than 20 minutes on this task.

The charts below show the percentage of their food budget the average family spent on restaurant meals in different years. The graph shows the average number of meals eaten in fast-food restaurants and sit-down restaurants per family.

Summarize[1] the information by selecting and reporting the main features, and make comparisons where relevant.

Write at least 150 words.

Percentage of Food Budget Spent on Restaurant Meals

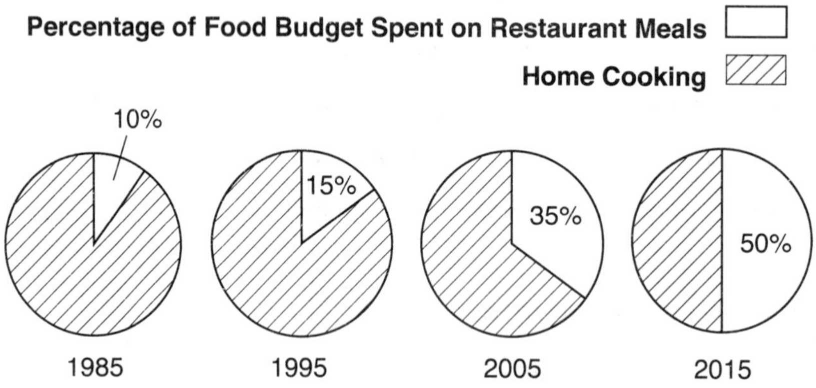

Fast-Food vs. Sit-Down Restaurants

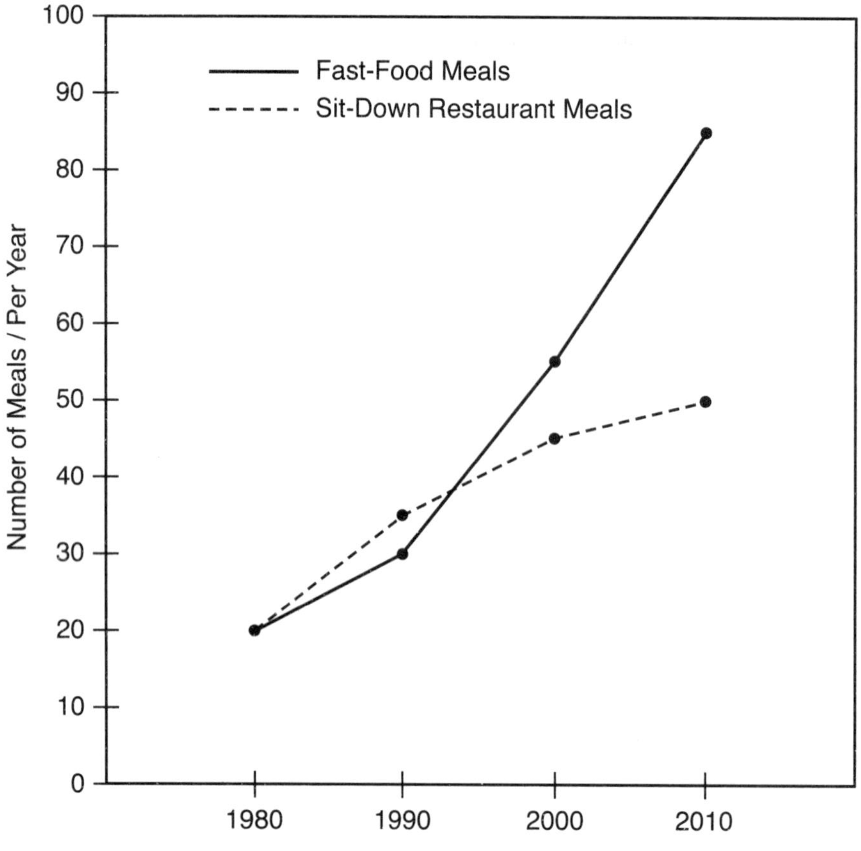

[1]BRITISH: summarise

WRITING TASK 2

You should spend no more than 40 minutes on this task.

Write about the following topic:

> ***By punishing murderers with the death penalty, society is also guilty of committing murder. Therefore, life in prison is a better punishment for murderers.***

To what extent do you agree or disagree with this statement?

Give reasons for your answer and include any relevant examples from your own knowledge or experience.

Write at least 250 words.

SPEAKING

Examiner Questions:

Part 1 (4–5 minutes)

Food

What kind of food do you enjoy eating?
What are some kinds of food you never eat? Why?
Do you generally prefer to eat at home or at a restaurant? Why?
What are some reasons that people eat at restaurants?

Free TIme

Describe some things you enjoy doing with your friends.
Do you think it's better to have a large group of friends or a few close friends? Why?
How do people choose their friends?
Have you remained friends with people from your childhood? Why or why not?

Part 2 (3–4 minutes)

You will be given a topic. You will have one to two minutes to talk about this topic. You will have one minute to prepare what you are going to say. You may take some notes if you wish. Here is your topic:

> Describe a teacher from your past.
>
> You should say:
> what grade you were in when this teacher taught you
> what things this teacher taught you
> what the teacher's special qualities were
>
> and describe why you remember this particular teacher.

Part 3 (4–5 minutes)

The Qualities of a Good Teacher

What kind of person makes a good teacher?
Why do you think people choose to become teachers?
Which is more important for a teacher—to be an expert in the subject he or she teaches, or to be very skilled at explaining things and motivating students to learn?

Changes in Schools

How are schools different now from when you were young?
How do you think schools will be different in the future?

ACADEMIC MODEL TEST 3—ANSWER EXPLANATIONS

LISTENING

1. *Patty.* In line 9 of the dialogue she says, "It's Patty, that's P-A-T-T-Y."
2. *17.* In line 11, she says, "I live at 17 High Street" and in line 13 she emphasizes this, "SevenTEEN."
3. *apartment.* In line 15, she says, "It's an apartment/flat."
4. *cell.* In line 19, she says, "It's my mobile phone."
5. (B) In line 23, when asked to describe her glasses, the woman says, "They're round. And they have a chain attached." (A) is incorrect because it shows round glasses without saying anything about the chain. (C) is incorrect because it indicates square reading glasses, and hers were round.
6. (A) In line 25, the woman says that she "had a window seat." So, she was by the window when she lost her glasses. (B) is incorrect because she was not near a door: "the door [was] at the other end of the car." (C) is incorrect because she "was sitting on the train reading," not in the station.
7. (C) In line 27, she "was [reading] a fascinating article in that new magazine." (A) and (B) are incorrect because those choices are never mentioned.
8. (C) In line 29 she says, "I've come here to visit my aunt." (A) is incorrect because she wasn't going home. In fact, she "left home at five o'clock this morning." (B) is incorrect because she wasn't going to work. She took "a whole week off work to make this trip."
9. (B) In line 31 she says, "At ten o'clock, I think. Yes, that's right." (A) is incorrect because that is the time she left home that morning. (C) is incorrect because in line 31 she says that her train arrived "just about 30 minutes ago. At ten o'clock." So her train arrived at 10 and she is making the lost report at 10:30.
10. (C) In lines 34 and 35, the man asks about what is in her coat pocket, and she finds her glasses then. (A) is incorrect because they were not in her purse/handbag. She does say, "I had my handbag," but her glasses weren't there. (B) is incorrect because she says, "I checked my seat to see if I had left anything on it, but I hadn't."
11. *mainly commercial area/fewer apartments.* The downtown is described as "mainly a commercial area."
12. *too far.* The downtown is described as "rather far from the university."
13. *prices are low.* The speaker says that in uptown "The prices there are quite low."
14. *a car.* The speaker says, "you'll need a car if you choose to live there" (in uptown).
15. *University's Student Center/Student Center wall.* The speaker says, "look . . . at the university's Student Center. There is a wall there devoted to apartment ads."
16. *Local newspaper/ The Greenfield Times.* He mentions, "The local city newspaper, *The Greenfield Times*, . . . lists apartment for rent ads."
17. *bus schedules.* He says the Student Counseling[1] Center (SCC) has "city bus schedules."
18. *roommate matching.* He says the SCC has a "roommate[2] matching service."
19. *inexpensive furniture stores.* He says the SCC can provide "a list of inexpensive furniture stores."
20. *meal.* He mentions that students can sign up "for a meal plan on campus" and that SCC has several different plans.
21. (A) The speaker says: "First, bicycle riding is good for your health."
22. (D) The speakers say: "Bicycles are a lot cheaper to use than cars. Or any other form of transportation when you think about it."
23. (E) The speaker says: "Bicycles don't cause pollution like cars and buses do."
24. (F) The speaker talks about rain and cold. She says: "So bad weather would be a problem."
25. (H) The speaker says: "It is difficult to ride your bike if your trip is long distance."
26. *make bike lanes.* The woman says, "I think the biggest thing is making bicycle lanes on roads."

[1]British: Counselling
[2]British: flatmate

27. *lock up bikes/lock bikes/leave their bikes.* The woman says, "They need a safe place to lock up their bikes."
28. *bicycling maps.* The woman says, "Some cities provide bicycling maps."
29. *helmet.* The woman says, "For safety you should wear a helmet."
30. *waterproof clothes.* The woman says, "For comfort you need . . . waterproof clothes when it rains."
31. *suggested topics list/list of topics.* In paragraph 1, the professor says, "I have a list of suggested topics . . . and I'd like you to look over it."
32. *final approval/professor's approval.* At the end of paragraph 1, the professor says, "You'll need to get my final approval on your topic."
33. *Gather information.* In paragraph 2, the professor says, "The next thing you'll do is gather information on your topic."
34. *magazines, and newspapers.* In paragraph 2 the professor mentions the "journals, magazines, and newspapers."
35. *encyclopedias/encyclopaedias.* In paragraph 2, the professor refers to the "online encyclopedias."
36. *Write an outline.* In paragraph 4, the professor says: "Now then, let's say you have your thesis statement . . . . Writing an outline will help you get focused."
37. *body.* Midway through paragraph 4, the professor explains there is an introduction and "then the body."
38. *conclusion.* At the end of paragraph 4, the professor explains there is "finally the conclusion."
39. *Organize/organise your notes.* At the beginning of paragraph 5, the professor says, "you can start organizing your notes."
40. *Revise your draft.* In paragraph 7 the professor says, "the next thing to do is revise your draft."

READING

Passage 1—Allergy Testing

1. (B) In paragraph 4, it states that the intradermal allergy test "involves placing the allergen sample under the skin with a syringe."
2. (A) In paragraph 3, it says that the "test is often done on the upper back of children."
3. (C) In paragraph 5, it says that a blood test (the RAST) "is used if patients have pre-existing skin conditions."
4. (B) In paragraph 4 about the intradermal allergy test, the text states, "People who have experienced serious allergic reactions called anaphylactic reactions are not advised to have these types of tests."
5. (A) In paragraph 3 about the skin-prick test, the text says, "Results from a skin test can usually be obtained within 20 to 30 minutes."
6. (A) In paragraph 3 about the skin-prick test, the text discusses a controlled hive known as a wheal and flare. "The white wheal is the small raised surface, while the flare is the redness that spreads out from it."
7. (C) In paragraph 5 about the blood test, the text states, "The RAST is a more expensive test."
8. *eating.* In paragraph 1, the text states: "Allergic reactions are triggered by the contact, inhalation, or *ingestion* . . . ."
9. *allergens.* In paragraph 1, the text states: "Allergic reactions are triggered by the contact, inhalation, or ingestion of a number of different *allergens*."
10. *signs.* In paragraph 1, the text states: "*Symptoms* of allergic reactions range from mild irritation such as itching, wheezing, and coughing."
11. *medicines.* In paragraph 1, the text states: "Serious allergic reactions are more likely to result from food, *drugs*, and stinging insects."
12. *anaphylaxis.* In paragraph 4, the text states: "*Anaphylaxis* is an allergic reaction that affects the whole body and is potentially life threatening." This sentence expresses that anaphylaxis is an allergic reaction, and a very severe one.

13. *identify.* In paragraph 7, the text states: "After using a reliable testing method, the cause of an allergic reaction is often *identified.*"
14. *avoiding.* In paragraph 7, the text states: "while those with food allergies learn to safely *remove* certain foods from their diets."

Passage 2—The Sacred Pipe

15. (A) Choice (A) is correct because paragraph 1 explains: "the sacred pipe was considered a medium through which humans could pray to The Great Spirit." The text mentions the pipe's "connection to the spiritual world." Choice (B) is incorrect because the reading passage mentions "a gift from the Great Spirit" and "gifts to the earth's first bears," but it does not describe using the sacred pipe in gift exchanges. Choice (C) is incorrect because paragraph 2 says that, "the sacred pipe was built with precise craftsmanship." But there is no mention of it representing traditional handicrafts.
16. (A) Choice (A) is correct because paragraph 2 states: "The bowl of the traditional sacred pipe was made of red pipestone . . . . The wooden stem." Paragraph 8 elaborates on the red pipestone by explaining that "the quarries must be considered a sacred place" and these quarries, where the pipestone was found, indicate that pipestone is a rock. Choice (B) is incorrect because those are the substances used in mixing tobacco–see paragraph 3. Choice (C) is incorrect because there is no mention of red clay in this reading passage.
17. (C) Choice (C) is correct because paragraph 2 states, "In many tribes the man and woman held onto the sacred pipe during the marriage ceremony." Choices (A) and (B) are incorrect because funerals and births are not mentioned.
18. (B) Choice (B) is correct because paragraph 3 states: "tobacco was mixed with herbs, bark, and roots . . . . These mixtures varied depending on the plants that were indigenous to the tribal area." So, the tobacco combined a variety of herbs as well as other plant life. Choice (A) is incorrect because this ceremonial tobacco was not plain. Choice (C) is incorrect because bark was only one of the ingredients in the mixture.
19. (C) Choice (C) is correct because paragraph 8 describes Pipestone, Minnesota. The text refers to its quarries, so this is a source of stone for pipes. Choice (A) is incorrect because there were no battles here. The text states, "Regardless of their conflicts, tribes put their weapons down and gathered in peace in these quarries." Choice (B) is incorrect because the text says that "According to the Dakota tribe, The Great Spirit once called all Indian nations to this location." No mention is made of the Dakota tribe originating there.
20. *pipe bowl/bowl.* Paragraph 4 states: "In a typical pipe ceremony, the pipe holder stood up and held the pipe bowl in his left hand."
21. *pipe stem/stem.* Paragraph 4 states: "In a typical pipe ceremony, the pipe holder stood up . . . with the stem held toward the East in his right hand."
22. *the East.* Paragraph 4 states: "he sprinkled some on the ground as an offering to both Mother Earth and the East. The East was acknowledged as the place where the morning star rose."
23. *the South.* Paragraph 5 states: "Before offering a prayer to the South . . . . The South was believed to bring strength, growth, and healing."
24. *Mother Earth.* Paragraph 6 explains the ritual. Read the first and last sentences.
25. *the four directions.* Paragraph 6 explains: "Finally, the stem was held straight up and the tribe acknowledged The Great Spirit, thanking him for being the creator of Mother Earth, Father Sky, and the four directions."
26. *smoke.* Paragraph 7 states: "Each member took a puff of smoke and offered another prayer."
27. *in separate pockets.* Paragraph 7 explains: "It was important for the stem and bowl to be stored in separate pockets in a pipe pouch. These pieces were not allowed to touch each other, except during a sacred pipe ceremony."

Passage 3—Bathymetry

28. *nineteenth century.* Paragraph 2 states: "During the nineteenth century, attempts to produce maps of the seafloor involved lowering weighted lines from a boat."
29. *depth.* Paragraph 2 says: "When the handline hit the ocean floor, the depth of the water was determined."
30. *single-beam sonar.* Paragraph 3 focuses on sonar and says it "was first used to detect submarines and icebergs." So, it was used for detecting objects underwater. The text explains, "By the 1930s, single-beam sonar was being used."
31. *sound waves.* Paragraph 3 states that "By the 1930s, single-beam sonar was being used to transmit sound waves in a vertical line from a ship to the seafloor."
32. *1960s.* According to paragraph 4, "The multi-beam sonar . . . was developed in the 1960s."
33. *the entire globe.* Paragraph 5 says: "The benefit of using satellites to map the ocean is that it can take pictures of the entire globe."
34. (A) Choice (A) is correct because paragraph 4 says: "The Ring of Fire . . . is famous for its seismic activity."
35. (B) Choice (B) is correct because paragraph 4 states: "The Mid-Ocean Ridge is . . . 1,200 miles wide."
36. (B) Choice (B) is correct because paragraph 4 explains: "The Mid-Ocean Ridge is a section of undersea mountains."
37. (A) Choice (A) is correct because paragraph 4 says: "This area [the Ring of Fire] . . . accounts for more than 75 percent of the world's active and dormant volcanoes."
38. False. Paragraph 6 states the opposite: "the topography of the seafloor is ever-changing."
39. True. Paragraph 6 states: "preserving the ocean's biosphere for the future will also rely on accurate mapping of the seafloor."
40. Not given. Predicting earthquakes is not mentioned in the article.

WRITING

Sample Responses

Writing Task 1

The charts and graph show information about the restaurant eating habits of the average family over the past 30 years. During this time, the number of meals that the average family eats at restaurants has dramatically increased. The percentage of the family's food budget spent on restaurant meals steadily climbed. Just 10 percent of the food budget was spent on restaurant meals in 1985 and 15 percent in 1995. That percentage more than doubled in 2005, to 35 percent, and rose again in 2015 to 50 percent.

Where families eat their restaurant meals also changed during that 30-year period. In 1985, families ate the same number of meals at fast-food and sit-down restaurants. In 1995, families ate slightly more frequently at sit-down restaurants. However, since 2005, fast-food restaurants serve more meals to the families than do the sit-down restaurants. Most of the restaurant meals from 2015 were eaten at fast-food restaurants. If this pattern continues, eventually the number of meals that families eat at fast-food restaurants could double the number of meals they eat at sit-down restaurants.

Writing Task 2—Agree

"Do as I say, not as I do." This is what society tells us when it punishes murderers with the death penalty. Society tells us that murder is wrong, and in our legal system, murder is against the law. Yet we still see our society kill murderers, and thus we are committing murder ourselves. For this reason, the death penalty should end, and instead murderers should be punished with life in prison.

Society needs to show a positive model of how our lives should be and how people should act. We should always strive to improve our situation, to be at peace and in harmony with others. However, when we kill murderers, we are not working to improve our society. Instead, we are stooping to the criminals' level.

It makes me think about the revenge that came when playing games with my brother. When we were kids/children, my brother would take my toys, so I would hit him and take my toys back. Then he would hit me harder and take the toys again. Thinking of the death penalty, I imagine a murderer kills someone. Society takes revenge by killing the murderer. This leaves behind the murderer's family and friends, who have tremendous anger inside of them, which they may release onto society. The cycle of killing goes on and on.

Society should not condemn people who are taking the same action that society is taking. Society tells us not to kill, and yet society kills when it exercises the death penalty. Because of this contradiction, we should end the death penalty and instead punish murderers by sentencing them to life in prison.

Writing Task 2—Disagree

I strongly support the death penalty for murderers. In today's society, life is very violent. There are many mentally ill people committing crimes and almost nothing will stop them. We have interviewed captured criminals who say, "I was going to kill him, but I knew that I could get the death penalty if I did. So I just left him there." Obviously, having the death penalty saves lives and prevents crimes from being committed, and that makes a positive difference to society.

If a criminal does murder someone and then gets the death penalty, that isn't society's fault. Everyone knows about the death penalty as a punishment for murder. So, the person who murders is really killing himself at the same time he is killing his victim. The murderer has made the choice to die.

It is important to remember that the death penalty is used only for people who have committed very serious crimes. For example, a woman shot a police officer when she was trying to escape from jail. She was already a convicted criminal when she committed murder. For all we know, she would continue committing violent crimes and possibly even more murders if given the chance. So, she deserves the death penalty and law-abiding citizens deserve to be protected from this type of criminal.

People need to accept responsibility for their actions. Punishing murderers with the death penalty is one way that society can help people to realize/realise the consequences of their decisions.

SPEAKING

Sample Responses

Part 1

What kind of food do you enjoy eating?
Most of the time, I enjoy healthy food. I like fish, salad, and vegetables. Sometimes I like something sweet.

What are some kinds of food you never eat? Why?
I never eat fast food. It's so unhealthy that I can't enjoy eating it. Well, sometimes I will eat French fries.

Do you generally prefer to eat at home or at a restaurant? Why?
I usually like to eat at home. It's less expensive than a restaurant, and I can make all of the food exactly the way I like it.

What are some reasons that people eat at restaurants?
Most of all, it's convenient. It's so nice to have someone make the food and clean up everything afterwards.

Describe some things you enjoy doing with your friends.
When I get together with my friends on weekends, we often have dinner together or we have a picnic lunch at a park. Most of us have young children, so that's really the easiest way to spend time together, because the children enjoy it too.

Do you think it's better to have a large group of friends or a few close friends? Why?
I like having a large group of friends. There's more variety that way. You don't always see the same people or talk about the same thing. And if you have a large group of friends, there's always somebody who has time to spend with you or who feels like doing what you feel like doing.

How do people choose their friends?
I think we choose our friends based on a comfortable feeling. You know, sometimes people just understand each other so easily and the conversation just flows. Of course, there's usually one thing that people have in common when they become friends such as work or school, or maybe their children are classmates.

Have you remained friends with people from your childhood? Why or why not?
No, I haven't really. I live in a different city now, so I'm not near any of my childhood friends. There are one or two I see when I go home to visit my family, but that's all. I don't think I have much in common with my childhood friends any more.

Part 2

There is one teacher that I remember very well. I went to school at age five, and she was my first teacher. She read stories to us and taught us our letters and numbers. She taught us a lot of nice songs, too. She taught us all the things that kindergarten children need to learn. I think she had a very good personality for a kindergarten teacher. She was a very kind person. She cared about all of us. She was very warm. I think these qualities are very important for a kindergarten teacher because kindergarten children are so young.

Sometimes it's hard for them to spend all those hours away from home. This teacher was also very patient. When we made a lot of noise or had disagreements or anything like that, she never yelled at us. She always helped us solve our problems in a calm way. I remember her because she was my first teacher and because she was so nice. I think it was because I had a good experience with my first teacher that I learned to like school. I learned that school was a nice place to be and that learning was fun and interesting.

Part 3

What kind of person makes a good teacher?
A person who is smart and caring makes a good teacher. Also, the person should like talking to other people and presenting information.

Why do you think people choose to become teachers?
There are many reasons, but I think that most teachers want to make a positive difference in others' lives. Many teachers have family members who were teachers.

Which is more important for a teacher—to be an expert in the subject he or she teaches, or to be very skilled at explaining things and motivating students to learn?
I think it's more important for a teacher to be an expert in the subject matter. How can you teach a subject if you don't know it very well? You have to know it in order to explain it. You have to be able to answer any questions the students ask. Anybody can read a book on any subject, but the subject matter expert is the one who can explain it well.

How are schools different now from when you were young? How do you think they will be different in the future?
When I was a child in school, we didn't have so much technology. We had computers, but they weren't in every classroom and a lot of the teachers didn't know how to use them. So I had a more traditional education. Now I believe computers are often used in schools. Children use the Internet now for research. That makes a very big difference. They can have access to a lot of information they didn't have before. In the future, I think there might not be any schools at all. Children will just stay home and do all their learning through the Internet

Academic

MODEL TEST 4

ANSWER SHEET
Academic Model Test 4

IELTS Listening Answer Sheet

1		✓ 1 ✗	21		✓ 21 ✗
2		2	22		22
3		3	23		23
4		4	24		24
5		5	25		25
6		6	26		26
7		7	27		27
8		8	28		28
9		9	29		29
10		10	30		30
11		11	31		31
12		12	32		32
13		13	33		33
14		14	34		34
15		15	35		35
16		16	36		36
17		17	37		37
18		18	38		38
19		19	39		39
20		20	40		40
				Listening Total	

MODEL TEST 4

Candidate Name ______________________________

International English Language Testing System

LISTENING

Time: Approx. 30 minutes

INSTRUCTIONS TO CANDIDATES

Do not open this booklet until you are told to do so.

Write your name and candidate number in the space at the top of this page.

You should answer all questions.

All the recordings will be played ONCE only.

Write all your answers on the Question Paper.

At the end of the test, you will be given ten minutes to transfer your answers to an Answer Sheet.

Do not remove this booklet from the examination room.

INFORMATION FOR CANDIDATES

There are **40** questions on this question paper.

The test is divided as follows:

Section 1	Questions 1–10
Section 2	Questions 11–20
Section 3	Questions 21–30
Section 4	Questions 31–40

Track 26

SECTION 1

Questions 1–2

*Choose the correct letter, **A**, **B**, or **C**.*

Example

Where will the man get the information he needs?

A The information desk

B The ticket office

(C) The Special Events Department

1 What does the man want to do?

A Look at art

B Hear a lecture

C Listen to music

2 What day will he get tickets for?

A Thursday

B Saturday

C Sunday

Questions 3–5

Complete the form.

Ticket Order Form

Customer name: Steven **3** ....

Credit card number: **4** ....

Number of tickets: 2

Amount due: **5** £ ....

Questions 6–10

Label the map below. Write the correct place names in boxes 6–10 on your Answer Sheet.

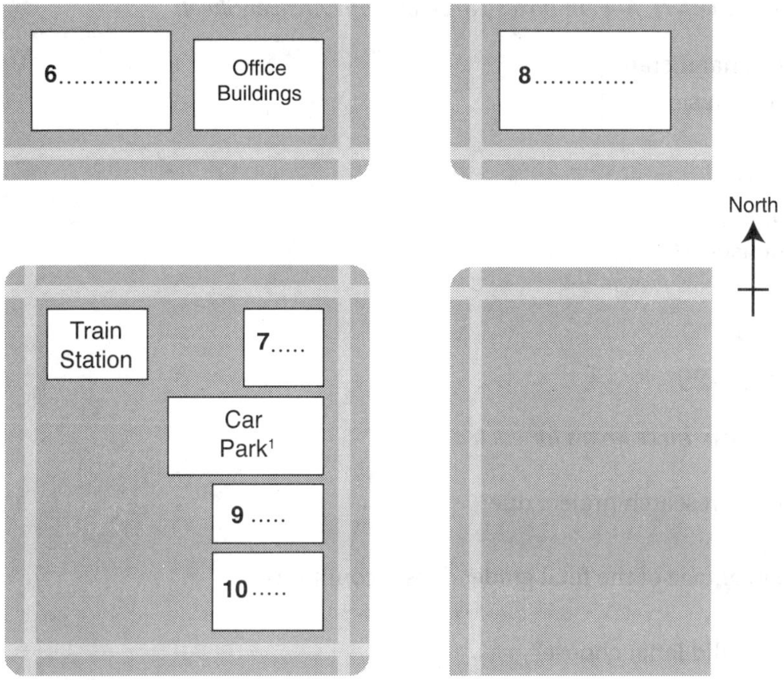

SECTION 2

Questions 11–17

Complete the table comparing the two towns. Write NO MORE THAN TWO WORDS *for each answer.*

	Ravensburg	**Blackstone Beach**
Population	**11**	12,000
Summer climate	average temp: **12** .... degrees weather: sunny	average temp: **13** .... degrees weather: **14** ....
Advantage	**15**	good seafood
Disadvantage	crowded in summer	**16** ....
Distance from airport	25 kilometers	**17** ....

[1]AMERICAN: parking garage

ACADEMIC MODEL TEST 4

Questions 18–20

Which three of the following do tourists usually shop for on Raven Island?

*Write the correct letters, **A–F**, in boxes 18–20 on your Answer Sheet.*

A native handicrafts
B native music
C perfume
D jewelry[1]
E fish
F fishing gear[2]

SECTION 3

Questions 21–23

Write NO MORE THAN THREE WORDS *for each answer.*

21 When is the research project due?

22 What percentage of the final grade[3] does it count for?

23 What topic did Janet choose?

Questions 24–30

Complete the chart showing the steps Janet took to complete her research project.

Write NO MORE THAN THREE WORDS *for each answer.*

A. Chose topic

B. Did **24** ....

C. Chose **25** ....

D. Wrote questionnaire

E. Chose **26** ....

F. Submitted **27** ....

G. **28** .... questionnaires

H. **29** .... and graphs

I. Wrote a **30** ....

[1]BRITISH: jewellery
[2]BRITISH: tackle
[3]BRITISH: mark

SECTION 4

Questions 31–34

*According to the talk, in which parts of the world do crows live? Choose four places and write the correct letters, **A–F**, in boxes 31–34 on your Answer Sheet.*

- **A** North America
- **B** South America
- **C** Antarctica
- **D** Hawaii
- **E** Europe
- **F** Asia

Questions 35–40

Complete the table with information about the American crow.

Write NO MORE THAN THREE WORDS AND/OR A NUMBER *for each answer.*

Length	**35** .... centimeters
Color	**36** ....
Favorite food	corn
Nest material	**37** ....
Nesting place	**38** ....
Number of eggs	**39** ....
Days to hatch	18
Days to fly	**40** ....

ACADEMIC MODEL TEST 4

ANSWER SHEET
Academic Model Test 4

IELTS Reading Answer Sheet

		✓ ✗
1		1
2		2
3		3
4		4
5		5
6		6
7		7
8		8
9		9
10		10
11		11
12		12
13		13
14		14
15		15
16		16
17		17
18		18
19		19
20		20

		✓ ✗
21		21
22		22
23		23
24		24
25		25
26		26
27		27
28		28
29		29
30		30
31		31
32		32
33		33
34		34
35		35
36		36
37		37
38		38
39		39
40		40
	Reading Total	

MODEL TEST 4

Candidate Name ____________________

International English Language Testing System

ACADEMIC READING

Time: 1 hour

INSTRUCTIONS TO CANDIDATES

Do not open this booklet until you are told to do so.

Write your name and candidate number in the space at the top of this page.

Start at the beginning of the test and work through it.

You should answer all questions.

If you cannot do a particular question, leave it and go on to the next. You can return to it later.

All answers must be written on the Answer Sheet.

Do not remove this booklet from the examination room.

INFORMATION FOR CANDIDATES

There are **40** questions on this question paper.

The test is divided as follows:

Reading Passage 1	Questions 1-13
Reading Passage 2	Questions 14-27
Reading Passage 3	Questions 28-40

Reading Passage 1

You should spend about 20 minutes on questions 1–13, which are based on Reading Passage 1 below.

One Hundred Days of Reform

Since the early 1800s, the term *one hundred days* has represented a political phrase, referring to a short period of concentrated political reform. In most cases, this period comes immediately after a new leader takes over a nation. The original Hundred Days took place between March and June of 1815, when Napoleon escaped from Elba, and King Louis XVIII reclaimed his throne. This was one of the results of the Battle of Waterloo. The Hundred Days of Reform in China (also known as the Wuxu Reform) was inspired by a similar event. After losing the Sino-Japanese war, the Emperor Guwangxu found his country to be in a major crisis. Desperate for change, the emperor hired the help of a young political activist named K'ang Yu-wei. At the age of only 27, K'ang had graduated with the highest degree (chin-shih), written two books on reform, and initiated several of his own political reform movements. K'ang impressed the court and convinced the emperor that China, like Japan, should form a constitutional government and do away with its monarchy.

On June 11, 1898, Emperor Guwangxu entrusted the reform movement to K'ang and put the progressive scholar–reformer in control of the government. Immediately, K'ang, with the help of a few other reformers, began work on changing China into a more modern society. Within days, the imperial court issued a number of statutes related to the social and political structure of the nation. First, K'ang planned to reform China's education system. The edicts called for a universal school system with an emphasis on practical and Western studies rather than Neo-Confucian orthodoxy. The new government also wanted to modernize[1] the country's examination systems and send more students abroad to gain firsthand knowledge of how technology was developing in other countries. K'ang also called for the establishment of a national parliamentary government, including popularly elected members and ministries. Military reform and the establishment of a new defense[2] system as well as the modernization of agriculture and medicine were also on the agenda.

These edicts were threatening to Chinese ideologies and institutions, especially the army, which at the time was controlled by a few governor–generals. There was intense opposition to the reform at all levels of society, and only one in fifteen provinces made attempts to implement the edicts. The Manchus, who considered the reform a radical and unrealistic idea, suggested that more gradual changes needed to be made. Just three months

[1]British: modernise
[2]British: defence

after the reform had begun, a coup d'etat was organized by Yuan Shikai and Empress Dowager Cixi to force Guangxu and the young reformers out of power and into seclusion. A few of the reformer's chief advocates who refused to leave were executed. After September 21st, the new edicts were abolished, and the conservatives regained their power.

Many Chinese civilians felt that the aftermath of the One Hundred Days of Reform was more detrimental to China than the short-lived failed attempt at reform. Immediately following the conservative takeover, anti-foreign and anti-Christian secret societies tore through northern China, targeting foreign concessions and missionary facilities. The violence of these "Boxer bands" provoked retaliation from the offended nations, and the government was forced to declare war on the invaders. By August, an Allied force made up of armies from nine European nations as well as the United States and Japan entered Peking. With little effort, north China was occupied, and foreign troops had stationed themselves inside the border. The court was ordered to either execute or punish many of its high officials under the Protocol of 1901. Rather than dividing up the occupied territory among the powers, the Allies settled on an "open door" trade policy. Within a decade, the court ordered many of the original reform measures, including the modernization of the education and military systems.

The traditional view of the One Hundred Days of Reform depicted Emperor Guwangxu and K'ang Yu-wei as heroes and Empress Dowager Cixi as the villain who refused to reform even though the change was inevitable. However, since the *One Hundred Days* has turned into a cliché related to political failures, historians in the 20th century often portray the Wuxu Reform as an irrational dream. The fact that the reforms were implemented in a matter of decades, rather than months, suggests that the conservative elites may have been more opposed to the immediacy of the proposed edicts rather than the changes themselves.

Questions 1–4

*Choose the correct letter: **A**, **B**, **C**, or **D**. Write your answers in boxes 1–4 on your Answer Sheet.*

1 The term *one hundred days* refers to

A the amount of time that is needed to introduce reforms.
B a brief time when political changes are initiated.
C a monarch's unusually short term of power.
D the first months a new leader is in power.

2 The original Hundred Days occurred as a result of

A the imprisonment of King Louis the XVIII.
B the Battle of Waterloo.
C the Wuxu Reform.
D a war with Japan.

3 K'ang persuaded the emperor to
   - **A** establish a constitutional government.
   - **B** distrust the military.
   - **C** attack Japan.
   - **D** go abroad.

4 The overall goal of the Wuxu Reform was to
   - **A** consolidate the emperor's power.
   - **B** gain power over the Japanese.
   - **C** educate the people.
   - **D** modernize China.

Questions 5–13

Complete the sentences below about the reading passage.

Choose your answers from the box below, and write them in boxes 5–13 on your Answer Sheet. There are more choices than spaces, so you will not use them all.

A	overthrew the government after the reforms were introduced
B	in charge of the reform movement
C	were voted in
D	in prison
E	were abolished
F	lost a war
G	began trade
H	foreigners in China
I	were executed
J	reform supporters
K	occupied China
L	were initiated
M	opposed the reforms
N	were reestablished

5 China .... with Japan.

6 Emperor Guwangxu put K'ang Yu-wei ....

7 After June 11, 1898, the reforms ....

8 People throughout China ....

9 Yuan Shikai and Empress Dowager Cixi ....

10 The reforms .... after September 21st.

11 Secret societies attacked ....

12 European, U.S., and Japanese troops ....

13 Eventually, the reforms ....

Reading Passage 2

You should spend about 20 minutes on questions 14–27, which are based on Reading Passage 2 below.

Sleep Apnea

Sleep apnea is a common sleeping disorder. It affects a number of adults comparable to the percentage of the population that suffers from diabetes. The term *apnea* is of Greek origin and means "without breath." Sufferers of sleep apnea stop breathing repeatedly while they sleep. This can happen hundreds of times during the night, each gasp lasting from 10 to 30 seconds. In extreme cases, people stop breathing for more than a minute at a time.

There are three different types of sleep apnea, with obstructive sleep apnea being the most common. Obstructive sleep apnea (OSA), which affects 90 percent of sleep apnea sufferers, occurs because of an upper airway obstruction. A person's breathing stops when air is somehow prevented from entering the trachea. The most common sites for air to get trapped include the nasal passage, the tongue, the tonsils, and the uvula. Fatty tissue or tightened muscles at the back of a throat can also cause the obstruction. Central sleep apnea has a different root cause, though the consequences are the same. In central sleep apnea, the brain forgets to send the signal that tells the muscles that it's time to breathe. The term *central* is used because this type of apnea is related to the central nervous system rather than the blocked airflow. The third type of sleep apnea, known as mixed apnea, is a combination of the two and is the most rare form. Fortunately, in all types of apnea, the brain eventually signals for a person to wake up so that breathing can resume. However, this continuous pattern of interrupted sleep is hard on the body and results in very little rest.

Sleep apnea is associated with a number of risk factors, including being overweight, male, and over the age of forty. However, like many disorders, sleep apnea can affect children and in many cases is found to be the result of a person's genetic makeup. Despite being so widespread, this disorder often goes undiagnosed. Many people experience symptoms for their whole lives without realizing they have a serious sleep disorder. Oftentimes, it is not the person suffering from sleep apnea who notices the repetitive episodes of sleep interruption, but a partner or family member sleeping nearby. The air cessation is generally accompanied by heavy snoring, loud enough to rouse others from sleep. Those who live alone are less likely to receive early diagnosis, though other symptoms such as headaches, dizziness, irritability, and exhaustion may cause a person to seek medical advice. If left untreated, sleep apnea, which is a progressive disorder, can cause cardiovascular problems, increasing the risk of heart disease and stroke. Sleep apnea is also blamed for many cases of impaired driving and poor job performance.

In order to diagnose sleep apnea, patients are generally sent to a sleep center for a polysomnography test. This test monitors brain waves, muscle tension, breathing, eye movement, and oxygen in the blood. Audio monitoring for snoring, gasping, and episodic waking is also done during a polysomnogram. Nonintrusive solutions for treating sleep apnea involve simple lifestyle changes. In many cases, symptoms of sleep apnea can be eliminated when patients try losing weight or abstaining from alcohol. People who sleep on their backs or stomachs often find that their symptoms disappear if they try sleeping on their sides. Sleep specialists also claim that sleeping pills interfere with the natural performance of the throat and mouth muscles and suggest patients do away with all sleep medication for a trial period. When these treatments prove unsuccessful, sleep apnea sufferers can be fitted with a CPAP mask, which is worn at night over the mouth and nose, similar to an oxygen mask. CPAP stands for Continuous Positive Airway Pressure.

In extreme cases, especially when facial deformities are the cause of the sleep apnea, surgery is needed to make a clear passage for the air. Many different types of surgeries are available. The most common form of surgery used to combat sleep apnea is uvulo-palato-pharyngoplasty (UPPP). This procedure involves removing the uvula and the excess tissue around it. UPPP helps about 50 percent of patients who undergo the procedure, while the other half continue to rely on the CPAP machine even after the surgery. Another type of surgery called mandibular myotomy involves removing a piece of the jaw, and adjusting the tongue. By reattaching[1] the tongue to a position about ten millimeters forward, air is able to flow more freely during sleep. This delicate procedure is performed only by surgeons with expertise in facial surgery and is almost always successful in eliminating the air obstruction. The latest surgical procedures use radio frequencies to shrink the tissue around the tongue, throat, and soft palate.

Questions 14–18

The passage describes three different types of sleep apnea. Which of the characteristics below belongs to which type of sleep apnea? In boxes 14–18 on your Answer Sheet, write

A if it is a characteristic of obstructive sleep apnea.
B if it is a characteristic of central sleep apnea.
C if it is a characteristic of mixed apnea.

14 Its root cause is a blockage at the trachea.

15 It is connected exclusively with the nervous system.

[1]BRITISH: re-attaching

16 It involves blocked airflow and a brain malfunction.

17 It is the most unusual type of sleep apnea.

18 It is the most common form of sleep apnea.

Questions 19–23

Do the following statements agree with the information in Reading Passage 2?

In boxes 19–23 on your Answer Sheet, write

TRUE	*if the statement is true according to the passage.*
FALSE	*if the statement contradicts the passage.*
NOT GIVEN	*if there is no information about this in the passage.*

19 Sleep apnea only affects men over 40.

20 Most people with sleep apnea have the problem diagnosed.

21 Often a relative of the sleep apnea sufferer is the first to notice the problem.

22 Sleep apnea is more common in Greece than in other countries.

23 Sleep apnea can cause problems at work.

Questions 24–27

Complete the sentences below.

Choose NO MORE THAN FOUR WORDS *from the passage for each answer.*

Write your answers in boxes 24–27 on your Answer Sheet.

Diagnosis of sleep apnea is made by observing the patient at a
24 ....

Intrusive treatments for sleep apnea may not be necessary as it can often be simply cured with **25** ....

Sleeping pills may be a cause of sleep apnea because they can prevent the
26 .... from performing normally.

One treatment for sleep apnea involves wearing a **27** .... while sleeping.

Reading Passage 3

You should spend about 20 minutes on questions 28–40, which are based on Reading Passage 3 below.

Adult Intelligence

Over 90 years ago, Binet and Simon delineated two different methods of assessing intelligence. These were the psychological method (which concentrates mostly on intellectual processes, such as memory and abstract reasoning) and the pedagogical method (which concentrates on assessing what an individual knows). The main concern of Binet and Simon was to predict elementary school performance independently from the social and economic background of the individual student. As a result, they settled on the psychological method, and they spawned an intelligence assessment paradigm, which has been substantially unchanged from their original tests.

With few exceptions, the development of adult intelligence assessment instruments proceeded along the same lines of the Binet-Simon tests. Nevertheless, the difficulty of items was increased for older examinees. Thus, extant adult intelligence tests were created as little more than upward extensions of the original Binet-Simon scales. The Binet-Simon tests are quite effective in predicting school success in both primary and secondary educational environments. However, they have been found to be much less predictive of success in post-secondary academic and occupational domains. Such a discrepancy provokes fundamental questions about intelligence. One highly debated question asks whether college success is actually dependent on currently used forms of measured intelligence, or if present measures of intelligence are inadequately sampling the wider domain of adult intellect. One possible answer to this question lies in questioning the preference of the psychological method over the pedagogical method for assessing adult intellect. Recent research across the fields of education, cognitive science, and adult development suggests that much of adult intellect is indeed not adequately sampled by extant intelligence measures and might be better assessed through the pedagogical method (Ackerman, 1996; Gregory, 1994).

Several lines of research have also converged on a redefinition of adult intellect that places a greater emphasis on content (knowledge) over process. Substantial strides have been made in delineating knowledge aspects of intellectual performance which are divergent from traditional measures of intelligence (e.g., Wagner, 1987) and in demonstrating that adult performance is greatly influenced by prior topic and domain knowledge (e.g., Alexander et al., 1994). Even some older testing literature seems to indicate that the knowledge measured by the Graduate Records Examination (GRE) is a comparable or better indicator of future graduate school suc-

[1]British: endeavours

cess and post-graduate performance than traditional aptitude measures (Willingham, 1974).

Knowledge and Intelligence

When an adult is presented with a completely novel problem (e.g., memorizing a random set of numbers or letters), the basic intellectual processes are typically implicated in predicting which individuals will be successful in solving problems. The dilemma for adult intellectual assessment is that the adult is rarely presented with a completely novel problem in the real world of academic or occupational endeavors.[1] Rather, the problems that an adult is asked to solve almost inevitably draw greatly on his/her accumulated knowledge and skills—one does not build a house by only memorizing physics formulae. For an adult, intellect is better conceptualized by the tasks that the person can accomplish and the skills that he/she has developed rather than the number of digits that can be stored in working memory or the number of syllogistic reasoning items that can be correctly evaluated. Thus, the content of the intellect is at least as important as the processes of intellect in determining an adult's real-world problem-solving efficacy.

From the artificial intelligence field, researchers have discarded the idea of a useful general problem solver in favor[1] of knowledge-based expert systems. This is because no amount of processing power can achieve real-world problem-solving proficiency without an extensive set of domain-relevant knowledge structures. Gregory (1994) describes the difference between such concepts as "potential intelligence" (knowledge) and "kinetic intelligence" (process). Similarly, Schank and Birnbaum (1994) say that "what makes someone intelligent is what he [/she] knows."

One line of relevant educational research is from the examination of expert–novice differences which indicates that the typical expert is found to mainly differ from the novice in terms of experience and the knowledge structures that are developed through that experience rather than in terms of intellectual processes (e.g., Glaser, 1991). Additional research from developmental and gerontological perspectives has also shown that various aspects of adult intellectual functioning are greatly determined by knowledge structures and less influenced by the kinds of process measures, which have been shown to decline with age over adult development (e.g., Schooler, 1987; Willis & Tosti-Vasey, 1990).

Shifting Paradigms

By bringing together a variety of sources of research evidence, it is clear that our current methods of assessing adult intellect are insufficient. When we are confronted with situations in which the intellectual performance of adults must be predicted (e.g., continuing education or adult learning

[1]BRITISH: favour

programs), we must begin to take account of what they know in addition to the traditional assessment of intellectual processes. Because adults are quite diverse in their knowledge structures (e.g., a physicist may know many different things than a carpenter), the challenge for educational assessment researchers in the future will be to develop batteries of tests that can be used to assess different sources of intellectual knowledge for different individuals. When adult knowledge structures are broadly examined with tests such as the Advanced Placement [AP] and College Level Exam Program [CLEP], it may be possible to improve such things as the prediction of adult performance in specific educational endeavors, the placement of individuals, and adult educational counseling.

Questions 28–34

Complete the sentences below about the reading passage.

Choose your answers from the box below, and write them in boxes 28–34 on your Answer Sheet. There are more choices than sentences so you will not use them all.

A	tests	**H**	thought processes
B	psychological issues	**I**	Ackerman and Gregory
C	new	**J**	social class
D	potential for achievement in school	**K**	recent research
E	knowledge-based	**L**	future job performance
F	knowledge	**M**	problem solving
G	Binet and Simon		

The psychological method of intelligence assessment measures **28** ....

Binet and Simon wanted to develop an assessment method that was not influenced by the child's **29** ....

The Binet-Simon tests have been successfully used to predict **30** ....

The Binet-Simon tests are not good predictors of **31** ....

According to **32** ...., the pedagogical method is the best way to assess adult intelligence.

The pedagogical method is a better measure of adult intelligence because most problems that adults encounter in real life are not completely **33** ....

In the area of artificial intelligence, **34** .... systems are preferred.

Questions 35–39

Do the following statements agree with the information in Reading Passage 3?

In boxes 35–39 on your Answer Sheet, write

TRUE	*if the statement is true according to the passage.*
FALSE	*if the statement contradicts the passage.*
NOT GIVEN	*if there is no information about this in the passage.*

35 The Binet-Simon tests have not changed significantly over the years.

36 Success in elementary school is a predictor of success in college.

37 Research suggests that experts generally have more developed intellectual processes than novices.

38 Knowledge structures in adults decrease with age.

39 Better methods of measuring adult intelligence need to be developed.

Question 40

Choose the correct letter, ***A–C****, and write it in box 40 on your Answer Sheet.*

40 The Advanced Placement and College Level Exam Program tests measure

A thought processes.
B job skills.
C knowledge.

ANSWER SHEET
Academic Model Test 4

Writing Answer Sheet

TASK 1

ANSWER SHEET
Academic Model Test 4

-2-

ANSWER SHEET
Academic Model Test 4

-3-

TASK 2

ANSWER SHEET
Academic Model Test 4

-4-

MODEL TEST 4

Candidate Name ______________________________

International English Language Testing System

ACADEMIC WRITING

Time: 1 hour

INSTRUCTIONS TO CANDIDATES

Do not open this booklet until you are told to do so.

Write your name and candidate number in the space at the top of this page.

All answers must be written on the separate answer booklet provided.

Do not remove this booklet from the examination room.

INFORMATION FOR CANDIDATES

There are **2** tasks on this question paper.

You must do **both** tasks.

Underlength answers will be penalized.

WRITING TASK 1

You should spend about 20 minutes on this task.

Write about the following topic:

> ***The table below shows the sales made by a coffee shop in an office building on a typical weekday.***
>
> ***Summarize the information by selecting and reporting the main features, and make comparisons where relevant.***

	Coffee	Tea	Pastries	Sandwiches
7:30–10:30	265	110	275	50
10:30–2:30	185	50	95	200
2:30–5:30	145	35	150	40
5:30–8:30	200	75	80	110

Write at least 150 words.

WRITING TASK 2

You should spend no more than 40 minutes on this task.

Write about the following topic:

> ***As compared to the past, children these days spend more of their leisure time indoors with computers and TV and less time outdoors.***
>
> ***Describe some of the problems this lack of outdoor leisure time can cause and suggest at least one possible solution.***

Give reasons for your answer and include any relevant examples from your own knowledge or experience.

Write at least 250 words.

SPEAKING

Examiner Questions:

Part 1 (4–5 minutes)

Home and Neighborhood

Describe the place you live in now.
Do you think it's better to live in a house or in an apartment? Why?
Describe your neighborhood.
How do people choose their place to live?

Family

Describe your family. Are you married? Do you have children? Brothers and sisters?
What are some things you enjoy doing with other members of your family?
Who in your family are you particularly close to? Why?
Do you spend more time with your family or with friends? Why?

Part 2 (3–4 minutes)

You will be given a topic. You will have one to two minutes to talk about this topic. You will have one minute to prepare what you are going to say. You may take some notes if you wish. Here is your topic:

> Describe a gift you have received that was important to you.
>
> You should say:
> what the gift is
> who gave you the gift
> why it was given to you

You will have one to two minutes to talk about this topic.
You will have one minute to prepare what you are going to say.

Part 3 (4–5 minutes)

Giving and Receiving Gifts

Do you think people generally enjoy giving and receiving gifts? Why or why not?
In your country, when do people usually give gifts?
What kind of gifts do they give?

The Meaning of Gifts

Do you agree or disagree: The price of a gift shows how much the giver cares about the recipient.

ACADEMIC MODEL TEST 4—ANSWER EXPLANATIONS

LISTENING

Example: (C) Line 3 has a woman ask, "Tickets? That's our Special Events Department. Let me transfer you." She directs the phone call to that number.

1. (C) Choice (C) is correct because in lines 5 and 7, the man says, "I'm interested in the series you have going on now . . . . Actually, I meant the concert series." Choice (A) is incorrect because in line 6, the woman thinks he is interested in the "lecture series on the history of art," but he isn't. Choice (B) is incorrect because he's interested in listening to music at the concert, not attending a lecture.
2. (A) All three choices are mentioned. Choice (A) is correct because in lines 8–11, the woman explains: "there's still a concert tomorrow, that's Thursday." The man asks, "The one tomorrow, is that when they'll be playing the Mozart concerto?" and the woman answers, "Yes, it is." Choice (B) and (C) are incorrect because the man does not want to attend the concert on those days, even though there are performances. In line 8, the woman says, "There's also one [concert] on Saturday, and then the last one is on Sunday."
3. *Milford.* In line 13, he provides his name, "It's Steven Milford. That's M-i-l-f-o-r-d."
4. *1659798164.* In line 17, he gives his credit card number, "1659798164."
5. *32.70.* In line 20, she says: "At 16.35 a piece that comes out to a total of 32 pounds and 70 p/pence."
6. Library
7. Bank
8. Post Office
9. Museum
10. Hotel
11. *56,000.* In paragraph 1, Sheila says: "Ravensburg is the major city on the island, though with a population of only 56,000 . . . ."
12. *26.* In paragraph 2, Sheila says: "Summer in the city of Ravensburg is warm with average temperatures reaching 26 degrees."
13. *23.* In paragraph 2, Sheila says: "Summer at Blackstone is a bit cooler, with average temperatures of around 23 degrees."
14. *windy.* In paragraph 2, Sheila says: "the weather is often windy because, of course, it's located on the coast."
15. *entertainment.* In paragraph 3, Sheila says: "so if entertainment is what you're looking for, Ravensburg has the advantage there."
16. *very quiet.* At the end of paragraph 3, Sheila says about Blackstone: "It's a very quiet town, which is a disadvantage if you're looking for excitement."
17. *75 kilometers.* In paragraph 4, Sheila says: "Travelers[1] to Blackstone Beach also use the Ravensburg airport, which is about 75 kilometers away."
18. (C) Sheila says, "Some very good deals can be found, however, in the perfume shops."
19. (D) Sheila says, "Jewelry[2] is also popular among tourists, and jewelry shops abound."
20. (E) Sheila says, "Since fishing is the major island industry, no tourist goes home without a package of smoked fish."

    For this section, choice (A) is incorrect because Sheila says, "Well, contrary to what one might think, native handicrafts are not a popular item." Choice (B) is incorrect because Sheila says, "there are not many CDs available of the native music, and the ones that are available are quite expensive." Choice (F) is incorrect because Sheila says, ". . . be sure to bring your own fishing gear.[3] Believe it or not, it's difficult and expensive for tourists to buy it on the island."
21. *next Thursday.* In line 6, Janet says, "It's due next Thursday."

[1]British: Travellers; [2]British: Jewellery; [3]British: tackle

22. *40.* In line 8, Janet says, "And it counts for 40 percent of our final semester grade"[1]
23. *TV watching habits/people's TV habits.* In line 10, Janet says, "I did my research about people's TV watching habits."
24. *library research/research.* In line 14, Janet says, "Well, after I decided my topic, I went to the library and did some research. I mean, I read about other studies people had done about TV watching."
25. *research method.* In line 16, Janet says, "So after I did the library research, I chose my research method."
26. *subjects.* In line 23, Janet says: "Well that's what I had to do next, choose my subjects."
27. *research design.* In line 23, Harry asks, "So then you just went around and asked people the questions?" Janet answers, "Well, first I had to submit my research design to Professor Farley. He had to make sure it was OK before I went ahead with the research."
28. *Sent out.* In line 26, Janet says, "So then I had to send out the questionnaire."
29. *Made charts.* After collecting the information, in line 28, Janet says, "I made charts and graphs."
30. *report.* In line 32, Janet says, "Well, I'll have to write a report, too, of course."
31. (A) In paragraph 2, the professor says, "You'll find crows in North America."
32. (D) In paragraph 2, the professor says, "There are several species of crows, for example, in Hawaii."
33. (E) In paragraph 2, the professor says, "And of course you'll find them in other parts of the world, Europe, Asia, and so on."
34. (F) In paragraph 2, the professor says, "And of course you'll find them in other parts of the world, Europe, Asia, and so on."
    Choice (B) is incorrect because in paragraph 2, the professor says, "You'll find crows in North America, although interestingly enough, not in South America." Choice (C) is incorrect because in paragraph 2, the professor says, "There are none in Antarctica."
35. *39–49.* In paragraph 3, the professor says, "[It measures] 39 to 49 centimeters in length."
36. *black.* In paragraph 3, the professor says, "the American crow is completely black, including the beak and feet."
37. *sticks.* In the first sentence of paragraph 4, the professor says, "Crows build large nests of sticks."
38. *trees/bushes/trees and bushes.* In the first sentence of paragraph 4, "Crows build large nests of sticks, usually in trees or sometimes in bushes."
39. *3 to 6.* In paragraph 4, the professor says, "The female lays from three to six eggs at a time."
40. *35.* In paragraph 4, the professor says, "Generally, 35 days after hatching they have their feathers and are ready to fly."

READING

Passage 1—One Hundred Days of Reform

1. (B) The first sentence of the passage explains that the term *one hundred days* refers to "a short period of political reform."
2. (B) The first paragraph explains that the original Hundred Days "was one of the results of the Battle of Waterloo."
3. (A) The first paragraph explains that K'ang "convinced the emperor that China . . . should form a constitutional government."
4. (D) Paragraph 2 explains that K'ang "began work on changing China into a more modern society."
5. (F) Choice (F) is correct because paragraph 1 states: "After losing the Sino-Japanese war, the Emperor Guwangxu found his country to be in a major crisis." So, China lost the war with Japan.
6. (B) Choice (B) is correct because paragraph 2 states: "On June 11, 1898, Emperor Guwangxu entrusted the reform movement to K'ang and put the progressive scholar reformer in control of the government."

[1]British: end of term mark

7. (L) Choice (L) is correct because paragraph 2 states, "On June 11, 1898, Emperor Guwangxu entrusted the reform movement to K'ang." The text states, "Within days, the imperial court issued a number of statutes related to the social and political structure of the nation."
8. (M) Choice (M) is correct because paragraph 3 states: "There was intense opposition to the reform at all levels of society, and only one in fifteen provinces made attempts to implement the edicts."
9. (A) Choice (A) is correct because paragraph 3 states: "a coup d'etat was organized by Yuan Shikai and Empress Dowager Cixi to force Guwangxu and the young reformers out of power and into seclusion."
10. (E) Choice (E) is correct because paragraph 3 states: "After September 21st, the new edicts were abolished."
11. (H) Choice (H) is correct because paragraph 4 states: ". . . anti-foreign and anti-Christian secret societies tore through northern China targeting foreign concessions and missionary facilities."
12. (K) Choice (K) is correct because paragraph 4 states: "an Allied force made up of armies from nine European nations as well as the United States and Japan entered Peking. With little effort, north China was occupied."
13. (N) Choice (N) is correct because paragraph 4 states: "Within a decade, the court ordered many of the original reform measures, including the modernization of the education and military systems."

Passage 2—Sleep Apnea

14. (A) Choice A is correct because paragraph 2 states: "A person's breathing stops when air is somehow prevented from entering the trachea."
15. (B) Choice (B) is correct because paragraph 2 states: "The term *central* is used because this type of apnea is related to the central nervous system rather than the blocked airflow." Immediately before this sentence, the passage is describing central sleep apnea.
16. (C) Choice (C) is correct because paragraph 2 states: "The third type of sleep apnea, known as mixed apnea, is a combination of the two."
17. (C) Choice (C) is correct because paragraph 2 states: "The third type of sleep apnea, known as mixed apnea, is a combination of the two and is the most rare form."
18. (A) Choice (A) is correct because paragraph 2 states: "There are three different types of sleep apnea, with obstructive sleep apnea being the most common."
19. False. Paragraph 3 states: "However, like many disorders, sleep apnea can affect children and in many cases is found to be the result of a person's genetic makeup." The paragraph does include risk factors related to sleep apnea, "including being overweight, male, and over the age of forty." So, people with those factors may be more likely to have sleep apnea, but all people can be affected by the disorder.
20. False. Paragraph 3 states: "Despite being so widespread, this disorder often goes undiagnosed."
21. True. Paragraph 3 states: "Often times, it is not the person suffering from sleep apnea who notices the repetitive episodes of sleep interruption, but a partner or family member sleeping nearby."
22. Not Given. This topic is not addressed in this reading passage.
23. True. Paragraph 3 states: "Sleep apnea is also blamed for many cases of impaired driving and poor job performance."
24. sleep center. Paragraph 4 explains: " In order to diagnose sleep apnea, patients are generally sent to a sleep center."
25. lifestyle changes. Paragraph 4 states: "Nonintrusive solutions for treating sleep apnea involve simple lifestyle changes."
26. throat and mouth muscles. Paragraph 4 states: "Sleep specialists also claim that sleeping pills interfere with the natural performance of the throat and mouth muscles."
27. CPAP mask. Paragraph 4 explains that sleep apnea patients can use "A CPAP mask, which is worn at night."

Passage 3—Adult Intelligence

28. (H) Choice (H) is correct because paragraph 1 states: "the psychological method [which concentrates mostly on intellectual processes, such as memory and abstract reasoning]."
29. (J) Choice (J) is correct because paragraph 1 states: "The main concern of Binet and Simon was to predict elementary school performance independently from the social and economic background of the individual student."
30. (D) Choice (D) is correct because paragraph 2 states: "The Binet-Simon tests are quite effective in predicting school success."
31. (L) Choice (L) is correct because paragraph 2 states: "However, they have been found to be much less predictive of success in post-secondary academic and occupational domains."
32. (I) Choice (I) is correct because paragraph 3 states: "Recent research across the fields of education, cognitive science, and adult development suggests that much of adult intellect is indeed not adequately sampled by extant intelligence measures and might be better assessed through the pedagogical method (Ackerman, 1996; Gregory, 1994)."
33. (C) Choice (C) is correct because paragraph 4 states: "The dilemma for adult intellectual assessment is that the adult is rarely presented with a completely novel problem in the real world of academic or occupational endeavors."[1]
34. (E) Choice (E) is correct because paragraph 5 states: "From the artificial intelligence field, researchers have discarded the idea of a useful general problem solver in favor[2] of knowledge-based expert systems."
35. True. Paragraph 1 states: "they spawned an intelligence assessment paradigm which has been substantially unchanged from their original tests."
36. False. Paragraph 2, states: "The Binet-Simon tests are quite effective in predicting school success in both primary and secondary educational environments. However, they have been found to be much less predictive of success in post-secondary academic and occupational domains." So, even though the tests predict elementary school success, we cannot make a connection between that predictor and a student's college success.
37. False. Paragraph 6 states: "the typical expert is found to mainly differ from the novice in terms of experience and the knowledge structures that are developed through that experience rather than in terms of intellectual processes (e.g., Glaser, 1991)."
38. False. Process structures, not knowledge structures, decline with age. Paragraph 6 states: "various aspects of adult intellectual functioning are greatly determined by knowledge structures and less influenced by the kinds of process measures, which have been shown to decline with age over adult development (e.g., Schooler, 1987; Willis & Tosti-Vasey, 1990)."
39. True. Paragraph 7 states: "By bringing together a variety of sources of research evidence, it is clear that our current methods of assessing adult intellect are insufficient."
40. (C) Choice (C) is the correct answer because paragraph 7 states: "When adult knowledge structures are broadly examined with tests such as the Advanced Placement [AP]."

WRITING

Sample Responses

Writing Task 1

The table shows the average sales of a coffee shop located in an office building on a weekday. Analyzing/analysing the coffee shop's sales report reveals some clear trends in the customers' buying habits. On a typical weekday, the usual morning foods and drinks are bought. More coffee, tea, and pastries are purchased from 7:30 to 10:30 in the morning than at any other time. At 10:30, fewer of these items are purchased; however, the number of sandwiches sold quadruples. The most sandwiches are sold from 10:30 to 12:30.

[1]British: endeavours; [2]British: favour

ACADEMIC MODEL TEST 4

Later in the day, all items reach their lowest selling point. Three of the four items: coffee, tea, and sandwiches sell their smallest amounts during the 2:30–5:30 block. The fewest pastries are sold from 5:30 to 8:30. However, the sandwiches and drinks sell more briskly from 5:30 to 8:30. It is their second-highest selling time period. This increase occurs when people are leaving work for the day or are working overtime and need to eat something convenient. By reviewing this table, it is clear that the office workers are using the coffee shop throughout the day and following a typical schedule.

Writing Task 2

Children are spending less leisure time outdoors than they did in the past. This can cause problems with their physical and social development.

Children spend the greater part of each day sitting in a classroom. If they then spend most of their leisure time at the computer or in front of the TV, this means they are sitting down for most of the day. They aren't getting much physical exercise. Physical activity is important for everyone, but especially for children. They need to move and run and breathe fresh air to help their body grow strong and healthy. They need to spend at least some time playing actively outdoors every day.

When children use the computer or watch TV, they are not interacting with other people. Even though they may use the Internet to communicate with friends, it is not the same as face-to-face interactions. Playing outdoors with others gives children many opportunities for social interactions. They learn to share and negotiate, to argue and cooperate. They learn social skills that they will need later on, in both their personal and professional lives.

Both schools and parents need to teach children to value outdoor leisure time. Schools should have children spend some part of each school day outdoors in both structured and unstructured activities. Parents should do more than only encourage their children to play outdoors. They should require them to spend a minimum amount of time doing so before they are allowed to use the computer or the TV. If schools and parents make the effort to teach children that playing outdoors is important, then children will learn to enjoy it.

SPEAKING

Sample Responses

Part 1

Describe the place you live in now.
I live in a small apartment that isn't far from the university. It has two bedrooms, and I share it with a classmate.

Do you think it's better to live in a house or in an apartment? Why?
For me, it's better to live in an apartment/flat. A house is too expensive. Anyway, even if I had the money for a house, I wouldn't have the time to care for it.

Describe your neighborhood.
The neighborhood/neighbourhood is in a good location. We're close to the bus and train. We have some good restaurants, and it's easy to buy food here. We're downtown/in the city centre, but it's safe.

How do people choose their place to live?
They choose where to live based on location, money, and what is available. If they need a roommate/flatmate like me, they also need to think about that.

Describe your family. Are you married? Do you have children? Brothers and sisters?
I'm not married yet. I have a younger brother who still lives at home with my parents. I have an older sister who got married recently. I don't live with my family now because I'm studying in a different city.

What are some things you enjoy doing with other members of your family?
When my brother and I are together, we always like to play soccer. We play it a lot at the park near my parents' house. We watch soccer matches on TV, too. Sometimes when I visit my sister, we cook a meal together, or we sit around and talk about old times.

Who in your family are you particularly close to? Why?
This might sound funny, but I am close to my mother. She is someone I can always count on. If I have a problem at school, I can tell her about it and she helps me figure out a solution. My father isn't like that. It's harder to talk to him.

Do you spend more time with your family or with friends? Why?
Right now I spend more time with my friends because I'm living away from home. Also, I have a lot in common with them. We take a lot of the same classes, so we help each other study. When we have free time, we enjoy doing the same things, like going to the movies or going to parties.

Part 2

NOTE: Gift/present
A really special gift I received was a set of cuff links and a key chain. My sister gave them to me when she got married. I helped a lot with the wedding arrangements. I helped organize everything, and I arranged for my friends' band to play the music at the reception. My sister gave me the cuff links and key chain to thank me for all my help. They are made of silver with a modern design, and the key chain has my initials on it. I use the key chain every day. I wear the cuff links on special occasions. They're really only for formal wear. I wore them at my best friend's wedding last fall, for example. Occasionally I go to a formal dance, and I wear the cuff links then. This gift is important to me because it has a personal meaning. I was happy to be able to help my sister on an important day in her life, and this gift reminds me of that. It reminds me of how important my sister is to me.

Part 3

Do you think people generally enjoy giving and receiving gifts? Why or why not?
Some people might enjoy giving gifts, but I think it has become an obligation in many cases. If it's a birthday or some other occasion, you have to get a gift. You may not have the time and money to spend shopping for a gift and wrapping it up, but you have to do it anyway. I think children like getting gifts, but adults don't always. Often the gift you get is something you really don't like and can't use. But gift-giving is a custom, it's a tradition, so we have to do it.

In your country, when do people usually give gifts?
In my country, the most important time to give gifts is on birthdays. This is especially true for children, but we often give birthday gifts to adults, too. Another important gift-giving occasion is weddings. If you are invited to a wedding, you have to bring a gift to help the couple start their new life. In everyday life, if you are invited to a special dinner, you might bring a small gift to the host and hostess. If you spend several days at someone's house, you definitely should give a gift to your hosts.

What kind of gifts do they give?
The kind of gift depends on the occasion and the people involved. Children, of course, get toys and sometimes clothes. For a wedding, you are supposed to give something for the couple's new home. If you are a close relative or friend, it is expected that you will give something more expensive. You might give a silver dish, for example, or an expensive appliance. For a host and hostess gift, you can give flowers or a bottle of wine or something small for the house. Grandparents and parents often give money to their children for birthdays or weddings. Everyone can give a gift of money for a graduation present.

Do you agree or disagree: The price of a gift shows how much the giver cares about the recipient.

I have to say that I disagree. Some people try to make an impression by spending a lot of money, but anybody can spend money. It's not hard to do! I think just the fact of thinking to give someone a gift shows that you care about the person. If you can find a gift that the person really likes, that will show that you really care. But it's hard to do that. I think that's why people buy expensive gifts. It's easier than figuring out exactly what would be the best gift for that particular person.

General Training: Reading and Writing

MODEL TEST 1

ANSWER SHEET
General Training
Model Test 1

IELTS Reading Answer Sheet

		✓		✕
1			1	
2			2	
3			3	
4			4	
5			5	
6			6	
7			7	
8			8	
9			9	
10			10	
11			11	
12			12	
13			13	
14			14	
15			15	
16			16	
17			17	
18			18	
19			19	
20			20	

		✓		✕
21			21	
22			22	
23			23	
24			24	
25			25	
26			26	
27			27	
28			28	
29			29	
30			30	
31			31	
32			32	
33			33	
34			34	
35			35	
36			36	
37			37	
38			38	
39			39	
40			40	
	Reading Total			

GENERAL TRAINING MODEL TEST 1

Candidate Name ____

International English Language Testing System

GENERAL TRAINING READING

Time: 1 hour

INSTRUCTIONS TO CANDIDATES

Do not open this booklet until you are told to do so.

Write your name and candidate number in the space at the top of this page.

Start at the beginning of the test and work through it.

You should answer all questions.

If you cannot do a particular question, leave it and go on to the next. You can return to it later.

All answers must be written on the Answer Sheet.

Do not remove this booklet from the examination room.

INFORMATION FOR CANDIDATES

There are **40** questions on this question paper.

The test is divided as follows:

Section 1	Questions 1–14
Section 2	Questions 15–27
Section 3	Questions 28–40

SECTION 1

You are advised to spend 20 minutes on questions 1–14.

Questions 1–7

Look at the five apartment advertisements, **A–E**.

Write the letters of the appropriate advertisements in boxes 1–7 on your Answer Sheet. You may use any letter more than once.

Which apartment is appropriate for a person who

1 owns a car?

2 is a university student?

3 has children?

4 likes to swim?

5 usually uses public transportation?

6 wants to rent for two months only?

7 often entertains large groups of people?

A

> Sunny 1 bedroom, central location, washer/dryer in building. Storage space, parking included in rent. One year lease required. Call 837–9986 before 6 P.M.

B

> Cozy one bedroom with study available in elevator building.[1] Near City Park. Amenities include exercise room, pool, and party room. Other apartments also available. One- and two-year leases. Call 592–8261.

C

> Small one-bedroom, reasonable rent, near shopping, bus routes, university. References required. No pets. Call Mr. Watkins 876–9852.

D

> Don't miss this unique opportunity. Large two-bedroom plus study, which could be third bedroom. Quiet neighborhood. Walk to elementary and high school, park, shops. Small pets allowed.

E

> Furnished flats,[2] convenient to central business district. Studios, one-, and two-bedrooms. Weekly and monthly rentals available. Call our office 376–0923 9–5 M–F.

[1]BRITISH: building with lift

[2]AMERICAN: apartments

Questions 8–14

Thank you for buying a Blau Automatic Coffeemaker. If you use and maintain your Blau product correctly, you will enjoy it for years to come.

A Preparing Coffee with Your Blau Coffeemaker

Your coffeemaker is guaranteed to make a perfect cup of coffee every time. First, fill the reusable coffee basket with coffee grounds, adding two tablespoons of grounds per cup. Next, fill the reservoir with eight ounces of water for each cup of coffee. Place the coffee pot under the coffee basket, making sure that it is directly underneath the drip spout. Press the "on" button located on the coffeemaker's base.

B Built-in Convenience

Your Blau Coffeemaker is equipped with a built-in timer. You can set the timer so that your coffee is ready when you get up in the morning, when you return from work in the evening, or at any other time you choose. Just follow the directions above for preparing your coffee. Then set the timer by pushing the button underneath the clock at the front of the coffeemaker. Push twice to put the clock in timer mode. The minutes will flash. Push the button until the minutes are set. Push twice again and the hours will flash. Push the button until the hours are set. Push twice to return the timer to clock mode.

C Maintaining Your Coffeemaker

Monthly cleaning will keep your coffeemaker functioning properly and your coffee tasting fresh. Just follow these easy steps. Fill the reservoir with a small bottle of vinegar. Turn your coffeemaker on and let the vinegar run through it, filling the coffeepot. Then fill the reservoir with fresh water and let it run through the coffeemaker. Do this twice to make sure all traces of vinegar are removed.

D Really Fresh Coffee

If your Blau Coffeemaker came equipped with a coffee grinder, then you can enjoy extra fresh coffee every day. Simply add whole beans to the grinder compartment, being careful not to pass the "full" line below the rim. Make sure the lid is securely in place, then press the "grind" button.

E Our Guarantee

Your Blau Coffeemaker has a lifetime guarantee. If your coffeemaker suffers any type of malfunction, just call our toll-free customer service line at 888–936–8721, 24 hours a day. If we are unable to help you over the phone, you may have to mail the coffeemaker to us for service.

Questions 8–11

Match each picture below with the appropriate section in the instructions.

Write the correct letter, **A–E**, *in boxes 8–11 on your Answer Sheet.*

8

9

10

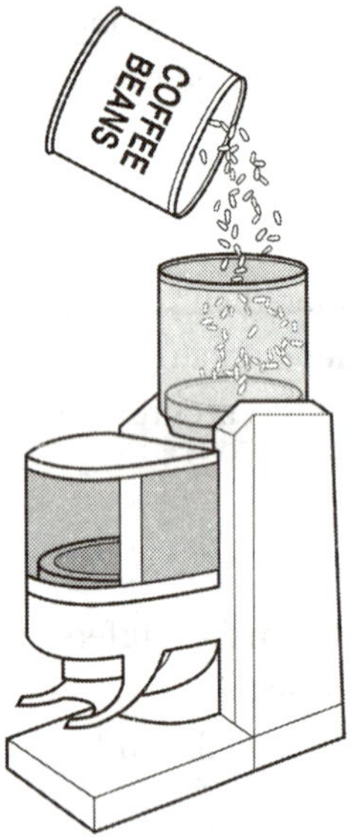

11

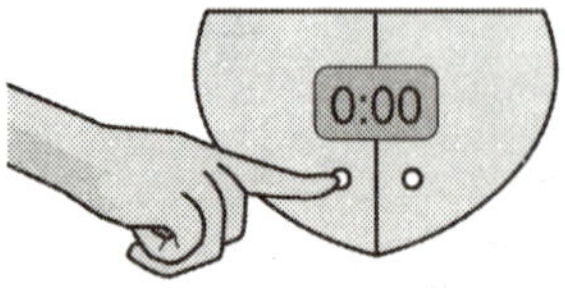

Questions 12–14

Answer the questions using NO MORE THAN THREE WORDS *for each answer. Write your answers in boxes 12–14 on your Answer Sheet.*

12 How much water should you use to make one cup of coffee?

13 How often should you clean the coffeemaker?

14 How can you contact the company for assistance?

SECTION 2

You are advised to spend 20 minutes on questions 15–27.

Questions 15–20

Look at the information from a company's employee manual.

There are six paragraphs, ***A–F***.

Choose the most suitable heading for each paragraph from the list below.

*Write the appropriate numbers (**i–viii**) in boxes 15–20 on your Answer Sheet. There are more headings than paragraphs, so you won't need to use them all.*

List of Headings

i	Vacation and Sick Day Policy
ii	Cafeteria Schedule
iii	Getting Paid
iv	Employee Discounts
v	Use of Conference Rooms
vi	Work Schedule
vii	Office Supplies
viii	Budgets and Accounting

15 Paragraph **A**

16 Paragraph **B**

17 Paragraph **C**

18 Paragraph **D**

19 Paragraph **E**

20 Paragraph **F**

The Mayberry Company
Employee Manual

A

Department heads distribute checks[1] on the first and fifteenth of every month. Each check is accompanied by a statement which shows wages earned and the number of vacation[2] and sick days taken so far for the year. Overtime hours are also indicated. Checks are issued by the accounting department. Please contact them if you have any questions about your check or to report errors.

B

All new employees are entitled to two weeks of annual leave. The number of annual leave days increases with each year of employment at the company. The dates when this leave may be taken are left to the decision of the employee in consultation with his or her supervisor. In addition, employees are entitled to take five days of paid leave per year for illness or other unexpected emergencies.

C

Our normal hours of operation are 8:30 to 5:30 Monday-Friday. Any employee wishing to modify his or her hours of work must have prior approval from his or her supervisor. All employees are entitled to a daily one hour lunch break to be taken between 11:00 A.M. and 2:00 P.M.

D

Rooms 101 and 102 may be reserved if extra space is needed for meetings or presentations. Please see the office manager to schedule this. The company cafeteria can provide snacks or lunches for your event with one week's notice.

E

Paper, envelopes, pens and pencils, ink cartridges, and other similar items are stored in the closet in the coffee break room. This closet is kept unlocked, and any employee may enter it at any time to take what is needed. If you cannot find what you need there, let your supervisor know. Department heads have a budget for ordering any extra materials you may need.

F

Company employees are entitled to purchase lunch at a reduced rate in the company cafeteria. The local health club has special reduced-rate memberships available for interested employees.

[1] BRITISH: cheque
[2] BRITISH: holiday

Questions 21–27

Read the information about applying for a job.

Employment at XYZ, Inc.

We are always interested in hearing from qualified applicants interested in working at XYZ, Inc. You must apply for a specific position as we do not accept general applications. Review the job openings listed on our website. If you see a position you are interested in, complete the Application for Employment form. Please do not apply for more than one position at a time.

We ask that you do not call or e-mail us after submitting your application. We receive a large number of applications and cannot personally reply to them all. Be assured that we will read your application and, if we feel you are qualified for the position you have applied for, we will contact you by e-mail. You can expect to hear from us within four weeks of receipt of your application. At that time, we will ask you to make an appointment for an interview. All interviews are conducted at our downtown office.

When you come in for your interview, please dress in appropriate business attire and bring the names of references who are familiar with your business experience and qualifications. Depending on the type of position you are applying for, you may be asked to take a language, office skills, or other type of test. Arrangements for this will be made at the time of your interview. Thank you for your interest in XYZ, Inc. We look forward to hearing from you.

Complete the summary of information about applying for a job at XYZ, Inc.

Choose NO MORE THAN THREE WORDS *from the text for each answer.*

First, look at the **21** .... online. Then fill out **22** .... If you qualify for the position, the company will send you **23** .... You may have to wait **24** .... before you hear from the company. You will need to go to the **25** .... for your interview. During your interview, you will be asked for **26** .... who know you and your work. Some job applicants may have to **27** .... This depends on the kind of job you apply for.

SECTION 3

You should spend 20 minutes on questions 28–40, which are based on the reading passage below.

Questions 28–33

Reading Passage 3 has six paragraphs, **A–F**.

*Choose the correct heading for paragraphs **A–F** from the list of headings below.*

*Write the correct number **i–ix** in boxes 28–33 on your Answer Sheet.*

List of Headings

i	Newer Subway[1] Systems
ii	Early Subways in the Americas
iii	Asian Subway Systems
iv	A New Device
v	The Longest Subway
vi	Subway Art
vii	Europe's First Subways
viii	The World's Largest Subways
ix	The Moscow Metro

28 Paragraph **A**

29 Paragraph **B**

30 Paragraph **C**

31 Paragraph **D**

32 Paragraph **E**

33 Paragraph **F**

A

People have been traveling by subway for well over a hundred years. The first subway systems began operating in Europe in the second half of the nineteenth century. London's subway system, known as "The Underground" or "The Tube," opened in early 1863. In 1896, subways began running in both Budapest, Hungary and Glasgow, Scotland. The Budapest subway ran from the center of the city to City Park and was just under four kilometers long. The city of Paris, France began operating its subway system in 1900. Its famous name, Metro, is short for *Chemin de Fer Metropolitan* or Metropolitan Railway. Many other cities have since adopted the name Metro for their own subways.

[1]British: underground

B

The city of Boston, Massachusetts boasts the oldest subway system in the United States, beginning operations in 1897. It had only two stations when it first opened. The New York City Subway, now one of the largest subway systems in the world, began running in 1904. The original line was 14.5 kilometers long and ran from City Hall in downtown Manhattan to 145th Street. The city of Philadelphia opened its first subway line in 1907. The oldest subway in Latin America began operations in Buenos Aires, Argentina in 1913. It is called the *subte*, short for *subterraneo* or underground.

C

The second half of the twentieth century saw new subway systems constructed in cities around the world. Many Korean cities have modern subway systems, the largest one in the capital city of Seoul, with 287 kilometers of track. The first subway in Brazil opened in the city of Sao Paulo in 1974. Since then subways have been built in a number of other Brazilian cities, including Rio de Janeiro and the capital, Brasilia. Washington, DC, began running the Washington Metro in 1976. Hong Kong opened its subway in 1979. This system includes four lines that run under Victoria Harbour. In 2000, a 17-mile long subway system was completed in Los Angeles, a city infamous for its traffic problems and resulting smog. Construction of this system took fourteen years to complete.

D

With a total of 468 stations and 656 miles of passenger service track, the New York City Subway is among the largest subway systems in the world. If the tracks in train yards, shops, and storage areas are added in, the total track length of the New York Subway comes to 842 miles. Measured by number of riders, the Moscow Metro is the world's largest system, with 3.2 billion riders annually. Other cities with busy subways include Tokyo, with 2.6 billion riders a year, and Seoul and Mexico City, both carrying 1.4 billion riders annually.

E

In some cities, the subway stations are famous for their architecture and artwork. The stations of the Moscow Metro are well-known for their beautiful examples of socialist-realist art. The Baker Street station in London honors the fictional detective, Sherlock Holmes, who supposedly lived on Baker Street. Decorative tiles in the station's interior depict the character, and a Sherlock Holmes statue sits outside one of the station exits. Each of the stations of the new Los Angeles subway system contains murals, sculptures, or other examples of decorative artwork.

F

A new feature now often included in the construction of new subway stations is the Platform Screen Door (PSD). The Singapore subway was the first to be built with the inclusion of PSDs. The original purpose was to reduce high air-conditioning costs in underground stations. Since then, there has been more and more focus on the safety aspects of this device, as it can prevent people from accidentally falling or being pushed onto the track. PSDs also keep the station platforms quieter and cleaner and allow trains to enter stations at higher rates of speed. The subway system in Hong Kong was the first to have PSDs added to an already existing system. They are becoming more common in subway systems around the world. Tokyo, Seoul, Bangkok, London, and Copenhagen are just some of the cities that have PSDs in at least some of their subway stations. PSDs are also often used with other forms of transportation, such as monorails, light rail systems, and airport transportation systems.

Questions 34–40

Look at the following descriptions of some of the subway systems mentioned in Reading Passage 3.

*Match the cities (**A–L**) listed below with the descriptions of their subway systems.*

*Write the appropriate letters, **A–L**, in boxes 34–40 on your Answer Sheet.*

A	Boston
B	Paris
C	Washington, DC
D	Sao Paulo
E	London
F	Tokyo
G	Seoul
H	Buenos Aires
I	Singapore
J	Budapest
K	Moscow
L	New York

34 has a station celebrating a storybook character

35 is the busiest subway system in the world

36 has lent its name to subway systems around the world

37 has the oldest subway system in the United States

38 was the first subway system constructed with PSDs

39 has a total length of 287 kilometers

40 was the first subway built in Latin America

ANSWER SHEET
General Training Model Test 1

Writing Answer Sheet

TASK 1

ANSWER SHEET
General Training
Model Test 1

-2-

ANSWER SHEET
General Training Model Test 1

-3-

TASK 2

ANSWER SHEET
General Training Model Test 1

-4-

GENERAL TRAINING MODEL TEST 1

Candidate Name ______________________________

International English Language Testing System

GENERAL TRAINING

Time: 1 hour

INSTRUCTIONS TO CANDIDATES

Do not open this booklet until you are told to do so.

Write your name and candidate number in the space at the top of this page.

All answers must be written on the separate answer booklet provided.

Do not remove this booklet from the examination room.

INFORMATION FOR CANDIDATES

There are **2** tasks on this question paper.

You must do **both** tasks.

Underlength answers will be penalized.[1]

GENERAL TRAINING MODEL TEST 1

[1]British: penalised

WRITING TASK 1

You should spend about 20 minutes on this task.

> ***You are going to spend your vacation in a city in a foreign country. You have never been there before. Your cousin has a friend who lives there. Write a letter to the friend. In your letter***
> - ***introduce yourself***
> - ***say why you are making this trip***
> - ***ask some questions about the city (e.g., places to see, things to do, things to bring)***

Write at least 150 words.

You do NOT need to write any addresses.

Begin your letter as follows:

Dear John,

WRITING TASK 2

You should spend about 40 minutes on this task.

Write about the following topic:

> ***Modern technology, such as personal computers and the Internet, have made it possible for many people to do their work from home at least part of the time instead of going to an office every day. What are some of the advantages and disadvantages of this situation?***

Give reasons for your answer and include any relevant examples from your own knowledge or experience.

Write at least 250 words.

GENERAL TRAINING MODEL TEST 1—ANSWER EXPLANATIONS

READING

NOTE: apartment (American)/flat (British)

1. (A) This apartment includes parking.
2. (C) This apartment is near the university.
3. (D) This apartment is big enough for a family and is close to elementary and high schools.
4. (B) This apartment has a pool.
5. (C) This apartment is near the bus lines/routes.
6. (E) This flat offers weekly and monthly rentals.
7. (B) This apartment has a party room.
8. (E) This section says that if there are any problems with the coffeemaker a customer can call the free service line.
9. (C) This section demonstrates how to clean the coffeemaker with vinegar.
10. (D) This section contains the warning that one should only pour coffee beans up to the "full" line.
11. (B) This section states that the coffeemaker comes with a built-in timer for convenience.
12. *Eight ounces.* Section A states: "fill the reservoir with eight ounces of water for each cup of coffee."
13. *Once a month/monthly.* Section C states: "Monthly cleaning will keep your coffeemaker functioning properly and your coffee tasting fresh."
14. *By phone/By telephone.* Section E states: "Just call our toll-free customer service line. . . ."
15. iii. Getting Paid. This paragraph gives information about paychecks.
16. i. Vacation and Sick Day Policy. This paragraph gives information about taking time off from work for annual leave (vacation) and for illness (sick days).
17. vi. Work Schedule. This paragraph explains the hours that employees are expected to work.
18. v. Use of Conference Rooms. This paragraph discusses the rooms used for meetings and presentations, normally called conference rooms.
19. vii. Office Supplies. This paragraph deals with paper, pens and pencils, ink cartridges, and other supplies used for office work.
20. iv. Employee Discounts. This paragraph describes discounts employees can get at the cafeteria and health club.
21. *job openings.* Applicants are asked to review, or look at, the job openings on the website.
22. *an application form.* Applicants are asked to "complete an Application for Employment form."
23. *an e-mail.* If you are qualified, the company will "contact you by e-mail."
24. *four weeks.* Applicants are told that they can expect to hear from the company within four weeks.
25. *downtown office.* At the end of paragraph 2, it is explained that interviews take place at the downtown office.
26. *references/names of references.* In the third paragraph, applicants are asked to bring "names of references who are familiar with your business experience and qualifications."
27. *take a test.* Some applicant may have to take a language, office skills, or other type of test.
28. vii Paragraph A describes the first subways/underground systems built in Europe in the cities of London, Budapest, Glasgow, and Paris.
29. ii Paragraph B describes the first subways in the USA and South America.
30. i Paragraph C describes subways built in the second half of the twentieth century.
31. viii Paragraph D describes the largest subway systems in the world, measured in terms of total track length and numbers of riders.
32. vi Paragraph E gives examples of several subway systems known for the art in their stations.
33. iv Paragraph F describes Platform Screen Doors, a safety device now becoming more and more common in subway stations around the world.
34. E The Baker Street Station in London honors the fictional detective Sherlock Holmes.
35. K The Moscow Metro has more riders than any other subway system.

36. B Many subway systems have adopted the name Metro from the Paris Metro.
37. A According to the article, "The city of Boston boasts the oldest subway system in the United States. . . ."
38. I The subway in Singapore was the first to be built with Platform Screen Doors. The subway in Hong Kong was the first to add PSDs to a system that was already built.
39. G The subway in Seoul has 287 kilometers of track.
40. H Buenos Aires has the oldest subway in Latin America.

GENERAL TRAINING WRITING

Sample Responses

Writing Task 1

Dear John,

I am planning a trip to Toronto and my cousin, Jake Vandelft, suggested I write to you since you live there. It has always been my dream to visit Canada, and I hope you can give me some suggestions for my trip.

My name is Irma. Jake may have mentioned me to you. Although we are cousins, we are more like brother and sister since we grew up in the same house. Jake told me that you and he were university classmates.

I am graduating from the university this summer and plan to take a month's vacation before I start work. I am really excited to have this opportunity to see Toronto.

I hope you can give me advice about a place to stay in Toronto. I don't have a lot of money so I would prefer to stay at a youth hostel or similar place. Also, what are some sights I should see? Do you think I could get a ticket to see the Blue Jays play baseball? That is another one of my big dreams!

I look forward to hearing from you and hope we can meet in person when I am in Toronto.

Best wishes,
Irma Klein

Writing Task 2

Modern technology has made the office less of a necessity. Rather than spending every working hour in the office, people can work at home on their personal computers. There are advantages and disadvantages to this situation for both the employee and the employer.

A big advantage that working at home has for employees is that it allows flexibility with child care. A parent can stay at home with a sick child and at the same time put in a few hours of work. A parent can leave the office early to attend a soccer game or school play and then work at home for a few hours in the evening.

Another advantage, for both employees and their employer, is that working at home eliminates lost work time due to transportation problems. Bad weather or a broken car might prevent an employee from getting to the office. However, by working at home, the responsibilities for the day can still be met.

On the other hand, working at home also has its disadvantages. For example, there can be many distractions throughout the day. A neighbor may call to chat, not understanding that he or she is interrupting work time. Children, quite naturally, expect and ask for attention from their parents, and this is difficult to ignore. It is also more difficult for employers to supervise their work-at-home employees. They cannot be sure how their employees are spending their time, and it is also harder to provide any needed support.

Employees and employers have to consider both the advantages and disadvantages of working at home and decide what works best for their own situation.

General Training: Reading and Writing

MODEL TEST 2

ANSWER SHEET
General Training Model Test 2

IELTS Reading Answer Sheet

1		✓ 1 ✗
2		2
3		3
4		4
5		5
6		6
7		7
8		8
9		9
10		10
11		11
12		12
13		13
14		14
15		15
16		16
17		17
18		18
19		19
20		20

21		✓ 21 ✗
22		22
23		23
24		24
25		25
26		26
27		27
28		28
29		29
30		30
31		31
32		32
33		33
34		34
35		35
36		36
37		37
38		38
39		39
40		40
	Reading Total	

GENERAL TRAINING MODEL TEST 2

Candidate Name ______________________________

International English Language Testing System

GENERAL TRAINING READING

Time: 1 hour

INSTRUCTIONS TO CANDIDATES

Do not open this booklet until you are told to do so.

Write your name and candidate number in the space at the top of this page.

Start at the beginning of the test and work through it.

You should answer all questions.

If you cannot do a particular question, leave it and go on to the next. You can return to it later.

All answers must be written on the Answer Sheet.

Do not remove this booklet from the examination room.

INFORMATION FOR CANDIDATES

There are **40** questions on this question paper.

The test is divided as follows:

Section 1	Questions 1-13
Section 2	Questions 14-27
Section 3	Questions 28-40

SECTION 1

You are advised to spend 20 minutes on questions 1–13.

Questions 1–7

Read the notice below. Complete the sentences below using NO MORE THAN THREE WORDS *from the passage for each answer. Write your answers in boxes 1–7 on your Answer Sheet.*

To all tenants of Parkside Towers:
Please be advised of the building painting schedule.

Dec. 1-4:	Main foyer. Please don't use the main entrance at this time. Use the parking garage entrance to access the building.
Dec. 5-8:	Garage stairway and elevator.[1] Please stay away from these areas at this time. If you park in the garage, you will have to walk outside to the front of the building to gain access through the main entrance.
Dec. 9-13:	East stairway and elevators. If your apartment is in the East Wing, please use the West Wing elevators or stairway at this time.
Dec. 14-21:	West and north stairways and elevators. If your apartment is in these areas of the building, please use the east stairway or elevator at this time.
Dec. 22-27:	Parking garage. The garage will not be available to tenants at this time. In order to avoid illegal on-street parking, spaces in the parking lot[2] across the street will be made available to all tenants.

We are sorry for the inconvenience. If you have any questions or complaints, please contact the building manager.

If you would like to schedule painting for your apartment,[3] please fill out a painting request form, available in the main lobby.

It's December the 3rd. The **1** .... is being painted.

It's December 7th. You can enter the building through the **2** ....

It's December 12th. You can reach a tenth floor apartment in the East Wing by the **3** .... or stairs.

On December 15th , you can reach a sixth-floor apartment in the North Wing by the **4** .... or elevator.

[1]BRITISH: lift
[2]BRITISH: car park
[3]BRITISH: flat

On December 24th, you can park your car **5** ....

If you are unhappy about the painting schedule, you can talk with the **6** ....

If you want to have your apartment painted, you should look for a **7** .... in the lobby.

Questions 8–13

Read the bill from the electric company and answer the questions.

Write NO MORE THAN THREE WORDS AND/OR A NUMBER *from the text for each answer.*

Write your answers in boxes 8–13 on your Answer Sheet.

ENVIROELECTRIC COMPANY

Date: 2 August

Customer name:
Oswald Robertson
15A Peacock Lane
Mayfield

For: 1 July–31 July—	Total charges:	£35
	Previous bill:	£29
	Payment:	–£29
	Total due:	£35

We must receive your payment in full by 21 August or a late fee of £2.50 will be assessed.
Please make out your check to EnviroElectric Company and mail it to:

EnviroElectric Company
PO Box 30682
East Bradfield

Or, pay by credit card:

Number: .... Expiration date: ....

Signature: ....

Cash payments may be made by visiting any branch of the Bradfield Bank.

Account questions? Call (01 223) 385–9387
For repair service, call (01 223) 385–9856

8 How much did Mr. Robertson pay on his electric bill in June?

9 When is his July bill due?

10 How much extra will Mr. Robertson owe if his payment arrives after the due date?

11 Where is the EnviroElectric Company located?

12 If Mr. Robertson wants to pay cash, what should he do?

13 If Mr. Robinson thinks the company has charged him too much, what should he do?

SECTION 2

You are advised to spend 20 minutes on questions 14–27.

Questions 14–20

Read the information about repetitive stress injury.

Repetitive Stress Injury (RSI) is the irritation of muscles, nerves, or tendons resulting from repetitive motions. In other words, it is an injury that comes from making the same movements again and again. It is a particular problem in the modern office, where workers spend hours a day in front of computers. In fact, the most commonly reported RSIs are related to computer use. In the past, office tasks were more varied. People had to stand up to go to the copy machine or filing cabinet. Now, almost everything is done on computers and as a result, people spend hours a day sitting in the same position and repeating the same motions.

Fatigue, numbness, and pain in the hands, arms, neck, or shoulders are signs of RSI. These symptoms arise during an activity which involves repetitive motion and often cease when the activity stops. If left untreated, however, the discomfort starts lasting longer and becomes more intense. The pain can eventually become so severe as to cause long-lasting damage.

Some common causes of RSI in an office setting are poorly designed keyboards and chairs, spending long hours in the same position, and the use of a computer mouse. Computer keyboards force the user to continually hold the hands with the palms down. This is an unnatural position and causes strain on the hands, fingers, and wrists. Desk chairs often do not support the user's posture, but instead encourage slumping, which results in poor circulation. Holding a computer mouse causes strain on the hand muscles. In addition, using a mouse requires the repetitive motion of one finger.

RSI can be a serious problem if ignored. Fortunately, it isn't difficult to prevent. The best form of prevention is to take frequent breaks from work. A minimum of five minutes every hour is recommended. This will give your hands, wrists, and back a chance to change position and rest. If you spend hours typing, a wrist rest from your computer keyboard will help protect your wrists from strain. You can also protect your wrists by holding your palms parallel to the keyboard and keeping your forearms in a horizontal position. You can support your posture by adding armrests to your chair. This will actually aid in supporting your back and help you maintain a good posture.

Complete the sentences below about the reading passage.

Choose your answers from the box below, and write them in boxes 14–20 on your Answer Sheet. There are more choices than sentences so you will not use them all.

A	supports the back
B	isn't difficult to prevent
C	using a computer mouse
D	protects the wrists
E	is never recommended
F	works on a computer
G	typing for long hours
H	uses a filing cabinet
I	taking a break
J	becomes serious and permanent
K	is not natural

In the past, people moved around the office a lot, but now the average office employee **14** .... all day.

When RSI is not treated, the pain **15** ....

Computer keyboards cause users to hold their hands in a position that **16** ....

17 .... causes repeated stress on one finger.

18 .... often can help prevent serious problems.

Holding your hands and arms in the proper position **19** ....

Using armrests on your chair **20** ....

Questions 21–27

Read the information about company policy

Comet Corporation
Vacation[1] and Sick Leave Policy
To all employees: Please read the following information carefully. If you have any questions, contact the Human Resources Department.

Vacation/Personal Leave

Employees may use their vacation days when they choose, with the permission of their supervisor. To apply for permission, Form 101A must be completed and submitted at least three weeks ahead of time. Forms are available in the Human Resources Department.

Sick Days

Sick days are to be used in the case of illness or for doctor's appointments only. They may not be used as extra vacation days. Permission is not required to use these days, but department heads should be notified as soon as possible about unexpected absences due to illness. Supervisors should also be informed in a timely manner when employees need to be absent to attend doctor's appointments. Supervisors may request written confirmation of appointments from the doctor's office if they desire.

Rolling Over Vacation Days

Any vacation days that are not used up by the end of the calendar year will not be lost. Instead, they may be rolled over and added to the vacation days for the following year. This policy does not apply to sick days.

Do the following statements agree with the information in the reading passage?

In boxes 21–27 on your Answer Sheet, write

TRUE	*if the statement is true according to the passage.*
FALSE	*if the statement contradicts the passage.*
NOT GIVEN	*if there is no information about this in the passage.*

21 Employees must get permission from the Human Resources Department to use vacation days.

22 All employees at the Comet Corporation get three weeks of vacation a year.

23 Employees may use some of their sick days in order to take a longer vacation.

24 An employee does not need to ask for permission before using a sick day.

[1]BRITISH: holiday

25 Employees must have confirmation from a doctor in order to use a sick day.

26 An employee may use fewer vacation days one year in order to have more the next year.

27 Sick days that are not used before the end of the year may be used the following year.

SECTION 3

You should spend 20 minutes on questions 28–40, which are based on the reading passage below.

Stonehenge

Approximately two miles west of Amesbury, Wiltshire, in southern England stands Stonehenge, one of the world's most famous megalithic monuments. The remains of Stonehenge consist of a series of stone structures arranged in layers of circular and horseshoe-like patterns. Theories and myths concerning this mysterious monument have flourished for thousands of years. The Danes, Egyptians, and Druids are just a few of the groups who have been credited with building Stonehenge. Some people have even made attempts to prove that aliens erected Stonehenge. Early historians believed that the monument was constructed as a memorial to nobles killed in combat, while other later theorists described Stonehenge as a place for sacrificial ceremonies. Regardless of who built the monument and why, all of the legends surrounding these megaliths are based on speculation. With the exception of archeological evidence, very little of what we understand about Stonehenge today can actually be called fact.

Stonehenge was constructed in three phases during the Neolithic and Bronze Age periods. Stonehenge period 1, also commonly referred to as Phase 1, is believed to have occurred sometime around 3000 B.C., during the middle Neolithic period. In this first step of the construction, picks made of deer antlers were used to dig a series of 56 pits. These pits were later named "Aubrey Holes" after an English scholar. Outside of the holes was dug a large circular henge (a ditch with an earthen wall). During this phase, a break, or entranceway was also dug on the northeast corner of the henge. Archeologists[1] today refer to this break as the Avenue. Two stones were set in the Avenue. The "Slaughter Stone" was placed just inside the circle, while the "Heel Stone" was placed 27 meters down the Avenue. The Heel Stone weighs about 35 tons and is made of natural sandstone, believed to have originated from Marlborough Downs, an area 20 miles north of the monument. The 35-foot-wide Avenue is set so that, from the center of Stonehenge, a person would be able to see the sunrise to the left of the heel stone. Just inside the henge, four other "Station Stones" were placed in a rectangular formation.

[1]BRITISH: archaeologists

There is great debate over how long the first phase of Stonehenge was used and when the original alterations were made; however, the second phase is generally placed between 2900 B.C. and 2400 B.C. and accredited to the Beaker people. It is thought that many wooden posts were added to the monument during this phase. One of the problems archeologists have had with Phase 2 is that unlike stone or holes in the earth, wood does not hold up over thousands of years. The numerous stake holes in the earth tell the story of where these posts were positioned. Besides the ones in the center of the henge, six rows of posts were placed near the entrance. These may have been used to mark astronomical measurements, or to guide people to the center. The original Aubrey holes were filled in either with earth or cremation remains. Many archeologists believed that the Beaker people were sun worshipers,[1] and that they may have purposely changed the main axis of the monument and widened the entrance during this phase in order to show their appreciation for the sun.

The final phase of Stonehenge is usually described in terms of three subphases, each one involving a setting of large stones. The first stones that arrived were bluestones, brought all the way from the Preseli Hills in Pembrokeshire, Wales. A horseshoe of paired bluestones was placed in the center of the henge, with a tall Altar Stone marking the end of the formation. In the next subphase, a 30-meter ring of sandstones called the Sarsen Circle was built around the bluestones. Only 17 of the original 30 stones remain. These sarasen stones were connected with lintel blocks, each precisely carved in order to fit end-to-end and form perfectly with the stone circle. Approximately 60 more bluestones were then added inside the original horseshoe.

How these enormous stones were transported and raised in Phase 3 remains a mystery. The fact that these monoliths were built before the wheel means an incredible amount of manual labor was used. It is believed that a pulley system using rollers still would have required at least one hundred men to operate. Raising the lintels and fitting them into one another would have been another major struggle without the use of machines. Stonehenge remains one of the world's greatest mysteries and one of England's most important icons.

[1] BRITISH: worshippers

Questions 28–31

Complete the labels on the diagram of Stonehenge below.

Choose your answers from the box below, and write them in boxes 28–31 on your Answer Sheet. There are more words than spaces, so you will not use them all.

Aubrey Holes Heel Stone Marlborough Downs Avenue Henge Station Stones

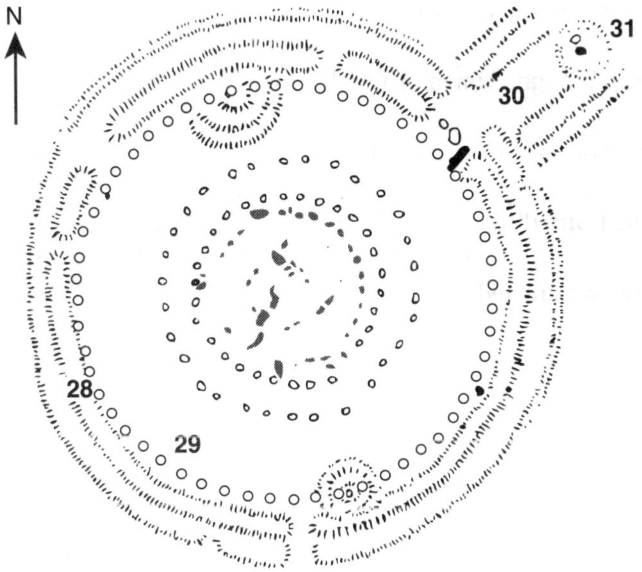

Stonehenge Phase 1

GENERAL TRAINING MODEL TEST 2

Questions 32–40

Stonehenge was built in three phases. During which phase did the following things occur? In boxes 32–40 on your Answer Sheet, write

A if it occurred during Phase 1.
B if it occurred during Phase 2.
C if it occurred during Phase 3.

32 The entrance was made wider.

33 The Slaughter Stone was erected.

34 Stones were placed in a horseshoe formation.

35 Wooden posts were set near the entrance.

36 Deer antlers were used to dig holes.

37 Bluestones were brought from a distant location.

38 A ring of sandstones was constructed.

39 Holes were filled with dirt.

40 The Altar Stone was erected.

ANSWER SHEET
General Training Model Test 2

Writing Answer Sheet

TASK 1

ANSWER SHEET
General Training
Model Test 2

-2-

ANSWER SHEET
General Training
Model Test 2

-3-

TASK 2

ANSWER SHEET
General Training Model Test 2

-4-

GENERAL TRAINING MODEL TEST 2

Candidate Name ____

International English Language Testing System

GENERAL TRAINING WRITING

Time: 1 hour

INSTRUCTIONS TO CANDIDATES

Do not open this booklet until you are told to do so.

Write your name and candidate number in the space at the top of this page.

All answers must be written on the separate answer booklet provided.

Do not remove this booklet from the examination room.

INFORMATION FOR CANDIDATES

There are **2** tasks on this question paper.

You must do **both** tasks.

Underlength answers will be penalized.[1]

[1]BRITISH: penalised

WRITING TASK 1

You should spend about 20 minutes on this task.

> ***You stayed at a hotel last week. After you got home, you realized that you had left your watch behind. Write a letter to the hotel manager. In your letter***
> - ***explain what happened to your watch***
> - ***describe your watch***
> - ***ask the manager to help you find it***

You should write at least 150 words.

You do NOT need to write any addresses.

Begin your letter as follows:

Dear Sir or Madam:

WRITING TASK 2

You should spend about 40 minutes on this task.

Write about the following topic:

> ***Children today spend more time watching television than they did in the past. Describe some of the advantages and disadvantages of television for children.***

Give reasons for your answer and include any relevant examples from your own knowledge or experience.

You should write at least 250 words.

GENERAL TRAINING MODEL TEST 2—ANSWER EXPLANATIONS

READING

1. *main foyer.* From Dec. 1–4, the main foyer is being painted.
2. *main entrance.* From Dec. 5–8, tenants cannot enter the building from the garage.
3. *West Wing elevator.* From Dec. 9–13, the East stairway is being painted. To reach the tenth floor one would have to take an elevator.
4. *East stairway.* From Dec. 14–21, the west and north stairways and elevators are blocked. The east stairway or elevator must be used.
5. *Across the street.* From Dec. 22–27, the parking garage is unavailable. Tenants will get fined if they park on the street, but there is a parking lot/car park across the street that will be made available.
6. *building manager.* Near the bottom of the notice it says, "If you have any questions or complaints, please contact the building manager."
7. *form/painting request form.* At the end of the notice it says that tenants can request a painting form if they want their apartments/flats painted.
8. *£29.* The invoice shows the last payment made. This bill is for the month of July, so the last bill was for June.
9. *August 21st.* The invoice says: "We must receive your payment in full by August 21st."
10. *£2.50.* The invoice states that a late fee of £2.50 will be charged for payments received after August 21.
11. *East Bradfield.* The mailing address for this company is given below the late fee information.
12. *Visit Bradfield Bank/ visit the bank.* The invoice states: "Cash payments may be made by visiting any branch of the Bradfield Bank."
13. Call *(01 223)* 385–9387. This number is given for any customer who has questions about a bill.
14. (F) Paragraph 1 states: "It is a particular problem in the modern office, where workers spend hours a day in front of computers" and "Now, almost everything is done on computers. . . ."
15. (J) Paragraph 2: "The pain can eventually become so severe as to cause long-lasting damage."
16. (K) Paragraph 3 states: "Computer keyboards force the user to continually hold the hands with the palms down. This is an unnatural position. . . ."
17. (C) Paragraph 3 states: "In addition, using a mouse requires the repetitive motion of one finger."
18. (I) Paragraph 4 states: "RSI can be a serious problem if ignored. Fortunately, it isn't difficult to prevent. The best form of prevention is to take frequent breaks from work."
19. (D) Paragraph 4 states: "You can also protect your wrists by holding your palms parallel to the keyboard and keeping your forearms in a horizontal position."
20. (A) Paragraph 4 states: "You can support your posture by adding armrests to your chair. This will actually aid in supporting your back and help you maintain a good posture."
21. False. Employees must get permission from their supervisors. The Human Resources Department has information and forms but doesn't give permission.
22. Not Given. There is no information about the amount of vacation time employees get.
23. False. Paragraph 3 explicitly states that employees may not do this.
24. True. Paragraph 3 says that permission is not required for sick days.
25. False. Confirmation from a doctor is not required for sick days but may be requested for doctor's appointments.
26. True. Paragraph 4 states that unused vacation days can be added to vacation days for the following year.
27. False. Paragraph 4 explicitly states that this is not allowed.
28. *Henge.* Paragraph 2 states that a large circular ditch called the henge was located around the Aubrey Holes.
29. *Aubrey Holes.* Paragraph 2 talks about the series of holes called Aubrey Holes that were dug with deer picks.
30. *Avenue.* Paragraph 2 says that archeologists called the entrance way the "Avenue."

31. *Heel Stone*. Paragraph 2 describes the Heel Stone as being placed along the Avenue.
32. (B) The last sentence in paragraph 3 states that the Beaker people likely, "widened the entrance during this phase in order to show their appreciation for the sun."
33. (A) Halfway through Paragraph 2 is the description of the Slaughter Stone addition in Phase 1.
34. (C) Paragraph 4 contains the description of the bluestones being placed in a horseshoe formation.
35. (B) The second sentence in paragraph 3 describes the wooden posts being added.
36. (A) Paragraph 2 states that the Aubrey Holes were dug with picks made of deer antlers.
37. (C) The second sentence in paragraph 4 states that the bluestones came "all the way from the Preseli Hills." The expression "all the way" means *a long distance*.
38. (C) In the middle of paragraph 4, the addition of the sandstone ring is described.
39. (B) Toward the end of paragraph 3 is a description of the Aubrey Holes being filled in: "The original Aubrey Holes were filled in either with earth or cremation remains."
40. (C) In the middle of paragraph 4, the addition of the Altar Stone is described.

WRITING

Sample Responses

Writing Task 1

Dear Sir or Madam:

I am writing about a lost item. While I was staying at your hotel last week, I lost my wristwatch. I hope you can help me find it.

When I arrived home after my stay in Honolulu, I realized that I didn't have my watch with me. I am sure I left it behind in my hotel room. I stayed in room 401, and I think I must have left the watch on the table by the bed.

The watch is a lady's wristwatch with a chrome band. There is a yellow moon on the face with a bluish-black background. The brand of the watch is TIMEOUT.

I would appreciate it if you would help me find my watch. Perhaps the staff found it when they were cleaning the room, or maybe someone turned it in to the lost and found office. Please call me if you find the watch, and I will send you a check to pay for the postage to mail it to me.

Thank you very much for your help.

Sincerely,
Therese Lim

Writing Task 2

Today most children in the world grow up with TV. This has both advantages and disadvantages.

Children can learn many interesting and valuable things from TV. There are programs that are designed specifically to teach young people. Some of them reinforce skills that children need for reading. For example, they might help children learn to read letters and common words. Or they might have actors reading or telling stories. Other programs teach children fascinating facts about the natural world or about life in other countries or about other interesting things. Through programs such as these, children can be exposed to information that they might not learn otherwise. Often I have seen children become excited about subjects they first heard about on TV. They then go on to seek out books and other sources of information about these subjects.

On the other hand, there are also drawbacks to TV. For one thing, watching TV is a passive activity. Children don't participate in TV programs. They don't ask questions or tell their own opinions or choose what to do next. They just receive the information or entertainment they are given. Watching TV is also physically inactive. When children spend too much time watching TV, they don't spend enough time running and playing actively. In addition, there are a lot of programs on TV that are inappropriate for children, but children can still see them. This can be confusing and even scary for some.

There are both good and bad sides to TV. One thing, however, is always true: too much of anything is never good.

Audioscripts

8

IELTS LISTENING MODULE

LISTENING SKILLS

Track 1

Skill 1—Making Assumptions (page 24)

PRACTICE 1 (PAGE 25)

Listen to the conversation between an apartment house manager and a man who wants to rent an apartment.

Questions 1–10

W1: Good morning. How may I help you?
M1: Yes, I was wondering, do you have any one-bedroom apartments available?
W1: Yes we do. Were you looking for yourself?
M1: Yes, it's for me.
W1: Let me just get some information from you then, for our application form. May I have your name?
M1: Yes. It's Kingston. James Kingston.
W1: And what's your current address?
M1: I live over on State Street. Number 1705 State Street, apartment seven.
W1: And your phone number?
M1: My home phone? It's 721-0584.
W1: Work phone?
M1: 721-1127.
W1: Great. I need to know just one more thing. What is your date of birth?
M1: December 12, 1978.
W1: Thank you. Now, you're interested in a one-bedroom apartment, correct?
M1: That's right.
W1: Did you want just a one-bedroom, or a one-bedroom with a den? We have several of those available, and a study is really nice. Having that extra room gives you space for a small home office or you can use it as a guest room.
M1: I don't think so. I live alone. I don't need an extra room.

W1: Right. Then I'll put you down for a simple one bedroom. With a balcony?

M1: No, I don't need that. I'll tell you what I do need, though, is a parking space.

W1: We have garage parking spaces available for a low monthly fee.

M1: Great. I really need that. Oh, and, um, something else. I need an apartment with lots of closets for storage.

W1: We actually have storage areas in the basement. You can rent your own storage space by the month.

M1: Hmmm. That sounds like a good idea.

W1: All right. So I'll put you down for a storage space in the basement.

M1: Sounds good.

W1: Are you interested in our exercise club? We have an exercise room with several pieces of equipment as well as a sauna.

M1: Is it included in the rent?

W1: It's available for a small extra fee.

M1: Then I don't think so. I can always go for a walk for free.

W1: All right then, one bedroom, no balcony. . . . I have several apartments you might like. One of them has a fireplace. Would you be interested in that?

M1: Do I have to pay extra for it?

W1: Actually no. That apartment is slightly smaller than our other one bedrooms, so even though it has a fireplace, the rent isn't any higher.

M1: OK then I'll take the fireplace.

W1: There is one drawback to that apartment. It doesn't have a washing machine. You'll have to go out to a laundromat.[1]

M1: Oh. Well, I suppose that doesn't matter. Can I see the apartment today?

W1: Certainly. I can show it to you now. However, we're still painting it, so it won't be available until next month.

M1: I was hoping to move next week, but . . . . maybe I can wait.

W1: And I'll need a small deposit to hold it for you, just 50 percent of the first month's rent.

Track 2

PRACTICE 2 (PAGE 27)

Questions 11–20

Now turn to Skill 1, Making Assumptions, Skill 2, Questions 11–20.

Practice 2. You will hear a recording of a tour of an art museum.

Listen carefully and answer the questions.

Female tour guide:

Good afternoon, everyone. I'm Lucy and I'll be your guide for today's two o'clock tour of the Jamestown Museum of Art. As a reminder, if you haven't purchased your ticket yet, please do so now. It's 15 dollars for adults, and for children twelve and under it costs just 11 dollars. If you're a senior, today's your lucky day because it's Tuesday. That's Senior Citizens Day, so admission is free for all people over 65. However, you'll still need to get a ticket before the tour starts.

All right now, does everyone have a ticket? Yes? Good, then, let's go. We begin our tour here in the Main Gallery. Here you can see our collection of modern art. We're quite proud of this collection, which includes some minor works by major artists, for example, you'll see over there a small Picasso. And on this wall you'll see works by some other well-known modern painters.

[1]BRITISH: laundrette

Moving ahead to the next room, now we're in the City Gallery. This is the room where we feature local artists, who have painted a variety of subjects. You'll notice here some local scenes, in addition to a few portraits, and right over there you'll see some abstract works. Most of these works are modern, although we have a few older paintings in this room as well.

Straight ahead is the Hall of History. In that room we have a wonderful collection of portraits of famous figures in our city's history. The oldest paintings date back to the 17th century, and there are some quite modern paintings in there as well, including a portrait of our current governor, who was born in this city. Unfortunately, the Hall is closed right now, so we won't be able to visit it today.

Here to our right is the East Room. Isn't this a beautiful room? The view of the garden is just lovely. You'll see there are no paintings in here because this room is devoted entirely to sculpture. That large sculpture in the center is by a well-known local artist, and over here you'll see several pieces by a modern European sculptor. You can see we have quite a number of lovely pieces in this room.

Just beyond the East Room is the gift shop. You may want to visit it after you have finished looking at the galleries. You can buy reproductions of art in the museum's collections, as well as souvenirs of the city, and many other lovely things as well.

All right then, we've visited all the open galleries in the museum. If you would like to return to any area of the museum now and look at the exhibits more carefully, please do so. Remember, the Hall of History is closed for repairs, but it should be open again next month. Also, please don't go up to the second floor. There's nothing up there but offices, and the area is off limits to visitors. Thank you for coming to the museum. Don't forget to visit the gift shop on your way out.

Track 3

Skill 2—Understanding Numbers (page 30)

Questions 1–5

Question 1

W1: Now, Mr. Wilcox, you can send us a check[1] or, if you pay now by credit card, I can process your order right away.

M1: I'll pay by credit card.

W1: Great. May I have your credit card number then?

M1: It's 8 6 double 7 5 3 2 1 4 8.

W1: 2 1 4 8. All right then, you should have your order within four business[2] days.

Question 2

M1: The university is very proud of its new theater, which is equipped with a state-of-the-art light and sound system and has a much greater seating capacity than the old one. The old theater had seats for just 250 people while the new one can seat an audience of 500.

[1]British: cheque

[2]British: working

Question 3

W1: I'm updating my phone list. Do you know Sherry's phone number by any chance?

M1: I know it by heart. It's 575-3174.

W1: Great. Thanks.

Question 4

M1: That room is only three hundred and fifteen dollars a night if you stay for three nights.

W1: Wow! Do you have anything more, uh, economical?

M1: Let me see . . . for next week . . . . Yes, I have another room that is just two hundred and sixty-five dollars a night. For a minimum three-night stay of course.

W1: That's still a lot of money, but I'll take it.

Question 5

M1: Is this the lost luggage office?

W1: Yes. How may I help you?

M1: How can you help me? By finding my luggage that your airline lost.

W1: All right, sir. Calm down. May I have your name and your flight number, please?

M1: My name is Richard Lyons and my flight number is X Y 5 3 8.

Track 4

Questions 6–15

6. S1: seven oh three six five double eight
S2: seven oh three six five eight eight
S3: seven zero three sixty-five eighty-eight

7. S1: seven double four one four nine two
S2: seven four four one four nine two
S3: seven forty-four fourteen ninety-two

8. S1: two oh two double nine eight three
S2: two oh two nine nine eight three
S3: two zero two ninety-nine eighty-three

9. S1: six seven one four five three two
S2: six seven one four five three two
S3: six seventy-one forty-five thirty-two

10. S1: eight two four one five six one
S2: eight two four one five six one
S3: eight twenty-four fifteen sixty-one

11. S1: six three seven oh double five oh
S2: six three seven oh five five oh
S3: six thirty-seven zero fifty-five zero

12. S1: two six five one eight double one
S2: two six five one eight one one
S3: two sixty-five eighteen eleven

13. S1: two eight seven six two one six
S2: two eight seven six two one six
S3: two eighty-seven sixty-two sixteen

14. S1: four double five three oh two one
S2: four five five three oh two one
S3: four fifty-five thirty twenty-one

15. S1: three oh five eight four eight oh
S2: three oh five eight four eight oh
S3: three zero five eighty-four eighty

Track 5

Skill 3—Understanding the Alphabet (page 32)

Questions 1–6

1. M1: My name is Tomas, t-o-m-a-s. I use the Spanish spelling.
W1: Oh, without the h.

2. W1: I live at 534 Maine Avenue. That's Maine with an "e" on the end.
M1: With an e. Not like Main Street with no e.

3. M1: Is that Patty, p-a-t-t-y?
W1: No, with an i. P-a-t-t-i.

4. W1: Excuse me. You spelled my family name wrong. It's Roberts. The last letter is s.
M1: Oh, I'm sorry. I thought you said Robertson.

5. M1: All right then, you live in the city of Springfield.
W1: No, that's Springvale, v-a-l-e.

6. W1: OK, that's Mr. Nixon, n-i-x . . .
M1: No, no, no. Dixson, d-i-x-s-o-n.

Track 6

Questions 7–12

7. M1: If you're paying by credit card, I'll need your full name.
W1: Sure. It's Miranda Green. That's m-i-r-a-n-d-a.
M1: A-n-d-a. Great. And what's your credit card number?
W1: 7-oh-4-3-2-1-8.
M1: 2-1-8. OK, you wanted two tickets, right?

8. W1: I'm looking up the number of the Bijou Theater. How do you spell that? With a g?
M1: No, with a j. It's B-i-j-o-u.
W1: B-i-j . . . . Found it. Write this number down for me: 2-3-2-5-4-double 8.

9. M1: Let me just get your name. That was Miss Roberta Johnson.
W1: Not Johnson, Janson. With an a. J-a-n-s-o-n.
M1: S-o-n. Got it. Now I can give you room 203. It's small but has a nice view. That room is only 245 pounds a night.
W1: I'd really prefer a larger room. I don't mind paying for it.
M1: Room 304 is the biggest we have available at the moment. It's 335 pounds a night.
W1: That's fine. I'll take it.

10. W1: All right, Mr. Park. May I have your address?
M1: It's 75 String Street. That's String Street S-t-r-i-n-g.
W1: That's an unusual name for a street. Well, would you like a seat near the front or more towards the middle?
M1: I'd like to be as close to the front as possible. Row B or C would be best.
W1: I can give you row B. Seat number 15 B.
M1: Fifteen B. Perfect.

11. W1: Good evening, class. Welcome to Introduction to Economics. I'm your instructor, Dr. Willard. That's W-i-double l-a-r-d. Please don't hesitate to ask for help if you need it. My office hours are Tuesday and Thursday from three to five. My office is here in this building. It's office number 70, on the first floor.

12. M1: Thank you for the opportunity to speak tonight about my passion, wildflowers. If anyone in the audience would like to know more about the subject, I recommend contacting the Wildflower Society. They're at 17-oh-five State Street in Landover. That's L-a-n-d-o-v-e-r. Landover. They issue a number of interesting publications and also host several events each year for wildflower enthusiasts.

Track 7

Skill 4—Distinguishing Similar Sounds (page 34)

PRACTICE 1 (PAGE 34)

bath – path	match – mash	math – mass	flow – flaw
cub – cup	tear – dare	din – ding	cat – cut
lice – rice	wet – wed	jam –yam	chit – cheat
chip – ship	thumb – some	west – vest	set – sat

PRACTICE 2 (PAGE 35)

1. This peach isn't ripe.
2. My back hurts.
3. Please staple these pages together.
4. We took a cab.
5. Rain has been falling all night.
6. They will arrive tonight.
7. The clown made us laugh.
8. Please turn at the light.
9. You can choose either one.
10. I need another sheet of paper.
11. Put the sauce in this dish.
12. They didn't eat much.
13. I tore my dress on a nail.
14. She dyed her hair black.
15. It's a very bright color.
16. We need another chair.
17. The sink is full of water.
18. This blanket is thick and warm.
19. You can follow this path.
20. Don't miss the train.
21. She loves to sing.
22. The sun is bright today.
23. The food is all gone.
24. We need one more thing.
25. He's feeling worse.
26. The vine grew up the tree.
27. A viper bit him.
28. It was a weird story.
29. Let me help you.
30. Set it on this table.
31. They ran home.
32. Put on your coat.
33. Please take a seat.

Track 8

Skill 5—Listening for Descriptions (page 36)

Questions 4–8

Question 4

W1: It's really easy to get here. Just take the bus to the corner of the High Street and Regent Avenue. Then it's the second house from the corner.

M1: Second house from the corner, OK. It's not the two-story duplex with two doors, is it?

W1: No, that's across the street. Mine's small, it's only one story. There's only one door, so knock or ring the bell. I'll be waiting for you.

Question 6

W1: This is the noon news report for Friday, April 12. Several stores in the downtown area of Jamestown were robbed[1] early this morning. Police are on the lookout for the suspect, who is described as about 45 years of age, bald, somewhat overweight, with a beard. If you see anyone meeting this description, please contact the Jamestown police.

Question 8

W1: May I help you?

M1: Yes, I'm looking for a present for my girlfriend. It's her nineteenth birthday. I was thinking maybe some jewelry.

W1: I can help you choose something that would look nice on her. What does she look like?

M1: Well, she's very pretty. She has really long dark hair and she's very thin. She almost always wears earrings.

W1: We have many nice earrings to choose from. Or, what about something different? Would she like a necklace?

M1: I don't know. Maybe . . .

Track 9

Skill 6—Listening for Time (page 38)

TIME (PAGE 39)

Questions 1–6

Questions 1 and 2

M1: Good afternoon class. There have been a number of questions about the time for our final exam. As you know, this class regularly meets from two thirty until four Wednesday and Friday. Some of you have realized that during exam week there is a different schedule, thence the questions. Our final exam will be on Wednesday of exam week. It is scheduled to start at one forty-five and should last about an hour and a half, so you'll be out of here at around three fifteen or so.

Questions 3 and 4

W1: Could you tell me what time the train to Chicago leaves?

M1: The next train is at five fifteen.

W1: Hm. That's a long wait. It's only three now. What time does it arrive in Chicago?

M1: The trip is a little over six hours. It arrives at 11:30.

Questions 5 and 6

W1: Hi Cindy. I wanted to see if you could meet me for lunch tomorrow.

W2: Let's see, tomorrow's Monday. . . . I have a Spanish class in the morning. . . . Yes, I think that's a good idea.

W1: OK. Let's meet at twelve.

W2: Well, I have a haircut at 11:30. Better make it quarter past.

W1: Quarter past twelve, great.

W2: I'm so glad we're getting together. I'll be really nervous because I have a job interview in the afternoon. You can help me get ready for it.

W1: You know what's good for nerves? Exercise.

W2: I have my exercise class tomorrow at four. That should help.

[1]BRITISH: shops in the city centre were burgled

Track 10

DATE (PAGE 40)

Questions 1–6

Questions 1 and 2

W1: The City Museum of Art was established in the year 1898. It first opened its doors to the public on August fifteenth of that year. There was a spectacular opening celebration, but it wasn't held until later in the year, on December first, to be exact. Now the reasons for the delayed celebration are very interesting . . .

Questions 3 and 4

M1: All right, Mrs. Katz. I need just a bit more information to complete your application. May I have your date of birth?

W1: It's twenty-second September.

M1: Your husband's name is George, correct?

W1: Yes, and he was born on seventh July.

Questions 5 and 6

W1: We're thinking about going to Silver Lake this year. When do you think is a good time to go?

M1: Well, most people don't like to go in July or August because it's so hot then. September is too. I think the most popular time to go is October.

W1: Is that when you plan to go?

M1: Actually, no. We can't get away till November this year. We've made our reservations[1] for then, and we're leaving on the seventh.

Track 11

DAY (PAGE 41)

Questions 1–6

Questions 1 and 2

W1: Hey, Jim. Are you going to history class?

M1: No, I don't have history today. I have English.

W1: It's Monday. Are you sure you don't have history today?

M1: Yeah. I have English today and Wednesday. My history class is on Thursday.

W1: Just one day a week for history, huh? Not bad.

Questions 3 and 4

M1: We're very glad that you are considering becoming members of the Urban Exercise Club. I'm sure you'll want to sign up for membership after you've enjoyed this afternoon here. Since today's Thursday, you could have a tennis lesson. The tennis instructor is here twice a week, Saturday as well as Thursday. You're lucky it's not Friday. You'll be able to enjoy the steam room. It'll be closed for its weekly cleaning tomorrow.

Questions 5 and 6

W1: Let me remind you of your assignments for next week. Don't forget that the final exam has been rescheduled, so it'll be on Friday instead of Thursday. And you have an essay due on Tuesday. You should have a lot to study over Saturday and Sunday. Don't forget that I have office hours on Monday afternoon, in case you have any questions.

[1]British: booking

Track 12

YEAR (PAGE 42)

Questions 1–6

Questions 1 and 2

M1: John James Audubon, the famous naturalist and painter of birds, was born on the island of Haiti in 1785. In 1803, he went to live in the United States. He was a self-taught painter and supported himself for a while by painting portraits. His famous work, *Birds of America*, was first published in England. Later, in 1842, Audubon published a version of this work in the United States. He died in 1851.

Questions 3 and 4

W1: That was a really interesting lecture on Maria Mahoney. I really admire her for being the first woman governor of our state.

M1: Yes, she was an admirable person. Let's go over our notes. I put down that she was born in 1808.

W1: Not eighteen. Nineteen. She was born in 1908.

M1: Whoops! OK, then, but I have this right. She became governor in 1967.

W1: Are you sure? Wasn't it 1957?

M1: No, 1957 is when she first decided to run for office, but she didn't win an election until 1967.

Questions 5 and 6

M1: The university began construction of the library in 1985. It was expected to take just two years, but by the end of 1987, the library was only three-quarters completed. Finally, by the summer of 1988, construction was finished and the new library opened in August of that year.

Track 13

SEASON (PAGE 42)

Questions 1–6

Questions 1 and 2

W1: Tourists visit the region only during certain times of the year. The winters are not harsh, but it rains a lot then and the temperatures are quite cool. Spring is quite a bit less rainy than winter, and the temperatures are warmer, so many tourists like to visit then. Summers are hot and dry, so hot that most tourists stay away. They return in the autumn when the weather is still dry but not as hot.

Questions 3 and 4

W1: Wow, Josh, I can't believe you hiked the whole mountain range. When did you start your trip?

M1: Well, you can't leave too early in the spring, because it's still late winter in the mountains then. Most hikers start in the late spring, and that's what I did too.

W1: And then you hiked all summer. What's summer like in the mountains?

M1: It's not too hot and you can see a lot of wild life, especially later in the summer when the birds start to migrate.

W1: It must have been winter by the time you finished the trip.

M1: Not quite. It was late in the autumn, which is almost as cold as winter in the mountains.

Questions 5 and 6

M1: I'd like to sign up for the beginning Japanese class.

W1: I'm sorry, all our Japanese classes are full. Fall is the busiest time of year here at the language school.

M1: Hm. Well, then, maybe I'll wait until next summer to take a class.

W1: That would be fine, but I recommend enrolling early. Summer is almost as busy as fall.
M1: Really? Well, when is your least busy time of year?
W1: Spring is a quieter time, but we have our lowest enrollment in the winter.

Track 14

Skill 7—Listening for Frequency (page 43)

Questions 1–6

Question 1

M1: Do you like dancing?
W1: Yes , but I don't go very much.
M1: No?
W1: Well, I go about once a month or so.

Question 2

W1: Do you smoke?
M1: No, I don't.
W1: Really? Not at all?
M1: Mmmm, maybe once or twice a year.

Question 3

M1: Another rainy day. Does it ever stop raining here?
W1: It's the rain forest. It rains every day.

Question 4

W1: Mike says he's a vegetarian. What does that mean?
M1: It means he doesn't eat meat.
W1: No meat at all? Not even on special occasions?
M1: Not even then.

Question 5

M1: How's your class?
W1: It's really hard. The professor loves giving tests.
M1: Really? Does he give a lot of tests?
W1: Oh, yeah. We have one or two a week.

Question 6

W1: Do these geese spend all summer here?
M1: Yes, and all winter, too. They don't migrate.
W1: So you can see them here any season of the year.

Track 15

Questions 7–12

Question 7

W1: For the first part of my research, I counted the number of shoppers who entered the store between 6 A.M. and 8 A.M.
M1: And you did this every morning?
W1: Yes, every morning for a week.

Question 8

W1: Are you interested in joining the chess club?

M1: Maybe. When does it meet?

W1: On the last Sunday of every month.

Question 9

W1: How often do you have your history class?

M1: Every Tuesday and Thursday.

Question 10

M1: Do you go to the movies much?

W1: I go when I get the chance, but not as often as I'd like. Maybe once or twice a semester.

Question 11

W1: How can I start managing my money better?

M1: First, you need to make a monthly spending plan.

Question 12

M1: While you're student teaching, I'll observe each one of you in the classroom several times.

W1: How frequent will your visits be?

M1: You'll get a visit from me once every two weeks.

Track 16

Skill 8—Listening for Similar Meanings (page 44)

Questions 1–6

Question 1

M1: How many tickets will you need?

W1: There will be three adults and two children in our party.

Question 2

W1: How's your French class? Do you like the instructor?

M1: Yes, she's great, but she gives us a lot of work to do in class.

W1: Then you have to wait weeks before you get your papers back, right?

M1: No, she always checks our assignments on the same day we do them.

Question 3

M1: I've heard that this area of the country is really growing.

W1: Yes, the population is increasing at a rate of about 10,000 people a year.

Question 4

W1: I understand that this area has suffered harsh weather conditions in recent years.

M1: Yes, for example, last year a severe drought killed much of the vegetation in the region.

W1: That must have had a devastating effect on agriculture.

Question 5

M1: If I give you a check for the first month's rent right now, can I move in tomorrow?

W1: I'm sorry, but the apartment won't be available until next week.

Question 6

M1: Let's see . . . I got your address and phone number. Oh, I need to know your occupation.

W1: Put computer programmer.

Track 17

Skill 9—Listening for Emotions (page 45)

PRACTICE 1

Questions 1–6

Question 1

W1: We'll begin the tour of Roselands Park with a bit about the history of the park. Local residents were thrilled when millionaire Samuel Waters announced that he would donate land for the park, including his collection of prized rose bushes. Some of his heirs, quite naturally, were a bit angry when they learned[1] that he had given away so much family property.

Question 2

W1: What's the matter with you? Yesterday you seemed really excited about your science experiment.

M1: That was yesterday. Today I just can't seem to get it to work right.

W1: Oh, don't worry about it. I'm sure it will be fine.

M1: I don't know. I keep trying and trying, but it isn't working the way I planned.

Question 3

M1: Our language lab is equipped with state-of-the-art equipment guaranteed to greatly improve your foreign language skills. Students are often confused when they first use our facilities because it seems complicated at first glance, but it's actually quite simple once you get used to it. Today I'll give you an orientation to the lab, and you'll see how easy it is to use this equipment to complete your class assignments and study for tests.

Question 4

W1: You didn't win the essay contest? Aren't you upset?

M1: Not really.

W1: I'd be really disappointed if I'd worked so hard and didn't even win second or third place.

M1: It's just a contest. It doesn't really matter.

Question 5

W1: In local news, children and teachers at Burnside Elementary School received an unexpected visit yesterday from Mayor Sharon Smith as part of her campaign to focus attention on the plight of city schools. Several school board members accompanied the Mayor. "We had no idea she was planning to visit us," said school principal[2] Roger Simmons. "But naturally we felt quite honored."

Question 6

M1: How is your research project going?

W1: Great. It's almost done.

M1: I'm impressed. I always get nervous when I have a big project like that to do.

W1: It's not so bad really. And I'm quite pleased with the results that I'm getting.

[1]British: learnt

[2]British: head master

Track 18

Skill 10—Listening for an Explanation (page 47)

Questions 1–12

Listen to the explanation of how cacao beans are processed.

W1: The rich flavor of chocolate that almost everyone loves comes from the cacao tree, which is grown in tropical regions around the world. The farmer harvests the ripe fruit of the cacao tree, then cuts it open to remove the seeds. These seeds are the cocoa beans from which chocolate is made. The beans are fermented in a large vat for about a week. Then they are placed on trays in the sun to dry. When the cocoa beans are ready, they are shipped off to the chocolate factory. At the chocolate factory, the cocoa beans are turned into all sorts of delicious chocolate treats.

Track 19

Skill 11—Listening for Classifications (page 49)

Questions 1–5

Question 1

W1: It's easy to upgrade your ticket from economy class to first class. It costs just a little bit more, and it will enhance your travel experience in several ways. While we have roomy seats in both economy and first class, our first-class passengers are also offered pillows and blankets so they can nap in comfort. Snacks are served in economy class, while full meals are served to all first-class passengers. As an economy-class passenger you'll be offered the most current magazines for your entertainment, but you'll have to bring your own DVDs if you want to watch movies. In first class, we show complimentary first-run movies.

Question 2

M1: Do you want to go to the movies tonight? There's a great film showing at the Royal Theater.

W1: The Royal Theater? I never like the movies there. They only show violent types like horror and war movies.

M1: So what kind of movie do you like?

W1: Oh, romantic movies and classic movies, like the ones they show at the Deluxe Theater.

Question 3

M1: Although butterflies and moths look very similar, they aren't exactly alike. There are several ways to tell the difference between them. The most well-known difference is that butterflies fly during the day, while moths are night fliers. Additionally, when butterflies rest, they fold their wings back. Moths at rest hold their wings in a horizontal position. The antennae are different also. Butterflies have thin antennae, and moths often have feathery antennae.

Question 4

W1: I have so much to do to get ready for the party. I have to clean the house, cook . . .

M1: You've bought all the food already, haven't you?

W1: Yes, the shopping's done. And I've planned all the decorations, too.

M1: When did you mail[1] the invitations?

W1: Mail the invitations? Oh, no! I guess I'd better do that today.

[1]British: post

Question 5

W1: Trees for landscaping your garden can be divided into three categories. Some trees we plant to add beauty to the yard. They are chosen for their beautiful flowers or interesting leaves. These are the ornamental trees. If you live in a sunny location, then you'll probably want to plant some shade trees. These are usually tall, broad-leafed trees. Finally we have the evergreens. Every garden should have at least one to provide a bit of green year round. Most evergreens are cone-bearing trees with needles instead of leaves.

Track 20

Skill 12—Listening for Comparisons and Contrasts (page 51)

Questions 1–4

Question 1

W1: How's your new job?

M1: It's great. Much better than my old job.

W1: Really? That's wonderful. You're earning more money now, aren't you?

M1: Yeah, the salary's a lot higher, but I have to work more hours.

W1: Too bad. I remember you had a really good schedule at your old job.

M1: Yes, I miss that. But the job itself is pretty similar. I have the same kind of responsibilities that I had before.

W1: That makes it easier. Are you still working in the same place?

M1: No, now I have to go to the other side of town. But at least I can still take the bus like I did for my old job.

W1: Well, that's convenient.

Question 2

W1: The new Riverdale Library will have its grand opening next month. The new library, which has been under construction for the past two years, stands on the same site as the old library. But there the similarity ends. The new library is much larger than the old two-story building, boasting four floors of books and two floors of offices, as well as an underground parking garage, which everyone agrees will be a great improvement over the old outside parking lot. With so much space to fill, we have greatly expanded the size of our book collection. You will continue to enjoy the same services as before. Online book renewal, free Internet access, and the Ask-a-Librarian Hotline that you enjoyed at the old library will also be available at our new facilities.

Question 3

M1: I'm interested in joining the health club, but I see you have two types of membership.

W1: Yes, we have both full and associate memberships. The full membership costs almost twice as much as the associate, and many members feel it's worth the extra cost.

M1: What's the difference between them?

W1: With both types of membership you are entitled to the use of all our club facilities and you can take advantage of all our fitness classes as well. You also get use of the locker room[1] with both memberships, but full members get extra locker room privileges, such as your own locker exclusively for your use and laundry service as well. May I sign you up for a full membership today?

M1: I'm not sure. The associate membership sounds fine to me.

W1: Let me point out that with the full membership you also get a complimentary individualized fitness plan tailored just for you. Associate members may take advantage of this service as well, but they have to pay extra for it.

M1: I'll have to think about it.

[1]British: changing room

Question 4

M1: Toads and frogs begin their lives in similar ways. The eggs hatch in or near water, and the babies, called tadpoles, spend the first part of their lives living in the water. When they become adults, frogs continue to live in the water, while adult toads usually live on the land. When you come across one of these animals, how can you tell whether it's a toad or a frog? The easiest way is to touch its skin. Frogs have smooth skin while the skin of toads is generally rough and bumpy. Their shape is somewhat different also, with toads being plumper and broader than frogs. What is a more typical sound on a summer evening than a chorus of croaking frogs or toads? Both these animals make their croaking sound by inflating a sac in their throat.

Track 21

Skill 13—Listening for Negative Meaning (page 53)

Questions 7–12

Question 7

M1: The flora and fauna of this region are adapted to the special climate. It hardly ever rains here, even in the winter. Most of the year, there is barely a cloud to be seen in the sky.

Question 8

W1: Your essay writing exam is coming up tomorrow, so I'd like to review some of the testing rules with you now. The good news is that you'll have an unlimited amount of time to write your essay. You won't, however, be permitted to consult a dictionary while[1] writing the exam. Neither can you take anything else into the testing room with you except a pen.

Question 9

M1: I'm in a bit of a hurry. Do you think you can fix the problem with my car today?

W1: I'm sorry, but I'm behind schedule. I won't be able to get to it until the weekend.

M1: Then I'll have to take a bus to work tomorrow.

Question 10

W1: What a restaurant! Never in my life have I tasted such delicious food.

M1: You really think so? But don't you think the service was too slow?

W1: Not a bit. I can't wait to go back there.

Question 11

M1: Botanists and other flower lovers enjoy visiting this area in the spring and summer to see the abundant variety of wildflowers. In the early spring it isn't uncommon to find violets and, later in the season, there is a profusion of wild roses as well. Many also come here seeking the wild iris, although that is more rarely seen in these parts.

Question 12

M1: I have so much homework this week. Not only do I have to write two papers, I have to read four books, too.

W1: Wow. That's a lot.

M1: Yeah, well, at least I don't have any exams to study for.

Track 22

Skill 14—Listening for Chronology (page 56)

Questions 1–5

Question 1

W1: I'm interested in renting an apartment in this building.

M1: OK, first you'll have to fill out[2] an application. Then, before you submit it, you'll need to get two references.

[1]British: whilst; [2]British: fill in

W1: References?

M1: Yes, from former landlords or your boss or someone like that who can vouch for your responsibility. All right, so you do that, then you'll have to have some money ready for a deposit. As soon as we have an available apartment, we'll notify you, and we'll ask that you pay a deposit to hold it for you.

W1: I have to pay the deposit before signing the lease?

M1: Well, of course we'll refund it if you decide not to take the apartment, but the deposit holds it for you while you look the apartment over and decide whether or not you want it.

Question 2

M1: Today we'll take a look at the life of classical composer Wolfgang Amadeus Mozart. Mozart was born in Austria in 1756. His father, Leopold, was a well-known music teacher and published an important textbook on violin playing shortly after Wolfgang's birth. Young Wolfgang showed his genius at an early age, beginning to write his own musical compositions at the age of 5. This was one factor that led to his father's decision to take Wolfgang and his sister on performing tours around Europe, beginning in 1762. After a childhood of touring Europe, Mozart visited Vienna in 1781 and decided to settle there. He had been greatly saddened during his tour of 1777 when his mother, who was accompanying him, died while they were abroad. He looked forward to a new life in Vienna.

Question 3

W1: How'd your trip to the beach go?

M1: Fantastic. Well, mostly. Of course, we had to leave home at five in the morning.

W1: Ouch! So early.

M1: Yeah, but, then, by lunchtime we were almost there.

W1: So where'd you have lunch? At that burger place, right?

M1: No, we just had a roadside picnic to save time. We'd made our sandwiches the night before we left.

W1: You're so organized.

M1: I guess. Whatever. So anyhow, back in the car after lunch we started arguing about a place to stay. We finally agreed on the White Sands Motel.

W1: I've been there. It's all right.

M1: Yeah, well, it's a good thing we left home early because by the time we got there, there was only one room left at the motel, so we were lucky to get it. We went swimming as soon as we'd checked in.

Question 4

W1: I have to do this research project for my sociology class, and I don't know how to begin.

W2: Is that Professor Miller's class? I took it last year. It's a great class.

W1: Really? Can you help me get started?

W2: Sure, well, I mean, I guess so. Well, I'd say the most important thing is get a partner. It's much easier working with someone else.

W1: So the first thing is to get a partner?

W2: You probably should choose a research topic first, then find a classmate who's also interested in your topic. Then you need the professor's approval.

W1: Approval for what?

W2: No, wait. OK first you and your partner design your research, I mean you write up your questionnaire and decide whom you will interview and all that.

W1: *Then* we get the professor's approval for our research design?

W2: Yes. And then you can start your research.

Question 5

W1: Welcome to Waterside Gardens. We'll begin our tour by walking through the rose garden, just as soon as everyone has shown me his or her tickets. Following the rose garden, we'll view the pond area. We'll visit the greenhouse after everyone who so desires has had a chance to photograph the butterfly garden. It is our most picturesque area. And that's it. I hope you'll enjoy the tour.

MODEL TEST 1

Narrator: IELTS Listening. Model Test 1.

Track 23

You will hear a number of different recordings, and you will have to answer questions on what you hear. There will be time for you to read the instructions and questions, and you will have a chance to check your work. All the recordings will be played once only.

The test is in four sections. Write all your answers in the Listening Question booklet. At the end of the test you will be given ten minutes to transfer your answers to an Answer Sheet.

Now turn to Section 1.

Section 1. You will hear a conversation between Mark Winston, who wants to learn Japanese, and Kathy Green, who is a receptionist at the World Language Academy.

First, you have some time to look at Questions 1 to 3.

Example

Narrator: You will see that there is an example which has been done for you. On this occasion only, the conversation relating to this will be played first.

Kathy Green: Good morning. May I help you?
Mark Winston: Yes, I'm Mark Winston and I...

(Telephone rings)

Kathy Green: Oh, Excuse me, Mr. Winston. World Language Academy. This is Kathy Green. May I help you? (pause). No this is a private language school, not a travel agency. (pause) No problem at all. Good-bye. I'm sorry, Mr. Winston. Now, may I help YOU?
Mr. Winston: Yes, I hope you can. I'd like to sign up now for a Japanese class next week.

Narrator: The man says he'd like to "**sign up now**" which means "register today" for a language class. The number 2 has been written in the blank. You should answer the questions as you listen because you will not hear the recording a second time. Listen carefully and answer Questions 1 to 3.

Questions 1–3

Kathy Green: Good morning. May I help you?
Mark Winston: Yes, I'm Mark Winston and I . . .

(Telephone rings)

Kathy Green: Oh, Excuse me, Mr. Winston. World Language Academy. This is Kathy Green. May I help you? (pause). No this is a private language school, not a travel agency. (pause) No problem at all. Good-bye. I'm sorry, Mr. Winston. Now may I help YOU?
Mark Winston: Yes, I hope you can. I'd like to sign up now for a Japanese class next week.

Kathy Green:	Classes start next week, and we have lots of Japanese classes to choose from. Have you studied Japanese before?
Mark Winston:	No, I haven't. I'm a beginner. I'm planning to visit Japan next summer so I want to learn a bit of the language.
Kathy Green:	That's great. Japan is a wonderful place to visit. I spent a month in Tokyo last year, actually, and I even climbed Mount Fujiyama.
Mark Winston:	Really? That's too much activity for me. I'm just planning to visit Tokyo. I think I'll find plenty to do there.
Kathy Green:	You certainly will. All right then, let me tell you a bit about our classes. They're all taught by native speakers, and they are all specialists in their field. You can choose a Japanese for Tourists class, Japanese for Business Travelers, or Japanese for University Students. You're not studying at a university, are you?
Mark Winston:	No, I graduated a few years ago.
Kathy Green:	Well, then, the tourist class is probably best for you.
Mark Winston:	Yes, I think you're right. I just want to learn enough to order food in restaurants and go shopping and things like that. When does the Japanese for Tourists class begin?
Kathy Green:	Let's see. We have a class for beginners that starts next week. I think there are still a few spaces left. You're in luck . . . we have 15 students enrolled, and there's room for three more.
Narrator:	Before you hear the rest of the conversation, you have some time to look at Questions 4 to 10. Now listen and answer Questions 4 to 10.

Questions 4–10

Mark Winston:	When does that class meet?
Kathy Green:	Every Monday, Wednesday, and Thursday from 5:30 until 7:30.
Mark Winston:	That's a bit early for me. I work until 6:00. Don't you have a class that starts later in the evening?
Kathy Green:	No . . . not for beginners. Let's see . . . we have an afternoon class on Monday, Wednesday, and Thursday, from one to three. Oh, but that's an intermediate class. What about mornings? We have a beginner's class that meets five days a week, Monday through Friday, from 9 A.M. until 10 A.M. Could you do that?
Mark Winston:	No, I work all day. I only have evenings and weekends free.
Kathy Green:	The advanced class is Tuesday and Thursday from 7:30 to 9:30, but you've never studied Japanese before, have you?
Mark Winston:	No, I don't know anything about it.
Kathy Green:	Well, we have a beginner's class on Saturday from 9 in the morning until 2 in the afternoon.
Mark Winston:	Nine until two? That's a long class.
Kathy Green:	We also have private tutors. Actually, I usually recommend private tutors because they give you individualized attention. You are the only student in the class, so the tutor teaches you according to your specific needs. It really is the best way to learn a language.
Mark Winston:	It sounds great! I'd learn a lot that way, wouldn't I?
Kathy Green:	You really would. And it's very convenient. You can arrange to meet with your tutor at whatever time suits you.
Mark Winston:	Fantastic.[1] How do I sign up?

[1] BRITISH: Brilliant

Kathy Green: Well, how many hours a week do you want to study? We usually recommend three to five hours a week for a minimum of four weeks.

Mark Winston: OK. I'll start with three hours a week.

Kathy Green: Great. You can send us a check to cover the first week of classes, or you can pay now by credit card. Three hours of private classes comes out to 300 dollars, plus a 25-dollar registration fee.

Mark Winston: Three hundred dollars? That's 100 dollars a class!

Kathy Green: And it's certainly worth it. You'll be studying with a native speaker of Japanese. And all our tutors are professionally trained in the latest teaching methods. You'll be getting the best instruction money can buy.

Mark Winston: But 100 dollars a class! That's over one thousand dollars for a month of classes. I'm sorry, but I just can't do that.

Kathy Green: Then take the Saturday class. It's only $300 a month. And it's small. There will be only four or five students in it.

Mark Winston: Great. I'll take that class. Can I pay by check?

Kathy Green: Yes. Just bring your check to the first class. See you next Saturday at 9:00.

(*Audio fades as last speaker continues to speak.*)

Narrator: That is the end of Section 1. You now have half a minute to check your answers.

Now turn to Section 2.

Section 2. You will hear a guided tour of an old mansion.

First, you have some time to look at Questions 11 to 13.

As you listen to the first part of the talk, answer Questions 11 to 13.

Questions 11–13

Barbara Wilson: Good afternoon. My name is Barbara Wilson, and I will be your guide for today's tour of Sumner Mansion. As a reminder before we begin, we ask that you not take photographs inside the building, and please turn off your cell phones during the tour. Also we request that you refrain from eating as well as drinking inside the mansion. Refreshments will be available at the end of the tour in the café next to the garden.

Narrator: Before you hear the rest of the tour, you have some time to look at Questions 14 to 20.

Now listen and answer Questions 14 to 20.

Questions 14–20

Now, to begin. Here we are at the main entrance. You will notice the elaborate Italian frieze installed by the original owner when the mansion was built in 1810. To the left of the entrance is the main living room. This was used by the Sumner family for entertaining guests, particularly for their tea parties. They were famous for the tea parties that they gave in this room. Here on display you can see the elegant chinaware they used for their parties. There are several sets of china imported from abroad.

Let's go over to the other side now. This room to the right of the main entrance is the dining room. Of course the family meals were served here, but the most interesting thing abut this room is the art. The Sumners collected a lot of art, and some of the finest pieces of their art collection are displayed in this room. On that wall opposite, you can see a large painting of a garden. Mr. Sumner bought that on a trip to China in 1825. You will also notice several smaller pieces of Chinese art as well as some portraits of the family.

Behind the mansion are the famous Sumner gardens. Right now you can see a spectacular display of roses. The tea roses are especially nice, and there are many other varieties of roses, as well. The guided tour will not continue into the garden. You can enjoy it on your own. Don't forget to stop in at the café before you go home for some tasty hot or cold tea and pastries. You enter it through the garden, but it's just behind the living room. There is also a small display there of kitchen tools used in the original mansion kitchen, which I am sure you will enjoy viewing. If you feel disoriented after walking around the gardens, don't worry. Remember that the parking area is just beyond the café, so it's a short walk back to your car.

Also, please remember that the grounds close at five P.M. as we are still on our spring schedule. If you come back next week, the summer schedule will have started and we'll be open a full ten hours a day from ten in the morning until eight in the evening. Thank you for visiting, and come back anytime. We're open seven days a week.

Narrator: That is the end of Section 2. You now have half a minute to check your answers.

Now turn to Section 3.

Section 3. You will hear a panel discussion between the panel moderator and two panelists, Dr. Karen Akers and Dr. Fred Williams, both transportation consultants. In the first part of the discussion, they are talking about the future of public transportation.

First, you will have some time to look at Questions 21 to 26.

Now listen carefully and answer Questions 21 to 26.

Questions 21–26

Moderator: Dr. Williams and Dr. Akers, I want to thank both of you for coming today and sharing your thoughts on the future of public transportation.

(Simultaneous thanks)

Dr. Akers: Glad to be here.

Dr. Williams: Thank You.

Moderator: Let me ask you first, Dr. Williams, traffic congestion is becoming more and more of a problem, and it's spreading. We're used to traffic jams in cities, but now we find traffic problems on many major highways[1] that run between cities. What solutions do you see for the future of transportation?

Dr. Williams: Many transportation experts, myself included, are excited about the potential of high-speed trains. These trains are having a great deal of success in Japan and in several European countries, as well. They've actually been around for a while—since 1964, in fact. The first high-speed train was put into operation that year.

Moderator: What would the speed be exactly of a high-speed train? How would you define "high-speed" train?

Dr. Williams: We usually call a train high speed if it's capable of traveling at 200 kilometers an hour or faster.

Moderator: That's very fast. It would seem to open up a lot of possibilities for transportation between cities.

[1]British: motorways

Dr. Akers: Yes, that's right. Fifty years ago or more, conventional trains were the major form of transportation between cities. Of course, they weren't high-speed trains, but nobody expected that then. Those old trains provided frequent, reliable, and affordable long-distance transportation, and most people used them. Then things changed. Cars and highways were improved, so more and more people started driving cars.

Dr. Williams: Cars are a great form of transportation. Everybody loves them because they're so convenient. But we usually use cars for local trips . . . shopping, and going to work, and things like that.

Dr. Akers: That's true. For long-distance trips, most people nowadays rely on planes. Plane service is more frequent and affordable now than it was in the past, so planes, like cars, have become more convenient for people. Meanwhile, trains have more or less fallen by the wayside as a common means of transportation.

Moderator: But with everybody driving cars and taking planes, we have a lot of congestion. And not just on the roads. Airports have become very crowded, too.

Dr. Williams: Exactly. We have congestion everywhere now, so we need to look at new forms of transportation.

Narrator: Before you hear the rest of the conversation, you have some time to look at Questions 27 to 30.

Now listen and answer Questions 27 to 30.

Questions 27–30

Dr. Akers: And that's where high-speed trains come in. They offer several advantages over both cars and planes. When you take everything into consideration—getting to the train station, boarding the train, and all that—a high-speed train gets you to your destination just about as quickly as a car. So speed isn't really an advantage. Cost isn't always, either. Depending on how many people are traveling with you, a train trip could be more expensive than a car trip. But, a train trip is much more relaxing than a car trip. You can read, sleep, eat, whatever, while the train carries you to your destination. And of course you're never delayed by traffic jams. To my mind, these are great advantages.

Moderator: Yes, I can really see the advantage of the train over the car. But what about planes? Planes are much faster than cars, so that's a big plus for planes.

Dr. Williams: Not necessarily. For trips shorter than 650 kilometers, high-speed trains can actually be faster. Checking in at the airport and going through security takes a long time. You don't have that kind of delay with a train. Also trains can carry more passengers than planes. They can also offer more frequent service. So for your medium-distance trips, they really are faster than planes.

Narrator: That is the end of Section 3. You now have half a minute to check your answers.

Now turn to Section 4.

Section 4. You will hear a lecture on Albert Einstein. First you have some time to look at Questions 31 to 40.

Now listen carefully and complete the timeline in Questions 31 to 40.

Questions 31–40

Lecturer: Today I want to talk about the early life of a man whose name is synonymous with genius—Albert Einstein. He is well known, of course, for his work in physics, especially his theory of relativity. This is a term that everyone has heard, but few lay people, . . . and I do not mean to include you in this group, . . . but few non-physicists understand. Equally incomprehensible to most people is why Einstein the genius did so poorly at school. There are some questions, actually misconceptions about his early life, particularly about his lack of success in school that I want to clear up for you. Let's look now at some true facts about the life of this famous man.

Albert Einstein was born in Germany in 1879. As a child in school, he had a reputation as a slow learner. Now there were a couple of theories about why he could not keep pace with his classmates. He may have had some sort of learning disability; we don't know for sure. Another theory about his slow learning is that he may have suffered from a condition related to autism.

Whether it was a learning disability or not, Einstein himself believed that his slowness actually helped him develop his theory of relativity. He said that he ended up thinking about time and space at a later age than most children, at a time when his intellect was more developed. He didn't even begin to study mathematics until he was 12. There are popular rumors that he failed his math classes, but this is actually not true.

Mathematics was a later passion; his first was the violin. Like many intellectuals, Einstein had a passion for music. He started his study of the violin during elementary school and continued playing the violin for the rest of his life.

When Einstein was fifteen, his family moved to Italy. Soon after that his parents sent him to Switzerland where, in 1896, he finished high school. After graduating from high school, he enrolled in a Swiss technological institute. In 1898, he met and fell in love with a young Serbian woman, Mileva Maric. Maric was a mathematician and Einstein considered her his intellectual equal.

Einstein received a teaching diploma in 1900. The next year he became a Swiss citizen. Although he had his teaching diploma, he had a hard time finding a teaching job. In fact, he never did find one. A friend's father helped him get a job at the Swiss Patent Office. He began working there in 1902. His job involved reviewing inventors' applications for patents. When he looked over the applications, he often found faults in the applicants' drawings. He would make suggestions so they could improve their designs and better their chances for receiving a patent.

The same year Einstein began working at the patent office, he and Mileva had their first child, a daughter, although they didn't actually get married until 1903. Their son was born the following year. There is no record of whether the two children inherited their father's learning disability.

Narrator: That is the end of Section 4. You now have half a minute to check your answers.

You will now have 10 minutes to transfer your answers to the Listening Answer Sheet. Pause CD for 10 minutes

This is almost the end of the test. You now have one more minute to check all your answers.

That is the end of the Listening section of Model Test 1.

MODEL TEST 2

Narrator: IELTS Listening. Model Test 2

Track 24

You will hear a number of different recordings, and you will have to answer questions on what you hear. There will be time for you to read the instructions and questions, and you will have a chance to check your work. All the recordings will be played once only.

The test is in four sections. Write all your answers in the Listening Question Booklet. At the end of the test you will be given ten minutes to transfer your answers to an Answer Sheet.

Now turn to Section 1.

Section 1. You will hear a conversation between an interviewer and a woman shopper.

First you have some time to look at Questions 1 to 7.

You will see that there is an example that has been done for you. On this occasion only, the conversation relating to this will be played first.

Example

M1: Excuse me, ma'am. Could I have a few minutes of your time?

W1: What do you need?

M1: First, welcome to Lougheed Mall, the largest shopping center in Vancouver. We're conducting a survey of the shoppers at this mall. We want to learn about when and how often people shop, the stores they prefer, in general, people's habits when they shop at the mall. Would you mind answering a few questions about your shopping?

Narrator: The man says he is conducting a survey of shoppers, so B has been circled. Now we shall begin. You should answer the questions as you listen because you will not hear the recording a second time. Listen carefully and answer Questions 1 to 7.

Questions 1–7

M1: Excuse me, ma'am. Could I have a few minutes of your time?

W1: What do you need?

M1: First, welcome to Lougheed (Lawheed) Mall, the largest shopping center in Vancouver. We're conducting a survey of the shoppers at this mall. We want to learn about when and how often people shop, the stores they prefer, in general, people's habits when they shop at the mall. Would you mind answering a few questions about your shopping?

W1: Not at all.

M1: Thank you. Today we're interviewing married women, that is women with husbands and children who shop for their families. So the first question is, do you fit this category?

W1: Yes, I do.

M1: Wonderful. Now, I need to know your age. Are you between the ages of 18 and twenty-five, twenty-six and . . . ?

W1: (interrupting) I'm 34.

M1: Great. OK. Now, how often do you shop here? Less than once a month, at least once a month, once a . . .

W1: I have a big family. I have to buy a lot of things. I'm here at least twice a week.

M1: Well that's just fine. You must be very familiar with the stores here.

W1: I certainly am.

M1: All right then. The next question concerns the things that you buy. What do you usually shop for here?

W1: Just about everything. I've been in all the stores at one time or another. The clothing stores are quite nice, though, frankly, their prices are a bit high, and I like the bookstore too, but . . .

M1: What I need to know, though, is what is the one type of thing you shop for most often? Would it be books?

W1: Oh, no. That's only occasionally. The reason I come here so often is for food. I told you I have a large family. I buy all our food at the supermarket here.

M1: OK. So, the next question is how much time do you usually spend at the mall?

W1: What do you mean? Do you mean every week?

M1: I mean, each time you come here, how long do you spend?

W1: Oh, I'd say about an hour and a half or so. Maybe a little longer, but I'm hardly ever here for more than two hours.

M1: Now there's one last question in this section. How do you usually come to the mall? Do you take the bus, the . . . ?

W1: I always drive.

Narrator: Before you hear the rest of the conversation, you have some time to look at Questions 8 to 10.

Now listen and answer Questions 8 to 10.

Questions 8–10

M1: Fine. OK, the next part of the questionnaire concerns your opinions. You say you've been in all the stores in the mall. In general, in which store would you say you've had the best shopping experience?

W1: That's easy. The shoe store.

M1: That's a big store, isn't it? They have a huge selection of shoes.

W1: They do, but I consider it a good store because the employees there are so polite. They give very good service.

M1: Now, you may have had a chance to eat at our new food court.

W1: Yes, I have, but I don't think I'll eat there again.

M1: Why not?

W1: Well, the food tastes fine, but it's very expensive. It shouldn't cost so much.

M1: I have just one last question. Do you have any suggestions for improvements to the mall?

W1: Yes. You should add more parking spaces. I can never find a place to park. It's really annoying sometimes when . . .

(Audio fades as last speaker continues to speak.)

Narrator: That is the end of Section 1. You now have half a minute to check your answers.

Now turn to Section 2.

Section 2. You will hear a recording of a tour of a health club.

First, you have some time to look at Questions 11 to 14.

Now listen carefully and answer Questions 11 to 14.

Questions 11–14

Good afternoon. Welcome to the Riverside Health Club. The purpose of today's tour is to let you become familiar with the different activities available at the club. I hope that by the end of the tour all of you will decide to become members.

When you become a member of the health club, you will have the opportunity to participate in a wide range of fitness activities. Over here we have our indoor tennis courts. There are three of them, and if you don't know how to play, we offer tennis lessons throughout the week. Right here next to the courts is the club store. It's quite small, you see, but we have it as a convenience. So if you need snacks or drinks after exercising, you can buy them here.

OK, now this is the exercise room. It's the most well-equipped exercise facility in the city. You won't find old-fashioned weights for lifting here. We have only the most modern exercise machines. All the machines are electronic. They automatically adjust to your weight and fitness level, so you get the workout that's just right for you. The exercise room is run by Peter Jones, who's an expert in both fitness and technology, so he can help you become familiar with the machines. Once you learn how to use them, and Peter makes that easy, they're really great. I work out on them myself just about every day.

OK. In here we have the swimming pool. We offer different types and levels of swimming lessons. Also you'll notice that the pool is Olympic size, so it's well-suited for competitions. In fact, our swimming team is well-known throughout the city. As a club member, you would have the opportunity to try out for the swim team if you're interested.

Narrator: Before you hear the rest of the tour, you have some time to look at Questions 15 to 20.

Now listen and answer Questions 15 to 20.

Questions 15–20

Over there at the other end are the locker rooms where you can change from your business clothes to your swimsuit or whatever. You can look in them later if you wish. They're very comfortable. We keep them well-stocked with the basic necessities such as towels and soap. You'll have to supply your own shampoo, however. There are plenty of showers, so you'll never have to wait your turn. We also have hairdryers for you to use. For safety reasons, we ask that everyone wear rubber sandals in the changing rooms. What else? Oh, you'll have to supply your own lock, of course. That's for your security.

Before we leave the pool area, I'd like to make you aware of some of our rules. The pool is the most popular place in the club, and it's often crowded, so we have rules for everyone's comfort and safety. The most important one, if you have children, please be aware that they are not allowed in the pool area alone. Children must be accompanied by an adult at all times. Naturally, there is no running near the pool. The floor is very wet, and it would be easy to get hurt. One last thing, for sanitary reasons, we ask everyone to shower before entering the pool.

All right, I hope you've enjoyed the tour. Are there any questions?

Narrator: That is the end of Section 2. You now have half a minute to check your answers.

Now turn to Section 3.

Section 3. You will hear a professor and her students discussing class assignments.

First, you will have some time to look at Questions 21 to 26.

Now listen carefully and answer Questions 21 to 26.

Questions 21–26

W1: In this class we focus on developing writing skills, so one of the most important things we do is practice those skills by writing essays. Today we'll go over the requirements for your essay assignments. You'll have to write one essay each week. They're not very long essays, just about 350 to 400 words apiece. Every week I'll assign a different type of essay, so I thought today we'd go over some of the important essay types. The first type of essay I'll assign will be an essay describing a process. So you'll need to choose something that you can describe step-by-step. Yes, Mr. Smith?

M1: Is that a "how to" essay? I mean, would a topic be something like "How to fix a car?"

W1: Well, you should be more specific. Remember, you have a limited number of words. A better example would be "How to change the oil in a car." Yes?

W2: How about friendship as a topic? "How to make friends." Would that be a topic for a process essay?

W1: It could be, but actually friendship is a better topic for a classification essay, which is the second type I'll assign. In a classification essay you present your idea by organizing it into categories. "Three types of friends" would be a good topic for a classification essay. The third essay type you'll write is compare and contrast. So, obviously, for your topic you'll pick two or more things to compare.

M2: (*laughing*) Like comparing the food in the student cafeteria to the food in a real restaurant.

W1: Why not? That could actually be quite a good topic. But it really doesn't matter which topic you choose, as long as you develop your argument well. The next essay type is argumentative, in which you'll present an opinion and prove or defend it.

M1: I like to argue.

W1: Then you should do quite well with an argumentative essay. When writing this type of essay, be sure to state your opinion in a clear, straightforward sentence. For example "Homework is necessary" could be a thesis statement. Yes?

Narrator: Before you hear the rest of the conversation, you have some time to look at Questions 27 to 30.

Now listen carefully and answer Questions 27 to 30.

Questions 27–30

W2: Will you give us the topics, or do we pick our own?

W1: I'd like you to pick your own topics. That way you can write about things that interest you. But be sure your topics are original. I want them to come out of your own heads, not out of any book on essay writing. So, any original topic is fine as long as it fits the assigned essay type. Are there any more questions? Yes?

M2: When are the essays due?

W1: Every Monday I'll make a new essay assignment, which you'll have to hand in to me the following Friday. Another question?

W2: Will the essays count toward the final grade?

W1: Of course. The essays are the most important thing we do in this class. All together your essays will count for 65 percent of your final grade. Other class work will count for 15 percent and your tests will be 20 percent of the final grade. One more thing. Please type your essays on a computer. Handwritten essays are not acceptable, and I don't want to receive any photocopied work either.

Narrator: That is the end of Section 3. You now have half a minute to check your answers.

Now turn to Section 4.

Section 4. You will hear a professor give a lecture. First you have some time to look at Questions 31 to 36.

Now listen carefully and answer Questions 31 to 36.

Questions 31–36

Good evening. I'm Professor Williams and this class is Introduction to Anthropology. This class meets every Tuesday evening from 6:45 until 8:15. Please be on time for each class session.

This evening we'll begin with a discussion of hunter-gatherer societies. This is an important topic because at one time all humans were hunter-gatherers. What are hunter-gatherer societies? They are groups of people that survive by hunting animals and gathering plants to eat. Typically in these societies the men's job is to hunt large animals while the women both gather plants and hunt smaller animals. Before twelve thousand years ago, all humans lived as hunter-gatherers. Now there are relatively few groups of people living this way, but there are some. Experts estimate that in about 50 years or so all such groups will have disappeared. Today hunter-gatherer societies still exist in the Arctic, in some desert areas, and in tropical rainforests. These are areas where other forms of food production, namely agriculture, are too difficult because of the climate.

Narrator: Before you hear the rest of the conversation, you have some time to look at Questions 37 to 40.

Now listen carefully and answer Questions 37 to 40.

Questions 37–40

In history, many hunter-gatherer societies eventually developed into farming societies. What are some of the basic differences between hunter-gatherers and farmers? The first is that hunter-gatherers tend to be nomadic. They travel from place to place. Once they have used up the food in one area, they have to move on to the next place to find more. Farmers, on the other hand, are more likely to be sedentary. They can't move often because, of course, they have to stay in one place long enough to plant their crops and harvest them.

Another difference is that hunter-gatherer societies generally have lower population densities. Farming can support much higher population densities than hunting and gathering can because farming results in a larger food supply. So you'll find smaller groups among hunter-gatherers. Another very important difference is in social structure. A characteristic of hunter-gatherer societies is that they tend not to have hierarchical social structures. They usually don't have surplus food, or surplus anything, and if they did they would have no place to keep it since they move around so often. So in a hunter-gatherer society, there is little ability to support full-time leaders. Everybody has to spend their time looking for food. These societies are more egalitarian than farming societies, where we see hierarchical social structures begin to develop.

Please bear in mind that everything I have said so far this evening is of a general nature. Next we will look at some specific examples of hunter-gatherer societies to see how these general concepts translate into reality.

Narrator: That is the end of Section 4. You now have half a minute to check your answers.

You will now have 10 minutes to transfer your answers to the Listening Answer Sheet. Pause CD for 10 minutes.

This is almost the end of the test. You now have one more minute to check all your answers.

That is the end of the Listening section of Model Test 2.

MODEL TEST 3

Narrator: IELTS Listening. Model Test 3.

Track 25

You will hear a number of different recordings, and you will have to answer questions on what you hear. There will be time for you to read the instructions and questions, and you will have a chance to check your work. All the recordings will be played once only.

The test is in four sections. Write all your answers in the Listening Question booklet. At the end of the test you will be given ten minutes to transfer your answers to an Answer Sheet.

Now turn to Section 1.

Section 1. You will hear a conversation between a lost and found agent and a woman who has lost something.

First you have some time to look at Questions 1 to 4.

You will see that there is an example which has been done for you. On this occasion only, the conversation relating to this will be played first.

Example

W1: Is this the lost and found department?
M1: Yes, this is Lost Property. Did you lose something on the train?
W1: Yes, I did. I lost something very valuable, and it's very important that I get it back.
M1: All right, calm down. We'll fill in a lost item report form. Now, when did you lose the item?
W1: Just now. Today. A few minutes ago.
M1: Today's Monday, OK, right.

Narrator: The item was lost today, which is Monday, so "Monday" has been written in the space. Now we shall begin. You should answer the questions as you listen because you will not hear the recording a second time. Listen carefully and answer Questions 1 to 4.

Questions 1–4

W1: Is this the lost and found department?
M1: Yes, this is Lost Property. Did you lose something on the train?
W1: Yes, I did. I lost something very valuable, and it's very important that I get it back.
M1: All right, calm down. We'll fill out a lost item report form. Now, when did you lose the item?
W1: Just now. Today. A few minutes ago.
M1: Today's Monday, OK, right.
W1: Can't you hurry? Can't you send the police to look for it or something?
M1: Now just relax. This will only take a minute. May I have your name, please?
W1: It's Patty, that's P-A-T-T-Y, last name Brown, like the color.
M1: Patty Brown. All right, Ms. Brown, your address?
W1: I live at 17 High Street.
M1: Seventy or seventeen?
W1: SevenTEEN.
M1: Is that a house or a flat?
W1: Oh. It's a flat, an apartment. Number 5. And the city is Riverdale.
M1: Just one more thing. I need a phone number.
W1: 305-5938.
M1: Is that home or office or . . .
W1: It's my mobile phone. That's the best number to use because you can always reach me there.

Narrator: Before you hear the rest of the conversation, you have some time to look at Questions 5 to 10.

Now listen and answer Questions 5 to 10.

Questions 5–10

M1: OK. I'll need a description of the lost item. What exactly did you lose?

W1: I lost my reading glasses. But you know I bought them in Italy, they're Italian designer glasses and very expensive.

M1: I see. And can you describe them? Are they square or round or . . .

W1: They're round. And they have a chain attached. You know, those chains on glasses so you can hang them around your neck.

M1: Where were you when you last had them?

W1: I was sitting on the train reading. I had a window seat. The train was just about to enter the station. I heard the door at the other end of the car open, so I looked up from the article I was reading to see what the noise was.

M1: So you had your glasses on then because you were reading?

W1: Yes, that's right. It was a fascinating article in that new magazine, you know the one, I can't remember the name now but anyhow . . .

M1: Which train were you on?

W1: Oh, dear. I don't remember the number, but it was the train from Riverdale. I've come here to visit my aunt. I've taken a whole week off of work to make this trip. I left home at five o'clock this morning, and I'm very tired.

M1: I'm sorry to hear that. Several trains have arrived from Riverdale this morning. What time did your train get here?

W1: Oh, just about 30 minutes ago. At ten o'clock, I think. Yes, that's right.

M1: So the last time you had your glasses was when you were reading on the train?

W1: Yes, and when I got off the train, I had my handbag and my suitcase, and I checked my seat to see if I had left anything on it, but I hadn't.

M1: And what's that in your coat pocket?

W1: What's what? Oh . . . oh, my glasses! Oh my goodness! I can't believe they were there the whole time.

(Audio fades as last speaker continues to speak.)

Narrator: That is the end of Section 1. You now have half a minute to check your answers.

Now turn to Section 2.

Section 2. You will hear a recording of a talk about student housing.

First, you have some time to look at Questions 11 to 14.

Now listen carefully and answer Questions 11 to 14.

Questions 11–14

M1: Good morning. Welcome to day two of Student Orientation Week. The subject of the first talk today will be off-campus housing. This is of interest to those of you who don't want to live in student housing and are not familiar with our city. I'll give you some tips about where to look for housing and how to go about it.

OK, first let's talk about where to look for an apartment. There are some places that I don't recommend. The obvious place to look, you might think, would be in the neighborhood of the university. However, that's probably not a very good idea because, unfortunately, this is one of the more expensive areas of the city to live in. The downtown area is a popular place to visit; however, that's not a good place to look for housing, either, because it's mainly a commercial area. There are very few apartments there. It's also rather far from the university. So where does that leave us? I can recommend a couple of good places to look. Many students rent apartments in the uptown neighborhoods. The prices there are quite low, and many buses go there, so it's very easy to get to the university from there. The Greenfield Park neighborhood is also popular. It's closer to the university, but not many buses run in that direction, so you'll need a car if you choose to live there.

Narrator: Before you hear the rest of the talk you have some time to look at Questions 15 to 20.

Now listen carefully and answer Questions 15 to 20.

Questions 15–20

M1: All right, so let's say you've decided on a neighborhood. Next you have to find out what apartments are available. There are a number of places where you can look for apartment ads. The best place to look is at the university's Student Center. There is a wall there devoted to apartment ads. You can also look in the university newspaper. It comes out every Friday, which gives you the weekend for apartment hunting. The local city newspaper, *The Greenfield Times*, also lists apartment for rent ads. Again, Friday and Saturday are the best days. That's when you'll find the most ads. Finally, of course, you can look on the Internet. There are several Internet sites devoted to apartment rental ads in this area.

The staff at the Student Counseling Center is always ready to help you in your apartment search. They have available city maps as well as city bus schedules to help you get around to the various neighborhoods. If you would like to find someone to share an apartment with you, the Counseling Center has a roommate matching service. Most students find that having roommates is the most economical way to rent an apartment. The Center can also provide you with a list of inexpensive furniture stores. We all know how expensive it can be to furnish an apartment, but it can also be done in a more economical way. Also you might want to consider signing up for a meal plan on campus. If you don't like to cook or are too busy, well, you still have to eat, right? If you live off campus you can still eat in the university student dining rooms. We have plans for buying meals by the week, month, or semester. The Student Counseling Center can give you all the necessary information on that.

Narrator: That is the end of Section 2. You now have half a minute to check your answers.

Now turn to Section 3.

Section 3. You will hear two students talking about their assignment.

First, you will have some time to look at Questions 21 to 25.

Now listen carefully and answer Questions 21 to 25.

Questions 21–25

M1: Have you decided what you're going to write your paper on? The one for Professor Anderson's class?

W1: The topic is transportation, right? I've been thinking about writing about bicycles as a way to solve our transportation problems.

M1: Really? I usually think of bicycling as a sport or recreational activity.

W1: Around here, that's what most people think. But in some parts of the world bicycles are an important form of transportation for many people. I think we have a lot to learn from them.

M1: So, what are you going to say in your paper?

W1: I'm not sure. Maybe you can help me figure some of it out.

M1: Sure. OK, well, I'd say if you want to persuade people to use bicycles more often, you have to start by thinking about the advantages and disadvantages.

W1: You're right. Let's see . . . well, I think the advantages are obvious. First, bicycling is good for your health.

M1: Yes, that's true. And another thing is that bicycles are a lot cheaper to use than cars.

W1: Or any other form of transportation, when you think about it. You don't have to pay a fare every time you ride your bike, like you do when you take the bus or the train.

M1: OK, another one is that bicycles don't cause pollution like cars and buses do.

W1: Yeah, that's a really important one. Bicycles are a clean form of transportation.

M1: OK, so what about the other side? What are some disadvantages, some reasons why people might not want to use bicycles?

W1: One thing I thought of is weather. Who wants to ride a bike in the rain? Or if you live where the weather is cold all winter, it would be hard to use a bicycle regularly. So bad weather would be a problem.

M1: Bad health would be too. Some people just aren't strong enough to ride bikes very much. You have to be in good shape.

W1: Yes, especially if you live far from your job or wherever you have to go. So that would be another problem, distance. It's difficult to ride your bike if your trip is a long distance.

Narrator: Before you hear the rest of the conversation, you have some time to look at Questions 26 to 30.

Now listen carefully and answer Questions 26 to 30.

Questions 26–30

M1: OK, so using a bike might not work for everyone, but for a lot of people it would. How can people be encouraged to use bikes for transportation?

W1: I think there's a lot cities can do. I think the biggest thing is making bicycle lanes on roads. It's really dangerous riding a bike where there's a lot of traffic, so special lanes just for bicycles would make things a lot safer.

M1: That's a great idea.

W1: Yeah, they already do that in some cities. And another thing is to make safe places for people to leave their bikes. I mean like at subway stations. A lot of people ride to the subway station and then take the subway to work. They need a safe place to lock up their bikes all day so they don't get stolen.

M1: That seems important.

W1: Yes, and another thing I've read about is maps. Some cities provide bicycling maps that show all the good routes. They show people how easy it is to get around by bike.

M1: OK, but what about equipment? Don't you need a lot of special stuff to ride a bicycle?

W1: I don't think so. For safety you should wear a helmet, and at night you should have lights or wear reflective tape so cars can see you. For comfort you need light clothes, and waterproof clothes when it rains. But that's all I can think of. Really, it's easy and inexpensive to get started riding a bike.

M1: I think you'll write a great paper. You've already persuaded me to get a bike.

Narrator: That is the end of Section 3. You now have half a minute to check your answers.

Now turn to Section 4.

Section 4. You will hear a professor explaining an assignment to the class. First you have some time to look at Questions 31 to 40.

Now listen carefully and answer Questions 31 to 40.

Questions 31–40

W1: Good afternoon, everyone. Today we'll talk about the most important assignment you'll do in this class, which is write a research paper. I'll start by going over the process step-by-step so you'll know exactly what I expect of you. All right, let's begin at the beginning. The first step is to choose a topic. I have a list of suggested topics related to the content of this class, and I'd like you to look over it to find a topic that interests you. Then, since they are somewhat general, I'd like you to narrow your topic choice down to something more specific. You'll need to get my final approval on your topic before you begin your research.

The next thing you'll do is gather information on your topic. There are two major places to go for that. At the library you'll have reference books and other types of books available, as well as journals, magazines, and newspapers. Don't forget to look at atlases and other similar sources too. They contain a lot of useful information. Then of course there is the Internet, where you'll find online journals and newspapers, as well as online encyclopedias, and much more.

After you have gathered some information and had the chance to start thinking about your topic, the next step is to write a thesis statement. This is a critical part of the process because the bulk of the paper will be about using your information to defend your thesis statement. I will be happy to help you with this, and, actually, with any other part of your writing process if you need it.

Now then, let's say you have your thesis statement and you have your information. How do you get started writing? It can seem overwhelming with all your ideas and notes floating around. Writing an outline will help you to start getting focused. Make sure your outline includes three important things: first your introduction, where you state your thesis, then the body, which is the bulk of the paper and where you make the arguments to support your thesis, and finally the conclusion. Here you'll restate your thesis and summarize your arguments.

So now that you have your outline, you can start organizing your notes. Organize them according to the outline. As you go along you'll start seeing what information is important to emphasize, what information you may actually not want to include, what you need to find out more about, etc. So organizing your notes helps you understand your information better and start to analyze it.

The next step is to write your first draft. If you have developed a good outline and organized your notes well, then this should not be too difficult. Following your outline, present your information and analysis of it.

Then, of course, the next thing to do is revise your draft. Read it over carefully, checking to make sure that you have explained your ideas clearly and presented your information correctly. You may want to reorganize some of your information at this point, too.

Finally, you'll type your final draft on the computer. Make sure that you check it for punctuation and spelling errors before you hand it in.

OK, that's a general outline of how to go about writing a research paper. Now let's talk about the proper format for footnotes and bibliographic entries.

Narrator: That is the end of Section 4. You now have half a minute to check your answers.

You will now have 10 minutes to transfer your answers to the Listening Answer Sheet. Pause CD for 10 minutes.

This is almost the end of the test. You now have one more minute to check all your answers.

That is the end of the Listening section of Model Test 3.

MODEL TEST 4

Narrator: IELTS Listening. Model Test 4.

Track 26

You will hear a number of different recordings, and you will have to answer questions on what you hear. There will be time for you to read the instructions and questions, and you will have a chance to check your work. All the recordings will be played once only.

The test is in four sections. Write all your answers in the Listening Question booklet. At the end of the test you will be given ten minutes to transfer your answers to an Answer Sheet.

Now turn to Section 1.

Section 1. You will hear a man buying tickets over the phone.

First you have some time to look at Questions 1 to 5.

You will see that there is an example which has been done for you. On this occasion only, the conversation relating to this will be played first.

Example

F1: Good morning. Municipal Museum of Art. Information Desk.
M1: Yes, I'd like to find out about tickets for . . .
F1: Tickets? That's our Special Events Department. Let me transfer you.

Narrator: The woman says she will transfer him to the Special Events Department, so C has been circled. Now we shall begin. You should answer the questions as you listen because you will not hear the recording a second time. Listen carefully and answer Questions 1 to 5.

Questions 1–5

W1: Good morning. Municipal Museum of Art. Information Desk.
M1: Yes, I'd like to find out about tickets for . . .
W1: Tickets? That's our Special Events Department. Let me transfer you.

(*telephone ringing*)

W2: Special Events.
M1: Yes, hello. I'm interested in the series you have going on now . . .
W2: Oh, you mean our lecture series on the history of art.
M1: Actually, I meant the concert series.
W2: Oh, yes, of course. It's already begun, but there's still a concert tomorrow, that's Thursday. There's also one on Saturday, and then the last one is on Sunday.
M1: The one tomorrow, is that when they'll be playing the Mozart concerto?
W2: Yes, it is.

M1: Then I'd like two tickets for that, if they're still available.
W2: Yes, we have some tickets left. Now, I'll need your name.
M1: It's Steven Milford. That's M-i-l-f-o-r-d.
W2: Since you want tickets for tomorrow there isn't time to mail in a check. You'll have to pay by credit card.
M1: That's not a problem.
W2: Then I'll need your credit card number.
M1: Oh, of course. It's 1659798164.
W2: . . . 8164. Got it. Okay, you wanted two tickets, right?
M1: Yes.
W2: At 16.35 apiece that comes out to a total of 32 pounds and 70 p. You can pick up your tickets at the door.

Narrator: Before you hear the rest of the conversation, you have some time to look at Questions 6 to 10.

Now listen carefully and answer Questions 6 to 10.

Questions 6–10

M1: Fine. Um, could you tell me how to get there? We're coming by train.
W2: Certainly. It's very easy. When you get out of the train station, you'll see the library right across the street. Just walk down to the corner . . .
M1: Do I go right or left out of the train station?
W2: Oh, sorry. Go right, walk down to the corner. Right there on the corner you'll see a bank and across the street on the opposite corner is the post office. There are some office buildings across the street, too. Anyhow, you just go right at the corner, pass the car park and you'll see the museum right there in the middle of the block. If you get to a hotel, you've gone too far.
M1: So right at the corner and pass the car park but not the hotel. All right I think I've got it.
W2: Great. Make sure you're here by 7:30.

Narrator: That is the end of Section 1. You now have half a minute to check your answers.

Now turn to Section 2.

Section 2. You will hear a recording of a radio show about tourism to Raven Island.

First, you have some time to look at Questions 11 to 17.

Now listen carefully and answer Questions 11 to 17.

Questions 11–17

M1: Good afternoon and welcome to Travel Time. Our guest today is Sheila Farnsworth, director of Raven Tours travel agency. She'll talk to us about travel to Raven Island.
W1: Thank you, George. Raven Island is becoming quite a popular tourist destination, and with good reason. The prices are still low, and there's so much to enjoy there. Most tourists to Raven Island usually spend their time in one of two places. Ravensburg is the major city on the island, though with a population of only 56,000, it's not large by most standards. But for those who enjoy a more urban-style vacation, Ravensburg is where they go. For those looking for a bit of peace and quiet, Blackstone Beach is a favorite destination. This town, located on the island's northern coast, has a population of just 12,000 people.

The weather on Raven Island is always nice, especially during the summer. Summer in the city of Ravensburg is warm with average temperatures reaching 26 degrees or higher, and the weather is always pleasantly sunny there during July and August. Summer at Blackstone is a bit cooler, with average temperatures of around 23 degrees, and the weather is often windy because, of course, it's located on the coast.

Ravensburg has a lot to offer visitors. Its clubs and theaters are well-known, so if entertainment is what you're looking for, Ravensburg has the advantage there. The disadvantage to this is that, particularly during the summer theater festival, the city can become quite crowded with entertainment seekers. Blackstone Beach, on the other hand, is famous for its many fine seafood restaurants, considered to be the best on the island. So if you like seafood, that's the place to go. Unfortunately, eating seafood is the major activity in Blackstone. It's a very quiet town, which is a disadvantage if you're looking for excitement.

How can you get there? The Ravensburg airport is actually located a bit out of town. It's 25 kilometers from the city, but frequent bus service, taxis, and car rentals make it quite easy to get downtown. Travelers to Blackstone Beach also use the Ravensburg airport, which is about 75 kilometers away. There are three buses a day from the airport to Blackstone or you can rent[1] a car, of course.

Narrator: Before you hear the rest of the talk, you have some time to look at Questions 18 to 20.

Now listen carefully and answer Questions 18 to 20.

Questions 18–20

W1: Because of the low prices on Raven Island, many tourists travel there with shopping on their minds. What are some of the best bargains available on the island? Well, contrary to what one might think, native handicrafts are not a popular item. And although Raven Island has a beautiful musical tradition, there are not many CDs available of the native music, and the ones that are available are quite expensive. Some very good deals can be found, however, in the perfume shops. Raven Island Scents, a local factory, produces several fashionable perfumes, which they sell at reasonable prices. Jewelry[2] is also popular among tourists, and jewelry shops abound. Since fishing is the major island industry, no tourist goes home without a package of smoked fish. If you want to try fishing yourself, however, be sure to bring your own fishing gear.[3] Believe it or not, it's difficult and expensive for tourists to buy it on the island.

Narrator: That is the end of Section 2. You now have half a minute to check your answers.

Now turn to Section 3.

Section 3. You will hear two students talking about a class project.

First, you will have some time to look at Questions 21 to 23.

Now listen carefully and answer Questions 21 to 23.

Questions 21–23

M1: Hi, Janet.

W1: Harry. What's up?

M1: You know that research project we have to do for Professor Farley's class? Have you started it yet?

W1: Started it? I'm almost done.

M1: Really? I'm having trouble. Do you think you could help me?

W1: You're going to need a lot of help. It's due next Thursday.

M1: I know.

W1: And it counts for 40 percent of our final semester grade.

[1]British: hire
[2]British: jewellery
[3]British: tackle

M1: I know! So I could really use your help. So, what topic did you choose?
W1: I did my research about people's TV watching habits.
M1: You mean which programs they watch?
W1: Yeah, and how often they watch. It was really interesting.

Narrator: Before you hear the rest of the conversation, you have some time to look at Questions 24 to 30.

Now listen carefully and answer Questions 24 to 30.

Questions 24–30

M1: So, how'd you get started?
W1: Well, after I decided my topic, I went to the library and did some research. I mean, I read about other studies people had done about TV watching.
M1: How did that help you?
W1: Oh, it was really important. It gave me lots of ideas about what questions to ask. So after I did the library research, I chose my research method.
M1: What did you choose?
W1: Well, I could do either interviews or just send around a paper questionnaire. I decided to use the questionnaire because I could get information from a lot more people that way.
M1: And then what?
W1: I made up the questions for the questionnaire.
M1: And who did you give it to?
W1: Well, that's what I had to do next, choose my subjects. You have to think about if you want data from people of a certain age or certain professions and things like that. I decided to ask people like myself—university students.
M1: So then you just went around and asked people the questions?
W1: Well, first I had to submit my research design to Professor Farley. He had to make sure it was OK before I went ahead with the research.
M1: Did he make you change anything?
W1: No, he pretty much liked it the way it was. So then I had to send out the questionnaire. I just put it in all the students' mailboxes. A lot of them responded. I got a lot of results—pages and pages.
M1: Well, what did you do with all that information?
W1: Well, I did what Professor Farley told us to do. I made charts and graphs. That helped me figure out what all that data meant.
M1: Charts and graphs, huh? Hmm, I'll have to look at my class notes.
W1: Yes, you'd better. The professor outlined the whole process for us.
M1: So then you'll just hand in those charts and graphs on Thursday?
W1: Well, I'll have to write a report, too, of course. I mean, the professor wants to see our interpretation of the results. That's the whole point, don't you see?
M1: Yeah, I guess. If I get started now, do you think I'll finish on time?
W1: Maybe, if you don't have anything else to do this week.

Narrator: That is the end of Section 3. You now have half a minute to check your answers.

Now turn to Section 4.

Section 4. You will hear a professor giving a lecture on the American crow. First you have some time to look at Questions 31 to 40.

Now listen carefully and answer Questions 31 to 40.

Questions 31–40

M1: Today I'll talk about the American crow, also known as the common crow. This bird has a bad reputation, and many people consider it to be a pest, but the American crow and many of its cousins in the corvid family are actually among the most intelligent of all the birds.

There are about 40 species in the crow family, and they can be found in most parts of the world. You'll find crows in North America, although interestingly enough, not in South America. While crows live in cold areas of the far north close to the Arctic region, there are none in Antarctica. They also like warm regions. There are several species of crows, for example, in Hawaii. And of course you'll find them in other parts of the world, Europe, Asia, and so on.

The American crow is one of the 15 species of crows found in North America and is also one of the most common. It's not a small bird, measuring 39 to 49 centimeters in length. Unlike some of its cousins—the magpie, for example, which is black and white, or the blue jay which is blue with white and black markings—the American crow is completely black, including the beak and feet. Because of their intensely dark color, some people dislike crows, or better said, fear them. Another reason people dislike crows is because they associate these birds with garbage. Crows love garbage and are often seen hanging around dumpsters behind restaurants and grocery stores. In addition to garbage left behind by humans, crows eat seeds, grains, eggs, fish, and carrion. They'll eat just about anything. One of their absolute favorite foods is corn.

Crows build large nests of sticks, usually in trees or sometimes in bushes. For safety reasons, they almost never nest on the ground. Mostly they nest alone, but in some places they have been seen nesting in colonies. The female lays from three to six eggs at a time. The eggs hatch in about 18 days. The babies stay in the nest for around a month. Generally, 35 days after hatching they have their feathers and are ready to fly.

Next we'll talk about some studies which have demonstrated the extreme intelligence of these animals.

Narrator: That is the end of Section 4. You now have half a minute to check your answers.

You will now have 10 minutes to transfer your answers to the Listening Answer Sheet. Pause CD for 10 minutes.

This is almost the end of the test. You now have one more minute to check all your answers.

That is the end of the Listening section of Model Test 4.

MP3 CD TRACKS

Track 1
Skill 1, Practice 1

Track 2
Skill 1, Practice 2

Track 3
Skill 2,
Questions 1–5

Track 4
Skill 2,
Questions 6–15

Track 5
Skill 3,
Questions 1–6

Track 6
Skill 3,
Questions 7–12

Track 7
Skill 4

Track 8
Skill 5

Track 9
Skill 6, Time

Track 10
Skill 6, Date

Track 11
Skill 6, Day

Track 12
Skill 6, Year

Track 13
Skill 6, Season

Track 14
Skill 7,
Questions 1–6

Track 15
Skill 7,
Questions 7–12

Track 16
Skill 8

Track 17
Skill 9

Track 18
Skill 10

Track 19
Skill 11

Track 20
Skill 12

Track 21
Skill 13

Track 22
Skill 14

Track 23
Model Test 1

Track 24
Model Test 2

Track 25
Model Test 3

Track 26
Model Test 4

INTERNATIONAL BEST SELLING TEST PREPARATION TITLES

BARRON'S EXCLUSIVELY PUBLISHED BY NEW AGE

Publishing Globally

GRE

1 

BARRON'S PASS KEY TO THE GRE

Green, Sharon Weiner
Wolf, Ira K
Seventh Edition

Contents: What You Need to Know About the GRE • Test-Taking Tactics for the Computer-Based GRE • Verbal Ability: Tactics and Practice • Building Your Vocabulary • Analytical Writing: Tactics and Practice • Quantitative Ability: Tactics and Practice • Test Yourself: Two Practice Tests.

ISBN: 978-81-224-3593-1 | Publication Year: 2014 | Edition: 7th
Pages: 272 | MRP: ₹ 199.00 | Paperback

2 

BARRON'S ESSENTIAL WORDS FOR THE GRE

Geer, Philip
Fourth Edition

Contents: Introduction: Mastering Advanced Vocabulary for the GRE • Pretest • Suggested Study Plans • 300 High-Frequency GRE Words • Essential Words for the GRE • Review: 300 High-Frequency GRE Words • Review: Essential Words for the GRE • 300 High-Frequency Word Roots • Common Suffixes • Posttest • Answer Keys: Essential Words for the GRE • Root Roundup • Root Roundup Review.

ISBN: 978-93-87477-01-8 | Publication Year: 2018 | Edition: 4th
Pages: 416 | MRP: ₹350.00 | Paperback

3 

BARRON'S GRE MATH WORKBOOK

Madore, Blair

Contents: The GRE General Math Exam • Strategies and Problem Solving • Numbers • Algebra • Data Analysis • Geometry • Sample Exams and Solutions • **Appendix:** Suggested Facts to Memorize.

ISBN: 978-81-224-3150-6 | Publication Year: 2011 | Edition: 1st
Pages: 280 | MRP: ₹ 299.00 | Paperback

4 

BARRON'S GRE VERBAL WORKBOOK

Geer, Philip

Contents: The New GRE • The New Verbal Reasoning Section • Examining the Questions • Diagnostic Test • Sentence Equivalence Questions • Text Completion Questions: Single Blank • Text Completion Questions: Double Blank • Text Completion Questions: Triple Blank • Reading Comprehension Questions • Practice Test 1 • Practice Test 2 • GRE Dictionary.

ISBN: 978-81-224-3576-4 | Publication Year: 2014 | Edition: 1st
Pages: 342 | MRP: ₹ 275.00 | Paperback

5 

BARRON'S 6 GRE PRACTICE TESTS

Freeling, David
Kotchian, Vince

Contents: Introduction • Practice Test 1 • Practice Test 2 • Practice Test 3 • Practice Test 4 • Practice Test 5 • Practice Test 6.

ISBN: 978-81-224-3572-6 | Publication Year: 2014 | Edition: 1st
Pages: 370 | MRP: ₹ 325.00 | Paperback

E-mail: sales@newagepublishers.com

6 

TAKING THE GRE WRITING ASSESSMENT

Avants, Tim

Contents: Introduction to the Writing Assessment • Punctuation • Transitions • Analysis of Argument • Patterns of Development • Logical Fallacies • Inductive vs. Deductive Logic • Sample Argument Questions and Essays • Analysis of Issue • Comparison-Contrast • Sample Patterns of Development Comparison-Contrast • Cause-Effect • Division-Classification Sample Paper • Definition • Sample Essay Questions and Answers.

ISBN: 978-81-224-1786-9 | Publication Year: 2006 | Edition: 1st
Pages: 100 | MRP: ₹ 95.00 | Paperback

GMAT

7 

BARRON'S PASS KEY TO THE GMAT

Bobby, Umar
Carl, S. Pyrdum III
Seventh Edition

Contents: The Basics • The Analytical Writing Assignment • Integrated Reasoning • Quantitative Section: An Introduction • Arithmetic • Algebra • Geometry • Statistics • Data Sufficiency • Problem Solving • Probability • Permutations and Combinations • Introduction to the Verbal Section • Critical Reasoning • Sentence Correction • Reading Comprehension • Sample Test with Answers and Analysis.

ISBN: 978-81-224-3571-9 | Publication Year: 2015 | Edition: 7th
Pages: 432 | MRP: ₹ 299.00 | Paperback

8 

BARRON'S GMAT MATH WORKBOOK

Markal, Ender

Contents: Getting Started • Arithmetic • Algebra • Word Problems • Geometry • Data Sufficiency • Model Tests.

ISBN: 978-81-224-3574-0 | Publication Year: 2014 | Edition: 1st
Pages: 320 | MRP: ₹ 199.00 | Paperback

NEW SAT

9 

BARRON'S PASS KEY TO THE NEW SAT

Green, Sharon Weiner
Wolf, Ira K
Stewart, Brian W
Tenth Edition

Contents: About the SAT • Tips and Strategies for the SAT • The Evidence-Based Reading Section: Strategies, Tips, and Practice • Building Your Vocabulary • The Writing and Language and Essay Sections: Strategies, Tips and Practice • The Mathematics Sections: Strategies, Tips, and Practice.

ISBN: 978-93-86418-57-9 | Publication Year: 2018 | Edition: 10th
Pages: 412 | MRP: ₹ 399.00 | Paperback

10 

BARRON'S SAT 1600 AIMING FOR THE PERFECT SCORE (1 CD FREE)

CD-ROM

Carnevale, Linda
Teukolsky, Roselyn
Fifth Edition

Contents: Welcome to the 1600 club. **Part 1: The Evidence-Based Reading Test:** 1600 Club Reading Strategies • Practice Reading Questions. **Part 2: The Evidence-based Writing and Language Test:** English Grammar and Usage • Practice Writing and Language Questions. **Part 3: The Essay:** Writing the 50-Minute Essay • Sample Source Texts. **Part 4: The Math Sections:** Getting Started • Strategies for Solving SAT Math Problems • 1600 Club Background Topics • Problems in Context • Heart of Algebra • Problem Solving and Data Analysis • Passport to Advanced Math • Additional Topics in Math.

ISBN: 978-93-859-2391-3 | Publication Year: 2017 | Edition: 5th
Pages: 464 | MRP: ₹ 499.00 | Paperback

INTERNATIONAL BEST SELLING TEST PREPARATION TITLES

BARRON'S **EXCLUSIVELY PUBLISHED BY NEW AGE**

Publishing Globally

11 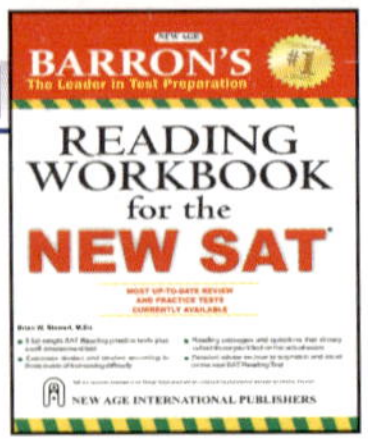

BARRON'S READING WORKBOOK FOR THE NEW SAT

Stewart, Brian W

Contents: Introduction • Diagnostic Test • Reading Strategies • Words in Context: Strategy and Practice • Graph Analysis: Strategy and Practice • Practice Exercises of Increasing Difficulty • **Practice Tests:** Practice Test 1 • Practice Test 2 • Practice Test 3.

ISBN: 978-93-859-2393-7 **Publication Year:** 2017 **Edition:** 1st
Pages: 248 **MRP:** ₹ 299.00 Paperback

12 

BARRON'S WRITING WORKBOOK FOR THE NEW SAT

Ehrenhaft, George

Fourth Edition

Contents: Section 1: The Writing and Language Test: Overview • Writing and Language Practice Tests. **Section 2: The Sat Essay:** Getting Acquainted with the SAT Essay • Getting Prepped to Write • How to Write an Analytical Essay in 3,000 Seconds • You Be the Ump: Essays for Evaluation • Practice, Practice, Practice.

ISBN: 978-93-859-2394-4 **Publication Year:** 2017 **Edition:** 4th
Pages: 384 **MRP:** ₹ 425.00 Paperback

13 

BARRON'S MATH WORKBOOK FOR THE NEW SAT

Leff, Lawrence S

Sixth Edition

Contents: Learning About SAT Math: Know What You're Up Against • SAT Math Strategies. **The Four Mathematics Content Areas:** Heart of Algebra • Problem Solving and Data Analysis • Passport to Advanced Math • Additional Topics in Math. **Solutions for Tune-up Exercises. Taking Practice Tests:** Practice Test 1 • Practice Test 2 • How to Evaluate your Performance on a Practice Test.

ISBN: 978-93-86070-15-9 **Publication Year:** 2017 **Edition:** 6th
Pages: 572 **MRP:** ₹ 499.00 Paperback

14 

BARRON'S 6 PRACTICE TESTS FOR THE NEW SAT

Geer, Philip
Reiss, Stephen A

Second Edition

Contents: New SAT Format and Test Dates • Countdown to the SAT • Introduction: Let's Look at the New SAT. **Practice Tests:** Practice Test 1 • Practice Test 2 • Practice Test 3 • Practice Test 4 • Practice Test 5 • Practice Test 6.

ISBN: 978-93-859-2392-0 **Publication Year:** 2017 **Edition:** 2nd
Pages: 512 **MRP:** ₹ 499.00 Paperback

NEW SAT SUBJECT WISE

15 

BARRON'S SAT SUBJECT TEST PHYSICS

Jansen, Robert
Young, Greg

Second Edition

Contents: Introduction • Diagnostic Test • Conventions and Graphing • Vectors • Kinematics in One Dimension • Kinematics in Two Dimensions • Dynamics • Circular Motion • Energy, Work and Power • Momentum and Impulse • Gravity • Electric Field • Electric Potential • Circuit Elements and DC Circuits • Magnetism • Simple Harmonic Motion • Waves • Geometric Optics.

ISBN: 978-93-86418-50-0 **Publication Year:** 2018 **Edition:** 2nd
Pages: 600 **MRP:** ₹ 550.00 Paperback

E-mail: sales@newagepublishers.com

16 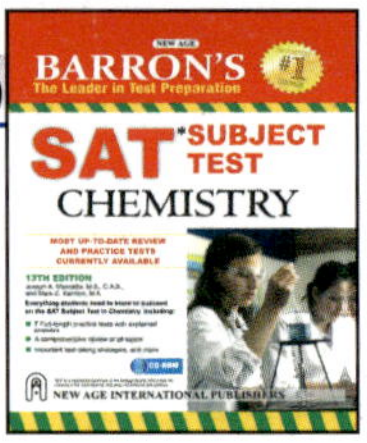

BARRON'S SAT SUBJECT TEST CHEMISTRY (1 CD FREE)

CD-ROM

Mascetta, Joseph A • Kernion, Mark C

Thirteenth Edition

Contents: Introduction: About the Test. **A Diagnostic Test:** Diagnostic Test. **Review of Major Topics:** Introduction to Chemistry • Atomic Structure and the Periodic Table of the Elements • Bonding • Chemical Formulas • Gases and the Gas Laws • Stoichiometry (Chemical Calculations) and the Mole Concept • Liquids, Solids and Phase Changes.

ISBN: 978-93-86418-51-7 **Publication Year:** 2018 **Edition:** 13th
Pages: 472 **MRP:** ₹ 499.00 Paperback

17 

BARRON'S SAT SUBJECT TEST MATH LEVEL 1 (1 CD FREE)

CD-ROM

Wolf, Ira K

Sixth Edition

Contents: Test-Taking Strategies: Important Tactics. **Math Review:** Basic Arithmetic • Fractions, Decimals, and Percents • Ratios and Proprotions. **Algebra:** Polynomials • Equations and Inequalities • Word Problems. **Plane Geometry:** Lines and Angles • Triangles.

ISBN: 978-93-86418-53-1 **Publication Year:** 2018 **Edition:** 6th
Pages: 402 **MRP:** ₹ 450.00 Paperback

18 

BARRON'S SAT SUBJECT TEST MATH LEVEL 2 (1 CD FREE)

CD-ROM

Ku, Richard

Twelfth Edition

Contents: Introduction. **Part 1: Diagnostic Test:** Diagnostic Test. **Part 2: Review of Major Topics:** Functions • Linear Functions • Quadratic Functions • Higher Degree Polynomials • Solving Polynomial Inequalities • Triangle Trigonometry • Trigonometric Functions • Exponential and Logarithmic Functions • Rational Functions • Parametric Equations.

ISBN: 978-93-86418-54-8 **Publication Year:** 2018 **Edition:** 12th
Pages: 360 **MRP:** ₹ 399.00 Paperback

TOEFL

19 

BARRON'S PASS KEY TO THE TOEFL iBT

Sharpe, Pamela J (1 CD FREE) MP3 CD

Ninth Edition

Contents: Orientation • Review of TOEFL iBT Sections • Academic Skills • Model Test 1: Pretest • Model Test 2: Progress Test • Model Test 3: Progress Test • Answers and Audio Scripts for Activities, Quizzes, and Model Tests • Score Estimates • Resources • Timetable for the TOEFL iBT.

ISBN: 978-93-86418-56-2 **Publication Year:** 2018 **Edition:** 9th
Pages: 620 **MRP:** ₹ 599.00 Paperback

20 

BARRON'S PRACTICE EXERCISES FOR THE TOEFL (1 CD FREE)

AUDIO CD

Sharpe, Pamela J

Eighth Edition

Contents: Plan for Success • Practice Exercises for Listening • Practice Exercises for Speaking • Practice Exercises for Structure • Practice Exercises for Reading • Practice Exercises for Writing • Explanatory Answers and Audio Script for TOEFL Practice Exercises • Model Tests.

ISBN: 978-93-86418-55-5 **Publication Year:** 2018 **Edition:** 8th
Pages: 576 **MRP:** ₹ 599.00 Paperback

21 

BARRON'S TOEFL STRATEGIES AND TIPS OUTSMART THE TOEFL (2 CD FREE)

MP3 AUDIO CD

Sharpe, Pamela J

Second Edition

Contents: Orientation • Strategies for the Reading Section • Strategies for the Listening Section • Strategies for the Speaking Section • Strategies for the Structure Section • Strategies for the Writing Section.

ISBN: 978- 81-224-3888-8 **Publication Year:** 2017 **Edition:** 2nd
Pages: 410 **MRP:** ₹ 475.00 Paperback

INTERNATIONAL BEST SELLING TEST PREPARATION TITLES

BARRON'S **EXCLUSIVELY PUBLISHED BY NEW AGE**

Publishing Globally

22 

BARRON'S OUTSMART THE TOEFL TEST STRATEGIES AND TIPS

AUDIO CDs

Sharpe, Pamela J (2 CD FREE)

Contents: Orientation • Strategies for the Reading Section • Strategies for the Listening Section • Strategies for the Speaking Section • Strategies for the Structure Section • Strategies for the Writing Section • Audio Scripts and Answer Keys.

ISBN: 978- 81-224-3573-3 **Publication Year:** 2014 **Edition:** 1st
Pages: 404 **MRP:** ₹399.00 **Paperback**

23 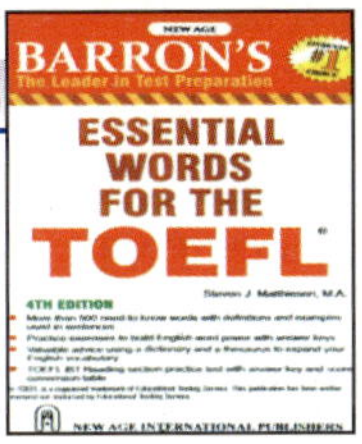

BARRON'S ESSENTIAL WORDS FOR THE TOEFL

Matthiesen, Steven J

Fourth Edition

Contents: **Introduction:** Success on the TOEFL • Getting to Know the TOEFL • Understanding the TOEFL Reading Section • Improving Your TOEFL Vocabulary • Building Your Vocabulary • Important Vocabulary Building Tools • The Essential TOEFL Vocabulary.

ISBN: 978-81-224-3151-3 **Publication Year:** 2011 **Edition:** 4th
Pages: 320 **MRP:** ₹250.00 **Paperback**

24 

DELTA'S KEY TO THE TOEFL iBT

AUDIO MP3

Advanced Skill Practice (1 CD FREE)

Gallagher, Nancy

Second Revised Edition

Contents: Introduction. **Part 1:** Reading. **Part 2:** Listening. **Part 3:** Speaking. **Part 4:** Writing • Test 1 • Test 2 • Test 3 • Test 4 • Answer Key • Audio Scripts.

ISBN: 978-81-224-3528-3 **Publication Year:** 2013 **Edition:** 2nd
Pages: 720 **MRP:** ₹499.00 **Paperback**

25 

DELTA'S KEY TO THE NEXT GENERATION TOEFL TEST

AUDIO CDs

(Six Practice Tests for the iBT) (6 CD FREE)

Gallagher, Nancy

Contents: About the Test • The TOEFL iBT • The TOEFL ITP • How to use this Book • To the Student • Reading • Listening • Speaking • Writing • Test 1 • Test 2 • Test 3 • Test 4 • Test 5 • Test 6 • Answer Key • Audio Scripts • How to Score Speaking • How to Score Writing.

ISBN: 978-81-224-2071-5 **Publication Year:** 2007 **Edition:** 1st
Pages: 390 **MRP:** ₹495.00 **Paperback**

26 

DELTA'S KEY TO THE NEXT GENERATION TOEFL TEST

AUDIO CD

(Essential Grammar for the iBT) (1 CD FREE)

Gallagher, Nancy

Contents: Nouns • Verbs • Infinitives and Gerunds • Clauses and Sentences • Conjunctions • Adverb Clauses • Adjectives Clauses • Noun Clauses • Conditional Sentences • Singular and Plural • Articles • Subject-Verb Agreement • Pronoun Agreement • Comparison • Prepositions • Word Order • Parallel Structure • Word Form • Common Word Errors • Punctuation.

ISBN: 978- 81-224-2806-3 **Publication Year:** 2010 **Edition:** 1st
Pages: 312 **MRP:** ₹395.00 **Paperback**

IELTS

27 

IELTS READING TESTS

(Academic Module)

McCarter

Ash

Contents: Reading Test 1 • Reading Test 2 • Reading Test 3 • Reading Test 4 • Reading Test 5 • Reading Test 6 • Reading Test 7 • Reading Test 8 • Reading Test 9 • Reading Test 10.

ISBN: 978-81-224-1744-9 **Publication Year:** 2006 **Edition:** 1st
Pages: 146 **MRP:** ₹195.00 **Paperback**

28 

A BOOK FOR IELTS

(Academic Module) (2 CD FREE)

CD ROMs

McCarter

Easton

Ash

Third Edition

Contents: Listening Module • Reading Exercises • Reading Tests • Section on Writing • Section on Speaking • Keys.

ISBN: 978- 81-224-2121-7 **Publication Year:** 2007 **Edition:** 3rd
Pages: 226 **MRP:** ₹295.00 **Paperback**

29 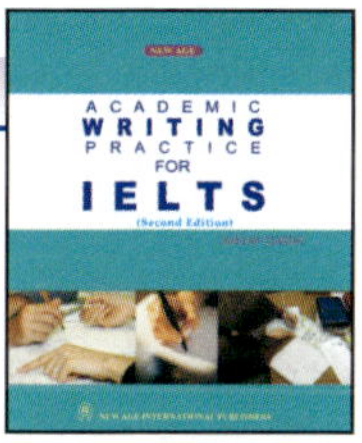

ACADEMIC WRITING PRACTICE FOR IELTS

McCarter, Sam

Second Edition

Contents: **Section 1:** Writing Practice for Task 1. **Section 2:** Writing Practice for Task 2. **Section 3:** Checking and Editing. **Section 4:** Practice Writing Tests • Answer Key.

ISBN: 978-81-224-2166-8 **Publication Year:** 2006 **Edition:** 2nd
Pages: 170 **MRP:** ₹245.00 **Paperback**

30 

A BOOK ON WRITING

(Useful for IELTS, TOEFL, SAT, GRE, GMAT etc.)

McCarter, Sam

Contents: **Section 1:** Focus on Coherence. **Section 2:** Focus on Cohesion. **Section 3:** Writing Letters. **Section 4:** Correcting Written English. **Section 5:** Punctuation.

ISBN: 978-81-224-1746-3 **Publication Year:** 2006 **Edition:** 1st
Pages: 152 **MRP:** ₹125.00 **Paperback**

31 

BARRON'S IELTS

International English Language Testing System

AUDIO CD

Lougheed, Lin (1 CD FREE)

Fourth Edition

Contents: Introduction • Preparing for IELTS • Listening Module • Reading Module • Writing Module • Speaking module • IELTS Model Tests • Audioscripts.

ISBN: 978-93-87477-00-1 **Publication Year:** 2018 **Edition:** 4th
Pages: 470 **MRP:** ₹499.00 **Paperback**

32 

BARRON'S IELTS PRACTICE EXAMS

AUDIO CDs

(2 CD FREE)

Lougheed, Lin

Contents: **Part 1: Academic Module:** Practice Test 1 • Practice Test 2 • Practice Test 3 • Practice Test 4 • Practice Test 5 • Practice Test 6. **Part 2: General Training Module:** Practice Test 1 • Practice Test 2 • Practice Test 3 • Practice Test 4 • Practice Test 5 • Practice Test 6. • Audio Scripts for Listening Parts 1-4 • How to use the Audio CDs.

ISBN: 978-81-224-3346-3 **Publication Year:** 2012 **Edition:** 1st
Pages: 452 **MRP:** ₹399.00 **Paperback**

33 

BARRON'S ESSENTIAL WORDS FOR THE IELTS

AUDIO CD

(1 CD FREE)

Lougheed, Lin

Contents: Introduction • The Natural World • Leisure Time • Transportation • Culture • Health • Tourism • Business • Society • Education • Technology/ Inventions.

ISBN: 978- 81-224-3402-6 **Publication Year:** 2012 **Edition:** 1st
Pages: 368 **MRP:** ₹350.00 **Paperback**

INTERNATIONAL BEST SELLING TEST PREPARATION TITLES

BARRON'S **EXCLUSIVELY PUBLISHED BY NEW AGE**

Publishing Globally

34 

BARRON'S IELTS STRATEGIES AND TIPS (1 CD FREE) AUDIO CD

Lougheed, Lin

Contents: Introduction • IELTS Listening Module • IELTS Reading Module • IELTS Writing Module • IELTS Speaking Module.

ISBN: 978- 81-224-3893-2 **Publication Year:** 2015 **Edition:** 1st
Pages: 278 **MRP:** ₹ 299.00 **Paperback**

ENGLISH SKILLS

35 

DANGEROUS ENGLISH

Claire, Elizabeth

Third Edition

Contents: What Makes Some Words Dangerous? • Is Your Pronunciation Dangerous? • The Social Classes of English Words • We All Do It, but We Can't Talk about It • Common Words with Dangerous Double Meanings • How Safe Is Your English? Test Yourself • More Dangerous Doubles • Religious Taboos • Safe Words for Dangerous Clothing: Our Underwear • Dangerous English Goes to the Movies • Your Body Talks. Is It Speaking Dangerously? • Sexual Harassment: Whats That? • Who are all these People ? • The New Taboo: Politically Incorrect Words • True Stories of Dangerous English • Dangerous Synonyms and Related Words: The Human Body • Male • Female • In the Bathroom • In the Bedroom.

ISBN: 978-81-224-1635-0 **Publication Year:** 2005 **Edition:** 3rd
Pages: 210 **MRP:** ₹ 125.00 **Paperback**

36 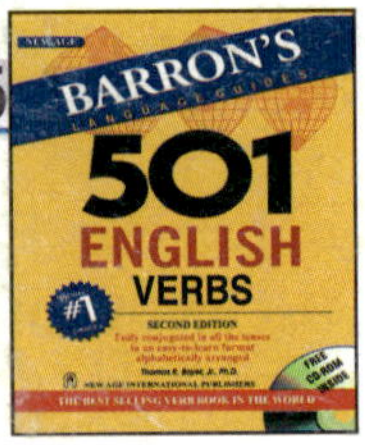

BARRON'S 501 ENGLISH VERBS (1 CD FREE) CD-ROM

Bayer, Thomas R

Second Edition

Contents: The English Verb • Auxiliary Verbs • Phrasal Verbs • Catenatives • Questions • Negations • Which 501 English Verbs? • Essential 55 Verb List • 501 English Verbs Fully Conjugated, Arranged Alphabetically • Appendixes • Phrasal Verbs • Another 550 Problem Verbs • 501 Verb Drills and Exercises • Index of the 501 English Verbs • Minimum System Requirements for the CD-ROM.

ISBN: 978-81-224-2132-3 **Publication Year:** 2008 **Edition:** 2nd
Pages: 672 **MRP:** ₹ 295.00 **Paperback**

37 

25 BUSINESS SKILLS IN ENGLISH (1 CD FREE) AUDIO CD

McCracken, Mark

Contents: Skills: Control a Conversation • Start a Conversation • Introduce Yourself • Describe Your Job and Your Company • Use Large and Small Numbers • Exchange Company Data • Have a Job Interview • Take or Leave a Telephone Message • Change Topics • Ask for or Give Advice • Make, Accept or Decline an Invitation • Offer Help • Make a Request • Apologize • Show Sympathy • Ask for and Give Examples • Hesitate • Ask for, Give and Support an Opinion • Rephrase a Question or an Opinion • Make a Toast • Ask for a Discount • Complain.

ISBN: 978-81-224-1657-2 **Publication Year:** 2005 **Edition:** 1st
Pages: 176 **MRP:** ₹ 120.00 **Paperback**

38 

BARRON'S AMERICAN ACCENT TRAINING

Cook, Ann

Fourth Edition

Contents: Introduction: Read This First • The American Sound • Word Linking & Phrasing • Cat? Caught? Cut? • The American T • The American R • The El • Reduced Sounds • Tee Aitch • S or Z? • Review and Expansion • More Reduced Sounds • "V" as in Victory • Tense and Lax Vowels • The Ridge • Grammar in a Bigger Nutshell • Practical Application • Nasal Consonants • Throaty Consonants • Review and Expansion • Nationality Guides.

ISBN: 978-93-87477-45-2 **Publication Year:** 2018 **Edition:** 4th
Pages: 210 **MRP:** ₹ 399.00 **Paperback**

39 

NEW AGE VOCABULARY FOR ACHIEVERS (Useful for SAT, TOEFL, IELTS, GRE, GMAT etc.)

Agarwal, Anjana

Contents: Adventure & Dare-What's life without risk and chance! • Art, Drama, Music, Culture-Finer aspects of life • Beauty-It lies in the eyes of the beholder • Communication-Make yourself heard • Deception or Lie-Speak truth or die • Determination & Strength, Energy & Power-You can do it if you want to • Difficult or Tough, Secretive Or Hidden-Can't quite figure it out! • Environment-Saving it is now or never • Evil-Get out of harm's way • Food-Hungry for more.

ISBN: 978-81-224-2748-6 **Publication Year:** 2010 **Edition:** 1st
Pages: 380 **MRP:** ₹ 295.00 **Paperback**

40 

POWERFUL VOCABULARY BUILDER: (Useful for SAT, TOEFL, IELTS, GRE, GMAT)

ANJANA AGARWAL

Second Edition

This book aims at helping students to fulfill their need for vocabulary building and retaining newly learnt words for long term usage. The book is particularly recommended for those students who are appearing for various competitive examinations like SAT, IELTS, TOEFL, GRE, GMAT etc. and those who wish to enhance their communication skills.

Contents: Adventure & Dare—What's life without risk and chance!. **Art, Drama, Music, Culture**—Finer aspects of life. **Beauty**—It lies in the eyes of the beholder. **Communication**—Make yourself heard. **Deception or lie**—Speak truth or die. **Determination & Strength, Energy & Power**—You can do it if you want to. **Difficult or tough, secretive or hidden**—Can't quite figure it out!. **Environment**—Saving it is now or never. **Evil**—Get out of harm's way. **Food**—Hungry for more. **Godly, Religious, Spiritual**—What's your spiritual quotient?. **Grand, Abundant, Huge**—Wow, that's some size. **Happiness & Contentment**— Smile and the world smiles with you. **Health, Fitness & Medicine**—Your health is in your hands. **History**—Past keeps coming back. **Knowledge & Wisdom**—Thinking ways to be a know-it-all. **Literature**—Who hasn't read any?. **Love & Friendship**—All is fair in love. **Money, Money, Money**—Its a rich man's world. **Negative Emotions**—Never did any body good. **Positivity & Praise**—Think well, do good, be optimistic. **Science & Technology**—How geeky are you?. **Small**—Judge me by my size, do you?. **Sorrow**—No use crying over spilt milk. **Vanity & Pride**—No one does better than me. **Violence**—When will man stop fighting?. **Some New Entrants in English Language**—New wine in old bottles.

ISBN: 978-81-224-4005-8 • Publication Year: 2016 • Edition: 2nd • Pages: 390 • MRP: ₹ 399.00 • Size: 21.5 × 28 cm • Paperback

NEW AGE INTERNATIONAL (P) LIMITED, PUBLISHERS

Publishing Globally

22, Golden House, Ansari Road, Daryaganj, New Delhi-110 002 (India) • Tel.: +91 (11) 23262368, 23262370 • Fax : 43551305

E-mail: sales@newagepublishers.com • Visit us at www.newagepublishers.com

Bangalore (080) 26756823 • Chennai (044) 24353401 • Cochin (0484) 2377303 • Guwahati (0361) 2513881
Hyderabad (040) 24652456 • Kolkata (033) 22273773 • Lucknow (0522) 2209578 • Mumbai (022) 24927869

(CIN: U74899DL1966PTC004618)